THE COYABA CHRONICLES

Reflections on The Black Experience in
The Twentieth Century

'Blood, race, colour and origin are not the only bonding agents in human relations. The trouble is that the others are not as easily defined.' It is seldom that one finds the depth of wisdom in personal reminiscences, but here is wisdom in Peter Abrahams' words. His exploration of the severing and bonding of human relations forms a kind of peripatetic auto-biography — not only of one man, an extraordinary writer, but of the concepts and attitudes that have interplayed between the countries and peoples of our time, preoccupied us and determined our lives. Abrahams is an African writer, a writer of the world, who opened up in his natal country, South Africa, a path of exploration for us, the writers who have followed the trail he bravely blazed.

Nadine Gordimer

THE COYABA CHRONICLES

Reflections on The Black Experience in
The Twentieth Century

Peter Abrahams

Ian Randle Publishers
Kingston

David Philip
Cape Town

First published in Jamaica 2000 by
Ian Randle Publishers
206 Old Hope Road, Box 686
Kingston 6

ISBN 976-637-014-1 hardback
ISBN 976-637-017-6 paperback

Published in 2000 in Southern Africa by
David Philip Publishers (Pty) Ltd,
208 Werdmuller Centre, Newry Street, Claremont 7708, South Africa

ISBN 0-86486-356-X paperback

Photo of Nelson Mandela (front cover) © Reuters/CORBIS

Set in 11/13pt Adobe Garamond
Book and cover design by Errol Stennett

Printed in the USA

God that made the world and all things therein,
seeing that he is Lord of heaven and earth,
dwelleth not in the temples made with hand.
Neither is worshipped with men's hands,
as though he needed any thing,
seeing he giveth to all life, and breath and all things;
and hath made of one blood all nations of men
for to dwell on the face of the earth,
and hath determined the times before appointed,
and the bounds of their habitation.

Acts 17: 24-26

Contents

A World At War

The Loved Ones

We are fast coming to the close of the twentieth century. By the time these chronicles are made public we will, I suspect, be into the twenty-first century. I did not expect to live this long. As far as I know, no other member of my family has lived to the ripe old age of eighty. My mother made it to her early sixties. My brother, Lolly, my sister, Tibby (Margaret or Maggie), and my cousin, Catherine, did not. Catherine died young, perhaps in her early forties. She suffered from 'St Vitus' Dance' and a wife-beating husband. My Aunt Mattie, Catherine's mother, she who accused me of stealing a half-crown all of seventy years ago, was an old person in her late fifties, with swollen legs and feet, when she died.

Why does that accusation linger? I knew it was false; she found that out later without telling me how.

Almost sixty years ago, when I last saw Aunt Mattie, just before I left South Africa for good, she apologised painfully, awkwardly. She was a shadow of the tough old Skokiaan Queen of my childhood days. We embraced. The intensely passionate hurt of youth had long since gone. All I remembered at that last meeting was how hard she had struggled to keep our family together.

Aunt Mattie, formally Margaret DuPlessis; her younger sister, Angelina, (Limmie to everybody) my mother; Lolly and Tibby, my elder brother and sister and Catherine, Aunt Mattie's only child; and me, the youngest: that was my circle of love, the people who made up my world, the first humans whose faces and sounds and smells and movements illuminated my consciousness. The two DuPlessis sisters, with four children between them, and no men to support them. There had been a fifth child, my sister Natalie, nearest in age to me, a year older, who died in early childhood, before she became part of my memory bank. There is the memory of my father; a tall, thin dark presence, a mineworker who died early. The most lingering image is of being lifted up to look my last on the dead face that I associated with my mother's laughter and the tranquil sounds of haunting music. As long as he was with us Aunt Mattie was not a dominant presence. When he died, she became the cornerstone of our lives.

My mother went to work in the homes of white folk, usually living in and looking after their children. The money was small. Aunt Mattie stayed home and managed the family. In the Vrededorp of my childhood that was difficult. Finding our daily bread was a struggle. Aunt Mattie tried all sorts of things. We sold vegetables, then firewood, from a pushcart. As long as Lolly was prepared to lead us through the streets of Vrededorp and Fordsburg, and Braamfontein, pushing the loaded handcart, it worked. When he found a girlfriend and a job for himself, and when he spent more time at his girlfriend's than at our place, the firewood enterprise collapsed.

So Aunt Mattie brewed the illicit Skokiaan, the 'kaffir beer', and sold it to the mine boys — a shilling for a small tin-full, one-and-six-pence for a slightly larger one — at weekends when they were allowed out of the mine compounds. I remember Aunt Mattie went to jail many times when she was caught in the Saturday night police raids.

The usual Monday morning magistrates' court sittings were packed with prisoners' relatives, come to pay the fines or to swear, nearly always in vain, that the accused was not the guilty person. The sentence, a monotonous routine, was fourteen days or twenty-one shillings; or, for the bigger fish, one month or forty to forty-five shillings. Those who could, paid up and went back to their trade. Those who could not, served their time then went back to their illicit brewing. The State collected quite a bit of money from these 'Skokiaan fines'. Once, I recall, we could not raise the twenty-one shillings and Aunt Mattie spent a fortnight in jail. It was a miserable fortnight for all of us. But we had a party the day she came home, and all the neighbours came to celebrate, bringing food and drink which lasted us for three days.

Aunt Mattie always stood out among the prisoners. She was one of those almost white Coloureds; all the others had the subtle variation of pigmentation — from a Mongolian light-yellow through to a rich reddish-brown or near-black — which the world of white folk sweepingly lumped together as black. So except for such rare cases as near-white Aunt Mattie, and the occasional other Coloured Skokiaan Queen, the Monday morning prisoner line-ups were all comprised of black women. But for all that, this near-white woman, dressed as voluminously as all the other black women prisoners, down to the elaborately tied kerchief or *Doekie* on her head, seemed not out of place.

Every now and then we had seen some other Coloured woman lined up in the dock among the Skokiaan Queens; not as fair as Aunt Mattie, not with grey-green eyes and 'European' hair, but seemingly much more awkward, embarrassed and out of place. I have a vivid memory of Aunt Mattie in animated conversation with her fellow prisoners before the white magistrate entered and the world became silent. There she was, wedged between a row of black women, all taller than she was. She was short, just over five feet, heavy-bodied, squarish and squat, as are Boer women after generations of walking the vast African veld and eating the heavy Dutch-style Afrikaner food. She could have been one of them — if she were not my Aunt Mattie. She and a very tall statuesque and austere-faced woman were talking 'nineteen to the dozen', as Tibby and her friends used to say. Those around them listened eagerly. It seemed normal at the time, but now I wonder what language they were speaking. Most of the black women who lived in the lower end of Vrededorp came from the countryside and were there to be near their menfolk who worked in the mines. They spoke neither English nor Afrikaans. I knew Aunt Mattie had a nodding acquaintance with English, but Afrikaans was her language; she thought and cursed in Afrikaans. She made it sound beautiful when she spoke softly to my mother when the two of them were alone and thought no one was listening. There was a hint of sadness when that gentleness was between them. Years later, and in strange and distant lands, I slowly grew to recognise that shared quiet gentleness. It was a thing of shared memories, of remembrances of other times and other lives. What were these memories? Where had these two sisters come from? Why was one near-white and the other as near-black as makes no difference? It is one of the great regrets of my life that I did not have the sense to ask these questions of Aunt Mattie and my mother. We do not ask the right questions when we are young, so we miss the important answers. Now it is too late to ask, too late for the illuminating answers, and the unanswered questions haunt us for a lifetime. In what language was she talking to that big and beautiful black Skokiaan Queen in the Marshall Square prisoners' dock that Monday morning? Why was she so at ease among those women? Questions without answers. That big woman became the prototype for Leah in *Mine Boy*.

Of all my immediate family Aunt Mattie was, looking back over more than sixty years, the least concerned with the colour and shade consciousness which defined every aspect of South African life. Perhaps, without my realising it, she helped to shape for me a way of looking at my world. I should have given her the credit for this in *Tell Freedom*. I did not because I did not recognise it at that time, or its influence in the shaping of my views on my world.

One day, in the cold Vrededorp winter, I returned to our yard. We were either living at 21st or 22nd Street, the lower and blacker end of Vrededorp, when I saw this little man, black as only one from Nyasaland could be. He did not look like a mine boy. I was between ten and twelve at the time but he was no taller than I was and not much heavier. He had small hands, tapering fingers, and there was a beakiness to his face: pointy nose, pointy lips, pointy ears. And then he smiled at something Aunt Mattie had said in a language I did not understand. And the whole world seemed to glow. Then, as suddenly as it came, the smile was gone and we were back in drab, shanty Vrededorp.

When the rest of the family came home in ones and twos they all looked surprised at the presence of the little black man. Aunt Mattie said nothing and behaved as though everything was normal; we all knew her so nobody said anything — within her hearing. Tibby and Catherine had much to say out in the yard, so that Aunt Mattie couldn't hear. She called him Pickanin — a variation on piccaninny — little one — so we called him that behind their backs. When my mother came from work that night Aunt Mattie silenced her with one of her 'looks'.

Pickanin stayed the night — with Aunt Mattie. When we got up next morning he was gone. We did not see him all day nor that night, nor the next night. But on the third morning, before sunrise, Pickanin was back. With him he brought a donkey cart piled high with firewood drawn by a big handsome strong Jenny. Aunt Mattie glowed as she welcomed him with a hot mug of coffee and a plate of cornmeal porridge. She warned us off with her eyes, and the two of them sat quietly talking and sipping coffee for the best part of an hour. Then Pickanin put on his battered trilby, adjusted his jacket, cracked his small whip and drove the cart in the direction of white Fordsburg.

For many days and weeks this new routine dominated our lives. Piccanin was the man of the house now and we all accepted it because Aunt Mattie would brook nothing else. Tibby was as irreverent as ever; she and Catherine were forever snickering about the strange little new black man in Aunt Mattie's life.

One day I was ordered to go with him on his selling trip. It was my first time close to him. We walked up one street and down another called out: 'Firewood! Firewood!' until we had sold more than half the wood. I noticed his gentleness with the donkey, how he caressed her neck when nobody was looking; how she nuzzled against his shoulder when he adjusted her harness or gave her a snack of fodder or a drink of water when we paused. At one point when there were no people about, no customers, and we had paused from calling 'Firewood! Firewood! Shilling a bundle!', the donkey was directly behind him and he could not see her face. She raised her head, pushed it forward and stretched out her lips as far as they would go, and bared her teeth at his back. I burst out laughing. I couldn't help myself. I had never seen anything like that.

Without turning, Pickanin said: 'She mock me', the words filled with laughter. And suddenly they were both my friends, the big beautiful grey donkey and the blackest little man I had ever seen up to then. I could see why Aunt Mattie liked him. In the days that followed, going out selling firewood with Pickanin and his donkey became an adventure I looked forward to.

It ended all too suddenly. One morning he did not load the little cart with firewood from the stockpile in the far corner of our yard. He and Aunt Mattie talked quietly for a while. Then he looked at me with a twinkle in his eyes.

'Bye, Lee. I leaving.'

'Why?' I cried.

'Family die me shamba. Must go take care.'

'Will you come back?'

A rare smile lit up the little face. He looked at me as he looked at his donkey when no one was looking.

'Don't know.' It was a whisper. 'Remember me...'

I nuzzled against the donkey's neck. And then Aunt Mattie and I watched him leading his donkey and cart out of our lives. This little incident had been out of my mind for all these years until just now, as I reflect on Aunt Mattie. So much I would have liked to ask, but I did not know how at the time. Who were they really, these two women who shaped me? Where did they come from? Where were they born? Where did they go to school? Who were their parents? Did they have any other relatives beside each other? Why were they the kind of women they were, who could turn poky little backyard rooms in Vrededorp, Johannesburg, racist South Africa, into homes filled with love and sanctuaries where strangers sometimes paused for rest before moving on? So much I would have liked to know about my Aunt Mattie and her sister, my mother. In a coldly hostile and cruel place they somehow taught us how to be gentle, how to laugh, how to love, how to survive.

One of the things about the Vrededorp of my childhood was the coming and going of strangers. All manner of people came, staying for a day or many days, or weeks, or even years. And then they left. I do not remember anyone in the family ever asking where they came from or where they went. We depended on Aunt Mattie's judgement. She decided who to give shelter and who to turn away. We did not always agree with her choices, but her decisions were final. We either liked it or lumped it. And, looking back, I think my Aunt Mattie was quite a judge of character, despite that mistake of accusing me of stealing her — or rather, the family's — half-crown. Wherever you are, dear stern and beloved old lady, thank you. I wish I got to know you and your background better. All the years of my life I have remembered how you cared for my mother, your little sister, after she was nearly burnt to death; how you and Tibby and Catherine brought her back to life by your sheer will for her to stay alive. Above all, I remember the deep passion for 'family' you instilled in all of us. I was hugely blessed in the strong women who raised and shaped my way of looking at the world during those key early years.

DuBois / Garvey

Outside that family circle of love, the reality of my childhood and early years in the second decade of the twentieth century was much the same as for all who were black or brown or yellow or 'red' throughout the world. A singular difference was that in my South Africa colour prejudice and discrimination were institutionalised in law as well as custom. W.E.B. DuBois' bold declaration at the end of the nineteenth century and the beginning of the twentieth that: *The problem of the twentieth century is the problem of the colour line; of the relations between the lighter and darker races of man* defined for me and my generation the terms of our engagement with the world in which we had to live and love and affirm our humanity. But before that point there were the years of the internal struggle to unshackle our minds, which was, I think, perhaps the hardest part of all in the effort to come to terms with DuBois' definition of the problem of our age. In 1897 DuBois had said: 'One feels his two-ness — an American, a Negro, two souls, two thoughts, two unreconciled strivings, two warring ideals in one dark body.' When

I met DuBois in London nearly fifty years later those 'unreconciled strivings' were still there. The great scholar, the natural aristocrat, the man of taste and refinement in the delicately featured, impeccably dressed, dark body was still the prisoner and battlefield of his 'two-ness' in a way that I, from an equally, if not more, brutal background could never be. We carried the debilitating burden of an imposed sense of inferiority, an enormous questioning of our self-worth, but not DuBois' sense of 'two-ness'. Many, if not most of us, infected by the racism which enveloped every detail of our lives, became 'pure"Zulus, 'pure Xosas, 'pure' Sothos, 'pure" Pedis, 'pure' Shonas, 'pure' Ndebeles, 'pure' Kikuyus — even 'pure' Coloureds. Never victims of a sense of 'two-ness'. Which made that perhaps the most terrible burden for any human being, any group of human beings, to have to bear.

The great difference, I realised then, was in the numbers. There is a qualitative difference between being a minority and being a majority. Majorities are stronger under psychological pressure because numbers count. But only if they are aware of it. Otherwise the reality of one young District Commissioner in the uplands of Kenya or Uganda or Tanzania controlling vast areas of land with populations in their thousands would make no sense. This, in my youth, when I got to know South and East and Central Africa by wandering about it on foot or cow- or donkey-cart or truck or van, was one of the great revelations. One young DC, in all likelihood just out of some British or European university, with six to twelve brightly uniformed black Askaris, could control huge stretches of land and vast numbers of people because he was *Bwana* and behind him, in a faraway but powerful place was a *Bwana Kubwa* whose orders he enforced and who was terrible towards those who resisted his authority. Their numbers, though far away and unseen, could be terrible if crossed. So the young DC, still wet behind the ears, but suitably stern and authoritative, was the representative and the symbol of terrible legions who were ruthless when provoked. They could 'talk big' and threaten the likes of Kenyatta in the days when they ran 'White Africa', which essentially belonged to their white settlers. The history of earlier encounters was there to confirm this reality of the unseen, but ever present, might of imperial power. The British, the French, the Belgians were faraway numbers symbolised by the young DC in control of vast numbers of blacks. Not DuBois' two warring ideals in one dark body, but the raw and brute power of an invisible but very real army that could unleash havoc, as had been done during the same period when DuBois, in distant America, was using his big brain to try to come to terms with being black in a world where the real and visible majority was white. In East, South and Central Africa, the minority manipulated the majority into believing the minority was the majority, that there were more whites in the world than blacks; instilled in the blacks a sense of inferiority, inadequacy, worthlessness. They had the power. They used that power to 'occupy' and condition the minds of black folk, to cancel their past and to define their future for them. If as brilliant a mind as that of the highly gifted and educated W.E.B. DuBois could be plunged into psychic crisis by it, who could escape that kind of 'mental slavery'?

One black man, born on the Caribbean island of Jamaica twenty-one years after DuBois was born in the United States, seemed to have come to grips with this problem with startling clarity and without his own mind being thrown into turmoil. No wonder black folk the world over see him as the Black Moses. That man was Marcus Mosiah Garvey. Perhaps Garvey's single most striking attribute was his detachment from all the traditionally accepted avenues of protest, struggle and representation of his time. He did not join any of the then established parties or movements. All the other black and brown leaders of the period tried to use or influence the centres of power. They became Democrats in the United States, socialists in European — or communists in both. Not Garvey. This black man was his own man at the dawn of the twentieth century, long before others had even begun the painful process of questioning and challenging the assumptions of empire on which the white man's domination of the world was based. Garvey had none of the 'two-ness' which tortured DuBois. Where did he get this strong sense of the inviolability of his own person, of his own mind? In America DuBois was part of the black minority; in Jamaica Garvey was part of the black majority. Was that it? Then why did the millions of Africans of Central, East and Southern Africa, who greatly outnumbered the whites of their countries, not have this same characteristic? Is this capacity to rise above the normal conditioning and brainwashing process one of the measures of greatness? If, on the other hand, there is something in the history of the Jamaican struggle to explain the extraordinary spiritual, mental and emotional independence of Marcus Garvey, then what is it? Where do you look for it? Garvey died alone and in poverty in London in 1940. DuBois died in independent Ghana in 1963, greatly honoured by Kwame Nkrumah and the leaders of West Africa. He was honoured all over Africa for his pioneering work for Pan-Africanism. But in 1940 there were no independent African states to honour Garvey other than Liberia and Ethiopia. Liberia, moreover, was an American puppet state, and Ethiopia had its own troubles with Italy and with convincing others that it was not black like the rest of us (or if it was, it was a special kind of blackness which came down from the line of Solomon and Sheba). My own father had been one of a group of young Ethiopians who would not tolerate this mindset nor the brutal conditions of near-serfdom of the low-caste majority, so some were driven, and some chose to go, into exile. A small group ended up in South Africa where this particular one met my mother and became my father, and died after a spell of working on the Rand gold mines.

Garvey was never allowed into Africa by the British government, though that for him was the home of all Africans 'those at home and

those abroad'. He built a mighty movement of black people in the
United States, the Universal Negro Improvement Association and
the African Communities League. His extraordinary success frightened
the government as well as many black American leaders, including
W.E.B. DuBois. All the American communists, black and white,
denounced Garvey's movement as 'black racism'. Garvey was
imprisoned by the Americans and then deported. He was not well
received by the power brokers in his native land. He stood for local
elections on the limited property franchise of the day, and was defeated.
And most Jamaicans seemed not to have any stomach for what many
saw as his 'race politics'. The strongest impulse among most Jamaicans
was towards peace and harmony and racial co-existence. So Garvey's
attempts to rebuild his movement in Jamaica failed. He tried within
the region. He could not muster the same kind of massive support he
had enjoyed in the United States in general and in Harlem, the black
metropolis, in particular. The black folk of the Caribbean and Central
America were too widely dispersed to fashion the same type of great
cohesive movement he had built in America. So he moved to London
where he died at 53, alone and in poverty. The great W.E.B. DuBois
died in Nkrumah's Ghana at the venerable old age of 95. How much
did Jamaica shape Marcus Garvey?

Garvey was the youngest of eleven children, all but two of whom
died at birth or shortly after. He and an elder sister were the only
survivors. He grew up and went to school in the verdant beautiful little
town of St Ann's Bay. In *The Philosophy and Opinions of Marcus Garvey*
he tells the story of his friendship with a little white girl until her parents
forbade her to play with him and told her why. He does not say how he
came to know about this. The little girl may have told him why she
could no longer play with him. This was his first discovery of prejudice
and discrimination. He tells it in a matter-of-fact manner, as one might
talk of the discovery of something new — a pretty coloured stone in a
riverbed or a new-born baby bird fallen out of its nest.

At fourteen Garvey left school and became a printer's apprentice. Six years later, at twenty, the former apprentice led a printers' strike. When that failed and work was hard to come by, he did what most Jamaicans under pressure have done throughout their history. He travelled. He went to Central America, to South America. He worked at a variety of jobs, and everywhere he found the conditions of black folk the same. They were always at the bottom of the heap. They lived in the poorest areas, earned the lowest wages, had the fewest social amenities, received the lowest level of respect in the societies in which they were, whether as citizens or as transient workers. Being black, anywhere, meant being at the bottom of the scale. And he noted, too, that the blacks themselves seemed to accept this state of affairs. This Garvey was determined to end.

Oddly, in all his travels there is no indication that Garvey ever visited Haiti, the one independent black republic in the Americas. Why? The French government could keep him out of their colonial island territories in the Caribbean. Not out of Haiti, the land of the Black Jacobins. So why did he not go to Haiti? The truth is that for all their long history of independence, the Americans, who had expelled Garvey from their own country, were the overlords in Haiti. They did not want Garvey in Haiti. I suspect language was another problem. He must have acquired a working knowledge of Spanish when he travelled and worked in Central America. Most Jamaicans who travelled to those parts did. And he did go to Cuba, the largest island of the Caribbean, despite the American influence. Even back then, in the 1920s, the Cuban relationship with the United States was different and difficult. So Garvey and his movement were welcomed. Indeed, the Garvey movement was so strong in Cuba that it was, at one time, the second largest UNIA centre in the world, after Harlem. And when Garvey visited Cuba in 1921 he was received with all the pomp and ceremony due to a visiting head of government. The Cuban blacks were a militant lot and in later years formed a core group when Fidel Castro launched his revolution against the American-backed Batista regime. Is it any wonder that the Cubans, at a critical stage of the Southern African struggle, sent soldiers and military and material support to stop the racist South African army and tilt the balance against the forces of Apartheid and in favour of the black freedom fighters of Angola? The earlier influences of the Garvey movement in Cuba surely had a bearing.

Language, particularly the spoken word, was Garvey's greatest tool. If he could not speak to the people he met he could not influence them. His presence, the power of his personality, the magnetism of his style of speech were part and parcel of his message. Without these he was just a short, tubby little black man with an air of authority. So language was key, and his was English, the language of the imperial British colonial masters who had brought his forebears from the Guinea Coast of Africa. In the process they had taken away the African languages of his ancestors; taken away whatever African name he could have been given; taken away whatever history, whatever culture they had; taken away the ancestral gods and spirits which guided tribal life, and replaced them with an austere, bearded white God who was without laughter. Tribal gods are gods of mischief and fun and laughter, as well as of dark wrath and great anger, much as were ancient Europe's own gods of the pre-Christian world. The language of imperial Europe and its imperial God, reinforced European overlordship and control. In the end it was that same language, the English language, and the Christian Bible which became the most powerful tools used by the descendants of the slaves in their liberation efforts and the forging of a place for themselves in an increasingly global environment. The language in which the black American DuBois defined the problem of the twentieth century was English. And he used it most gracefully and eloquently. The language in which Garvey exhorted black folk to self-awareness, black self-respect, black dignity, black enterprise, was English. And he used it as shock therapy to redefine black awareness.

The language of the British Empire became, in Asia, in Africa and in the islands of the seas wherever the Union Jack flew, the language of emancipation, of the struggle for freedom. Gandhi used it. Nehru used it like a poet. Mandela used it — though these three, and others, had not been deprived of their own native languages. Only those whose forebears had endured the Middle Passage, like Garvey and DuBois, had no other.

So the English language, in this century, long before it became the world's first language, was mobilised and used in the service of the freedom struggle. The spreading world-wide importance of English as the language of politics, business, commerce and technology, ensured the centrality of the struggles of those who spoke that language. Language, almost more than anything else, made the struggles of the French-, Spanish-, Dutch-, Portuguese-speaking anti-colonial freedom fighters marginal compared to those of the English-speaking freedom fighters. So the young Indonesians and Vietnamese and others were sent to London to learn English as part of their preparation as freedom fighters. Thus the struggle, in its turn, spread the language and helped make it the world language it is at the start of the twenty-first century. What would have been the shape and nature of the Indian and African struggles if Gandhi, Nehru, DuBois, Garvey, Nkrumah, Kenyatta and Mandela had been colonial subjects of non-English-speaking empires? Would the world have looked the same? Would world politics, would the United Nations and its multitude of agencies, have looked the same? Would our world be the same today if some language other than English had been the primary instrument of change? Indeed, in the process of becoming a major instrument of change, the English language itself has undergone profound change. Read Nehru's *Glimpses of World History,* read *The Philosophy and Opinions of Marcus Garvey,* read DuBois' *The Souls of Black Folk,* read the flowering of literature in English from Africa, Asia and the Caribbean, then ask: whose language is this? Certainly, W.E.B. DuBois wrote English with a grace and elegance only a small minority of those born in Britain can match. And beside the great Churchill, few could mobilise the English language and send it into battle as Marcus Garvey could. And Garvey's audiences were the most dispossessed and denied and mentally and emotionally crushed of the earth. Yet he used the English language to straighten their backs and turn them into men and women of self-regard and dignity. And he chastised them verbally into becoming proud hard working and co-operative human beings instead of sullen, sneaky and servile puppets in a white world with no respect for them. For me, this straightening up of the spines of the black men of the Diaspora, was Garvey's greatest contribution to the emancipation from mental slavery. It defied and contradicted, at the level of the individual, the whole superstructure on which the notion of the inferiority of black folk was based. It was the antithesis of everything South Africa's racism was. A Garveyite, by definition, and I have, over the years, met many of them in many parts of the world, is a free man, a free woman, who knows his/her own measure. He is a good husband and father. She is a good wife and mother. Garveyism condemns drugs and strong drink. It puts a high premium on clean and healthy living, on education, on family life, on discipline and self-discipline. It teaches hard work. It is Christian, but its God is not the conventional white patriarch with the flowing white hair and beard. He is a dark God on whom the sun has shone.

We knew a Jamaican Garveyite a very long time ago. He was a quiet, gentle, smiling man called Mr White. He was a carpenter. We met him at a public meeting at Miss Amy Bailey's private school, where young girls, usually from poor rural backgrounds, were trained in the skills of domestic work: how to become proficient household helpers and managers. Records were kept of the careers of those who passed through Miss Bailey's school and the school helped place them in jobs, helped negotiate their pay and conditions and make periodic visits to their workplace to ensure compliance. Miss Amy Bailey's young women were in great demand as helpers in the homes of the well-to-do of Kingston and St Andrew.

We had just completed the building of the shell of our home, Coyaba, high up in the hills of West Rural St Andrew. I told Mr White we needed some carpentry done. Without hesitation he offered to do the work. I had told the meeting of how I had discovered the writings of Marcus Garvey while still in South Africa. This, I suspect, was the reason for Mr White's prompt offer.

'But we are more than twelve miles up in the hills, Mr White.'

'No matter.'

'How will you get there?'

'My bicycle.'

I had just bought a small second-hand old car. I offered to pick him up.

'No need to. It's easier if I come. You won't have to make two journeys.'

'But it's far and very steep', Daphne protested.

'No matter. I'll come. Not tomorrow or the next day. I have work doing. The day after.'

I was not sure we would see Mr White again. But three days later, on a cold, slightly damp, November morning, a little after six o'clock, there was Mr White, his tools strapped to the frame of his bicycle. He had kept his word and made the long steep journey up to Coyaba. Daphne was awe-struck, trapped between tears and laughter.

At that earlier meeting where I had spoken, Mr White had told us that he had met 'Mr Garvey' personally and worked with him at Edelweiss Park in Kingston during his brief sojourn in Jamaica after his expulsion from the United States.

As Daphne gave him a glass of fresh orange juice because he did not drink coffee, I whispered to her:

'Mr Garvey's man.'

All the people who had met and spoken or worked with Marcus Garvey had this one thing in common. They all talked of 'Mr Garvey'. Never Garvey or Marcus Garvey. Even his second wife, Amy Jacques Garvey, the keeper of his record and his memory until her death, talked of 'Mr Garvey'. And when I tried, once, to get her to tell me what kind of a human being the man was, what made him laugh, what made him angry, what kind of father, what kind of husband he was, she could not. You talked about 'Mr Garvey's' ideas, his vision, his words, struggles, not about 'Mr Garvey' himself. When I tried to ask the same questions of the first Mrs Garvey, Amy Ashwood Garvey, the playgirl of his younger life, she also 'choked up'. She could call him Garvey and recall some of the conspiracies and intrigues around him at the height of the power of his organisation. But the personal details of an ordinary, living breathing human being with the characteristics common to all people — those she could not evoke. The nearest we get to Garvey, the ordinary mortal, is in his autobiographical writings of early childhood, printed in *The Philosophy and Opinions*, which Amy Jacques had compiled and a copy of which she presented to me when I first arrived in Jamaica in 1955. A few years later, when we had settled in Jamaica, she asked for the return of the book and subsequently sent me her later work, *Garvey and Garveyism,* as a replacement. The little personal vignette about the little black boy and his little white playmate and why their friendship ended, was not part of the later work. It was all politics without any human touch. Today there is a large and impressive body of scholarly works on the life and times and struggles and significance of Marcus Garvey, mainly by a new generation of black scholars. And, willy-nilly, those of the western world who in his time had scoffed and mocked and belittled his efforts are going to be forced to recognise him as one of the most profound influences of the twentieth century. I think the judgement of history will be that this was an enormously good influence for all humanity. Of how many others can we say that in these closing days of this century whose central problem DuBois identified as the problem of the relations between the lighter and darker races of mankind?

And how they had to suffer and endure, these two, DuBois and Garvey, just to affirm our common humanity! Why? Why was colour the most crucial issue of our century?

Would it have been any less traumatic for more than half the human race if the problem of the twentieth century had been something else?

3

The London Days

I arrived in wartime London on a cold damp foggy day in late October 1940. Between that day in Durban in 1939 when I signed on as a stoker's trimmer and my arrival in London, I had spent more than a year at sea. I never had much fat on my body, and the little I had was quickly sweated out in the over-heated stoke-hold where the furnace which powered the merchant ship had to burn day and night. My thin body soon became hard bone and muscle held together by a layer of skin. No amount of water I drank could quench an endless thirst. I developed a craving for salt. After three weeks of physical distress my body adjusted. I was at ease with my parched, dry, hard new body, with the almost mindless new me who was always too tired and worn down to think or dream.

My first ship was an old tramp travelling between the Suez Canal, the East coast of Africa and the ports of the Bay of Bengal. I got to know the poky little drinking places of Suez and where you could get the best coffee any early morning after a booze-up the night before. I once won, and lost, a small fortune of several tens of thousands of

Piastres at the casino in Suez. I remember a small, pretty, English-speaking young woman in western dress sticking close to me while I was winning and fading away suddenly when I had lost all. I also remember the older Egyptian men at the gambling table consoling me when I lost. I felt more at home in Suez, more at ease, than I had ever felt anywhere in South Africa except within the family circle. I was completely oblivious to anyone's colour, except as a way of describing a person. *She was a small dark-brown woman with her eyes circled in deep greenish blue, her hair henna coloured, her fingers and toenails a matching ochre. Or he was a tall thin near-black man with long tapering fingers, dressed in a flowing, almost glowing white Jellaba.* It was fun to be able to think and talk about colour without its racial overtones and undertones. And the areas around the Suez Canal and the Red Sea, and particularly the town of Suez, were where I first experienced that delight. I never got to like camel flesh but I enjoyed the very many ways in which fish, rice, and cornmeal could be cooked.

Mombasa, Aden, the small settlements inland from the ports and the small, neat and trim habitations on the edge of the desert made me feel back in Biblical times. There were places and people in that part of the world who seemed unaffected by DuBois' or Garvey's preoccupation with the *problem of the twentieth century.* I have not been back to those places in all of sixty years. I wonder if they are still as free of that *problem* as they were when I was there. But then, Israel with its surprising and distressing brand of racism had not yet emerged. The Jews, then, were just another set of victims of racism and discrimination and, under the Nazis, subject to the most brutal repression next to slavery, in the twentieth century. Such people are not expected to become racists when they throw off the yoke of racism. That was the conventional wisdom. It is not all that true or wise. Suffering, exploitation, discrimination do not confer special wisdom and understanding. They only teach how to do it to others; how to be racist; how to brutalise the weak and the vulnerable. In the same way, beating a child or a spouse only teaches the victim how to become a child or spouse abuser when he/she becomes a husband, a wife, a parent, a policeman, a teacher or an occupation soldier. Brutalisation of any kind is a 'How To' lesson. It does not deepen anybody's humanity. It is most unlikely that the Aden-Suez region of those early years is still the same today.

It was, of course, a time of war and every now and then the war intruded dramatically, usually at night. Whenever we were in port, the harbour was crowded with other ships and only a few — two or three — could lie at dockside. Most times we were a distance out in the water and went ashore by little Arab ferries. Time was strictly observed. We never knew when we might be ordered to join a convoy or where we might go next. Only the man on the bridge knew that. So when the shore pass said be back by such and such a time, we were back. Once, three seamen were late returning to ship. We watched them waving and shouting frantically from dockside. We had been ordered to move at a certain hour and only the man on the bridge knew that secret hour. Shore leave was carefully timed with that hour in mind and we learned the importance of obeying instructions strictly.

One clear moonlit night we were the lucky ones at dockside. Most of the other ships were lying in 'the stream' with cargo and people having to be ferried from shore to ship. In wartime and on all the waterfronts we knew work went on all the time, night and day. When one group of workers, seamen or dockhands, broke from work another group took their place. The faces and bodies changed, but the work did not stop. In easy times on board ship we had a routine of eight hours on and eight hours off. Under pressure it was changed to four hours on and four hours off. And under attack we just worked until the attack was over, whatever its duration. Suddenly we heard the eerie sound of air-raid sirens. We all knew what to do and rushed to our duty stations. The lights went out everywhere, but the moon was so big and bright that the town, the docks, the shape of the ships must all have been clearly visible to the incoming planes. After a few minutes of the kind of silence in which you hear the thumping of your own heart, the world exploded into sound. The planes and the bombing started from what seemed a great distance. Then suddenly it was on us. Searchlights from shore and some ship traced the moonlight night and picked up a small dark object which seemed to slide down the shaft of bright light till it was near the ground then broke free of it and a huge explosion shattered the night. A ship near us was hit. It lit up the clear night. We heard the whine of a plane coming down from almost overhead and the single anti-aircraft gun on the stern of our own ship peppered the sky. A bomb blast nearly lifted us out of the sea and at the same time our gunner let out the kind of scream that was like an imaginary roar from hell as we watched flames spurting from the little plane now streaking away. But then another near-miss started a fire on our own deck and there was no time for thought; only the frantic battle to control and put out the fire. When we did, morning was on us.

Our gunner was a giant of a man. I think he was Scandinavian. In my many months on that particular ship I never once heard him speak. He seemed a law unto himself, not over-awed by the Captain and First Officer, as were all the rest of the ship's crew. There was a nurse, a middle-aged woman, I guessed, rather dumpy and motherly looking. The Belgian officer corps of the ship treated her with protective deference. I came to realise that these people, the huge Scandinavian gunner and the Belgian officer corps, and the few key lowers ranks like the Mate, his two assistants and half a dozen or so highly experienced Belgian seamen, were people at war, pursuing that war with grim intensity. I learned the reason for this much later. These people's homelands were under German occupation; homes, families, loved ones were under occupation, which made whatever they were doing part of the grim and bitter war against the Nazis. This single-minded passion made them different from those of us for whom this period on the high seas was either adventure or a means to escape, as in my case, from some monstrous home background.

The ship which took a direct hit in Suez harbour that bright moonlit night sank with three or four of its crew perishing. When we steamed out, we passed its submerged hull, part above water.

This time we went further south than on our previous trips. We spent twenty-four hours in Cape Town. I did not go ashore — just in case. Other merchant ships steamed into the harbour, all laden with cargo and sitting deep in the water. I watched them gather and remembered other such convoys. But this time we were not going up and down the Suez Canal, the Red Sea and through the Bay of Bengal. This time, with the huge British battleships as the mother ships in front, behind, and on the side away from land, we left the Cape of Good Hope and steamed slowly up the Atlantic, hugging the west coast of Africa. It was cold and the sea was rough. Working in the furnace-like stoke-hold was a great relief.

I knew that at long last I was on the way to Europe — if the submarines did not get us first. We were to the back of the convoy of the largest gathering of merchant ships I had ever seen. It was not a good position. The German submarines had the habit of picking off the slow ones and the tail-enders. But we were also on the inside, nearer the land, which was often visible. Halfway up the Atlantic we began losing ships. A pack of submarines, like hunter sharks, nightly picked off one cargo vessel after another. The warships dropped their depth-charges, but there was no way of knowing with what effect. It was not until we were near where the West African bump of Nigeria-the Gold Coast-French West Africa jutted into the Atlantic that extra help came in the form of low-flying planes skimming the ocean and dropping their own depth-charges. I watched at least one grey dark submarine, frighteningly close to us, put its nose up into the air and then sink with an explosion which shook the sea and the ships on it for miles around. A hooting British warship hustled the merchant ships closer together. Stokers were put on the round-the-clock four hours on, four hours off emergency regime. I lost count of the days and nights. I think everybody did. Then, one morning, everything suddenly relaxed. The sea was calm. The world seemed brighter, though still very cold. There was land on the far horizon to the right of us. Then I saw the convoy dispersing. Groups of ships took different directions approaching the distant land.

I had made it. That land had to be Britain. It had taken me the best part of two years to get this far. The dreams which had been suppressed almost to the point of not being there at all began to stir again. I was twenty-one. My body was thin and dry and hard and strong. I had worked physically harder than I had thought myself capable of. The palms of my hands were hard, coarse and calloused. I once opened my skin rubbing the side of my face. Once or twice I had to fight fiercely to ensure my right to remain my own person. There was a huge scar across my back, made by a hot stoker's iron, which stayed on my body for more than twenty years before finally fading away. I had made good friendships with young men who had decided that the security and relative peace and comfort of life at sea was for them and that being merchant seamen would be their jobs henceforth. I saw the sense in that. Being at sea had been a good, maturing experience. It had helped me become a man. But it was only one phase of my life, a phase which was now ending. Soon, it would be behind me. There were the promises I had made to be fulfilled: some to me, some to others. So, all day long, I watched the land draw near and remembered the promises. It took an enormous time, and the slow old ship seemed slower than ever. Somebody said we would be docking in Liverpool where our precious cargo would be discharged. It did not matter where we docked or when. It would, in any case, take time, to let go of all the many pent-up emotions. I remember fleetingly thinking of my mother and Tibby. I must write to them; they would be worried. Then I had my first sight of the rolling green fields of England, soft, gentle, inviting from that great distance. I felt a little apprehensive, but not greatly so. This, after all, was what I had chosen for myself. And there is something liberating about completing a long, difficult and, at times, seemingly impossible journey of your own choosing. Now it was over. Now it was time for the new beginning.

After a long day of processing, after growing a little more relaxed with the reality that everywhere I turned I saw only white faces, I finally boarded the train for London. We talk of 'white' faces, but in strict terms of colour as a thing of the spectrum, no human beings are 'white' just as no human beings are 'black'. No living human being I have ever seen looks like the colour 'white'. I have seen variations from a very pale pink through to a near-red or a complexion tinged with a creamy yellow. Never 'white' — except when they are dead and all blood is drained from their bodies — and that I have not seen. But, surely, even then a residual touch of colour must remain. I think when we finally get around to putting this thing behind us, we will stop talking about any group of living human beings as 'white' or 'black'. They looked far more interesting in their variety of creamy coloured-ness than any 'white' person could possibly be. But being white in a racist world is part of the foolishness that takes pride in describing oneself as looking like some bloodless sheet!

The people themselves were quiet and carefully, delicately friendly, as if anxious not to risk rebuff. I learned later that it was different when you travelled first-class. There, no one looked at anyone else, no one spoke. Everyone hid their faces behind newspapers. Not so in the crowded second-class carriages. They seemed to know I was a stranger in a strange land and they carefully avoided saying or doing anything that might upset the stranger in their midst. This was wartime Britain, and war, it seems, has this odd way of pulling people together.

The neat and tidy landscape rushed by; acre after acre of green fields, all looking beautifully managed and controlled. The hand of man, here, was in control as I had never seen it in Africa. There, the battle to control was continuous and the land seemed still to resist. There, if you left the land alone for a season, it reverted to jungle. There, the forest took back its own. Here, the jungle had given up and the land belonged to man, not to itself anymore. The rolling green acres flashing by would, it seemed, of their own volition, remain cropped and green and tidy even if left alone for a long time. But for how long? Could England ever revert to jungle in the same way I have seen in Africa?

I had, growing up, seen England through the eyes of its poets and dreamers. Wordsworth's England, Byron's England, Shelley's England, venerable old Williams Blake's England. The London I entered was a great bustling metropolitan city at war, an imperial power fighting to hold on to that empire. And the teeming colonial subjects of that empire did not, on the whole, want England to lose that war, but they also did not want the empire to emerge unchanged from it. This, for very many of us, was the hard dilemma.

The contact address had been given to me in Durban nearly two years earlier. It was somewhere off Hampstead Heath and I did not know if the person would still be at the same address. When I tried earlier in the day, there was no reply. I crossed the road, hoisted the light suitcase with all my worldly belongings onto my shoulder and climbed the slightly sloping hill to the top of the Heath. It was all familiar from my readings. I felt oddly at home on Hampstead Heath. Being colonial and missionary-trained meant, in my case, knowing more about the 'mother country' than about the country in which I was born. The missionary schooling inevitably imbued me with the English vision of the way things are. My teachers at St Peter's in Rosettenville, outside Johannesburg and at Grace Dieu, outside the northern Transvaal Boer town of Pietersburg, had been graduates of

Oxford and Cambridge, products of English religious orders. They transmitted their values to several generations of black South Africans. So I was freer on Hampstead Heath on my first day in London than I had been in any public park in the land of my birth.

I found a huge shade-giving tree and using my small suitcase as pillow, I raised the collar of my overcoat which I had bought for three pounds at a second-hand clothes store off the Liverpool dockyard, lay down and immediately went into a deep sleep.

When I woke I was chilled to the bone and the sun was going down. It was that special time just before the day ends and the night begins: the magical twilight hour — which is never as sharply defined and clear-cut in tropical lands. People were about, but a black man sleeping on Hampstead Heath at twilight seemed not unusual to them. I found a public toilet and wash place, washed my face, tidied myself and walked down to the street facing the Heath to try again.

This time someone was home. A plumpish young woman with hardly any chin. Yes, it was the right place; yes, I was expected. I was escorted to a sparsely furnished upstairs flat and given a cup of tea. There was a sense of dormitory living about the place. This was how things felt at St Peter's and at Grace Dieu. I was offered another cup of tea. I accepted gratefully. The English habit of the cup of tea began and stayed with me until, many years later, Jamaican Blue Mountain coffee took over as completely. The young woman told me her name, which I immediately forgot. While she busied herself in the kitchen I browsed through the books on a single home-made bookshelf. They were all paperbacks, all 'Left Book Club' editions, a combination of Marxist studies and left-wing novels. Among them, I remember *Love on the Dole, Studies in a Dying Culture* and George Orwell's *Down and Out in Paris and London*.

A little over an hour later, two more women of the house arrived from work. Then, shortly after, my contact came: the person I knew from South Africa. I was shaken by the warmth and freedom of her embrace. I had not been that close to any woman for more weeks than I cared to remember, and the soft closeness roused me. I was embarrassed but no one noticed, or if they did, they did not let on. Memory throws back odd little details across time and space: a flash of arousal, sharply recalled more than sixty years later.

These four women shared the flat overlooking Hampstead Heath. It was a crowded two-bedroom, kitchen and bathroom and spacious living room which was the communal centre. Two women shared each bedroom. Three were white South Africans, one was English. The South Africans were open, loud, forthcoming; the English woman was naturally quiet and reserved. I noticed how the speech patterns of the South Africans, their way of speaking English, had changed subtly, become more akin to the English way of speaking. They were now English women, though born in South Africa, able to fade into the English landscape as no black South African could. Being born white in South Africa or anywhere in the empire and Commonwealth automatically conferred this special status. You had no problem finding a place to live, a job, trade union membership, access to social services. Being white, speaking English, you were accepted as English, entitled to all the rights of citizenship. This sharp difference in how the 'mother country' received its black and white children of empire lingers to this day, making for resentments and bad feelings between black and white in the former colonies.

When white Africans were under pressure in later years to justify their possession of all the best land of what they claimed was 'White Africa', they insisted they were Africans, 'white Africans' as entitled to Africa as anybody else, part of the African landscape. I sympathised with the claim. It had merit, but not enough to justify the 'alienation' of the land from its original inhabitants and certainly not enough to excuse the elaborate legal and constitutional structures of racial discrimination they inflicted on their fellow Africans who were black. And the 'mother country' condoned these practices, whether of the 'white Africans', the 'white Australians', the 'white Canadians', or the 'white West Indians'. In this sense the 'mother country' fostered inequity.

I slept on the living room sofa that first night in London. During the evening and next morning my contact made several phone calls and told me a friend of theirs, 'a comrade' with a flat of her own in Belsize Park, was prepared to rent me a room. I might be able to get a job at a place called Central Books.

'It's a party set-up and they don't pay well but it's a start,' she said. Then: 'Frankly, Peter, you'll meet discrimination in finding a good job.'

They fed me well that first night. The only thing was that they were vegetarians and the African in me missed the taste of meat. But I was grateful to these women who had taken me in, fed me, found a room for me and promised to help me find a job. Other new arrivals, I learned later, had not fared so well.

I spent the next few days settling in and getting the feel of London. Belsize Park was as obviously working-class as Hampstead was middle-class. My landlady, Dorothy, was from Yorkshire and had come to London when she was twenty, more than a decade earlier. She was a tenant herself, renting the flat from a stocky Irish immigrant builder who had made good in London. When I met him I concluded that he was a supporter of the Irish independence struggle. Dorothy was trim, self-contained, businesslike and made no bones about being 'in the movement'. She, too, was vegetarian, but she would not mind if I cooked the occasional meat dish. My room had a large window from which I could see a small sliver of the green of Belsize Park — nothing remotely like wonderful Hampstead Heath, but a welcome green glimpse all the same. I often took a book and spent a few quiet hours reading in Belsize Park, while children played and women pushed prams and old folk strolled. At such times the war seemed far away and London seemed the most peaceful place on earth.

But at nights, sometimes, that peace was violently shattered. First we heard the air-raid sirens, wailing like the damned, then the eerie waiting, then the sound of planes, then the thud of bombs, usually far away, nearer the centre of London but occasionally very close and — at least once — down our street and shattering our windows. We all carried some form of identity. I had received identity papers when I signed off the ship. Once or twice in my wanderings about London at night some policeman had stopped me with 'Can I see your papers, mate?' Such encounters had usually been cordial. There had not been many black faces on the streets of London in those days, especially at night. The great influx from Africa, the Caribbean and the Indian sub-continent was still in the future. Most of the blacks seen in London were in uniform, part of the country's fighting forces, 'our boys', there to defend the 'mother country'; the empire in solidarity against the Nazis who would enslave the world. The racism of the Nazis threatened to make whatever we had experienced look like child's play. If they could be so brutal to the Jews, what would they do to the blacks? So large numbers of black young men and women rallied to the defence of the empire. The mood of a shared enterprise in defence of freedom was tangible.

Soho became one of my favourite places. It had the feel and air of a cosmopolitan village. I loved the variety of food displayed on the open window stalls and I loved the dark little cafés where you could get a simple but sumptuous meal for about five shillings. Above all, I loved the strings of sausages, salamis and crusty fresh 'French' loaves that you could take home and turn into a feast with a cheap bottle of Chianti. When day-to-day English food — meat, butter, milk, cheese — was being rationed, the off-ration stuff of Soho made life more interesting.

In one little dead-end Soho corner I discovered what looked like an ordinary food joint with a licence to sell drinks. That, indeed, was what it was in daytime. At night it became a hot little club, crammed with pretty girls and more black men than I had seen in London up to then. Drinks flowed freely and the men and women fraternised. My experience at sea told me that these pretty young English women were what we now call 'sex workers'. This, I learnt, was Bah's club. Bah was a tall, thin, elegantly black-suited West African who drove up to his club in one of those sleek and swanky cars you see in newsreel pictures. A chauffeur, white, opened the door and first one beautiful blonde, then tall black Bah with two gold teeth, rings on three of his fingers, a chain on his left wrist, and then another beautiful young woman with striking red hair followed him out of the car. The two women flanked Mr Bah into the bar. In any of the *Saint* novels or the *Bulldog Drummond* tales, Mr Bah would have been the powerful villain who had to be brought down by the end of the story. I had read about this type of man in my sister's pulp magazines. Now I was seeing him in real life.

In real life it turned out that Mr Bah was basically a gambler. London was full of gamblers, but they were white and thus not much noticed. Mr Bah was. On my second visit to his club, a white man, an apparent regular, once offered me a drink.

'You're new here.' It was more a statement than question.

'Yes.'

'Be careful. Bah's dangerous.'

'How? Why?'

'Just be careful. Not your kind.'

I did not see that undercover stranger again. But I did check and found out that Mr Bah had served time in a British prison. Now, he had a collection of beautiful young women he had set up at various 'good' addresses as 'sex workers' whom he managed. It seemed a mutually willing arrangement between the 'workers' and Mr Bah. And Mr Bah flourished, owned a stable of racing dogs, one or two racehorses and several fancy cars. This was successful black enterprise with a vengeance. And I did not like it. Mr Bah tried to recruit me into his 'business' with the promise of big money and any 'beautiful gal' I wanted. When I said no, our budding friendship died and then one of his workers warned me off Mr Bah's club.

When I turned him down, Bah had snapped:

'What wrong with you? You John Bull nigger?'

'No.'

'Then what?'

I shrugged. 'This is not right.'

'They do it to us. They use our women. Been to Lagos?'

'Yes.'

'Accra?'

'Yes.'

'Freetown?'

'Yes.'

'Cape Town?'

'Yes. You been there?'

'Me been everywhere. Cape Town, Cairo, everywhere. They do it with our women, so I do it with their women. Only I treat them good. Join me?'

'No.'

'Damn John Bull nigger!'

Mr Bah had no time, no patience, for John Bull niggers.

I was not sorry when months later Mr Bah was convicted, given a heavy sentence and then deported back to West Africa.

Any way you look at it, racial exploitation is ugly, whether coming from white or black. I have often wondered, over the years, what triggered Mr Bah's particular form of black racism. West Africans are not usually as preoccupied with race and colour as those of us who have had daily living contact with white racism. So what started Mr Bah's? Is he still around? He was older than me by a good ten years, I would guess. I have come across other expressions of black racism, but not in Mr Bah's extreme exploitative form. There is no virtue, no goodness in hurting, abusing, degrading someone white because you have been abused, degraded and hurt by someone white. The hard moral issue is where and how to begin to break this impulse to mutual denigration and degradation between black and white. How to stop Mr Bah's use of the flower of English beauty to degrade the English? Surely, how it began, what caused Mr Bah to do it, must be a cardinal part of the answer. To just want to put everything behind you, to say it is in the past and we must forget the past and get on with the future, is to say that the Jews must forget the Holocaust, must forget their six million dead; or that the Palestinian Arabs must forget being driven out of their homeland and must get on with living in peace with the Jews. It is to say slavery was in the past, that the loss of the millions in the Middle Passage and after is part of an old history that is to be forgiven and forgotten. If we accept that, the social and moral sickness of a century and more of racial exploitation will be covered over like a cancerous boil waiting to erupt at the first opportunity. We are seeing signs of this eruption of old and uncleaned cancerous social boils in many places. The bombings and terrorism of the aggrieved of the Middle East; the murders of white farmers by the land-hungry dispossessed blacks of once 'white Africa'; the 'senseless' vengeful acts of murder, robbery and violence in the choicest tourist areas. These are symptoms of the festering of unresolved social, moral and economic sores which must be addressed if we are to move past DuBois' *Problem of the Twentieth Century,* past the sense of the 'two-ness' of American black men.

Garvey saw the possibility of a wholeness in self-respect and mutual respect between all peoples and all races and colours. Not based on ideology, or the notion of power blocs, or North and South, or East and West, but starting with the simple acceptance of the inviolability of the dignity of the human person. This view of a common personhood goes far back in human history to a time before our monkey-clever ancestors thought they were masters of creation, back to a time when human survival was a matter of touch and go, when any serious mistake could have meant the end for our species. To survive, early man had to think clearly, come to terms with his own limitations and with the environment, and try to not offend the creatures with whom he had to co-exist in that dangerous, fragile, delicately balanced early world. Was it luck, instinct or conscious choice which led to the survival and ultimate triumph of our species? Probably a combination of all three. As a group, with rare exceptions, we are still too clever by far for our own good.

Marcus Garvey was one of those rare exceptions in the evolution of our species. By some historic or genetic miracle, or both, Garvey survived all the horrors of three hundred years of transplantation and transition with his psychic personality more intact than that of any other black man of our time. Which is why he did not need other men's intellectual crutches to think things through and define a way out of the problems of his own black folk.

By the time I got to London, Garvey had died. I never met the man alive. But I soon began to meet the many other blacks, who, for all sorts of different reasons, had made London their temporary home. There was a strong body of West African students who had their own Students' Union. There I met some of their future leaders, their future doctors and lawyers, the two professions most favoured by black students. West Indian students made up a smaller group. The West Africans were a dour lot who seemed to withdraw into themselves during the cold English winters. Their faces turned ashen, their dark skins purplish, their eyes sunk deep back in their heads as though trying to withdraw independently from the cold. A walking West African on a very cold London winter's day was a body wrapped in dark covering from head to toe with only a little opening at the top for eyes, nose, mouth and the steaming breath. They growled and grunted for speech.

The West Indians escaped into sounds and laughter — in Langston Hughes' words, 'laughing to keep from crying'. It made the

West Indians better company in the cold, cold days of an English winter. The West Indians were the operators of the small nightclubs and little restaurants where blacks and their friends congregated to eat and drink and pass the time and exchange the news from 'home'. A few East Indians, usually seamen who had decided to stay, also had their little 'curry houses'. Amy Ashwood Garvey, the first wife of Marcus Garvey, had turned a rented London suburban house into one of the most popular eating places. She was a gay spirit filled with pealing laughter, and she used men as men usually used women. Her neighbours resented this conversion of a residential home into a popular, loud nightclub. They brought a lawsuit against Amy, so Amy packed up and transferred to Harlem, New York, where she could do the same kind of thing without trouble. London's loss was Harlem's gain and there were many other converted London homes where blacks in Britain could go and for a modest price get a highly seasoned West Indian meal in good company.

This, looking back, was the seedbed of the later unity of African, American and Caribbean black folk. The students got to know each other personally. They had a West African Students' Union and a West Indian Students' Union. They shared classes, meals, parties. There were very few women students from Africa and the Caribbean in those early days, so they dated English young women, as well as the large body of European refugee students, mainly Jews who had fled the Nazis. The future lawyers, doctors, civil servants, teachers, got to know each other and each other's problems intimately and personally. Some, like our later younger friends, Ruth and Victor Kadalie (son of the great Clements Kadalie, the Nyasaland-born pioneer of the black South African trade union movement), inter-married. Ruth was a refugee student, Victor an African British colonial student. London was the critical point of contact where Pan-African, socialist and anti-colonial ideas were shared and enlarged.

When I got to London, the likes of George Padmore and Jomo Kenyatta were already there. Kenyatta's *Facing Mount Kenya,* first published in 1938, was still a great talking point among those interested in African affairs, and he himself was something of a lion in certain left-wing socialist circles. He was a regular lecturer at the network of adult workers' educational schools, colleges and workers' holiday camps all over Britain. But Padmore was the man to whom the politically-inclined among the blacks in Britain gravitated. He had a London County Council flat on Morningside Crescent in Camden Town. It was up two flights of narrow stairs, a dark place with small rooms leading off a tiny entrance space. I think there were three doors. There was the familiar smell of West Indian cooking. And what I guessed to be the largest room was where Padmore worked and met his visitors.

George Padmore seemed taller than he was because he held himself so ramrod straight. He was thin, austere, always neatly dressed, with crease-lines in his usually dark trousers and spotless white shirt under jacket and tie. His shoes always shone. I cannot remember Padmore without jacket and tie. I knew him for many years, but I never saw him in an open-necked shirt. Yet I recall seeing a picture of a much younger George Padmore in an open-necked shirt in Nancy Cunard's huge 1930s tome, *Negro:* a half-smiling, good-looking young man with a long pipe in his mouth.

When we met in late 1940 he had just recovered from an operation on his palate performed by Belfield Clarke, a Jamaican physician and surgeon practising in South London, near the Elephant and Castle underground station. Blacks from all over London, and even further afield, regularly took the long underground journey to be treated by Dr Clarke. He was 'our' doctor in London. Padmore had developed some throat ailment which had robbed him of speech. Dr Clarke had either himself performed the operation, or supervised it, and then guided Padmore's treatment until he was able to speak once more. His speech was impaired, but the iron will of the man was such that he forced himself back to public platform speaking.

Padmore was a totally political animal. His work room had one large table piled high with books and papers and a large old office typewriter that could make many copies at once. On that old machine he typed his 'dispatches' which were sent to the small local newspapers and magazines in Africa, Asia, the Americas and the Caribbean. I had used some of the Padmore dispatches when I edited a cyclostyled little magazine in Durban for the largely Indian Liberal Study Group. All the Padmore dispatches said 'please pass on to other periodicals'. This was the way most of the independent little papers and magazines in the colonies received a non-European perspective on what was happening in the world. Except for his English lady, also named Dorothy, who sometimes helped with the typing at weekends when she was not at work, Padmore did it all himself. He was the news-gatherer, the copy-taster, the sub-editor, the editor, the printer. He used thin paper that could take six to eight carbons, so a two-, three-, or four-page article, typed twice, could be sent anywhere from a dozen to eighteen destinations all over the world, and these were then reproduced by other little publications. He kept a record of those who had paid the nominal fee of five shillings for the dispatches. From time to time he clipped tiny reminder slips to the dispatches of those in arrears. Postal orders usually followed such reminders. That small, one-man operation was a major early version of a new, Third-World way of looking at the news. I have seen copies of these articles coming back to Padmore in the printed papers and magazines to which he had sent them. The only other influence in print I can recall which was as widespread as the Padmore dispatches was Marcus Garvey's *Negro World*, a proper printed newspaper which black seamen made a habit of leaving in every seaport where they stopped.

The George Padmore I met and knew did not talk much about his past and all he had done during that past. I knew he had been a very important person in the pre-war Moscow Soviet, that he had been an important functionary in the Communist International. I knew he was one of those who left Moscow at the time of the Soviet-German Pact between Stalin and Hitler — before the Soviet Union later joined the Western alliance against the Nazis. He had somehow found his way across Europe without falling into the hands of the Nazis. From the little information he dropped, I got the impression he spent a short time in Nazi Germany before reaching Britain. This was not stuff he ever talked about. When I asked, he became the stern, withdrawn stony-faced 'other man' whom all of us — Makonnen, Kenyatta and, later, Kwame Nkrumah (in those days Francis Nkrumah) — recognised quietly among ourselves as 'the Comintern man', the man we never argued with, never crossed. It was the 'Comintern man' who was contemptuous when Jomo had too much to drink. Or when Kwame was late for a meeting because of some woman. Or when I was too caught up in writing fiction to complete an assigned job.

There was a striking little painting on Padmore's wall. When Daphne, many years later, asked him about it, he said it was one he had himself painted.

'But why did you stop painting?' she exclaimed.

He silenced her with the cold contempt of the 'Comintern man'.

She appealed to me with her eyes. I shook my head imperceptibly. I did not want to get involved. In any case, he did not have much time for her. As far as he was concerned, she was not a 'comrade', not part of the 'movement', and she had diverted my interest from politics and the real issues. He was not hostile to her, but just very clear about his own priorities and what he saw as best for me and the movement. And this wild, free-thinking young bourgeois woman did not fit into his scheme of things. But I am ahead of myself.

Way back before Daphne, at the very beginning of my London days, Dorothy and her circle of women comrades, of whom my South African contact was one, guided me through the complexities of settling down in wartime London. I had to be registered to get my ration cards. I had to become part of the civil defence network of my area. I had to learn how to go about getting my rations. The women helped and guided me. I got a job as a dispatch clerk at Central Books, a socialist wholesale book outlet. I think the pay was about three pounds a week. The work was easy and monotonous, but I liked it because I could do a lot of reading on the job.

I realised, for the first time, what a truly vast body of writing there was on communism and socialism. I came to realise how deeply, passionately and fiercely the disagreements between communists themselves — Stalinists versus Trotskyites — and socialists were argued. It was war — with words, cutting, slashing, brutal, with the communists always on the offensive. The polemics in the left-wing magazines could be fierce. The bitterness of the written battles between Trotskyites and Stalinists was startling, almost more savage in intensity than the real war in which Britain was engaged. The isms and schisms within Marxism itself at times seemed larger than the struggle against 'the class enemy'.

One night, after one of the pre-Christmas parties we had gone to and where we had both taken too much of the available wine, Dorothy and I ended up in her bed. I woke alone in her bed next morning. I had a fierce wine headache. I knew I had been drunk, but I also knew we had made love. So what now? Would she want me to leave? Would we try to go back to how it was before?

Then she came in, wrapped in a pretty dressing-gown, carrying a tray of tea and buttered toast. She was smiling and relaxed, eyes glowing.

'Morning, darling.'

We were married at a registry office a couple of weeks later. I was twenty-one, she was thirty-two. A couple of her union pals were our witnesses.

Padmore approved of the marriage. He said now I would settle down and get on with the real work with a good comrade to support me. And she was a good comrade. Padmore visited for lunch on many Sundays and sometimes he and Dorothy talked about me almost as though I was not there.

I settled into a routine. I had a table by the sitting room window where I wrote for two hours every morning before going to work at Central Books, just off the Holborn underground station. It was a short trip. I had acquired my first typewriter at one of those all-purpose second-hand shops in Soho. It was a sturdy heavy-duty old thing on which I wrote *Dark Testament, Mine Boy* and *The Path of Thunder*. I had got it thanks to Charley Lahr, a Jewish East Ender who ran a second-hand bookstore and knew everyone and everything in the area. Whenever I needed something at a reasonable price, I told Charley Lahr. Within a day or two, he would tell me where to find it.

In the evenings I usually reached home about five, brewed a pot of tea and wrote for two more hours. Then I did some reading. Dorothy worked in the City, which was more than twice the distance I had to travel, and she was involved with after-work union and party chores, so she rarely returned home much before eight or nine in the evening. The basics for dinner were usually prepared in the morning before going to work so we could always eat within half an hour of her getting home. Then we settled down to reading, or listening to a BBC radio play before ending the day. Sometimes friends visited in the evenings. Sometimes air-raids forced us to the shelters. Radio was still primitive and the BBC did an extraordinary job of keeping us informed and entertained in those wartime days and nights. Television was still somewhere in the offing. And we had not yet heard of the computer.

Dark Testament was published about this time. Allen and Unwin gave me an advance of five pounds and a ridiculous contract in which I signed away world copyright. I was so keen to be published that I accepted it anyway. Charley Lahr and I had a quiet little booze-up at the back of his bookshop on publication day.

When I first met Padmore in 1940 I was still Dorothy's tenant and he knew her, having met her at various meetings. Even before our marriage he approved of her as a 'good comrade'. Looking back, he always got on better with the women of the Communist Party than with the men. He was no longer a part of them, but he was not against them. He had no time for others who had fallen out with the Communist Party and then turned against it. For him the fault was not in the party and its principles, but in the men who ran it. If they had been as honest, as hardworking, as committed as the women communists, things would be different. He had a higher regard and healthier respect for the women of the 'movement' than any other Marxist, black or white, I have met. So, in those early days, I now realise on looking back, he had always wanted me to be more than just Dorothy's tenant. It was a form of control, and it worked for the best part of eight years.

The newspaper of the British Communist Party was *The Daily Worker,* and at some point my work at Central Books took me to the paper and I met their respected columnist, Walter Holmes, who struck me as a warm, friendly and naturally kind person. He had read *Dark Testament,* and the Russian wife of the editor of the paper had told Holmes that the style and content had reminded her of some famous Russian short stories. So Holmes put me in his column. A reviewer of another paper, the *Manchester Guardian,* was not as kind. He said to see a dog dancing would be a noticeable event and people would not be too concerned about the quality of the dancing; the mere fact of the dog dancing would be remarkable. For a while I was known as the dancing dog among my friends. But then they called the London-based Indian writer, Mulk Raj Anand, a Baboo writer because his novels were written in the English spoken by Indians.

The competition to be published was fierce, fiercer, if anything, than the competition for certain jobs. And any means to put down the competition was used. Racial prejudice, sex discrimination, belittling and sneering at each other's work were all fair game. Book reviews were means for cutting down some and promoting others. The home-grown kept out the expatriate, while the white claimed preference over the black. It was so in the job market and it was also so in finding a place to live — the two most critical needs for the shaping of a good life. I could not get a full-time job on a paper or magazine because I was not a member of the National Union of Journalists; and I could not become a member of that union because I did not have a job on a paper. I had not been apprenticed and brought into the fold. Was it just the 'closed shop'? And why was it always possible for South Africans who were white, or for Australians and Canadians, or for 'white Africans' from East and Central Africa, or for white West Indians — or even for foreign Americans — to break into that 'closed shop'? Why not for the blacks?

The English Working Men's Clubs were among the most exclusive groups I came to know in London. The West End clubs of the high and the mighty have nothing on them when it comes to exclusivity. I have been invited to West End clubs for a meal or drinks, never to a Working Men's Club. The only time I entered one was to go and make a speech about South Africa because a section of the Afrikaner population supported the Nazis and the members of that Working Men's Club wanted to know why. How could anybody, anywhere in the empire, side with the Nazis? I tried to explain. I do not think I succeeded. I was supposed to speak for half an hour, with another half an hour for questions and answers; then I would be escorted out and the Brothers would get on with their business. In the event, we argued stubbornly, sometimes harshly, for something like three hours. That man Smuts had it right. The Boers should follow him. The war with the Boers was in the past and Britain had treated them well since, as well as the Canadian, Australians and New Zealanders, all of whom were fighting for Britain. Everybody, even the Indians and the blacks, were rallying around the flag and supporting the war effort.

When I talked about racism, a curtain came down. You cannot sweep aside the fact of the differences between black and white: different ways, different habits, different cultures. Nothing you can do about that. Treat each other 'proper' and go back to your countries when the war is over and be friends. But we'll always be different. It was not said, but the Boer 'will of God' justification for the 'colour bar' was a strong undertone to my one and only formal encounter with a body of members of an English Working Men's Club in London in the 1940s. It left me depressed for days. If this was the outlook of ordinary decent English working men, what hope for a future free of prejudice? Perhaps the communists were right, Perhaps the whole structure had to first be torn down and then completely rebuilt. Perhaps that was the only way to create a world free of racism and prejudice.

Then Bill Rust, the editor of *The Daily Worker*, put a dent into that idea. I do not remember the details of how it happened, but I found myself in his office one day. It was the holy-of-holies, to which only the most senior people at the paper were admitted. I might have been sent to deliver some copy or special article. It was not one of those occasions when he worked on the daily editorial and his door was firmly shut and his secretary kept even the most senior staff at bay. His door was wide open and the great man leaned back in his big chair. He ordered me to sit.

Out of nothing and nowhere he started talking about colour. He had nothing against coloured people, but he did not see why he had to like them. Coloured people did not like all white people, did they? I was too startled and surprised to respond. People are people and you should treat them as people, but I don't see why I should have to like or approve of black people. I wanted to talk back, to ask what was behind these remarks, but he *was* the editor of *The Daily Worker*, possibly the most important communist after the party leader, Harry Pollitt, and the party theoretician, R. Palme Dutt, an Indian or part-

Indian intellectual recluse whom I never met. Dutt occasionally published an article in the *Worker*, but his main works appeared in more weighty party journals. So there was I, being lectured, out of the blue, on Bill Rust's views on colour, without knowing why or what had brought it on, and too intimidated to talk back.

What came across clearly to me was that communists, leading communists, no less than the members of the Working Men's Clubs, saw a difference between black and white, because they were black and white. The brave new communist world of the future, if it ever came, would not necessarily be a world free of race and colour. This was the first of many encounters with colour consciousness among communists, socialists and other left-wing radicals. The movement, as a movement, said it did not recognise colour, yet the people in it, those who led and controlled it, as well as those who followed it, were as colour-conscious as were the empire-builders. Marxism, communism, socialism — the ideologies — did not have the automatic answers to the problem of the relations between the lighter and darker races of mankind. They did not even have an answer to anti-Semitism. Was there an answer to prejudice? And if there was, what was it?

I asked George Padmore and he said it was a matter of power. The world only respected power. The moment the Africans and Asians and Jews had political power, the world would respect them. Kwame Nkrumah with his great gift for sloganeering turned it into: *Seek ye first the political kingdom and all else will follow.* Pan-Africanism was to be the way to that political kingdom.

We started planning for the Fifth Pan-African Congress in 1944. Once the decision was agreed on, Padmore, the master planner, was in his element. We were each assigned specific tasks and had to make written reports at our regular weekly meetings. The planning organisation was the Secretariat of the Pan-African Federation. A room in Makonnen's restaurant in Manchester was the head office. We also had a small place in London. Padmore's network of contacts throughout the Commonwealth and empire was alerted, fact sheets, newsletters, bulletins went out in a steady stream. I was put in charge of publicity. Nkrumah, recently arrived from the United States and burning with impatience, set up a West African Secretariat. When things moved too slowly for him, he went off on his own for a time. Azikiwe visited from Nigeria; Wallace Johnson came in from Sierra Leone. A very young Julius Nyerere from what was then Tanganyika came; so did Tom Mboya from Kenya. Then the great man, W.E.B. DuBois himself, descended on us. And in 1945, in the city of Manchester, he opened the Fifth Pan-African Congress. Nominally, the Mayor of Manchester did it, but that was simply a doffing of our hats to the host city. The real opening was DuBois' and we all knew we were in the presence of a great moment in black history.

DuBois had been there since the beginning of the Pan-African idea. He was there in 1919, the year I was born, for the First Pan-African Congress. He was there for the Second Pan-African Congress in 1921, for the Third in 1923, and for the Fourth in 1927. Those had all been Congresses called by individuals representing the hopes and ideals of individuals. The African people had not yet found their voice. These individuals were the forerunners, like John the Baptist, for our Fifth Pan-African Congress, with its delegates and representatives from all over Africa and the African Diaspora. The Fifth Pan-African Congress was the first truly representative one. As W.E.B. Dubois stood on that platform in the Manchester City Hall and traced the long and difficult journey of the mind and spirit by which we had come to this point, it was one of the most moving moments of my adult life. And if it was of such importance to me, what must it have been for DuBois? What were his feelings that night? Had he thought this day would ever come when he would be speaking to a group of representative Pan-African delegates from all the regions of Africa? That he would live to see the dream handed over from a small group of expatriate black intellectuals to the representatives of

Africa itself? That he would be the agent of that transfer? All his life, from way back before I was born, he had been at it: dreaming about it; talking about it; writing about it. On this vision, for all their many differences, for all the harsh words they had written and spoken against each other, Garvey and DuBois, the dead and the living, were at one.

It was a moment of great hope for me. I was sure, now, that one day, no matter how far in the future, Africa would be free. Up to then I had not dared think about that possibility. The imperial European stranglehold seemed too strong to break. Those who controlled us were too skilled, too determined to hold on. Their confidence had undermined mine — and ours. But that night the West Indian proverb — Time Longer than Rope — became part of my mental and spiritual baggage and I had no more doubts. Africa, all of Africa, would be free one day, whether I lived to see it or not. This new certainty gave me a sense of inner peace such as I had never known before.

When the great conference was over, the mood of tension, of high excitement, gradually evaporated. We returned to our daily routine. The glitter, the only sign of his excitement, went from Padmore's eyes. Delegates spent a few days then left for their homelands. Azikiwe, one of the biggest financial supporters of the conference, went back to Nigeria to look after his newspapers and continue the struggle for Nigerian independence. Trade unionist Wallace Johnson returned to Sierra Leone. Kwame Nkrumah decided it was time to go home to the Gold Coast and start making things happen. After taking afternoon tea and whole-wheat biscuits with me at our flat in Belsize Park, DuBois slipped out of England as quietly as he had slipped in.

Under their wartime regulations the British government could have found some way of stopping us having that Congress. It did not.

The struggle against colonialism was entering a new phase. Within two years, the Indian National Congress, which had expressed its solidarity with our Fifth Pan-African Congress, moved towards independence for India. Kenyatta returned to Kenya to prepare for what became known as the Mau Mau war. The African and Asian freedom fighters were going home. London was gradually ceasing to be the centre of our struggle. The Second World War was coming to an end. The extraordinary alliance of convenience between the Soviet Union and the Western Powers from the very outset did not look like lasting. Even as they prepared to bring the defeated Nazis to trial at Nuremberg, the fissures in the alliance were showing. When Churchill went to America to make his famous speech about an Iron Curtain coming down over Europe we entered the long years of the Cold War. The world was changing. The position of black folk in that changing world surely had to change as well. Many of us saw the opportunities offered by the Cold War. Few of us recognised the dangers.

—— 4 ——

The Cold War Years

The period from the end of World War Two in 1945 till the end of the Cold War in 1991 marks the most dangerous years of the twentieth century. Several times, during that period, any major mistake or miscalculation by either the Soviet Union and its allies or the United States and its allies, could have resulted in a nuclear war of mutual and, perhaps world-wide, destruction. Toward the end of the war, on 6 August, 1945, a single American airforce plane dropped the first atom bomb on the Japanese city of Hiroshima. One hundred thousand people were killed in one massive flash. Three days later the Japanese city of Nagasaki became the second city to be destroyed by an atom bomb dropped by the Americans. Forty thousand people were killed in that fireball flash. Those who were not killed suffered the most horrible radiation burns and endured years of lingering pain. The shock reverberated throughout the world. We saw, suddenly and clearly, the possibility of the end of life on earth at the hands of man himself. A number of people, writers and artists, one or two of whom I knew, were so overwhelmed by the horror that they committed suicide. It was a stark and chilling vision of how time could end for all of us. And one man, in one country, had made the decision and given the order. What price the long and difficult centuries of human effort, the creation of great works of art and literature, the vast body of human scholarship stored in museums and libraries, if all could be wiped out in one blinding flash on the order of one human being? If Hitler's Germany had been the first to produce the atom bomb, would the London I had come to love still be standing? Would the Paris I was preparing to visit for the first time since its liberation still be standing? How much of the treasures of human history, stored in both London and Paris, would survive such an atomic firestorm? Try as I would, I could not, for days and weeks, banish these nightmare thoughts. They lingered with me throughout the Cold War years, just below the surface of consciousness. Nothing was sure, nothing was secure, not even human history or our sense of that history. All could be cancelled as though it never existed. It made real for me Bertrand Russell's view of the smallness, the unimportance of our species in the bigger scheme of things. We can turn our earth into a barren, lifeless minor star spinning in space, waterless, with little or no atmosphere, with not even cockroaches left on it. To face this possibility and still behave with decency; to still create beautiful things as though they will last forever; to still make music and poetry and paint pictures; to still consciously cultivate the gentler, tender side of our lives is to aspire to a grace which makes us more than the animals we surely are. It raises us to a level near the Godhood our species seems to need. To have the ability to destroy all and not to do it was one of the hard tests humanity passed — but only just — in the middle of the twentieth century.

That first summer after the end of the war was beautiful. Perhaps we wanted it to be so after the years of horror. I still remember the warm friendliness of everyone on the long train journey to the South of France. Somebody we knew — a woman artist, I seem to remember

— had a little peasant cottage up in the high mountains near the French-Italian border. She had not seen it throughout the war years and was eager to go and see if it was still there and in what state. We were among a group she invited to join her and 'rough it' in sleeping bags or tents or whatever — if the place was still standing. At the last minute Dorothy could not make it — something special had come up in her trade union. She urged me to go anyway.

At the change of trains at Paris' Gare St Lazare I noticed a young English couple. The man carried an artist's easel and both had rucksacks on their backs. I took a chance and accosted them. They were on their way to the same place. They told me the owner of the cottage should be at the place already, and another couple who were supposed to join us had dropped out. The man had been given a small part in a West End play. So it was just the three of us.

My new companions — I had a mental block about their names from the outset — soon turned out to be what we now call hustlers or scufflers. I remember the young man as about my own age, perhaps an inch or two shorter, round-faced, with an unruly mop of thick black hair. He smiled often but it never reached his eyes; they were always calculating what he could or could not get away with. His girlfriend had the physical grace and freshness of a healthy, strong young woman at her peak. They could have been the same age or he could have been a little older. They seemed well matched that summer as we left the train at Menton.

We bought a huge dry salami and half a dozen freshly baked long thin loaves of bread, all stuffed into a large brown paper bag together with two big bottles of red wine and started the long climb. After I had been manipulated into paying for the cushions we rented on the long train journey (we could not afford the sleeping car cost) and for most of the snacks we had, I decided firmly to stop being had. When my friend cocked his head and smiled at me, eyes calculating, almost invisibly rubbing his hands, I shook my head.

'Fifty-fifty.'

There was a long pause. He turned to his girlfriend. She opened her handbag, took his wallet from it and handed it to him. He counted out his half of the bill and stuffed the wallet into his hip-pocket. It was visibly there for the first time. He could no longer pat his empty pockets, tilt his head, smile and make me pay the whole bill. It was fifty-fifty from then on. He was still getting the better of the deal. She was his, not my, girlfriend. It stayed fifty-fifty whenever we shopped together. In the two weeks that followed I did as much of my shopping as I could on my own. Apart from that they were pleasant enough and I enjoyed their company. The only embarrassment I experienced with them was their open, almost exhibitionist, brand of having sex. Sex was a private thing for me.

It took us all day and many stops, and many a snack and many swigs along the ancient mountain track before the land levelled off. All day long we met mountain folk leading their laden donkeys, turning off the main track into side-tracks and taking them to settlements and houses that were scattered all about. Everybody greeted us; we returned everybody's greeting. We could not speak each other's language but we knew we were all friends. These mountains had been fierce partisan country not so long ago. Now they were all peaceful and the stranger was not the enemy.

Then, at about fourteen or fifteen thousand feet we began to see the Saracen architecture. My friend surprised me with his sudden enthusiasm. He had studied this stuff at art school and the rest of the way up he gave me an absorbing lesson on the Saracens and their mountaintop fortifications as they conquered this part of Southern Europe. The Africans had been here, I smiled.

'What you smiling at? What did I say that's so amusing?'

'I was just impressed by your knowledge.'

He looked appeased.

It was dark when we reached the cottage. The moon was up. The land was bathed in the shadowy light that makes for fantasy and dreaming, for seeing visions and ghosts and silhouettes. We were so high up we could not see the twinkling lights of the coastal strip with its gambling houses. Only the pale sky above; only the rolling, undulating mountains in every direction.

A small light, as from an oil lamp, appeared and filtered through cracks in the wooden building. A voice, vaguely familiar to me, but more so to my companions, shouted from the cottage. My friend, call him Joey, screamed back and dashed for the door. We had grown anxious as night approached and we were alone on the high mountain. Now it was over, and Joey's scream was one of pure relief. Two women were on the only bed in the far corner of the large room. The embers in the fireplace near the bed glowed faintly. The room was at least twice as warm as the chilly outside night air. The woman who sat up in bed, the owner of the cottage, was naked, her bare breasts, big and round, exposed. She ordered Joey to shut the door and made no attempt to cover her breasts. Just like an African mother, I thought. Her companion stayed deep under the bed covers, seemingly anxious to hide from our eyes. The Earth Mother got out of bed, wrapped herself in a thick dressing gown and welcomed us by reviving the fire and bringing out a flagon of wine. The one in bed rolled over, face to the wall, pulled the covering over her head and went to sleep, or pretended to. We ate and talked and drank far into the night. She and her companion were moving on in the morning. She instructed Joey to lock up the cottage when we left and take the key back to London. What was I going to do? I told her I wanted to do a little writing. She said I would find a typewriter and some paper tucked under all the rubbish in the cupboard. She had done that in case thieves broke in and ransacked the place. The typewriter had belonged to someone called David who used to come to the mountains with her to write. David had died in the war. I got the sense that David had been someone special to her. We finished the wine. She went back to bed. The young lovers unfolded their big sleeping bag, stripped naked and crawled into it. I wrapped myself in a blanket from the cupboard, fully clothed, as near the fire as I could without catching alight. I blew out the lamp. The young lovers almost immediately began the noises of love-making. It went on till I fell asleep.

When I awoke, a watery morning sun had not yet warmed the world. The lovers were still in their sleeping bag, looking relaxed and spent as two over-indulged children. The two women were nowhere in sight. The bed was made. A note on the pillow said there was hot tea and porridge and that they were on their way to the Italian side of the border.

I spent the next ten days using David's typewriter and the ream of yellowing newsprint-type copy paper to write *The Path of Thunder*, a passionate inter-racial love story set in rural South Africa. I wrote it in ten days up there in the mountains the Saracens once controlled. It was not a good novel; it was a first draft which needed a deal more work done on it. But my mind had shifted to a much more important theme. I began the careful, much slower, much more measured first draft of *Mine Boy*. That one, I knew, could not and would not be dashed off. It was too important for that. And already, the dim outlines of *Tell Freedom* were beginning to take shape. I owe much to those two weeks in the high mountains in the South of France, and to the peasant folk among whom I lived while these ideas germinated.

I also realised that I had slipped into a rut. Apart from writing, I needed a family. Not the 'family' of the 'movement' which seemed all that people like George Padmore and Dorothy wanted. I wanted a family in the old African way: a man, his woman and their children. I would talk to Dorothy to see if we could start a family. She had told me of the great love of her life. The committed man of the 'movement' who had gone to jail over the breaching of some official secrets and who had, after serving his jail sentence, written a best-selling book about it. She still saw him occasionally. When I met him in Charley Lahr's bookshop one day, it dawned on me that she had told him about me. He was careful, polite and charming, but he obviously knew about me. When I asked her about it that night she was evasive. It surprised me because she had always been open and straightforward about her past. I asked if she was still seeing him. She said sometimes. I left it at that. Up there in the high mountains, I decided to ask her about our starting a family. She was approaching forty and if we were to do so it would have to be soon. I had a premonition that she would not want this.

France in those days was de Gaulle's France. He had led the fight during the long German occupation. He had capped the liberation of France with his historic march into Paris while the guns were still firing in the streets and from the rooftops of Paris. France was de Gaulle, de Gaulle France. His pictures, larger than life, were everywhere. And de Gaulle's greatest and staunchest ally in the struggle against Nazi Germany was a black general in the army of France, Félix Eboué.

Eboué had been one of the first black governors of a French Overseas Department. Where other imperial powers had colonies, France named her colonies Overseas Departments of France. Huge chunks of West Africa were at one time Overseas Departments of France. Algeria, parts of Morocco and Libya, in the far east massive French Indo-China and an assortment of islands were all Overseas Departments. The French-held little islands of the Caribbean as well as huge French Guyana were also Departments of France. And France Overseas, in the main, rallied behind de Gaulle and fought for the liberation of France.

This, in part, was due to French policy in her Overseas Departments. Assimilation, turning the élite of her overseas possessions into French men and women, was at its heart. The educated, those who spoke French, were citizens of France. The illiterate who did not speak French were subjects, not citizens of France. But the children of subjects could become citizens by turning themselves into black or brown or yellow Frenchmen and women. This was the complete opposite of British, Belgian and Dutch colonial policy; they were against assimilation; they were for segregation. The peoples of their colonies were subjects, not citizens.

Except in Indo-China, where France was up against a much more powerful culture than Europe understood, assimilation worked. Black Frenchmen of talent rose to high positions in the service of France and they married into French society. If they served in the Departments, they sent their children to school in France. They planned for their sons and daughters to marry 'well' in France. There were no blacks in British, Dutch or Belgian high society. Blacks from the Overseas Departments were normal in French high society, usually married to French women of the right social class and background. The French managed the 'arranging' of marriages very well. Any potential Governor of an Overseas Department would somehow meet just the right kind of young woman who would make a good wife and hostess for a man holding such a high position. It seemed to happen even at the literary level. When Daphne and I moved from London to Paris in 1948 a well-known playwright took me up and introduced me to everyone in his circle: fellow playwrights, actors, artists, musicians. I thought it was because of a book I had just published. Then he discovered I was married. He dropped me so fast I did not know what had happened. I discovered later he was looking for a suitable husband for his very beautiful milk-and-coffee coloured daughter.

The French policy of assimilation, it seemed then, was of greater benefit to France in her hour of greatest need than were the segregationist policies of the Dutch in Indonesia, of the Belgians in the Congo, of the British in Africa. But the young men and women of the British West Indies did join Britain's armed forces in relatively great numbers. The only comparable figure to Félix Eboué for the British Commonwealth was the South African Boer General Jan Smuts, who opposed those of his own people who supported Germany. But he was white. All the others, the Governors-General, the Governors, the High Commissioners were, at that time, Britons or, if born where they served, white and of British descent. The most important of these was always the Governor-General of India. So the black Governor Eboué who declared 'France lives on!' after the fall of France, remains the highest symbol of the success of the French policy of assimilation. French Indo-China in general and Vietnam in particular, as well as Algeria, are the clearest symbols of the failure of that policy.

Implicit in the idea of assimilation is the notion of the strong absorbing the weak. There is never assimilation between equals. Inter-marriage and co-existence, yes; never the notion that the one can take in and so transform the other that it ceases to be, or to show any traces of what it was before the assimilation. The French succeeded in transforming a minority of blacks into Frenchmen. They failed singularly with black women. The offspring of black Frenchmen and their French wives, the French 'brownings', were French by definition, but surprisingly many made the choice to be, to see and proclaim themselves as black. They chose to become part of the unassimilated black majorities in the far-flung empire and, in the end, became the leaders in the anti-colonial struggle. They were the most educated, the most politically aware. As political control by the metropolis loosened, the trend away from assimilation with Europe grew stronger. That which was once so desirable no longer attracted. The centres of power, in terms of race and colour had shifted. The Anglo-Indians, the 'Eurasians', who once clung to 'the British blood in their veins' became Indians, proud of Mother India. The West Indians who once jeered at Africans as 'monkey chasers' and who derided Marcus Garvey and his 'Back-to-Africa' movement, rediscovered their blackness and found a new black pride, a new black beauty, and the 'wee-dropper' stuff of the British Caribbean quietly died. Africa replaced Britain as the mother country, the mother continent. It did not happen all at once. It was as gradual as the shift in political power. In South Africa the brown offspring of black and white at first clung to 'the privilege of the white blood in their veins', then became 'Eurafricans', a 'pure' new race of people, and then, reluctantly in many instances, part of South Africa's black community. As late as at the end of Apartheid, though, a sizeable segment of the Cape Coloured community voted against Mandela's African National Congress and with the whites.

In the United States the blacks had moved from being Negroes to being 'coloured people' to being 'Afro-Americans', to being 'African Americans' to being black people who wanted Africa to be great and powerful so that they would be respected in America. There was a movement away from hair straightening, skin bleaching and all the efforts to look as near white as possible. Looking African was ceasing to be seen as being ugly. Black was becoming beautiful. The long period of self-contempt, of being ashamed of what you were and how you looked, was beginning to come to a close. It was only the beginning, though, for emancipating ourselves from mental slavery, from the occupation of our minds by others, was a longer-term thing. The end of physical occupation does not mean the simultaneous end of generations and centuries of mental indoctrination. However, the convergence between colour and power was becoming clearer in our time. Its starkest expression was when the South African white racists made the citizens of the economically strong and growing Japan 'honorary white men'. These were the first signs that colour was ceasing to be colour in the old accepted way.

Back in London after my fortnight's holiday in the Southern French mountains, what had become a set routine of early morning writing then going to work, then returning to write some more before the end of the day, suddenly stopped. I had moved from Central

Books to regular sub-editing at *The Daily Worker*. I had made friends with the people at Central Books, so I spent most of my lunch hours there helping out. The mood and atmosphere were less tense than at the paper where everybody always seemed on the verge of exploding. Perhaps it was the tension of meeting the daily deadline.

One day the office secretary-typist called me to her office. Another woman was there. The secretary introduced me then left us alone.

The woman said: 'We've been checking our records and you're not on our files.'

I did not understand. I looked blank.

'Your party record, comrade.' She sounded impatient. 'Where and when did you join? Can I see your membership card? I'm from the Control Commission.'

My heart sank. ' I don't have a card.'

The woman stiffened. Her voice rose: 'Not a party member?'

'No.'

'Then what are you doing here?' She stormed out of the little office, telling everybody in earshot: 'He's not a party member!'

I lost the job on the spot. I left feeling guilty, as though I had committed some grave crime. Nobody asked me any question or said anything to me. Everybody withdrew. The cashier made out my pay slip and shoved the money at me from behind her grille. It was the middle of the week, as I remember, and the amount I received was a little over two pounds. I walked round to Central Books. The news had preceded me. Nobody looked at me and nobody said anything. So I walked to Soho and told Charley Lahr what had happened. He comforted me with a cup of tea. As an old socialist, he said, he knew the ways of the communists. Would the socialists give me a job on their paper, I wondered? They were in power and I could be of use as a sub-editor.

'Have you got a union card?' Charley Lahr asked, eyes twinkling.

'No.'

He shook his head. I was to discover, over the following weeks and months, just how hard it was for a black person to find a job in London after the war.

Neither Dorothy nor Padmore was surprised by the loss of my job. She said it was my fault; I should have joined despite my reservations. She thought if I tried to join the party now, they would be suspicious and might turn me down. Padmore's surprise was that I had been there that long without them finding out I was not a party member. To him they were just slack, careless. Nothing like that could have happened in the Comintern or in the Soviet or any other party. I tried to explain I had not intended to deceive. I just felt that anyone who wanted to be a writer had no business joining political parties. Sympathies, yes; preferences and inclinations, yes. However, the need for the writer to see all sides of an issue or situation or person demanded the greatest detachment and objectivity humanly possible. Membership of any political party, especially one as rigidly immersed in ideological dogma, as the Communist Party, inevitably meant subordinating detachment and objectivity to the interests of the party. Neither George nor Dorothy agreed with me. They cited the great Maxim Gorky. I questioned whether he was a card-carrying party member. Not even George knew the answer. After hours of heated argument we agreed to disagree. It may be different for other writers. For me, from the very outset, being a writer was incompatible with membership of any serious political party which demanded strict adherence to its principles and policies. They said this was 'escapist', 'idealist', 'ivory tower' stuff. Being involved in the anti-imperialist struggle and the nationalist movements of that struggle was altogether different. The pursuit of human freedom is a writer's natural commitment, entered into freely, irrespective of the approval or disapproval of any political party. I could disagree with and criticise specific policies or tactics of the African National Congress or the Indian National Congress without being accused of, or having a sense of, betraying the movement. That is not possible with any more narrowly based political party.

'Bourgeois nonsense!' George snapped.

Arguing with dyed-in-the-wool Marxists can be difficult.

I have, over the years, criticised things done by parties of the nationalist movements throughout the world without any sense of ambivalence. Kenyatta, when in power in Kenya, did not like my criticisms of female circumcision; the tendency, in the early days, to keep all levers of power in the hands of the Kikuyu, 'the tribe that won the war'. They said some harsh things about me in return. But because I was not 'the enemy' I was given the opportunity to talk back on their own controlled radio station. Those who were hostile to African independence tried to turn these criticisms into my 'pessimism' about African freedom. They were still trying to divide and rule. They did the same when I published *A Wreath for Udomo*. Kwame Nkrumah got word to me via Sam Morris, when he visited Jamaica on his way to Guyana, to express his disturbed appreciation. Nkrumah was overthrown a few years later. When I wrote critically about the situation in Liberia long before the vast later changes, they again saw it in terms of my 'pessimism' about African freedom. They turned my freedom to criticise my own into yet another tool to belittle and undermine the struggle for African freedom. Fortunately, the nationalist movements of the world, from the mid-1940s on, had matured too much for that kind of playing off against each other. I could now look inward and criticise with love. I still, psychologically, looked over my shoulder to see how 'they' were reacting, but less so than in earlier times.

The freedom to say 'I love you, but you are wrong here and you are wrong there', and to know that they understand and do not see you as a traitor, is a wonderful freedom. It is a freedom I hope the Irish revolutionaries will achieve before this century's close. It would stop their internecine bloodletting. It would lead them out of their present cul-de-sac. It is the kind of freedom which is essential for the writer to function at his or her best. If there is any residual anger left in me, it is that it took so long to work my way through to the point where I could recognise and so use this freedom. This looking inward, this holding up of a mirror, critically, harshly at times, but always with love, is, for me, the most important function of the writer. Those of us who are black writers have spent far too much time in protest, in polemics, in attack, in the struggle for freedom. It had to be done. It was a necessity, not a virtue. It was also inhibiting and crippling. Now, at last, there is the prospect of the black writer being just a writer who happens to be black and whose job, in the main, is to explore our black humanity and our black experience as part of the whole spectrum of the human condition. What a pity we had to struggle so long and so hard to get to this point. I think of all the poets and dreamers who had to fight their way past this psychological barrier of colour erected by Europe and its imperialism. Now, at last, in the closing stages of this twentieth century, the end to that barrier seems in sight. The end of the day of the protest novel promises a healthier new literature for the descendants of DuBois' darker races of mankind. And that, surely, must be good for all mankind.

It should make it possible for us to rid ourselves of the vast mythological superstructure of blood and race and colour which has been part of 'the black man's burden' in the twentieth century.

There is no pure 'race', no pure blood. The entire human race is a mixed race or, if you prefer, a single race, said to have come out of Africa at the beginning of human time. After a fragile period of survival, that race spread throughout the world, changing its environment and being changed by its environment: not evolving into a different species here and a different species there, but the same species with the same genetic make-up, changing and adapting to survive. So when 'Mr Garvey' wrote about the purity of the black race or the yellow race, it was a psychological and emotional response to the white racism of the times. Black men were lynched in parts of the United States for 'raping' white women by the mere act of looking at them. How do you respond to that if you cannot stop the lynching? You say I do not have to look at your women, let alone rape them, I don't want anything of yours, I have my own and I am proud of what I am and what I have. This is a racist response to racism. It could not be otherwise in a world where skin colour had been invested with such exaggerated qualities. I am my colour; my colour defines me, determines whether I am good or bad, rich or poor, high or low, free or slave, beautiful or ugly. In such a context, anyone, of any colour, would want his particular colour to be the dominant one, the preferred colour, the colour of God's chosen people.

So Garvey redefined colour to serve our interests. He wanted his black folk to be the equal of all other colours. He wanted all blacks — and for him it included all shades of black — to be as proud of their colour as were the whites of theirs: no intermarriage, no mixing of blood. Yet all humanity, in all its variety is of one blood. Our genes, our genetic make-up, our blood types, in all their variety, are the same for all people of all colours. Blood knows no colour. And still we, all of us — black, brown, yellow, white — have carried this debilitating burden of colour throughout this century. It is, historically, unsustainable in the centuries ahead. Those who would exploit their fellow beings in that future will have to devise new means of manipulation and management. Early signs of these new forms are beginning to take shape in the new economic vision being offered. The nature of things is changing, and the greatest, and in a sense the most foolish, of all the tools of control in our century, is on its way out. Its going is not without pain but the problem of the twenty-first century will not be the problem of the colour line. This does not necessarily mean that relations between the lighter and darker races of mankind will become 'normal', without further grief and pain. The scars, visible and invisible, are too deep for that. The psychological effects of three hundred years of slavery followed by a century of racism will linger long into the new century. If we understand this we may help make the process of mental liberation easier and less damaging than it might otherwise be. What is important is to finally put an end to the beast of racism, in all its shapes and forms: white racism, its responsive black racism, and the massive edifice of racial stereotypes built up over time to justify a manifest evil. As with all great evils, atonement must be part of the resolution and the settlement.

I began thinking seriously about this when we finally found Coyaba, the place of tranquillity, in the high hills of Jamaica, where contemplating the nature of things came more easily than anywhere else on earth I have been. The matter of atonement will be the substance of the final part of these chronicles of the remembrances, recollections and reflections of one black man of the events, places, people and experiences over the best part of this century. The perspective will be 'Third-World' non-Western, non-European; not as protest or criticism, but as part of the ongoing search for 'balance' in the desire to assert our place in tomorrow's world.

The history of our time has been, in the main, the story of Europe and, more lately, North America. This is natural: history has always been what happened to the dominant groups, those who conquered and controlled. All accounts, all records, all the news, were always from their perspective. They decided what was or was not news, what was or was not important. They owned the newspapers, the radio and television networks; they decided what was printed and broadcast and shown. They published the books and the magazines. They controlled the means of communication and so communication itself. Their wars were the world's wars, their heroes the world's heroes, their villains the world's villains. What happened elsewhere was judged and evaluated by how it affected the interests of Europe and America. They determined how we saw their world and how we saw our own world. For East Africa to know about West Africa, East Africans had to read or listen to the news by way of Europe. Our history, our news and our current affairs programmes, the 'think pieces' in our newspapers came from Europe and America, written by Europeans and Americans. Experts on Africa and Asia were Europeans and Americans. Foreign correspondents who reported on the Third World from faraway places were Europeans and Americans. Only a tiny fraction, a token group, in these latter days, are natives of the countries from which they file their stories. Then their stories are filtered through the prism of European-American interests. This century belonged to them. They determined how we saw it, what was important, what we thought of it.

To the extent that there were divisions among them, we had some small choice. We could decide which view of that history to see and hear and accept. We were the passive receivers, not the active participants in the making of that history. Even where we were allowed to participate, it was on their terms. George Padmore, the important operative of the Comintern became dispensable when Soviet interests changed. Félix Eboué, the black man born in French Guyana, who became Governor of French Equatorial Africa and played a pivotal role in the Western allies winning the war in Africa, does not get a footnote in the history of that war as written by most Americans. The French, with their assimilationist policies do better. Eboué is a hero of France, buried in the Panthéon in Paris. Not even Jan Smuts, a Field Marshal of the British Empire, is buried in Westminster Abbey, let alone any black servant of the British colonial empire and Commonwealth.

I found Jan Smuts in a popular American computer CD encyclopaedia. Félix Eboué was not in it. I did, however, find Eboué in the more recent *Encyclopaedia Britannica 98* CD. The European accounts of people and events tend to be better, though not all that much. I could find no reference to George Padmore in either European or American encyclopaedias, and he was an important and influential political operative of our time, like him or not. The perspectives, the choices, what is included or left out, how it is presented, made the world of the darker races of mankind peripheral to the history of our time.

The new world of the computer with its instant communication is fast changing all that. Is it surprising that the Indians in particular and the Asians in general are emerging as the great 'techies' of the computer age? You sit at a little machine, plug it in to your normal household electricity supply, and you can talk to anyone anywhere in the world who has a similar little machine, without either person knowing the other's colour or looks. That same little machine hooks you up to the main news centres of the world and you see and hear, at the same time, what the natives in Moscow, Peking, London, Paris, Berlin, Washington, Tokyo, Cairo, Lagos, Johannesburg are seeing and hearing. Management and control become less possible. Any smart young person anywhere in the world, sitting in front of his/her computer, can launch a web page and tell the world what they think. That was not possible till now. Time, space and distance have been conquered! What a difference it would have made if George Padmore had been able to use the computer to run what, in retrospect, was the first world-wide, and perhaps still the most successful, non-aligned news service. His clients would have had instant access to the news by themselves, needing only Padmore's interpretation or editorial slant. Is some latter-day Padmore providing this service now?

DuBois' darker races can now speak to each other directly. The Indian National Congress and South Africa's African National Congress have their own websites, and the expatriates of Africa and India, and all the others who want to, can now speak directly to these bodies. Wherever I am, I am no longer a long way from home. Wherever home is and whoever I am, European, African or Asian, I can stay in touch. With little effort, at little cost, the peoples of the earth, of all races and colours, can now talk to each other across time and space with minimal interference from political parties or powerful governments. Censorship is embattled. The little personal computer is the most potent antidote to exploitation by the use of fear and ignorance.

I once watched a tall skinny young black boy, about twenty or so, in a small room in a modest home in the St Andrew hills 'chatting' to three friends in rural North America by way of an Internet hook-up, the sophistication of which I still do not quite understand. It was young people stuff: a mixture of serious information interspersed with light banter and the kind of flirting common when young people get together — even in cyberspace. It was easy and familiar.

After he signed off I asked: 'Ever met any of them?'

'No, but they'll be visiting. I'll meet them on the North Coast.'

'Black Americans?'

'Don't think so.' That question didn't really interest him.

We turned to the problem with my computer.

Thanks in very large measure to the arrival of the computer, history will, before too long, cease to be what Europe and America decides it is.

When I lost my job because I did not carry a party card, and when I found it impossible to find another, short of the kind no one else wanted, I turned to what Langston Hughes described as 'literary sharecropping'. I armed myself with a copy of the *Writers and Artists Yearbook* and studied its list of magazines and their requirements. Then I started sending out articles with stamped self-addressed envelopes. It was weeks before one of them was accepted by, I think, *Reynolds News,* a now defunct weekly of the British co-operative movement. The fee just about covered what it cost to write and send out the three or four articles I wrote for the week. I became, in time, an almost regular contributor to the paper published by Fenner Brockway's Independent Labour Party. George Padmore introduced me to a key person in the Workers' Educational Association and I travelled to wherever WEA groups wanted to hear about South Africa. All these efforts brought in enough for me to keep up my end of the rent and household expenses. Since I now worked at home full-time, I did all the housekeeping and cleaning. I had always been a better shopper than Dorothy; now I did it all, making sure of my good piece of meat every week. The wartime shortages were easing. Life was becoming more pleasant, more normal. The people were also becoming less friendly and open. The wartime camaraderie was disappearing

After the publication of *Mine Boy* in 1946, the pressure eased. I earned a little more money, which allowed me to let up on churning out articles. I kept up the WEA lectures because they had turned into happy encounters for me. I met a large variety of working English, Scots and Welsh people away from London and in their own settings. This was an education for me. These people met me and dealt with me as just another human being. There was usually an organiser for the area who took charge of arrangements: a place for me to stay overnight, a meal before or after the meeting. Usually, I stayed at some private home and had dinner with the family in the evening either before or after the meeting, depending on the time of the meeting, and breakfast next morning before my departure. In scattered, widely dispersed small rural population centres we often had an informal session of darts and billiards, laced with draft beer, at the local pub. Most of the people at the Workers' Educational Association meetings were socialists of the old William Blake kind: Christian, humane, caring. They helped me see what Blake's 'green and pleasant land' was and how its people lived and worked, away from the great industrial cities. The 'gentry' of the area did not usually attend these WEA gatherings, but occasionally someone from 'the other side' with a special interest in Africa would come to the meeting. When that happened they were always treated with deference, were introduced to the 'visiting lecturer' and invited onto the 'platform'. Most often they declined and took a centre seat in the front row. Now and then they joined the platform and took part in the discussion after my talk.

Once the couple from the village 'great house' who had lived in Kenya attended. The man was big and red-faced, someone who had spent time in the African sun. The woman was small and wiry, less burned by the sun The man argued strongly that there was no colour bar in Kenya, only a 'culture bar': 'Fellows like you would be welcome everywhere provided you obeyed the rules and showed manners. That chap Kenyatta is just a troublemaker. He can live at peace with his white neighbours if he wanted to.' Then, deliberately, 'damned troublemaker! That's all!'

My WEA host signalled to me with his eyes, so I let it be. I learned later that this son of the gentry had tried farming in Kenya and failed. He had returned to Britain after serving in the war. He had stood for parliament as a Conservative. He had been heavily defeated by the candidate of the Labour Party, the son of a former farm hand of his father's. All this, my hosts suggested, explained his behaviour. He was one of them, in their midst, but isolated in his big house with its many acres of land. Farm hands in the area refused to work for him because he wanted to treat them as he had treated his African workers in Kenya.

Most often, though, these gatherings of Workers' Educational Associations all over Britain were concerned with British affairs, British conditions, and with the gradual transforming of the British mind and outlook to bring it closer to the dreams and visions of the early, pre-Marxist, English socialism of the days of William Blake and his fellow visionaries.

The men of empire, I discovered, were a tiny, highly visible, immensely powerful minority. To us, to the world outside Britain, the British people seemed part of one imperialist monolith. In reality, the majority were not interested in being the overlords of any people anywhere in the world. The business of empire was, essentially, a minority business. Power and the use and manipulation of power are almost by definition the function of minorities of strong and acquisitive individuals. Nations may benefit from the spoils of empire and so come to accept, condone, or turn a blind eye, to its worst manifestations such as turning vast numbers of Chinese into drug addicts for the benefit of trade or grabbing other people's lands and resources. So where do we draw the line? Do we say because they did not do these things directly, or, because they did not know, they cannot be held responsible? Most Germans said they did not know the Nazis operated slave camps. Even some who had slave labourers working in their homes and factories said they did not know it was slave labour. They were prisoner-of-war labourers who, they believed, were working voluntarily for some small return and to escape the boredom of confinement. Does that absolve them from the crime of benefiting from slave labour? These were some of the hard questions I found being discussed among ordinary British people in Workers' Educational Associations all over the country more than fifty years ago. To be preoccupied with such matters so soon after a great war, and at the level of the ordinary working people, says much to the good of that country and its people. So I came to feel a great warmth, a great affection for that Britain and its people with whom I had shared, in small measure, some of the fears and agonies of war. When you really get to know people, when you share the small daily problems of life and living with them, it becomes impossible to classify them by race, colour, class or status. You cannot do it even when some of them insist on imposing these classifications on you and on themselves.

This seeing of the British, and people in general, as people rather than as white people was one of the great virtues of George Padmore. He seemed incapable of seeing or judging people in racial terms. People were good or bad: capitalists or socialists or communists; backward and reactionary; enlightened and progressive; never black or white

— except as straight descriptive terms. His enemies were the people who served capitalism, imperialism, fascism, colonialism. His allies were the 'progressive forces', whether he agreed with them on all points or not.

For me, his one great blind spot was his dismissal of Garvey as a 'black racist'. Looking back, I think his years as a key functionary of the Communist International had given him a jaundiced view of human beings. He tended to put them into neatly labelled compartments from which he could select those he approved of as useful and reject those he saw as no good. It was clear, simple, black-and-white. In later years I came to wonder why so many of the black intellectuals in Britain and Europe at that time seemed so uncomfortable and ambivalent about Garvey. The impulse was to scoff at him, to mock him, to jeer at his ideas, to dismiss them as unreal, far-fetched black racism. For a time I was one of those. Looking back, I think now that our discomfort with Garvey and his ideas stemmed from a subconscious awareness that he was different from all the rest of us in one singular respect. He was his own man as none of us was. We thought, functioned, formulated ideas in a European context. Our ideologies came from Europe: we were socialists, communists, would-be capitalists, liberals, democrats — creatures of the West. The only thing Garvey took from the West — he had no choice — was its language and its mode of dress and living, otherwise he fitted no Western label. Where did a black man born near the close of the nineteenth century find the inner resources to be his own man in a world controlled and dominated by white men?

DuBois with his sense of 'two-ness', Padmore with his Marxism — and all the rest of us — with love or hate or a mixture of both, were dependents of Europe, its ideas, its ideologies. Only this one black man seemed free of this dependence. Was this why our responses to him were so often the same as those of the Western dealers in power and the Western news media? Is this why George Padmore did not want to talk about him? Why the communists detested and denounced him? Those who are in mental bondage are never comfortable with those who are mentally free. One of the good things about these closing years of the 'century of the colour line' is that at long last scholars — mainly black — are examining, assessing and re-examining the role and influence of Marcus Garvey as the emancipator of black minds in the twentieth century. The first one who said, clearly and sharply, 'don't look at him; look at yourself; see how good and beautiful you can be'. Quite a message for a people degraded and mired in self-contempt. Only a truly free man could do that.

Where and how did he find that freedom, three centuries removed from his African roots? Twentieth-century history has belittled this man. The great body of literature on Garvey now being produced in America and the Caribbean ensures that the people of the twenty-first century will look at him again and pass a different judgement. I think that this new judgement on Garvey will reflect the change in the way we humans see each other, deal with each other, live with each other in the centuries ahead. Garvey's teachings on family, on a drug-free culture, on social behaviour and hard work — which the Black Muslims of the United States have adopted – is, and will remain relevant, for poor and depressed communities all over the world, no matter of what colour or creed. Part of the troubles of our time stems from the suppression of such teaching. In the end, the politics of control and denial punishes all, not only the black.

5

Daphne / Paris

My relations with Dorothy were quietly turning bad. We shared the same flat, but it was no longer much of a shared home. During Christmas 1946 and the early months of 1947 we talked several times about my wish to have a family. She never rejected the idea outright. She scoffed at it gently, talked of the problems children could cause, talked about her own unhappy childhood in Yorkshire: the youngest of three, two girls and a boy in the middle, with a father who spent all his life working in a bank and a mother who had borne him those children and in whom he had no interest — an unhappy woman till the day she died. Now retired, the father lived in the small family home with the eldest sister as his housekeeper. I was never quite clear on the point, but I think the eldest sister had married and the husband had died. The eldest sister was mother to both Dorothy and the brother who was a few years older than Dorothy and who had followed the father into a career in banking. The brother was married to a strong-willed Yorkshire lass and they had one small daughter when I met them. A combination of the pressures of life at the bank and resisting the domination of a strong wife led the brother into a state of withdrawal and depression and he had just emerged from a session in a mental hospital when I met him.

The father was a small man, a few inches shorter than me and beanstalk slim. He had a sharp, beaky face and Dorothy's hooded eyes. Though retired from the bank, he was always dapperly dressed, as befits a middle-rank officer of the city's most important bank. Every morning, on our week's visit at Christmas, he came down from his room fully dressed as though for business, had breakfast over the morning paper, then left at precisely nine. He returned at twelve, had lunch, retired to his room for an hour, then changed and went out again. He returned in the evening, had a light supper, then retired to his room. That was his routine. Dorothy's eldest sister, Muriel, saw that everything facilitated that routine. The only one who seemed to get past this facade of the man was his strong-willed daughter-in-law. He seemed to have little time for his son and younger daughter. And they, it seemed, had no more time for him. It was a small household of order, controlled emotions, little show of feeling. My mother, I think, would have described it as a house without feeling. This, in part, was Dorothy's reason for shrinking from the idea of family. She saw family as a form of oppressive tyranny, a means by which men gained dominance over women. When, many years later, I told Daphne of these discussions with Dorothy, she suggested that perhaps Dorothy could not have children, which made me feel bad. I would not have left Dorothy if we had had a child.

My problems with Dorothy made 1946/7 a difficult time and it affected my writing. I made several false starts with *Wild Conquest* and gave it up. I also put away my early notes for *Tell Freedom*. I was not in the right mindset for any long and sustained writing effort. I did better with journalism and earned a little more money than in the earlier days. Royalties from *Mine Boy* began to come in regularly and steadily, as they have to this day. It was fascinating watching this book take on a life of its own and I was happy with its translation into many languages. I had reached the point where I needed a literary agent to look after the business side of my work. Having an agent turned out a mixed blessing, good for business, not so good for one's faith in human nature. After more than forty years I discovered a betrayal of trust and found it necessary to end relations with this agent with whom I had started doing business way back in 1946/7. In those early days, though, that agent served and protected my interests well.

Relations at home grew more distant and difficult and I spent increasingly more of my free time in the streets and cafés and clubs and private house parties which littered the post-war London landscape. There was a rush of South Africans into London. I went to several of their house parties. At one of these I met the Afrikaner poet Uys Krige, and it was amazing how much we had in common. The South African environment had made such meetings impossible; we had to meet in a foreign land to relax, have a few drinks and get to know each other. He, in South Africa, was as much a prisoner of his colour and the structures built around it, as I was. We needed to be a long way from home to discover how much we shared. I had begun to lose my Afrikaans. Krige was an Afrikaner poet who handled the English language better and more gracefully than most Britons. I remember him as quiet and gentle and soft-spoken. More than fifty years later, I can still close my eyes and see his face.

I spent time going from one to the other of the wide variety of student and youth hostels found all over inner and outer London. One of my favourites was Youth House, the Quaker hostel on Camden Road. It was residential, with a good little vegetarian restaurant. Prices were modest and many workers in the area lunched there. It had between ten and fifteen small rooms rented to students and young Quakers of both sexes. It held weekend dances to which the West

African students flocked from their all-male hostel up the road. There were lectures, discussions, musical sessions, poetry readings and the occasional organised trip to galleries, museums; more rarely there were day trips into the countryside or weekends with some hiking group. I got to know parts of Wales and climbed Mount Snowdon as a member of one of these groups.

I also made regular visits to the London Zoo, more to sit and watch the children enjoy themselves than to look at the animals. I always felt uncomfortable with caged animals, particularly with the big ones, the apes and monkeys. Whenever I made eye contact with one of these I was always startled by the sadness and despair I saw. Once, a few years later, I was driving through Kenya's Rift Valley, along a wide curving road snaking between two hills. A huge gorilla suddenly came out of the bush and loped into the road as though not seeing the oncoming car. I slammed on my brakes and came to a stop about ten or fifteen feet from the great animal. It paused, turned its head slowly, looked at the car, looked at me. Our eyes met. Then it loped across the road like a jay-walker. I felt a sense of terrible sadness. Then the animal disappeared into the bush on the other side of the winding road. That was years after my visits to the London Zoo. So the sadness could not be just the sadness of confinement. It reminded me of the sadness of my Aunt Mattie when she and my mother remembered things and times and places we had never known of. Was the sadness I sensed with these huge animals the same kind of sadness? The sadness of remembrances of other times when there were more of them? When they were freer and more in control of their world? Before man had pushed them to the point of near extinction? Do such animals sense when their species is on the decline and there is no future ahead for them? Will we humans, one day in the distant future, exhibit the same sense of despair and sadness when we come to the end of our line?

As always, I was shaken out of this mood by the joyous shouts and squeals of the children as they played in the great Zoo. For some odd reason we were all, children and adults, very quiet on our brief, seemingly compulsive, visits to the snake houses. It was as though we had to go and be frightened and unsettled by these slithering creatures of no emotions and dead, unblinking eyes. I usually had nightmares after such visits. I am sure the children did. I never wanted to go there; I always did.

I met Daphne at Youth House. It was the spring of 1946, warm enough for her to wear a floral dress which outlined her body, and for me to be in slacks and tweed jacket — without overcoats. She was a student at an art school in South London, newly moved into Youth House. She worked part-time at Youth House in return for a discount on her rent. One day she was serving from the little hatch through which we ordered our food, and, as was usual at the place, she introduced herself to the customers. 'I'm Daphne.' Then, serving over, she brought her own food and came and shared the table. This time she and a friend shared the table where I sat. It was a simple, commonplace beginning to a lifetime's friendship and love.

She was born in Djember, Java, Indonesia on 23 July, 1927. Her father, a Scotsman called 'Willie' by his family, managed a rubber plantation for a British company. The Dutch were the colonial masters at the time and she spent her first seven years in the special world of the colonial plantation manager's child, surrounded by 'natives', alone, isolated, with no playmates. Her mother was her teacher, yard animals were her friends. She learned Dutch and Malay in the way children soak up languages. Our youngest daughter, for instance, was never 'taught' to read; reading just happened because she lived in a world of books. Daphne also absorbed other things: the way Javanese women walked; the graceful movements of hands, head, feet, hips shoulders, neck; even the speech patterns.

I was raised by women who loved me. It made for a comfortable ease with women. I could listen to them, deal with them as friends, even at times be unaware of the sexual differences. With Daphne, right from the outset, I was always acutely aware of the woman. There was more sheer sensuality between us than I had known with any other woman. At the same time I was more completely at ease with this woman than I had ever been with any other.

I told her about Dorothy at the outset. We went for long walks and I took her to all my favourite places: the little tea-house off Hampstead Heath run by two elderly sisters who made buttery scones and served the most delightful strawberry jam with tea and toast, all for one-and-six-pence. I took her to Charley Lahr's in Soho and glowed in his approval of her; to the club where my fat Russian friend with the unbelievably common English name of Watson over-ate for several months then spent two weeks at a fat farm to take it all off before beginning all over again. We went to the Zoo. We went to concerts. We read books together.

She had a wider circle of friends, male and female, than I had, and I found myself increasingly impatient of the time she spent with them. I was, I realised with dismay, becoming possessive. I fought against it and against my newly aroused sense of jealousy. A wild, impulsive streak in her and her tendency to 'forget' or play games with the truth to get out of awkward situations worried me. I realised this woman could damage me grievously and I did not like the feeling of deep emotional dependence invading my life. I had never been jealous or possessive of any person before and I did not like the feeling. When I confided this to Charley Lahr, he smiled dreamily and said: 'It happened to me nearly fifty years ago and there's never been anyone else for me.' His wife had died a few years earlier, so I changed the subject.

About a year after our first meeting I finally admitted to myself that this was the woman with whom I wanted to share the rest of my life; this was the one I wanted to be the mother of my children. If it was not this one it would be no other. This deep, total emotional commitment to one person could not be repeated and it would not be fair to turn to any other woman as second or third best.

She had had chicken pox, was isolated in her little upstairs room, and could see no one who had not had chicken pox. I had it as a boy, so I went up to her room with a small bunch of flowers and some chocolates. She looked terrible and I could see she felt miserable. She was not allowed to wash, so she was dirty and smelly. At other times with other people in such a state I had kept my distance and removed myself as soon as possible. I embraced her, held her close, wanted to comfort her. This, for me, was the final confirmation.

'I want you to be the mother of my children,' I said.

'I smell,' she said.

'I know.'

'And you want me?'

'Forever.'

Tears glistened and she nodded, suddenly looking like a frightened little girl in the body of a strapping, smelly, pock-faced woman. The die was cast.

That night I asked Dorothy for a divorce. She refused flatly. We had an ugly, bitter row. I moved out of the flat.

Daphne and I moved to Paris on 1 June 1948. I was, now, more committed to one human being than I had ever been in my life; more responsible for another life than I had ever been. As we waved farewell to the small group of friends who had come to see us off I found myself silently praying that this venture would be a success. It was everything for me and, I hoped, for the beautiful young woman beside me. She was twenty, I was twenty-eight. This was a new beginning.

We found a room in a narrow, cobbled street where the houses leaned like drunken men bracing against the wind; what kept them up, kept them from falling over, was a miracle. The Rue Servandoni began just below the Gardens of Luxembourg and ended near the church of Saint-Sulpice; a short, narrow little street not far from the

Boulevard Saint-Michel. It was the Left Bank of Paris; the students' quarter, though mainly elderly lower middle-class French folk seemed to live on our street. The men looked in their mid-forties and over, the women in their thirties and over. The little hotels, like ours, had small courtyards surrounded by drab structures going up as far as they could without falling over. Ours went up five floors. Near the end of our stay we rented a tiny attic on the fifth floor where I could work in relative silence. Our concierge, Madame Garne, was a thin, raspy Russian émigrée, whose French was as weird to Daphne as her schoolgirl French was to the old lady. They both seemed to think that raising their voices made things more comprehensible. I had not learnt French at school, so I looked and listened and held my peace. Daphne and the old lady somehow got to understand each other and there were negotiations about hot water and where to bathe and about removing the smelly, infested overstuffed heavy settee from the cluttered room. I helped Madame Garne's only son and his wife, looking even younger than Daphne, prise the big and ugly thing out of the room and two flights down the narrow stairs into their own room. They seemed pleased to have the thing. Its removal made our room twice as big as before, and when Daphne opened and removed the dark curtains to reveal our little balcony the place was transformed into a bright sunny room with a view into the living room across the narrow street. A florid woman, hair like a wild bush all over the place, in what looked like a night-dress, looked at us from her own look-alike little balcony a few feet away. No need for peeping Toms; the bedroom next to the balcony had see-through lace curtains. The neighbours were close, within hailing distance, easy, forthcoming, without the familiar British reticence.

Our hotel had a grand name. The Hotel of the Nations, or something similar. We were in the left wing overlooking the courtyard. The right wing seemed occupied mainly by Vietnamese and other Indo-Chinese. I recall a French writer and an Irish musician also stayed on upper floors of the right wing. A Dutch couple, a runaway husband and his girlfriend, anxious to make friends, stayed in our wing. We also had glimpses of a big, burly, distinguished-looking white-haired middle aged man who was always well dressed, a slim elegant walking-stick on his left arm and a dark felt hat with its brim at a precise jaunty angle. He usually carried the hat in his left hand, partner to the walking stick. I could never decide which was more impressive: the hat on his head or in his hand. Either way, it added up to a striking presence. In the eighteen months we lived at the Rue Servandoni, I never once heard this man speak to anyone. He left his room on the floor above ours near midday and returned about sundown every evening. We rarely saw him at weekends. I tried to make contact with the writer in the Vietnamese wing. Language was a problem and he did not seem to want contact. There was a young, string-bean tall American with buck-teeth and friendly laughing eyes. His name was Lyle and he was in Paris on a government scholarship for American ex-servicemen. He was from Spartanburg, South Carolina. He was working on his thesis on John Adams, one of two former US presidents of that name; I cannot now remember which one, the second or the sixth. We struck up a warm friendship and gradually slipped into the habit of reading each other's writing of the day before over coffee and croissants. *The Path of Thunder* had just been published in the United States, had spent a week or so on the *New York Times* best-seller list, and was then knocked of its perch by Alan Paton's *Cry The Beloved Country*. There had not been a novel out of Africa for a very long time and my US publishers thought they were on to a winner. But though I did reasonably well, Paton was the winner. I realised then how important the commercial, money-making aspect of publishing was in the United States. But we were, for the time being, well off by Paris standards, where the US dollar was worth a small fortune in French francs. It was a good time to be young and alive and happy and writing in an attic in Paris. I was working on Wild Conquest.

Daphne spent her mornings keeping house, drawing or painting whenever she could, strolling down the road to the little market of Saint-Sulpice to buy strings of sausages, the occasional steak or chop for me, crisp lettuce, endives, tomatoes, and, on the way back, the freshly baked long French loaves. We always had two big flagons of ordinary wine, one red, one white. Wine was the cheapest drink in Paris; only water was cheaper and nobody, it seemed, drank water. The pavement cafés of Paris all had glasses of water on their outdoor tables; only the very broke who could not afford a glass of wine sat sipping water while watching the world go by. Even the black Americans we met in Paris 'made faces' when we drank water and offered them some.

The most famous black American in Paris at that time was the writer Richard Wright. I had first met him in London on his way to Paris a year earlier. A thickset, heavy man, looking shorter than his actual height due to his shape, with a soft voice and a Southern drawl, he was obviously relishing his status as the most famous black American writer of his day. His *Native Son* had won national acclaim in the US and earned him a fortune. He had been generous in his help to get *The Path of Thunder* published in the United States. When we got to Paris, he was settled in and had bought an apartment in a fashionable section of the Left Bank immediately behind the Boulevard Saint-Michel. They gave him the freedom of Paris, and the friends and cronies with whom he was seen in the cafés and nightclubs were household names in literary and intellectual circles all over the world. Jean-Paul Sartre, his great female companion, Simone de Beauvoir and the existentialist group around them fascinated Wright. He found existentialism intoxicating and was ready to talk about it until everybody was turned off, then that charming smile of his would light up his face and he would offer drinks all round and change the subject. He was a great buyer of books and usually carried a large leather bag into which he stuffed the books. I once felt the weight of it as it grew heavier each time we stopped at a bookshop on London's Charing Cross Road. Now he was into Kierkegaard's philosophy made popular by Jean-Paul Sartre. Behind it all, though, I was always conscious of an enormous anxiety and touchiness about colour and any show of prejudice.

People were always visiting us at Rue Servandoni and hardly a week passed without anybody 'dropping in': complete strangers from South Africa, usually whites on tourist visits to Paris; our own friends of all races and colours from London; political acquaintances; and, almost constantly, the Vietnamese students from the other section of our building, practising their English on Daphne. She made sure that nobody disturbed me when I was up in the little attic pounding away at the typewriter. Once a man from my seafaring days found his way to Rue Servandoni. We had a meal and a drink and a long chat, then he found his way back to wherever his ship was docked. I did not know him, I did not remember him from any of the ships on which I had worked, but he knew me and he recalled events and details I did remember. Every now and then the past came back.

My agent wrote to say Dorothy had filed for divorce, claiming a share of my future income. Another friend wrote to tell me that another man, also a South African, had moved in with her, not just as her tenant. I passed the information to my agent, who had engaged a lawyer on my behalf. A little later, my agent wrote to say the lawyer had investigated and confirmed that Dorothy was living with this other man. He had dealt with Dorothy's lawyer, and there would be no claim on any of my future literary earnings.

Wright introduced me to Sartre and Beauvoir; it was casual, off-hand, at some small gathering for Paris' latest hot topic, the 'little man', Gary Davis, who had symbolically destroyed his American passport. The context was bizarre: a bunch of French left-wing intellectuals aiding and abetting a politically naive young American to renounce his American citizenship. I found it embarrassing as such introductions sometimes are. Perhaps I did not say the right words. I was not as impressed by either the foolhardiness of the 'little man' or the originality of existentialism as Wright was.

Daphne liked Wright and he sometimes came to visit us at Rue Servandoni. I was always a little surprised at how impressed, almost envious, he seemed of the pleasures and small luxuries we enjoyed. Our food, sausages with fresh salads, a variety of three or four kinds of cheese and all kinds of fresh fruit seemed the epitome of luxury and he ate with relish, and drank large quantities of our cheap *vin ordinaire*. It was all from the little market down the road, carefully chosen and determined by Daphne's very tight budget. I once heard Wright complain to his wife that they did not eat the kind of food the Abrahams' did. They could not, in their luxury apartment with a French cook and at least two maids. Perhaps he was hankering back to 'soul food'.

Another black American writer who slipped in and out of Paris in those days was James Baldwin. At that time Baldwin's main claim to fame was an essay on Richard Wright, *Everybody's Protest Novel*, in which he savaged Wright cruelly. It was published in one of the most popular American magazines and gained wide currency. The attack hurt Wright deeply. He had befriended the younger Baldwin, had been as generous and encouraging with him as he had been with me and, indeed, with most aspiring black writers. So this, for Wright, was a Judas kiss. When I met Baldwin, I told him of my disappointment at his attack on Wright and we had a long, at times angry and bitter argument about the reasons and motives behind it. Baldwin was honest. Wright was the most famous black American writer of the time. There was room at the top for only one. That was 'the system', the way 'the man' had set it up for us. It worked that way at every level. If you are black and want to get to the top, you have to work to displace whoever was now at the top. Those were their rules we had to live by to survive. Even if it is your friend and mentor, I wanted to know? Even if it is your brother, he replied. I did not think Wright would do it, I suggested. He didn't need to, Baldwin retorted. Not even if he needed to, I insisted. You don't understand the ways of American racism, Baldwin said. People like Langston Hughes, with whom I had corresponded for years, would never do it, I insisted. They've used him, discarded him and pigeon-holed him, he snapped. The communists, the American literati, high society have all used the Harlem New Negroes and then discarded them. Langston was one of those. He's given up on trying to make it in their world. I was not satisfied; we parted in anger. But I had a better understanding of Richard Wright's enormous anxiety and touchiness. A black American writer at the top was no easy position. Was that why he left America?

Years later, Baldwin publicly expressed regret for that attack on Richard Wright. But the hurt had been inflicted, the damage done, That could not be undone. This notion of room for only one black at the top, in any field at any one time, in the struggle for white approval and white reward made life for the one at the top difficult, cruel, precarious. For me it was a subtle and complex new twist to racism and racial manipulation. It brought back memories of the time, long ago, in Vrededorp, when a couple of young white policemen ordered my brother and his friend to fight each other for their entertainment. They refused to. But they were in a land where they were part of the exploited majority, and there were no vast sums of money, no high positions of fame at stake. Where the blacks are a minority and fame and fortune required that they destroy each other, the choices were crueller. I understood much better than before that argument with James Baldwin the harsh complexities of being a black minority in a racist American society. It determines how you deal with each other, how you see and treat each other, even away from direct white supervision. The reality of DuBois' sense of 'two-ness' was more than an intellectual's view of things. It was part of the nature of being black in America.

One day George Padmore showed up at Rue Servandoni. I came down from the attic and there he was, sitting upright in the one big old velvet-covered armchair left in the stripped down room. He was as immaculately dressed as ever, with a tiny fresh red rose in his buttonhole. Daphne's little grey tabby cat was perched on his knee and he was sipping a cup of coffee. The mood in the room was chilly. Had he quarrelled with Daphne? Daphne told me later about the high-handed manner in which he had ordered her to make him a cup of coffee. These two would never be friends. My arrival relaxed the atmosphere somewhat. It transpired that a socialist conference on a united Europe was to take place in the little town of Puteaux the following week. The Pan-African Federation had been invited to attend and to deliver a fraternal message. Since I was now resident in France, I had been chosen to represent the Federation at the conference. We spent over an hour discussing what I should say, then Padmore left. When I offered to see him off at the station he refused. He had to see a couple of comrades and do a few things. He looked at his watch, went on talking for another ten minutes. Daphne was getting the lunch together; he picked at the blue cheese on the table, carefully separating the blue from the white and only eating the white bits. Then he looked at his watch again and got up. He did not even want to be accompanied down the stairs. We looked from the little balcony. A black official-looking limousine crawled up the narrow street and stopped outside our hotel. Padmore emerged from our courtyard, the car door opened. He got into the back and the car moved slowly up our little street. Even in Paris, George Padmore moved in a mysterious way. His world had changed; he was no longer the Comintern's man, but the old contacts and the old ways lingered.

Daphne was pregnant. A young Vietnamese doctor from the other block confirmed it. It explained her sudden bouts of periodic sickness which had worried me. A friend of Daphne's from Bournemouth, Iris, came to help out when the baby arrived. Madame Garne, who had difficulty pronouncing Daphne's name and who had forged an odd bond with her, found a little room for Iris a floor above us. Our friend Lyle was immediately taken by Iris. When Richard Wright met her, he too liked what he saw. Iris was flattered by the attention of the two men: Lyle's gracious and fun-filled Southern charm; Wright's fame and wealth and the attraction of being seen with such a man, being flattered by him in the presence of others, made the visit special for Iris. So she dated each in turn and had a wonderful time. Daphne and I were amused by what we saw as a bit of friendly rivalry between two men for the attention of an attractive young woman who would not be around for too long. Before Iris left, though, it blew up in our faces one day when Wright took me aside and bitterly denounced Lyle and our friendship with him. For him, the contest for Iris' attention was a thing of race and colour. This guy was from the South and you must never trust them, no matter how friendly they seem. If you were back where he came from, he would not be your friend. It was depressing. We had sensed a stiffness between them whenever they met, but the harsh racial judgement by my black friend of my white friend in our essentially non-racial context, was unsettling. Certainly, as far as Iris was concerned, the thing was non-racial and not all that serious. She was in her twenties, intelligent, sophisticated, a self-confident young woman who knew herself and what she wanted. She was having fun in Paris, enjoying the company of two men whose attention was flattering. Which one she preferred, which one she slept with, if either or both, was her business and would not be based on colour. Besides, Wright was not lacking in other women friends. There was one particular and very beautiful and self-contained young French woman to whom he introduced me with great pride and a hint of possession. So the thing with Lyle over Iris was odd and disturbing, a kind of war for other darker, deeper reasons of the mind and spirit that we would try to hide even from ourselves. Looking back to what happened more than fifty years ago I am still appalled by the terrible emotional and psychic turmoil someone like Richard Wright must have suffered. Colour should never be that kind of burden on any human spirit.

An obviously pregnant Daphne insisted on coming with me to that socialist conference in Puteaux. I remember it as a drab place, about an hour out of Paris by train. The meeting was in the town hall. When we arrived, the place was already crowded and noisy. If it was a conference of delegates, then most of them were working-class, going by speech and dress and behaviour. The upper-class French were, if anything, more controlled and self-contained than their British counterparts, the middle class more austere and self-conscious. The French working class, on the other hand, are as relaxed, uninhibited and noisy as a Jamaican crowd at some fun-filled public event. An usher spied us out at the crowded doorway and elbowed us into the huge hall. The Mayor, the chain of office round his neck, was on the platform to open the proceedings. This could have been any city hall in Britain, except that the British ones were much less drab. But Britain had not been occupied by the Nazis. A number of socialist dignitaries shared the platform with the Mayor. Daphne firmly refused to get on the platform with me, and with sketch pad in hand, sat in a corner from where she could get a good view. I was introduced to the person who would translate my remarks. It was a woman who spoke excellent English and who had spent the years of German occupation in Britain. She was an ardent socialist in her middle years.

My brief from Padmore was clear. Sooner or later, preferably sooner, the need for a united Europe would become so self-evident that nobody would be able to resist it. Either that or another war, between the Soviet Union and the Americans this time, to decide who would control Europe. In their own collective self-interest, the Europeans should agree to bury their differences and create a united Europe. Our main interest, the interest of the African, Asian and Pacific colonies, was to have a free, strong and united Europe, shaped on socialist principles which repudiated imperialism and colonialism and offered a new and healthier relationship between Europe and its former colonies. I was to tell them about the deliberations and decisions of the Fifth Pan-African Congress we had held a couple of years earlier in Manchester, England. I was to conclude with the abiding wish of the Pan-African Federation and all those on whose behalf it spoke, for good relations between Africa, Asia, Latin America and the Caribbean and a free and united Europe.

Everybody who spoke before me had used the platform megaphone to be heard above the din in the conference hall. It was a battle of noise against noise. When it came to my turn, the translator whispered into my ear to wait until they stopped talking. So I stood up. Megaphone in hand, the translator beside me, we waited. The chairman stopped pounding his gavel. Gradually the room grew quiet until there was complete silence. Only then did I begin my message, speaking quietly and clearly and waiting for the lady beside me to complete every sentence before I started a new one. It was the most captive, enthralled audience I had ever addressed, and I warmed to it, throwing in some asides of my own. When it was over, the hall exploded in applause. Everybody rose to their feet. I knew that much of it was for the quality of the translation. We had achieved a moment of symbiosis and my mood, my spirit, my passion for freedom, had become as real for that French audience as if I had said it all in their own language.

Afterwards, a very high-up personage from the Socialist International who was on the platform wanted me to be a guest on a European speaking tour to spread the message of the importance of European union and how it should relate to the former colonies. I declined politely, but agreed that they could make copies of the speech, which someone had taken down in shorthand, and use it as they wished. I would like to think that this message from the Pan-African Federation, given to me by George Padmore, to deliver to the movement for a united Europe at its early beginnings helped to shape Europe's relatively enlightened attitude to later unfolding events in her former colonies. Thanks to George Padmore, the internationalist throughout his life, the Pan-African movement made its contribution to the shaping of today's united Europe.

1948 was the year Yugoslavia's Tito broke with Joseph Stalin's version of communism and defied Stalin's world-wide control of all communist parties. The Cold War was at its height and the fall-out between the two communist giants threw communist parties everywhere into a period of confusion. The non-communist left, the socialists and other radical groups reacted with a mixture of approval and apprehension. The French and British communist parties quickly fell in line behind Stalin. Nobody thought that Stalin would do nothing about Tito's defection. The disturbing question was what he would do. The Americans and British warned carefully about interference in the internal affairs of states and offered aid to Yugoslavia. The Soviet Union made threatening noises. There was some propaganda about the Yugoslav Communist Party itself getting rid of the 'traitor'. When this did not materialise, the Yugoslav Communist Party was expelled from the Comintern. I wished I were nearer Padmore then. He and Tito had both been Comintern operatives about the same time. They must have run into each other in the course of their work. I would have liked to hear Padmore's reading of the situation.

Paris was buzzing with rumour: a Stalinist agent had been sent to kill Tito; Stalin was planning an invasion; the Americans and British were ready to intervene; a new war was in the making. We all frightened ourselves silly.

In the event, America did provide much moral and material aid to Tito, and as the weeks passed and Tito remained alive and in control of his country, it slowly dawned on us that it was possible for some communist or communist party to defy Stalin and survive. One of communism's most powerful myths had been shattered. But the apprehension lingered. Stalin had stalked another of his enemies for years. Leon Trotsky, one of the architects of the Russian revolution, had lost out to Stalin in the leadership fight after the death of Lenin. He had been driven into exile. When he persisted in his opposition to Stalin's policies and launched his alternative communist Trotskyist movement with its anti-Stalinist body of literature which I first read in South Africa, Stalin's agents hunted him down and he was chopped to death near Mexico City in 1940. Stalin's hate was long-term, his reach without limit. Tito, from now on, would always have to be on guard.

The most important long-term consequence of the Tito-Stalin fall-out was not, as most European intellectuals thought at the time, the greater independence of non-Russian communist parties. It was the beginning of the Non-Aligned Movement, that world-wide grouping across ideologies and cultures in defiance of the prevailing Cold War politics.

The Cold War dictated that the world was divided into two power blocs: the Soviet power bloc led by Russia in the name of Soviet communism and the Western power bloc led by the United States in the name of Western democracy. Eastern Europe, China and the communist parties of the West fell in line behind the Soviet Union; the rest of the world fell in line behind the United States. Soviet interests were the interests of all who fell within her sphere of power. American interests were the interests of all who fell within the American sphere. This determination of interests was, where necessary, enforced by a combination of political, economic and even military action. India, always inclined to non-alignment, was economically 'punished' by US policy almost from her independence. So the Soviets provided more aid to India than they might otherwise have done. In the main, the policies of countries during the Cold War period were decided by the power bloc within which they fell. Africa and the

Indo-Chinese peninsula, and Central America, were among the worst political victims of this Cold War period, which lasted from about 1945 until the collapse of the Soviet Union in 1991.

This was the period of the terrible carnage in the former Belgian Congo, where colonialism was replaced by chaos, slaughter and the massive manipulation of developments by both the United States and the Soviet Union. One of the major victims was the brilliant young Patrice Lumumba, who might, under other circumstances, have evolved into one of Africa's major statesmen. I still carry the mental picture of the young Lumumba, 36, handcuffed, on the steps of the American plane surrounded by CIA operatives, which was the last picture seen of the young Congolese first Prime Minister. If he had lived, he would have been 77 today, in 1999. The Cold War was wasteful of human life and human talent, as wasteful as any war. Only, no tally was kept. There is no 'body count' of the victims of the Cold War in Africa, Asia and Latin America. Nations and peoples were destroyed, countries were ravaged, economies laid waste, infrastructures wiped out in the name of the communist revolution or in the name of Western democracy. It was the cruellest of times for the Third World, the black, the poor and those who aspired to avoid being part of either power bloc.

The political witch-hunts were not only a feature of Stalinist Russia. They took place in America, too, where writers and artists and film-makers and actors were hauled in front of a Congressional Committee on Un-American Activities, were denounced as communists or agents of a foreign power and deprived of their reputations and abilities to make a living. Many famous American names, black and white, were tarnished. An idea, an identification, had become criminal. Paul Robeson was one of the victims. Richard Wright, an admitted communist earlier in his life, seemed to have escaped the witch-hunt. Perhaps that explains his later denunciation of communism in *The God That Failed*. I could not imagine Padmore ever denouncing the Comintern.

The Cold War turned African against African, Asian against Asian, Latin American against Latin American. It developed its own language: proxy wars, client states, satellites.

The Prime Minister of Iran, a committed nationalist desiring that the people of Iran be the primary beneficiaries of Iran's oil wealth, was overthrown in the cheapest ever political coup stage-managed by the American CIA. The Americans themselves were surprised at the ease with which they had overthrown and changed a government.

Tito's defection from his power bloc offered the first sign of a way out. If he succeeded, it might be possible for others to break free of the two power blocs. They all knew Tito could not do it alone. He either received quick Third-World help or one or the other of the power blocs would get him. The West had already begun to draw him into its power bloc. Nehru of India and Nasser of Egypt were the first to make contact with Tito. George Padmore's little news releases took on a new urgency and frequency. Tito, the communist, became a Third-World hero and the message was published in little papers and magazines all over the Third-World and talked about at political and trade union meetings. An idea was being let loose among us, and Padmore, as usual, was one of the key messengers. I do not think Wright ever met Padmore, but the next time I saw Wright he was full of Tito and the unfolding idea of a non-aligned gathering. He it was who first told me that Indonesia's Sukarno had contacted Nehru and Tito and offered Indonesia as the venue for a non-aligned gathering. I wrote and checked with London and Padmore confirmed that 'the fellows' were planning something big for Bandung. It would take time but it was important and they were planning it at government level. Did I want to be attached to the Indian end of the planning? I replied no; Daphne was too far into her pregnancy and I did not want to leave her and go on such a long trip. I got back a vast amount of information about the early planning. India would give full backing and some financial support, though it would not play a prominent role. Nasser had come on board altogether and there was a plan for him and Nehru to meet with Tito. Perhaps Kwame could be there too. The covering note was faintly disgusted, something about writers missing the making of history if they put family matters first. My news that Wright was planning to go did not mollify him. Was he that black American turncoat who joined with Koestler in that anti-Soviet book? What did he know about our movement? Padmore obviously knew more about Richard Wright than I had thought.

So our first child, Anne, Biddy to us, was born at the British Hospital in Paris in February 1949 in the midst of the unsettled turmoil of the Cold War and Tito's opening of an opportunity for those who wanted to be neither for Soviet communism nor for Western capitalism. It was a dangerous time. Our first child's birth was also dangerous: she was premature, weighed about five pounds and for the next six months and more Daphne and I had time for nothing except fighting to keep our tiny daughter alive. But on that night of her birth, Lyle and I had a grand celebration booze-up. The news of the birth of our daughter soon spread among our friends in Paris. They somehow found the bar where we were and the party lasted till daybreak. We went to the hospital as dawn broke, and I became aware of the problems that lay ahead if we were to keep this tiny little miss alive and help her grow. Daphne was tired but relaxed. We comforted each other, as we have at important times ever since, first with our eyes, then in quiet gentle embrace. The coming of Anne was the final cementing of our bond.

Daphne and our little girl stayed for ten days during which one cross-eyed nurse almost convinced her that our baby was too small and frail to survive. I think I protested to the Matron and the cross-eyed one was removed. After that I took them home to Rue Servandoni where they were received with great fanfare by the regulars who knew us. Madame Garne found a cot in the caverns of her ground-floor storing area. I think it had been originally acquired for her own hoped-for grandchild, who did not come because, the old lady insisted, her daughter-in-law was spiting her. Other women in the immediate neighbourhood, the lady across the road who nightly undressed by her lace-covered window, presented us with embroidered baby clothing; someone else gave rattlers to attach to the cot; someone else little cushions; a pair of knitted booties. Every woman in the neighbourhood told Daphne how best to look after the baby. Our Vietnamese friends brought oriental delicacies and flowers for Daphne. After negotiations to which I was not privy and the passing of some French francs, we had a grand Rolls Royce of a pram parked in the tiny passageway of Madame Garne's 'office', waiting for the day that Daphne and Anne would take their first stroll to the Gardens of Luxembourg a couple of hundred yards up the road. I did not work on their first morning up in the gardens.

Whenever it was warm and sunny, Daphne removed the covering so Anne could get the full benefit of the sun. I cannot remember the number of outraged French mothers, grandmothers and nannies strolling by with warmly-clad babies, covered from head to toe, who warned of the dire consequences for our baby, naked in her grand pram, being so exposed. One old dear even offered us the spare knitted woolly hat of the baby she minded. Daphne fought them all off, politely, firmly, even the old policeman who patrolled the gardens and tried to persuade her that it was not legal to have the baby naked in the pram. Over the weeks and months the *habitués* of the Luxembourg Gardens grew used to the strange young English mother who strolled or sat in the park with her baby stark naked as long as the sun shone on her. As the child flourished, grew stronger and started practising her voice scales, the ladies of the garden came to accept the strange ways of this young mother. One or two even stopped covering their babies' heads all the time. Anne, meanwhile, flourished and became beautiful; she soaked in everything around her and bonded with her mother and, later, her father. We measured our contentment and happiness by the remarkable growing of her little body, the improving of her health and the unfolding and growing interest, curiosity and awareness of a little human mind and intelligence. Anne and her happy morning noises as she practised her musical scales from our little balcony, bringing the neighbours to their balconies to watch and listen, made that one of the happiest, most memorable, periods of our lives.

Lyle became her first friend and she welcomed his arrival with high squeals, waving fingers and kicking legs. She doubling her weight in the first two months, doubled it again in the next three months.

Gerrard Sekoto, the black South African artist, was a frequent visitor and became Biddy's second great friend. Her eyes lit up whenever he came and she would stretch out her arms inviting him to pick her up. Perhaps she instinctively felt a bond between Sekoto and me. He was from the Transvaal, grew up in the same environment I did, had experienced the same hardships and discrimination. We had shared memories of people and places of childhood and youth. I was six years his junior, but he remembered the same Johannesburg and Vrededorp and Braamfontein and Orlando I did; the same Cape Town and District Six where he met and knew the same people I met later. We shared many memories at that room in Rue Servandoni, Biddy on Sekoto's knee, quiet and attentive for long stretches, then suddenly demanding attention and she and Sekoto would play some noisy game.

Our one room was not very big, probably about ten-by-twelve, or slightly larger, but by getting rid of most of the heavy furniture, swapping the old bed for a divan, using one simple wooden table, and stools and cushions, Daphne turned it into a spacious one-room apartment. The only relic of the old furniture was the heavy velvet-covered armchair tucked in the farthest corner of the room. Madame Garne had fought these changes every step of the way, especially the tearing down of dark wallpaper, but when it was over she grudgingly admitted that it made the room bigger and fresher, more like a salon. Then she snapped: 'But what will happen when you leave? Not everyone likes this emptiness! I will have to bring back everything.' We had grown used to her ways by now, so Daphne turned on her special smile and the stern old lady threw up her hands and smiled back. I once heard her upbraiding her daughter-in-law for not following the example of the young English woman upstairs. I understood because her French was almost as bad as mine and the point of the cussing out was for the world and her son to hear. Madame Garne, her son and her daughter-in-law were in a permanent state of family warfare. We remember her warmly for all her many kindnesses despite her stern exterior. We remember the tenderness of her love for our daughter. She was a wonderful old *émigrée* Russian mother figure. Not even Daphne dared to ask about Monsieur Garne!

Too many visitors, too many people we did not know, were finding their way to Rue Servandoni. Daphne was in the early stages of pregnancy with her second child. We had agreed on four children: two as close together as possible, a gap of five years, then our last two. That would be our ideal family. The first two close enough to keep each other company and old enough to help bring up the second two. It was fine in theory. In practice, we had the first two as planned, we had the five-year break, then the third one, and then Daphne said enough. So we ended up with only three. I was not complaining

It was time for me to write *Tell Freedom*. We decided to find a place in the country. We were also running low on money and neither of us had a permit to work in France. Our friends began searching for a place in the countryside, not too far from Paris. The mother of a young woman, Jenny Koso, about the same age as Daphne, who had married a rising young West African diplomat in the service of France, came up with the village of Paley in the Seine-et-Marne département. We met the owner who showed us pictures. It was an old bungalow in its own small walled-in grounds. It even had a name, *Lilac Close,* but in French. The owner had been set up at *Clos des Lilas* by her gentleman when she got pregnant. When her gentleman died, she and their child lived in the village until the child, too, died. Then she moved to Paris, renting out the place. The rent was low and we took the place, as the Americans would say, sight unseen except for the pictures. Another friend, Hannah Schramm, a long-time German anti-Nazi resident in France, persuaded a taxi driver she knew to take us all the way to Paley, again at a very modest price.

It was a sight to remember. We somehow piled everything we possessed into the taxi: the fancy pram that folded up, pots and pans, suitcases. Even the few household articles Daphne had bought at the market down the road — a mop, a broom, the big zinc pan in which we bathed — were stuffed into the taxi or tied to its top. Madame Garne and our friends who were not at work, saw us off. Neighbours in the narrow street came to say goodbye. Then Hannah and Daphne and Biddy and I left Rue Servandoni for Paley on a warm morning in July 1949. Stern old Madame Garne had tears in her eyes when she kissed Biddy goodbye. Two hours later, shaken and ratty and hungry and tired we reached our new home. There was someone from the village to hand us the keys. They had lit a fire and the place looked comfortable and warm. Hannah helped us settle in. Then, after a last long chat and a quick snack, she and the taxi driver made the long trip back to Paris.

Hannah, when we met her, was nearing fifty. She was an old-style German radical going back to the days of the Weimar Republic. She had, as a young woman in her early twenties, been close to the revolutionary writer and political activist, Ernst Toller. She loved him as a woman loves a man. Whether he returned that love, whether anything happened between them, was never clear; she did not say and we did not ask. We had no right to intrude on that intimately personal area of her memory bank. I did, however, ask many questions about the political side of their relations. We spent many days and nights with Hannah recreating for us how Germany looked and felt after World War One, what went into the making of the short-lived Weimar Republic, and one writer's involvement in those events. Through Hannah's eyes, through Hannah's words and the emotions evoked by her memories, I came to know the German writer Ernst Toller as well as I have any other writer I had known personally. Knowing the man made *I Was A German* a very special document for me of the spiritual sadness and sickness of Europe in the early years of this century. Toller's suicide in New York in 1939 underscored the tragedy of the Weimar Republic and the dreamers and idealists who tried to make it work, and failed. After the high hopes of the Weimar Republic came Hitler and the Nazis. And Hannah, and many like her, fled into exile

Hannah had been interned by the Vichy government when the Germans occupied France. Her great and constant dread at that time was that she might be deported back to Germany and one of its concentration camps. She was lucky and remained in the French prison camp until the liberation. Now she was a citizen of de Gaulle's new French Republic, growing old with the memories of what had been and what could have been. Hannah was a big woman: about five-ten or eleven, broad, big-boned and heavy. She must have weighed more than two hundred pounds of flesh and bone and very little, if any, fat. She had a huge thorax; she was a chain-smoker and one of those strong-smelling, spiky little French cigarettes, *Gauloises* I think they were called, was a permanent feature of her face. As one came to an end she lit another from the butt. Her lungs were so good she lived to eighty-two despite this terrible habit. When she visited us at Coyaba in 1968, she was still smoking as heavily, still as robust as ever. We took her to the university beach and she took to the sea like a huge mermaid, swam away until she was a dot on the horizon, then disappeared. For the best part of an hour Daphne watched the horizon anxiously before the dot reappeared and Hannah swam back to land.

We had never seen her as happy, as exhilarated. She had made the long journey to see how we, 'my best beloveds', were doing in an island so far from Europe. She loved it so much she stayed for many weeks and only left when she could extend her return ticket no more. She stayed in the small flat with its own kitchen, toilet and shower we had built next to our home for just such a purpose, and she was as happy in the sun as we had ever known her. She struck up a friendship with one of our big Labradors, Max, and they went for long walks into the bush country around, often returning with rare orchids Hannah had found.

At times, when reliving the excitement of the Weimar days for me, and recalling the comrades with whom she and Toller had shared the struggle, and the endless mugs of coffee and cigarettes, and those who had dropped out, and those who had turned traitor, and those who had died, and the young women who had worked at anything that furthered the cause — from typing leaflets and manuscripts and speeches to standing on street corners handing out leaflets to being couriers on dangerous missions — I saw the young Hannah in her twenties, a big and strong young woman of enormous commitment, living through a crumbling dream and remaining strong. We shared some magical moments with Hannah, up here at Coyaba nearly twenty years after our Paris days. Now, Daphne is approaching what was Hannah's age on that last visit, and I am older than she was then. When we remember her, though, we see her as she was then and we were then — with the extra magic, in our little flat, of seeing her as the young woman she conjured up for us by her remembrances of past dreams and hopes and of those, all now gone, who peopled that past. This, for Daphne and me, was our favourite German, a human being who kept faith with the dream of a different kind of world. When we received news of her death in faraway Paris, it hurt as it hurt each time we received news of the death of a loved one linked by blood and family ties. Hannah was one of those rare ones, an ageing

German socialist exile who became as dear as any of my loved ones. Blood, race, colour and origin are not the only bonding agents in human relations. The trouble is that the others are not as easily defined. Hannah made us aware of the underlying sadness among European dreamers, artists and intellectuals as we had not been before. It influenced the way we look back on Europe. And this, too, this sadness of the best of European dreamers, will become part of the problem of the twenty-first century.

In Paley, meanwhile, back in that distant July of 1949, we settled in to what was a nice old house built of porous sandstone. It was cool and dry when we moved in. Things changed in the winter as we discovered that any time it rained, the damp watermark seeped up the walls like a thermometer's mercury. We needed a fire going constantly to keep the damp at bay, to keep our clothes and bedding dry. We took to putting out everything to catch the morning sun.

Our village was small, about twenty houses on sloping land with a river running through its lower end. It had a general store and post office all in one and a butcher's shop which was opened once a week when the butcher came from our nearest neighbouring village, which was bigger and more prosperous. Men and women worked the land. Our nearest neighbour, across the wide dirt road was a woman who had lived in the French possession of New Caledonia, in the Pacific. Her husband had died there and she was living off his pension which stretched further in a small village than it would in Paris. She had been happy in New Caledonia and hoped to return there one day; a vain hope, she admitted on her first visit, but something to hang on to. Below her, unoccupied, closed for the coming winter, was Jenny Koso's mother's house. Jenny had had her baby, a strapping golden brown little miss who looked enormous beside Biddy, when they visited us a week before Koso was to leave for Senegal. The plan was for him to go first, prepare a place for them, then Jenny and the baby would join him. That never happened. The plane in which Koso flew home exploded in mid-air over Africa and everybody died. The young mother with her baby was widowed in her twenties. The village was devastated; so were we. Daphne still remembers the young Kosos. He was big, well over six feet, handsome, as near black as a human can be. Jenny was statuesque and almost as tall, dark-haired, a lovely olive skin and a winning, shy smile. They made a striking couple. Suddenly Koso was not there and she was lost. She had her mother and a brother for support, and the state was not ungenerous in the face of such disasters. But Jenny remained lost.

Then there were the Armands, a family from Alsace — part German, part French — an old couple with a young son, who was the travelling village butcher and woodsman. He lived in the nearby village with his wife and children and he saw his parents regularly on his meat and firewood rounds in an old van. Madame Armand helped Daphne one day a week with housework. She loved baking and nearly always brought a small basket of freshly-baked cookies or biscuits or bread, wrapped in a spotless white cloth. Her old husband, then, moved with the heavy stiffness I feel today at eighty, though I do not think he was that old then. The Armands were as happy an old couple as we had known. He worked hard on the land for her; she worked equally hard to make him the best-run home in the village, with the choicest meals every day. Biddy soon slipped into the habit of running to the gate to meet Madame Armand to look for her freshly-baked cookies. She was speaking now, and chattered away in a mixture of French and English. One day down at the farm near the river where we went to buy our Gruyère cheese she saw two cows, one to the left of her, the other to the right. 'Mummy! Mummy! Look!' she cried, tossing her head from side to side and crossing her arms to point in both directions at the same time.

Within a week of our settling in I began writing *Tell Freedom*. I slipped back into my old routine of getting up at about five in the morning, writing for at least two or three hours, having a first cup of tea with Daphne, going back to work while she prepared breakfast. Breakfast was brief, then back to work until about midday. There were slight variations in this routine, but it was basic. After lunch we usually went for a long walk, then two hours of reading; the rest was family time and trying to keep up with what was happening in the world. Paley made keeping contact with George Padmore and developments in the Pan-African movement even more difficult than they had been in Paris. We became dependent on short-wave radio. I had an old one and getting the BBC — our main news source — was difficult. When Lyle and Sekoto visited, I spoke about this difficulty. Sekoto smiled, raising his left shoulder in a slight twitch:

'I can fix that.'

'How?' He was, if anything, poorer than we were.

'I have rich would-be patrons,' he said. 'I take from them a little of what they took from us to get rich. Makes them feel good.'

We went on to something else.

A week later, a rich South African woman, her Italian *beau* in tow, arrived in Paley by taxi. She had a spanking new short-wave radio for me. Sekoto had told her of my need. The deal was that I would help her with the script for a documentary she was planning. It was the quality of radio I could not afford otherwise, so I happily traded three or four days of my time to get it. Now we could get the news on the BBC and follow world developments and we were also glad to be able to listen to the good radio plays and entertainment programmes put out by the World Service. So I traded our old radio for meat and firewood from young Armand. I left it to him to put a value on the radio. We received at least two weeks worth of choice beef and pork cuts, a vast amount of deliciously seasoned sausages made from leftover unsold meat, and enough firewood to last us for the entire year we spent in Paley. He and his family were very happy with their radio; we were even happier with our food and firewood riches. Our daughter flourished. Daphne was less prone to the spells of sickness she had in Paris; the friends who were dear to us visited at weekends; the Americans had agreed to publish *Wild Conquest* in which I attempted to put a non-white perspective on the Great Trek of the Boers into the lands of the black people; *Tell Freedom* was growing steadily. We were happy, productive, at peace in the closing months of 1949.

Into that peaceful period for us, on 1 October, 1949, the early morning BBC news bulletin brought the news of the proclamation of the People's Republic of China. I felt sure this was another great turning point in the affairs of our world. On the way to the post office, Daphne and I talked about it. She was born in Asia, had a stronger feeling for it than I had. Mine was essentially ideological and based on my visits to a few of its seaport cities during my time as a seafarer. Hers was the commitment of being born there. We knew this was the beginning of the breaking of old bonds, old power relations, and the start of new ones. We knew it would be long, perhaps longer than our own lifetime, for this to come to full fruition, but it would come. India was independent and in communal chaos, but it was clear about its direction. The Indian National Congress would see it through its problems. Now China had overcome the Kuomintang and its American backers. It was only a matter of time before these changes, followed by the coming changes in Africa, rearranged the balance of power in the world, and with it, the balance in the relations between the lighter and darker races of man. DuBois' dream was in the making. Looking back, I realise how grossly we under-estimated the obstacles and problems ahead; how long it would take to overcome them; above all, how the nature of the coming change would itself be changed in the unfolding process. Our vision was too simple, too clear-cut, too free of uncertainty and doubt. Our world looked promising on that first morning of October 1949. The Cultural Revolution and its years of horror and confusions were still to come. So we celebrated a very happy Christmas, 1949, in what for us was a world full of hope and promise. Our friends came to celebrate Christmas with us. At our New Year's Eve party the potent village-brewed *eau de vie* flowed so freely and we piled the firewood so high, the chimney caught fire and the whole village turned out to help quench the fire by flooding the place and then finishing off what was left of our two gallons of firewater. It was a good Christmas, a warming start to the New Year. I had completed the first draft of *Tell Freedom*, Daphne was preparing for her second child, seeing a boozy old family doctor from the bigger village; Biddy was preparing for her first birthday for which Madame Armand was baking a fancy cake.

Aron was born at the end of January 1950. When the time came, the old doctor was so drunk that we, 'Granny' Armand and I, had to do most of the delivering. Lyle, who had come for the weekend, was in the background, eager to help and not to be in anybody's way. He entertained Biddy, and when she slept he tucked himself into a corner in the kitchen with a book. Nearly fifty years after, I still have nightmares about that day. Daphne's contractions started in the morning, so I rushed to call Granny Armand, then down to the post office to phone the doctor. It took at least fifteen minutes to get through to him. Yes, he would be on his way. Be calm; make her comfortable; give her a sedative. I went back. Granny Armand was there, Biddy was crying. Lyle was rocking her on his knee. Our nearest neighbour had come in and was trying to persuade Daphne to sip a little cognac. It was good for relaxing the muscles for the hard work ahead. Daphne refused. How was I supposed to get her to take a sedative? I could see Daphne getting 'steamed up' at the persistence of our neighbour. Then she exploded. 'I do not like cognac, Madame. I never have! And I know it is not good for anybody about to have a baby. I will not drink it! Stop pressing me!' Then, to me, in English: 'She's driving me up the wall. Do something!' Between us, Lyle, Granny Armand and I got the neighbour into the kitchen where she had a cup of coffee laced with a shot of her cognac. She was excited, trembling. Another woman, a friend of Granny Armand's popped in to give a hand. Our neighbour showed disapproval of the new arrival and told me to call her immediately if we needed anything, then left — with her bottle of cognac.

'The colonies turned that one's head,' Granny Armand's friend snapped. 'Too big for us now.'

Morning turned to midday, to mid-afternoon, still no sign of the doctor. From time to time Daphne cried out. I sat with her, held her at times, combed her hair — anything to distract her. I read to her: the *Sonnets from the Portuguese*, a chapter from my latest manuscript, Blake's *Songs of Innocence* and *Songs of Experience*. She drank a cup of Granny Armand's rich tasty beef soup, then she dozed off and the rest of us had soup at the kitchen table. So the day dragged on — a day of waiting, which made it a long day. Lyle went down to the post office to check the doctor. He came and said the doctor was on his rounds and could not be reached.

As the cold winter's sun was setting, the doctor's long big old car drove slowly, weaving slightly, up our dusty road. As he struggled out of it, Granny Armand groaned, panic in her voice: 'He is drunk, very drunk.' So he was. This old man was in no state to deliver our child. Daphne was in one of her calm painless spells. I told her our problem. What are we to do? She became clinically calm. She called for Granny Armand and gave her quick instructions. Then, to me: 'Remember, no drugs of any kind; no pain-killers no injections, no matter what.'

'What if...?'

She did not allow for my fears. 'No matter what.'

'Yes, mum.'

The doctor staggered in, opened his black bag and laid out his paraphernalia on the bedside table. He put the thermometer in her mouth, held her wrist, checked his time. Everything was satisfactory. Granny Armand came in, went straight to the doctor's black bag and took out a three-quarters-full hip flask. The doctor watched in silence.

'Till the work is done.'

He gave a slight shrug. She obviously knew the doctor.

More than an hour passed. I sat beside Daphne, holding her hand. The doctor seemed asleep in the chair by the window. The room was comfortably warm. Whoever had designed this house had built the fireplace so that it heated every part of it. Lyle was in Biddy's room, telling stories till she fell asleep. Papa Armand had come to keep his wife company in what turned out to be a very long night. From time to time other people dropped into the kitchen, had a mug of coffee, left something — usually fruit or vegetables — then went. The village was sharing in the long vigil before the coming of our son. It was very African, very tribal, very comforting.

The doctor was sobering up visibly by now. Perhaps he would be fit to do the job when the time came, I hoped fervently. We had jointly resisted all his efforts at sedation. Daphne had been particularly firm in rejecting his suggestion of an injection to hasten the process. Her stubbornness was mulish in face of his invocation of medical authority. In despair he reached for his black bag, then remembered his comforter had been removed. He half-shouted for Granny Armand, who brought him a mug of coffee. Was it laced with anything? I wondered because Daphne shrieked with pain and the old doctor suddenly seemed as high as ever. This time it was real. The child was coming.

The next hour or so was a blur. Daphne in agony, with the child coming down but seeming stuck somewhere. The doctor said it was big and she would need help to eject it. He reached for his hypodermic needle. Between her screams came the insistent command: 'No injection! No injection!' I took the needle from the doctor and Granny Armand took it to the kitchen, returned with the doctor's hip-flask and poured a small shot in his mug of coffee. Then we went to work. It must have been after midnight when Aron was finally born. He was big, several times bigger than Biddy had been at birth, and he had everything in place.

The doctor looked utterly drained and very old. Granny Armand returned his flask and he took a long swig and seemed better for it. Daphne was exhausted, but relaxed and free of the pain. A woman helped Granny Armand clean up the place, change the bedding. She was sent out while Granny helped clean up Daphne herself. After one baleful glare at a world he did not like, the strapping new baby boy shut his eyes and went to sleep. Granny wrapped him up and tucked him beside his mother, washed and clean after her long night of hard labour. Then mother and child went to sleep and the rest of us were released from the night of tension. I could not sleep, neither it seemed could Lyle, so after the Armands and the neighbours had left, and after looking in on Daphne and her new child, we went back to the warm kitchen and celebrated the arrival of my son with laced coffee and a long talk, which lasted till daybreak, about life and birth — and the fear of death which had been an unspoken part of that long night.

A week later, I made my one and only trip to what we had referred to as our neighbouring village. It was, in fact, a small town and the administrative centre for our part of the area. I had to go to this place to register our son's birth. In Paris the birth of our daughter had been automatically registered from the British Hospital and Daphne received the certificate when she was discharged. With this home birth, I had to do it. I was armed with the doctor's signed form.

The place had the drabness of a small industrial town: a few streets, a few shops, a school with a dusty, grassless school playground, an infrequent bus service, no trees, no green grass. The look-alike houses, as though built by the same person without imagination, were made striking by the lurid, bright and clashing colours. Each loudly screaming at the other: Here I am! Look at me! Only the town hall, in the heart of the place, was drab inside and out.

I climbed the wooden stairs to a series of offices; the ground floor was one big hall where council meetings were held. A tired-looking woman looked at the doctor's paper, then made me sit in a corner. She called a messenger boy and sent him for what she described as the leader of the council. It was a long time before the man arrived. He was an ordinary worker, dressed in working clothes, the traditional cloth cap shoved back on his head.

The man looked me over and I recognised the manner. This was how I had been looked over in any South African police station I, or any other black person, had the misfortune to enter. But this man was a communist. The French communists had won most local elections in the small industrial and farming areas of the country and they controlled most of the local government system with its vast network of social security for the French working class and peasantry. So why this open hostility towards me? In South Africa the communists had been the only whites free of the prevailing prejudice and racism. All communists, we had assumed, were without prejudice. This one was not. He went out of his way to make me know he did not like me. Why was I in his country? His English was as bad as my French. Was I running away from some crime? He had heard about me. What kind of writer was I? The good writers are in Paris or in the south, not in an unknown small village. So what was I up to? He had worked himself into a rage and I was by now shouting back. The woman at the desk caught my eye, showed sympathy and gestured slightly for me not to react. I could not help myself. The man had got under my skin and I kept on shouting back. People from the other offices came to watch the spectacle. That was it. It was a spectacle. This man, this leader of a communist local council, was putting on a show.

I calmed down and so did he. We glared at each other. Then, for the benefit of the onlookers, he told me why he did not like people like me. The French workers had struggled long and hard for the privileges they now enjoyed. The Africans, the Algerians, the Chinese did not contribute to that struggle. Now they come here and demand the same services and benefits which rightly belong only to French workers and peasants. The government in Paris may condone this; we do not. We do not want you here. Go back to your own country, sponge off them, not us. I want to see your birth certificate, your father's, your mother's, your grandfather's, your grandmother's; and if you can bring all those, I will find other documents to ask for to prevent your child being registered to enjoy our benefits. Bring me all those papers and we will talk again. He left with a flourish. The onlookers drifted back to their offices. The drab woman began to apologise. I left the place, depressed. This was a South African experience a world away from South Africa. I decided that this one I would withhold from Daphne, for now at least. She had enough problems of her own. She did not have to be part of this one. My past experience told me that this man was not singular, except perhaps in the brutal bluntness and relish with which he expressed his prejudice. This was the other side of the civilised and sophisticated France we had come to know. Which was dominant: this aggressive racist France which used the word 'chinois' as its strongest form of condemnation? Or the other France which Félix Éboué declared lived on when she herself, and people like this communist leader of this local council, were under the Nazi jackboot? In which one would Jenny Koso's big beautiful brown baby grow up? And what of communism, which in those days was seen by many of us as a moral and social as well as a political force? All the way back to Paley I grappled with these questions. I decided then that it would be best for the children not to grow up in this type of environment. We would have to find a place where they could grow as 'normally' as is humanly possible.

In Paley I stopped at Granny Armand's place on the way home. They were both at home and she wanted to know how the registration had gone. I gave them a bare outline of what had happened. They looked at each other and it dawned on me that they too had been the victims of prejudice, in all likelihood at the hands of the same local council leader. Their crime would have been that they were from

Alsace, which had been seen as pro-German, pro-Nazi. It is hard, the old man said, but you must try to ignore these things. It was a long speech for him.

At home, Daphne brought me up to date with the day's world news. Times were turbulent and one or the other of us was always monitoring the news. War could break out any time and we might have to move fast to get back to Britain. There had been a few scares. The Berlin blockade had been one such, as had the earlier Tito affair. The Congo was in chaos and the news out of the rest of Africa was not much better. I had, for the time being, lost regular contact with the Pan-African Federation, though I was still its nominal publicity officer.

I talked to Daphne about our returning to England. The divorce from Dorothy had been finalised and we could get married and London seemed the logical place for that. She agreed. Her experience with our second child had shaken her. We had both realised how precarious things could become, so we began planning and setting things in motion for the return to Britain. Finding a place to live was the first priority. We agreed I should go to London on my own, find a place, then she and the children would follow. I knew I could depend on Hannah to see them off.

One day down at the river, before my departure, a gust of wind blew some dust into my eyes. My left eye was particularly affected. I scooped up some water from the river and dashed it into my eyes to flush them out. The right eye cleared but the left one stung, so I washed it some more. The irritation persisted for days then eased, leaving the left eye slightly bloodshot all the time. In that state I made the journey to London. Finding a place turned out more difficult than I had expected. Youth House could let us have a room, but not with the babies. In the end, a South African, not long arrived, who had shacked up with a young woman who had inherited her own house, offered us a room till we found a place of our own. I sent for

Daphne and the children and we moved into Croydon, a London suburb.

It was not comfortable. That couple acted more like a pair of boxing rivals than people in love. There was a brawl almost every night and the woman gave as good as she got. But we were caught in the crossfire, and Daphne and her babies grew more depressed, no matter how much they stayed out of the couple's way. My eye trouble grew worse, so I took the family to see our old friend Dr Belfield Clarke. He did not like the look of my eye and insisted that I see some specialist friend of his at Moorfields eye hospital. I told him of our housing problem and he gave Daphne a note to somebody in the welfare section of the London County Council. While I went to Moorfields, Daphne went to the LCC, where they put her and the children into what they called a Rest Centre, a place where women with children were sheltered, usually because they had nowhere else to go, or their husbands or partners had abused them, or were in jail, or, as in my case, incapacitated or undergoing medical treatment. The men were not allowed to be with the women and children. I slept at Youth House and made the daily trip to the hospital. My sight, by this time, was so impaired that I was unable to read. The stuff they put in my eyes dilated the pupils so that daylight, let alone sunlight, became painful. For several months my left eye had to be completely covered from the light. Penicillin was the new wonder drug then and I was injected with massive doses. The other new drugs were the steroids which the doctors used as eye drops. I was warned that some of this was still in the experimental stage and there was the risk of any one or any combination of them backfiring. The long months of treatment without any noticeable improvement led to a point where I was not sure I would ever again see well enough to write or to be of any use to my family.

At the outset, the doctors, or so it seemed to me, assumed that my eye trouble had a venereal origin. So they tested my blood, which read positive. I tried to explain that I had Yaws as a child and this would show up in any blood test. They insisted that Daphne and the children be tested. Only after their tests proved negative did they seem to believe me.

As my eyes improved, I grew more hopeful and our prospects became less gloomy. Daphne and the children were moved from the Rest Centre to a large upstairs high-ceilinged room in an old Victorian building in Chelsea. And, best of all, after several months of separation which had felt like several lifetimes, I was allowed to move in with my family. Then, shortly thereafter, the London County Council assigned a house to us in a new housing settlement called Debden, near Loughton in the county of Essex. It was a new, two-storey, two-bedroom house with space in front, a garden at the back and a green hill across the road. It had a big window facing the road and the green hill beyond. The sitting-room fireplace was one of those convection heating jobs which warmed the whole house and made hot water as well. Our children each received free medical treatment, supplementary feeding, as well as a small weekly cash allowance. Britain's Welfare State had come to our rescue.

When I had made my last visit to Dr Belfield Clarke's eye specialist friend at Moorfields, I asked him what the treatment for my eyes would have cost if I had not received it under the National Health Service.

'Hundreds of thousands, laddie.' His eyes twinkled. 'Think no more about it. We owe our colonies much more than that.'

But then, he was Belfield Clarke's friend.

Debden was a product of the British Welfare State. Our neighbours were case studies of how the Welfare State functioned. In the house to the left of us was a Jewish family of three: mother, father and daughter. They were caricatures of how anti-Semites saw all Jews. The man worked in the garment industry, the woman was loud-mouthed and intrusive, the teenage daughter was round-shouldered, skinny and allergic to going to school. Below them was an English couple with a son a little older than Biddy. The man was tall, very thin and had the hacking cough of a consumptive; his hobby was playing the violin. The woman was small, very tense, very protective of her husband and child. I remember once making some inoffensive remark which she misread as criticism of her husband. She flew into a temper and Daphne had a hard time placating her and explaining what I had in fact said. When she understood, she went into an equally strong emotional scene of apology for misunderstanding. Dealing with her was even more demanding than with our Jewish neighbours. Below the tense neighbour's house was the corner of our row of houses with a special bungalow for old folk. Facing it was another bungalow as the end point for another row of houses at a right angle to our row. Thus, there were homes for two old couples at every corner of two rows of houses, with everything on the same floor and no need for old people to climb stairs. Each house had storage space for about a ton of coal. Each house had a stove, cupboards and all the toilet fixtures. All tenants needed to bring were beds, tables, chairs and their personal possessions. The only serious drawback to the Debden houses was that some of the pipes were on the outside and froze in winter, despite being lagged. Gas was from the common source and each home had its own meter. The rent for all this was three pounds a week.

Our neighbours to the right were a young couple — the man very tall, very polite and for months on end fully dressed in jacket and tie whenever we saw him. He was a departmental manager in a large West End store and always being properly dressed was part of the job. He did, later, appear in shirtsleeves in his garden at weekends. His wife was a warm generous and friendly fair-haired young woman, who, with her younger sister, had grown up in an orphanage. She had an equally fair daughter, Lorna, gregarious and clumsy and about Biddy's age. The two little girls became close friends and brought our two households together. Next, above them, was a Welsh couple. Only the man was Welsh, but when he married the woman, he told me one boozy night, she too became Welsh. He was proud and cocky about being Welsh. The woman was the perfect foil for his cocky Welshness. She was stocky, a devoted wife and mother, open and friendly with all her neighbours, and became close to Daphne. She had, it turned out, a long history of illness: tuberculosis, high blood pressure, and had spent time in a sanitarium. They had a little boy, David, perhaps a year older than the girls, a strutting little carbon copy of his dad. The woman's greatest fear was of what might happen to her two men-children if she were not around to take care of them. Above, them, a world unto themselves, lived a cockney truck driver, his cockney wife and their brood of five or six children — all separated from each other by anywhere between ten to fifteen months. A man who drives a big truck at times develops a big truck ego. This one had, and he looked with disdain on all his family and all his neighbours.

Above them was the house of the little greengrocer, a man of about thirty-five who looked middle-aged. He had a small van turned into a thing of shelves on which his fruit and vegetables were beautifully displayed. He drove slowly up one street and down another, stopping at every second or third house. Women came out to shop, then he drove on. We were great buyers of fruit and vegetables, so the front of our house became the stopping-point for our immediate neighbourhood. At weekends, his quiet reserved little wife or one or two of his many children travelled with him to help. He always wore a cloth cap and a spotless white apron. The wife, when we saw her, always wore a long-sleeved dark dress, almost reaching down to her ankles. The children were always scrubbed clean, whether going to school or playing on the hill across the road. Most of them were older than our children and David and Lorna. But the youngest of the greengrocer's brood, an open-faced little boy called Mellie, came running down the pavement one day, crying his heart out. It was the crying of the desolate, the inconsolable, the desperate. When we managed to get a word out of him, it turned out that he had cut another boy's finger. He did not mean to do it, but the boy might die and his dad would kill him. He thought he might have cut the finger right off. Then his mother and an elder brother came. His wailing grew worse. They reassured us that it was a small cut. There had been a lot of blood and that was what had made Mellie flee in panic. He was still weeping heavily as they led him away.

Another incident that aroused our section of Jessel Drive (the name of our road) was when the truck driver's wife went into hospital to have her seventh or eighth baby. Instead of visiting his wife, the man went to spend the time with his mistress somewhere in the East End of London. When the woman returned, and as soon as she was back on her feet and back in voice, she went out onto the pavement and 'traced' her man for the entire neighbourhood to hear. Behind all of us who made up this new community was some story of trouble and need and the response to it by the Welfare State.

In the 1950s the Welfare State, a by-product of the most destructive war of our century, if not in all of human history up to that point, was a noble attempt to make things right for the survivors of that war and for the children of those who died in it. Of all the social action of our century this, for me, was the noblest attempt yet made by a section of mankind to create an environment of justice, social security, human decency and equity for all the citizens of one country. We shared, and watched in Debden, over the next five years, a community of values emerging from people who had been as different from each other as can be imagined. Children from the slums of London now attended the sprawling, clean, well-managed Debden school with its big classrooms and small classes. With its nutritious lunches for all, with its clinic and nurses in attendance during school hours, it transformed the children, who, in turn, transformed the outlook of their parents. Those who were handicapped, the spastic, those with Down's syndrome, received free physiotherapy. Those in need of nutritional support received it. The school system insisted on compulsory attendance by all school-age children and enforcement was strict. School officials made frequent visits to our Jewish neighbours' house. At one point, they faced the threat of court action. In the end, the girl attended school regularly. What happened in our neighbourhood happened all over Debden and wherever any such new housing scheme was established and wherever any new town was built. This was a quiet social revolution which changed people's attitudes and lifestyles.

Up to that point I had seen revolution as political action of a violent nature. In Britain, after the end of the war and into the 1950s, when we left, I came to see revolution as the social transformation of individuals and families and communities by creating the best living conditions possible. The problem, in a sense the dilemma, was that this could only be done by the state. But in order for the state to do this, it had to take unto itself vast powers to manage resources, regulate, redistribute and make choices and conditions for how people should live. In effect, individual people, especially those most in need, had to surrender much of their freedom of choice. We, like our neighbours, had no choice in being located in Debden. We could, of course, refuse to go. If we did, we would remain in the temporary places where we were until something else turned up. That could be months or years away, and there was the risk that the local authority might tell us to get out and try on our own. We did not have the money to make choices. If we did not accept Debden, and if we could not afford to make other choices, where would we be? Freedom of choice is only possible if you have the money to pay for your choices. Freedom of choice and poverty are incompatible. It was a hard lesson.

Loughton, the old English town on the edge of Epping Forest, was our 'mother town' and its people did not like the swarm of newcomers suddenly thrust among them. The newcomers, especially their young, tended to be loud, crude and vulgar — and many of us were. We were noisy at the normally quiet near-country pub on Saturdays. In the small, sedate shops and restaurants we were inclined to raise our voices for attention. In contrast to their children, ours were destructive of plants, trees and even road signs. Some of us had little regard for other people's property. In time, all this changed, We became almost as quiet and sedate as the old residents of Loughton. They influenced us. We did not influence them. They were set in their ways. In the end, by the time we left Debden, the integration of Debden into the semi-rural, ecology-minded community on the edge of Epping Forest was well on the way. In time, Debden would become just one of a series of suburbs clustered around the town of Loughton, no different from any other. The environment would gradually change the people.

For us, as a family, Epping Forest became our special picnic ground. The children were fascinated by the animals. We carried picnic hampers, blankets, Daphne's sketch pad or easel and spent days playing, reading, drawing, painting in Epping Forest. Sometimes friends visited and we took them on the short walk to the forest to talk and watch the game roaming freely and hear the happy laughter of children. The Debden days were good and healing for us as individuals and for a society picking itself up after the terrible devastation of a war whose consequences were just beginning to be seen. By 1950 it was clear that the British empire, as we had known it, was on its way out. Still, Mr Attlee, Mr Bevin, Mr Morrison and the fiery Mr Bevan and their cohorts were keeping their promise to those who had died in battle to make Britain a better place to live in. William Blake's vision of a new Jerusalem in England's green and pleasant land was being made reality.

England had not yet become the multi-racial, multi-cultural society it is today. The signs, though, were there. Many from the Commonwealth and colonies who had fought in the war elected to stay. Prejudice had always been there, but tiny minorities pose no serious threat to jobs or housing or social amenities. As the minorities grow, the threat grows and prejudice hardens into discrimination. It was in the 1950s that friction and tension between black and white in Britain came seriously into focus. Migration from the Caribbean had begun and there was trouble in northern England. *Reynolds News,* the newspaper of the British co-operative movement, commissioned me to write a series of articles on these early signs of racial friction. A black man in Manchester was charged with murdering someone, a white person, I think, and Norman Manley, the eminent Jamaican barrister was brought to England to defend the man. Money for his legal fees was raised by public subscription from the black community. Brixton was slowly changing its colour.

I met Manley at a reception organised by The League of Coloured People, a London-based West Indian group. He had been a soldier in World War One, seen his brother die in battle, experienced the prejudice and discrimination which was part of being a black person in a white society. He was very thin, which made him look taller than he really was, with fine features and an austere presence. His wife, a distant cousin, on the white side of the highly mixed Jamaican bloodline, was with him. She was as open and forthcoming as he was austerely withdrawn. I took an instant liking to the man; I was not sure of the woman whose reputation as an artist I knew.

Manley was the leader of Jamaica's People's National Party, which was leading the struggle for self-government. He was eager to know all about Pan-Africanism, developments in Africa and the non-aligned movement which was still in the making. He was particularly concerned about developments in Kenya and the reports of a secret society being built among the Kikuyu, Kenya's largest tribe, for the purpose of killing all that country's white settlers. I visited him at his hotel the morning after the reception and we talked about Kenya and the white settlers of East and Central Africa. Manley's information had been essentially European. He saw what was happening as reported in the European press which, for faraway Jamaica, meant the London *Times*, the *Manchester Guardian*, the Fabian Society literature and the BBC. He had no other source material, no other perspective, no other interpretation. He was Oxford-educated, had not travelled in the Third World. He read widely. We talked that morning of how the Pan-African movement saw what was going on in the Third World. His questions were searching. What kind of person was Kenyatta? What schooling did he have? He was not familiar with our type of missionary education. The Jamaican missionary tradition had been at an earlier time, so the changes in the approach of the missionaries had also been earlier. In addition, the missionaries did not have the problem of combating African tribal beliefs and traditions. Language was not a factor. All Jamaicans spoke the same language. Had he, I asked, read Kenyatta's *Facing Mount Kenya*? Manley's eyes lit up and I realised that this was a reading man, a man of the book. I promised to lend him my copy. Throughout our conversation he had jotted down notes. I knew he would check every point of fact I had given him. The accuracy of my points of fact would determine the weight he would place on my opinions. As we parted, I asked him about Marcus Garvey. I knew he was one of the lawyers who had prosecuted Garvey. 'I was wrong,' Manley said quietly. 'I did not understand at the time.'

He was out when I delivered Kenyatta's book that night. He read it over two days and returned it. A few years later in Jamaica, at his only private dinner with us up at Coyaba, when he headed the government, he, his wife Edna and their friend Robert Verity spent a quiet evening with us, talking and listening to music. After dinner the two of us went into my small study. He saw Kenyatta's book, leafed through it, looked at me with a twinkle in his eyes and said it had opened his eyes to what was behind the Mau Mau. He had said nothing when he had returned the book to me in London after our first meeting. Norman Manley's influence and support became an important factor in the African struggle.

As part of my freelance journalism I did a series of talks on the BBC's Third Programme. The subject was colour and culture. Under pressure from a new militancy in the black nationalist movement, the whites of East Africa were claiming they were not practising any kind of colour bar. The bar, they said, was cultural. Anybody of any colour who had attained an acceptable cultural level, would find no barrier anywhere in East Africa. This was not true, but for a good while the notion of the 'culture bar' became widely popular and received tacit support from a faction of the mandarins at the Colonial Office. These Third Programme talks were designed to explode the new myth of the culture bar.

Almost inevitably, someone suggested that I visit East and Central Africa to test the 'culture bar'. If I passed it, perhaps it was real. The Observer, the BBC Third Programme and, later, the Paris edition of the *New York Herald Tribune* backed the enterprise. Then we decided to throw in South Africa as well. It would be interesting to see how they would react to a native son returning as correspondent for such a media combination. So on a warm spring morning of 1952, I left my family in peaceful and happy Debden for the return journey to an Africa in turmoil. When I left Africa, everything had been under control: the Pass Laws, Kipandi, land control, the movement of people. Now, nothing was certain, not even Mr Churchill's hoped-for thousand years of the British empire and its Commonwealth. The result of that journey was the impressionistic *Return to Goli*, which was published within twelve months of that trip.

In Kenya I found the so-called 'culture bar' to be a fraud, a cruel racial hoax. I did a BBC broadcast listing all the handicaps under which Mr Eliud Mathu, then the only black appointed member of

Kenya's Executive Council, had to function. Mr Mathu experienced the same racial discrimination every black Kenyan did, except when he was shielded from it by some senior white colonial official. That had been so before I left Africa; it was still so.

One of the saddest experiences of my life has been to watch, over time, some fine men being changed by changed circumstances. On that first journey back to Africa, when she was still in bondage, Kenyatta was the old friend from our London days. We walked the beautiful mountainous land together, met the people, shared our ideas with them, were close to them — which was why so many fought and died for the vision of the freedom and land he promised them. More than 11,000 mainly Kikuyu died in what the British government and the white settlers called the Mau Mau rebellion and the blacks called their freedom struggle. It was both a physical and a propaganda war, with the propaganda at times seeming the bigger war. Kenyatta, in particular, and the Kikuyu in general were demonised. The Kikuyu were the largest tribe in Kenya, then approaching three million in numbers, a larger community than any one of the English-speaking British Caribbean island colonies. They were the most rebellious, the most educated, the most defiant and, for these reasons, the most detested by white settlers and Colonial Office officials alike. The campaign of vilification of the Kikuyu at that time was as savage as anything out of the Nazi wartime propaganda. In retrospect, it was understandable. If the Kikuyu prevailed, the days of settler dominance in 'White Africa' would be numbered. If they were defeated, the dream of Rhodesia's Ian Smith of a thousand years of white settler control would become a feasible possibility. So Johnny Kuke had to be crushed — and all means justified that end. Even Norman Manley, in faraway Jamaica, had been appalled by the horror stories of Kikuyu brutality and bloodthirstiness he heard in his dealings with Colonial Office officials: which was why he had that searching session with me in

London. In that propaganda war the fact that more than 20,000 Kikuyu were being brain-washed in concentration camps did not come out till very much later. Nor did the fact that about 100 whites and 2,000 black 'loyalists' of other tribes were the entire casualties on the government side. We heard about the blood rituals of the Kikuyu, but we heard and read nothing about the equally horrible brain-washing rituals. I know Jews who still grow cold when they meet a German. I know Kikuyu who turn cold when they meet a white settler, just as I know black South Africans whose faces become masks when they meet their white fellow countrymen and women. These things of the heart and mind and the spirit cannot be overcome in the short run. But the apparently automatic gulf which opens between leaders and led, a few days or weeks or months after independence, is something else again.

In 1952, on my first visit to South and East Africa after my years in Europe, Jomo Kenyatta and the entire leadership of the Kikuyu tribe welcomed me when I stopped over in Kenya. The Mau Mau war was in the making. The white settlers seemed determined to put down the brewing revolt with force. In the event, the Kikuyu, with a little help from their other African tribal friends, won that war at great cost.

When I revisited Kenya in 1965, after Kenyatta had been transformed from long-time demonic political prisoner and instigator of the dark Mau Mau blood-rituals into first the Prime Minister and then the first respected President of the independent Republic of Kenya, the gulf between leaders and led was already in place. Whenever the President had to travel from his official residence to Parliament or to some other official function, the streets were cleared. Traffic came to a halt. Police motorcycles patrolled the Presidential route. The Presidential limousine, led by an armed police car, flanked by police motor-cycles, and followed by two or three more police cars, had to pass before traffic could move again.

The President had ceased to be my friend, Jomo, the man of the people who had shared their struggles and suffering with them. Now, every business house, every store, every office I visited had the obligatory picture of the President hanging on the wall. The Kenyan Asians, in particular, made sure the portrait of the President was big, prominent, the first thing one saw on entering. The new *Bwana Kubwa* was the former freedom fighter. This, with less ostentatious fanfare, was how we had shown loyalty to imperial kings and queens. I saw the same thing when I visited the Gold Coast after my friend Kwame Nkrumah had been transformed from 'Prison Graduate' to the first Prime Minister of the Gold Coast and later the President of the Republic of Ghana. Somewhere along the road to freedom, the leaders of our freedom struggles had become like those they had fought against. We had become like our enemies, cloaked in the trappings of our enemies — only, more glaringly so.

In Nairobi, on that second visit in 1965, when I phoned to pay my respects to an old friend, Eliud Mathu, now head of the 'palace guard' welcomed me to Kenya and promised to arrange something and get in touch. I did not see Kenyatta.

The tribe that won the war was in charge. Everywhere, in all the key positions, the Kikuyu predominated. In the Gold Coast, Nkrumah still saw political power as the means to a greater end. All of West Africa had to be free of colonial rule, then, all of West Africa would unite in a federation of West African states which would lead the rest of Africa in the struggle for freedom. The ultimate aim: the United States of Africa. Nkrumah had spent years studying in the United States and I thought he had been impressed by the vast size of that unitary state. He had not travelled to South, Central and East Africa and did not know the vast differences, so the vision of a United States of Africa seemed feasible to him. But despite his strong visionary commitment, a gap was opening between the leader and the led. The 'mammy traders', that strong core of businesswomen, who had been the base of Nkrumah's support, were becoming disenchanted with their 'Show Boy'. He was not among them as frequently as he had been in the early days. He was taking more advice from his key British civil service people, less from the top people in his Convention People's Party. People left his party and some worked to replace him. He never lost sight of our Pan-African dream and sponsored all kinds of efforts to promote it. Blacks from other parts of Africa, the United States and the Caribbean — some of them of questionable intent — flocked to the Gold Coast, the first West African colonial state to win self-government after the British were forced to hold general elections in 1951.

Winning political power had not been easy. In East Africa, except for Tanganyika, soon to become Tanzania, the casualty rate had been higher than in West Africa. Against Kenya's full-scale war the Gold Coast agitation was 'small beer'. Retaining power and using it to improve the lot of the people turned out to be much more complex and difficult than gaining political power. When we talked in his cool spacious office that sunny morning in Accra, Nkrumah had begun to recognise some of the hard problems. But he was still optimistic, confident that he could overcome them, that he would prevail. He had, he said, a few good people around him, even a few British he could trust. The problem was with the tribal chiefs who were jealous of their positions. He would take his time and deal with them. I thought he underestimated them and said so. He was sure he could handle them: wait and see. Then the efficient Miss Gittens came in, apologised and said she could not keep the VIP waiting any longer. Nkrumah said he was planning for George Padmore to come, but that it might have to wait till independence. He was also in touch with DuBois. This one, I felt, was keeping faith with our dream. I also felt he took his political enemies dangerously lightly. The idea for *A Wreath for Udomo* was born.

— 6 —

Leaders & Leadership

The movement from colonialism to independence threw up a generation of nationalist leaders with no rule book by which to go. To be a nationalist leader was, almost by definition, to be someone who had broken with the old traditions of subservience to white domination. To reach that point, however, also meant a rejection, to some degree or another, of the old traditional African ways, or else being able to control and manipulate them. Kenyatta was a master at using tribal traditional ways in the service of modern political needs. But Kenyatta was born toward the end of the nineteenth century and was old and wise by the 1950s. Most of the others were young. Nkrumah was born in the early years of this century, ten years before me, in 1909, Nnamdi Azikiwe, Nigeria's first major black newspaper publisher, an ardent Pan-Africanist supporter of George Padmore, was five years older than Nkrumah. Obafemi Awolowo, one of Nigeria's best political thinkers, was the same age as Nkrumah. The two major French-speaking West African leaders of the time were Léopold Senghor, who was born in 1906, and the much younger Ahmed Sékou Touré, who was born in 1922, the same year as Nyerere. Milton Obote and Idi Amin, the two tyrants of Uganda, one civilian, the other military, were born in 1924 and 1925. Kenya's brilliant Tom Mboya, whose political career was cut short by assassination, was the baby of the lot, born in 1930. Oginga Odinga, Mboya's fellow Luo tribesman, the genius of a political leader whose career was systematically frustrated by Jomo Kenyatta's Kikuyu operatives, was born in 1911. Dr Hastings Kamuzu Banda, who ended up as dictator of Malawi, was born in 1902, and like all the others received his education mainly through the missionaries. Like most of the others, he worked his way up and went for further training in Europe and America. Banda became a doctor of medicine. We knew him well in London between 1945 and 1953. He was mild-mannered, benign, humorous, very friendly, always helpful to expatriate Africans with problems. The later dictator was not the man Daphne and I had known in London.

With the exception of Kenyatta and Banda, the key shapers of African independence were all born within the first quarter of this century. They grew up and were themselves shaped by the European occupation of their lands and their minds. In the early days the occupation was as savage and brutal as were the times. Notions of civil liberties and human rights had not yet come into play. Europe, at that time, had no doubts about its right to occupy Africa, put down its peoples by force, and determine what was right and good and best for them. That first generation of twentieth-century African leaders had the hard task of coming to terms with the prevailing climate in which Europe claimed the right to empire. It also justified the occupation of peoples and their lands, and the indoctrinating of all to its view of the world, its history, its right to determine the nature of the relations between races, nations and colours. That world was so set in its ways, the power and authority of the Europeans so absolute that to question it was a form of madness. Racism, the judgement and determination of the nature and status of man by the shade of his colour, was institutionalised, made legal by laws and regulations.

All this was the by-product of empire. In the name of empire the Germans had wiped out a whole people in what was then German South West Africa. When, in my youth, I wandered over the desert lands of what is now Namibia, where it bordered on South Africa, I met survivors and the children of survivors of the aftermath of German colonialism in South West Africa. In later years the Rev. Michael Scott told the world of the genocide committed by Germany against the Herero people, an 80,000-strong tribe which was reduced to fewer than 20,000 people and then expelled from its tribal homeland to facilitate mining for the vast mineral wealth under its land. German colonialism was no better in Tanganyika on the east coast of Africa, Julius Nyerere's homeland, which was to become Tanzania. There, too, there was massive slaughter of people. The rest, the British, the French, the Belgians, the Portuguese, were less murderous, but not much better in their dealings with the natives. The manner in which they dealt with the natives was more a matter of national traits and habits and behaviour patterns than differences of principle on how colonialism should function. The Portuguese, as a consequence of their own history, were least racist. The assimilationist French were as brutal on the unassimilated as the others. The British were most paternalistic; the Belgians cold-bloodedly concerned with self-enrichment. All had a vested interest in controlling hearts and minds.

To grow up educated into such an environment is to grow up mentally crippled. You are effectively separated from your own roots without having any real roots in the dominant occupying culture. You are the classic outsider. Not the man of two worlds or two cultures as portrayed by the historical romantics, but the man trapped between two worlds and comfortable in neither, accepted by neither. To break free of this situation you must either tear down the structures of domination and control or take them over and reshape them to your heart's desire.

For Kenyatta and Banda, both men born in the nineteenth century, the answer was relatively straightforward. They entered the new century shaped and defined by their own traditional cultural patterns. The European occupation had little impact on the shaping of their own personalities. They coped with this new reality of the white presence without any self-doubts about their place in the world. The whites, for the moment, had control of power. That did not change their world. It made it difficult, awkward. But they had knowledge, direct or received, of a time before the ascendancy of the whites. And what was once can always be again. Kenyatta had such impatience with the overlordship air of the Provincial and District Commissioners with whom I saw him deal that he drove those officials up the wall with frustration. Nothing frustrates the slave-master more than the slave who does not see himself as a slave, does not accept the fact of his slave state. Those are the ones who have to be killed. Banda, too, had this attitude, which for me explains why he had no difficulty making an alliance with white racist South Africa. The early African rulers, after all, made such alliances with the whites when they first came to Africa. Implicit in this was the non-acceptance of the white man's view of his status and his place in the scheme of things. They had knowledge of how it once was, so they could see a time after the passing of the white man's days of power. It made for a self-confidence and self-assurance not known by the leaders born in the first quarter of the twentieth century. So when Kenyatta and Banda came to power, they used power in the old ways, as it was used before the coming of the whites. The big difference is that they inherited modern twentieth-century states, structurally different from the African tribal states with their built-in checks and balances to the use of power.

It was not so for those born in the first quarter of the twentieth century. They had no, or very little, knowledge, direct or received, of how it was before the white occupation. This was less so for the west coast than it was for the east coast of Africa, but it was so everywhere as a general rule. The occupiers and their missionaries had done a great job of obliterating and undermining the tribal past and what it had been. They were educated to a system of government in an empire on which they were made to believe that the sun would never set. They learned more about the history of Britain than about the history of their own countries. West Africans knew more about Britain than about East Africa; East Africans more about Britain than West Africa. In the French colonies they knew more about France than about their own West African neighbours. The pattern of control of what we learned, what we thought, how we saw the world, was pervasive to the point of being commonplace, something not thought about, not talked about.

How to free themselves from such a state of conditioning was the first great hurdle. In the end, the same tools which were used to 'occupy' their minds were the tools which 'liberated' their minds. Literacy, the greatest gift of the missionaries to Africa, and the Bible, the story of a people's struggle to be free, were the beginnings. Once they could read and explore ideas from other people's struggles and cultures, the emancipation of the mind became possible. Scholars received the ideas of W.E.B. DuBois and Marcus Garvey. They became familiar with the struggles of other people in other lands of the empire. People like India's Mahatma Gandhi became their heroes and exemplars. Slowly, their view of the world changed, and so the world itself began to change, and they became part of the process of making that world change.

One of the greatest influences for change in our century, which in time turned out to also be a great distraction, was the Russian Revolution and the birth of the Soviet Union, which led to the Cold War, and the division of the world into two hostile ideological camps, dominating much of the middle years of the century. The Soviet system promised an alternative to capitalism and its exploitation of the peoples and countries of the under-developed world in the interest of the metropolitan countries. This was naturally attractive to the poor, the under-developed, the marginalised. We all seemed to have forgotten that the slogan of Liberty, Equality, Fraternity, had not prevented the growth of the French colonial empire. So, for many of us, the Soviet Union became the new beacon of freedom and opportunity for all. Its ideas were intoxicating. Many of us fell out among each other in support of the subtle variations in Marxist dogma. Some became Stalinists; some Trotskyites. We grew learned in the polemics of the differences between the factions of the communist international movement. For some, the objectives of African freedom were tied to Soviet communist interests. This did not happen only in Africa. In Asia and all over the Third World, the conflict of ideas between capitalism and communism, symbolised by the conflicting postures of the United States and the Soviet Union on the world stage, influenced and, at times overshadowed, our own native problems and issues. Our world was divided into satellites of either the capitalist camp or the communist camp. The two big powers exploited the situation to the full. They gave economic aid to those considered to be in their camp and withheld aid from those regarded as in 'the other camp'. Socialist groupings, like Julius Nyerere's party — by no means remotely communist — were starved of sorely needed aid by the United States. Its neighbour Kenya, considered more pro-capitalist, was helped generously, with much of the aid ending up in private hands. The Soviets did the same in the service of their own interests.

Later, Africans, Asians, Latin Americans, were manipulated into 'proxy wars' reflecting the prevailing state of the Cold War. The Russians and their allies armed one side, the Americans and their allies the other, and Africans killed Africans, Asians killed Asians, Latin Americans killed each other. They bombed and mined their own lands; killed and maimed their own women, children and old people; destroyed their own schools and hospitals; their own agriculture, their own factories, their own homes. The Big Two had devised a form of warfare in which they were the puppet masters, in which none of their own people were killed, none of their own lands suffered the ravages of war. The struggle for freedom and for better conditions for the poor was subsumed in the struggles of the great powers, played out in the lands of the poor, with the lives of the poor. With rare exceptions, the leaders of the poor and dispossessed were accomplices in this grotesque, most costly and wasteful of distractions.

It was not a good time for the peoples of the Third World. It was not a good time for Third-World leadership, despite the Non-Aligned Movement. That movement itself was divided on how its non-alignment should be 'tilted'. Should the superpowers be condemned equally? Should the Soviet Union, the anti-imperialist superpower, be treated with more sympathy than the pro-imperialist United States? That master Chinese diplomat and negotiator, Zhou En Lai, otherwise Chou En-lai, personally attended the Bandung Conference and ensured that any anti-communist sentiments were muted. So, 'colonialism in all its manifestations' was condemned. The communists could claim that since the Soviet Union was not a colonialist power, the condemnation did not include it.

Richard Wright went to that first Bandung Conference and I looked forward to discussing it with him on his return. In the event, we met only once, and for the last time, on London's Charing Cross Road, on my return from East Africa. He had been on one of his book buying sprees and his bag was bulging and heavy. It was not one of our usual friendly encounters. He was distant, almost aloof. We chatted for a while then parted. I found out, later, that he had applied to the British government for permission to live in Britain. Permission had been denied. I could not understand why. We were already settled in Jamaica when we heard of his death in Paris in November 1960. It was like a loss in the family: a dear, difficult, complex, at times trying, member of the family, but family nonetheless. When we heard the news that November night in 1960, sitting on the long verandah on Coyaba's high hill, we recalled with sad warmth our encounters with this very special, very passionate, very tormented man. Daphne wept when she recalled the sheer joy and envy with which the rich man shared our simple inexpensive food. What would this man have been, what would he have done, if he did not carry the burden of his colour? He was not as polished, learned, wise as DuBois. He was as sensitive, as American, as damaged.

That whole generation of African leadership which led the way to political independence was, to some degree or another, as damaged by its encounters with the Europeans. It was personal for black Americans. It was both personal and national for black Africans. The Cold War and how the African leaders were manipulated by the superpowers showed up the weaknesses of the damaged personality. It was not as easy for their enemies to set the Indians against each other. Even at the height of the Cold War, the Indian communists did not launch a civil war against their fellow Indians. To be sure, the Chinese had such a civil war, but it was of a different character and quality and it preceded the Cold War. In the islands of Asia, except for the American-controlled Philippines, the struggle was against controlling minorities — ethnic Chinese, ethnic Indians — not against each other. It was in Africa and, to a slightly lesser extent, in Latin America that the dogs of war were successfully let loose within the house. This was our great failure of leadership during the Cold War years.

It was easy to set us against each other because we had been overcome psychologically. The capacity to resist manipulation, to assert a counter set of values, a world view of our own which repudiated their concept of the nature of things, had been so undermined that we saw our world through their eyes, as they wanted us to see it. We measured ourselves by their yardstick. In the language of gambling we were into a situation where the dealer handled the cards, invented the game, made the rules. This, he said, is my game; I make the rules; you play by my rules; no other. We played his game. And when you play another man's game by that other man's rules, you do not win. The rules are made for him to win. It is only if the rules are made together and agreed on together that you have a chance of holding your own, even of winning once in a while. The cards were stacked against the African leaders in the power game of life. Each time they lost a round they grew weaker and those whom they opposed grew stronger.

In the 1960s, in that great rush to independence for a whole continent, there were brief glimpses of new possibilities. We saw black men dominating the proceedings in the General Assembly of the United Nations by the sheer weight of their numbers. It seemed the world was finally coming to an acceptance of Africa as an equal in the scheme of things. African embassies sprang up all over the world. Some of the smallest and poorest countries in the world staged some of the biggest, most lavish, diplomatic receptions in Washington, London and Paris. Resources were squandered on palaces for Presidents and their hangers-on while national infrastructure deteriorated. A handful, such as Nkrumah and Nyerere, used state power to further the interests of their people and the Pan-African ideal. Poor Tanzania, under Nyerere's leadership, supported the largest centre for South African freedom fighters. Tanzania set up a powerful short-wave radio transmitter to carry the ANC message to South Africa. The catch was the very few short-wave receivers in black South African possession. Wealthier Kenya, under Kenyatta, had given limited support early in its independence, but pressure from its donor friends ended in the quiet cancellation of that support. Ghana, under Nkrumah, remained the strong arm of Pan-Africanism, though the exiles it harboured were at ideological odds among themselves, and alienated the Ghanaians with whom they had to work. The aggressive arrogance of some of these foreign Pan-Africans in public places hurt Nkrumah's authority among many in his own party.

Elsewhere the leaders treated independence as the opportunity to replace predatory white regimes with predatory black regimes, to replace white overlords with black overlords; in some cases the shift from white to black rule was used as the battleground for tribal ascendancy.

In London, the very polished, charming Liberian Ambassador to the Court of St James invited me to settle in Liberia. I would be given so much land and other help to settle in. What about my family? Oh, they would be able to inherit the land after me. My wife? She was white, wasn't she? Under Liberian law she would not be able to own property. Not even inherit from me? No. Apartheid in reverse. Is black Apartheid any better than the white variety? That only the natives and the citizens of a country should own its primary resources is not the same as only one ethnic group or only one racial colour having that right.

I returned to Debden in August 1953 and spent the next year with Daphne and the children and the regular weekend visits of friends from London. The journey from London to Debden by the underground took three-quarters of an hour, then a long fifteen-minute walk to our home at 37 Jessel Drive. We had planted apples and a cherry tree in our back garden. I had arranged with our off-licence liquor-store to regularly deliver a couple of wooden casks, one of Bulmer's cider and one of light ale, so we were always in good supply. On spring and summer and autumn Sundays, we and our friends would sprawl on the cut grass under the fruit trees and drink and munch while we talked the world's troubles away. Sometime we would carry hampers of food and drink and spend the day in Epping Forest. The community in which we lived was always possessed of a great curiosity to see so many dark faces together strolling up to the Forest. We sensed no resentment, only interest, only curiosity; so the exhibitionists among us at times showed off. Colour prejudice, such as was manifested later when dark folk congregated in groups, was absent in our Debden days. Indeed, there was one other 'coloured' family in another part of Debden: mother, father and man-child. The child was obnoxious and caused trouble at school and chaos at our newly opened supermarket. He was the most widely known child in the area, 'the troublesome little black boy'. Everybody was embarrassed; everybody was consciously tolerant. When we met the family, it emerged that the mother was at the root of the trouble. She was born in Liverpool, the child of a West African seaman who met a young working-class woman for one night, had a good time and then sailed away. An unwanted child was the result. Neither the young woman nor her family wanted the child. She grew up neglected, unloved. The man was from Jamaica. When we met them, the marriage was already on the verge of collapse. The straight, upright young man, anxious to get along in his post office job, anxious to live in peace with his neighbours, was embarrassed by the ways of his wife and son. In the end he left them. He later divorced her and married a quiet fellow worker, English and white. His marriage to someone black like him, but born in Britain, had been a disaster.

Among the people who visited us at Debden was a group of young West Indian writers: John Hearne and Andrew Salkey from Jamaica; Jan Carew and Edgar Mittelholzer from then British Guiana; Vidia Naipaul from Trinidad. Among the Africans I remember Tom Mboya, Peter Koinange, Charles Njonjo and Sadru Rahimtulla from Kenya. Sadru was a member of the Ismailite Muslim sect in Kenya, whose leader, the Aga Khan, periodically received tribute from his followers in the form of gold or precious stones equal to his own body weight. I remember as a young man in South Africa hearing about this dark prince, the richest man in the world, living among the aristocracy of Europe, marrying their women, and using his great fortune to do good works for his followers all over the world. The Aga Khan had instructed his scattered followers to become good citizens of the countries in which they lived, to foster education and give to charity. Sadru was trying to live by these injunctions and was as Kenyan as the most patriotic Kikuyu. In the end, though, even his most sophisticated African friends, like Njonjo, used him and then treated him as an outsider. Vidia Naipaul, in those days, was quiet and modest, with an air of friendly anxiety about him. Carew was tall, very handsome, with one of the most captivating smiles and completely irresistible to a certain type of woman. The Africans — and there were so many of them from South, East and West Africa that it is hard to remember them all — were either students or exiles in need of a few hours of congenial warmth in an otherwise cold and lonely place. So Debden became a small temporary haven for lonely people a long way from home. More than forty years later, Daphne still laughs out loud when she remembers the two Coloured South Africans who turned up one crowded Sunday morning. They had just arrived in London and the wonder of being free of the colour restrictions of home was still on them. At one point in a lively discussion one of them insisted that the Coloureds of South Africa were 'a pure race'; they were 'pure coloured' like unto no other people. The place erupted into verbal chaos. They persisted in their vigorous defence of the indefensible.

When it was all over and our other friends had departed, the two 'pure Coloureds' lingered behind. They could not understand why I had not supported them. Everybody else — black and white — boasts about their racial purity, the purity of their blood. 'We Coloureds' have to do the same thing if those others are to respect us. Did they really believe in this 'pure blood' stuff? They wanted to believe in themselves, to be proud of themselves, to stop being belittled as mixed breeds and half-breeds and half-castes by others. But did they really believe that any human beings were 'pure' anything? If others say they are, then we must too.

Our first two children were approaching five and four. One day they approached us as a little delegation. Mrs So-and-so down the road was making a baby. Could they have a new baby of their own? Daphne stopped using her contraceptive device. I think she knew how seriously I had been frightened by the difficult birth of our second child. We had not talked about it, but she had, through all her pain of that moment, seen my own panic that night in Paley.

Now, by popular pressure and demand, she was pregnant again. This third one was the most wanted of children. She tried to reassure me by describing the excellent quality of service she had watched pregnant young women get at the Debden clinic. The Epping Hospital was a first-class facility set in a spacious green environment. Everything would be different this time. And for family doctor we had a big, very friendly, charming, obviously aristocratic Pole, Dr Julius Cieszynski, who lived in Debden and made his Debden rounds in a grand old Rolls Royce, which, he said he had 'picked up for a song' from an upper-class British car salesman. You had, he said, to be of the upper classes to sell second-hand Rollses. All of which was comforting, but not wholly reassuring. I did not want to lose the mother of my children, my best friend, my one love.

About the time the new baby was due, everything that could went wrong. Biddy got tonsillitis. Aron fell over an inch-high front door ledge and broke his leg and I had to take him to Epping Hospital to have it set. It was set wrongly and had to be broken again and reset. I came near to doing violence to the person who had botched the first setting. Our Polish family doctor said it happened from time to time, and this was not a bad one. Then he told me of a little boy with multiple fractures whose cast had to be set and reset four times. 'And he was an upper-class little English boy.' He had assumed, rightly I think now, that part of my anger was at the possibility of carelessness because of the child's colour. That Polish doctor in the British National Health Service was a great fan of Joseph Conrad, a good family doctor to the predominantly working-class people of Debden. He became a good friend after he discovered I wrote books. He borrowed and read a couple of mine. 'All writers start out poor; you are not to worry; you will be alright in the end.' He supervised the midwife who handled Daphne's pregnancy and treated Biddy's tonsillitis with antibiotics, insisting there was no need to remove the tonsils. He saw Aron through his period in plaster and the exercises which followed. Then, in November 1954, he supervised the delivery our third child, Naomi. It was an easy happy birth; no problems, no complication, no long labour. The two children created a party atmosphere around the birth of their baby sister. The big upstairs bedroom where she was born was full of flowers and the invisible sunshine of happy laughter. But I could not contain the fear and the hint of panic aroused by that night in Paley. When, months later, Daphne said she wanted to go back on our agreement to have four and settle for the three we had, I agreed with relief. In later years, once or twice, I reminded her of our original agreement. I tried to make it seem like pressure. I do not think I fooled her. The two children took over the raising of Naomi in all but the bare essentials.

Tell Freedom was published in the United States with much fanfare in 1954. It received front-page treatment in the *New York Times Book Review*. It was well received by most of the influential literary critics. So Blanche Knopf of Alfred A. Knopf Inc., who was in London at the time, had Peter Du Sautoy of Faber and Faber, my British publishers, introduce me to her at lunch in Soho.

Blanche Knopf was a small, bird-like and very intelligent and sophisticated woman, the kind whose age seemed indeterminate. She seemed more European than American. I was on guard. Peter Du Sautoy was his usual calm, detached self; and the food at the upscale Jewish restaurant was superb. She was used to handling diffident writers on guard. They were all excited about the book, not about the money side, though that was important. What they wanted was quality.

Quality may not make the best-seller lists but it usually outlasted the best-sellers and sold more books over time. Then, suddenly, would I come to New York to help promote the book and give a few lectures? I looked at Peter Du Sautoy. His expression was neutral, an 'its up to you' expression. So I said, can I tell you tomorrow? I wanted to first talk it over with Daphne

When I called Du Sautoy the next morning, he told me Blanche had left for Paris but had left a contact name and number for the American Embassy. She had anticipated my agreement. The Americans were at the height of their anti-communist witch-hunt at home. Communists and anybody remotely associated with them were, we all assumed, routinely denied permission to enter the United States. So people who wanted entry usually denied any contact with communists. I was not a communist myself, but I had worked for the communist *Daily Worker.* I had friends who were communists. Would they give me a visa despite all this? It seems Blanche Knopf had influence. The person I called made a quick appointment, saw me a day later, and, with no 'third degree' and minimal formality, I was issued with a visa stamped 'Unlimited' and 'GRATIS'. It was dated 18 July 1955.

About the same time I had a call from the British Colonial Office. Would I accept a commission from the Corona Library series to visit the Caribbean and write a book on Jamaica? If I was interested, could we set up a meeting to discuss the project? I was interested and we did set up a meeting, At no point did anybody hint that Mr Norman Manley, now the Chief Minister of self-governing Jamaica, was behind my choice for writing the book. The Corona Library series had traditionally been written by British authors, usually people who had lived or worked in the particular territory about which they wrote. No natives of the territories concerned had ever been commissioned for such a task. It was a choice assignment with a good flat fee, free travel and subsistence, and the assistance of the local colonial bureaucracy. I would have the opportunity to visit all the islands of the English-speaking Caribbean to familiarise myself with the region. My agent tried to re-negotiate the fee part, not for more money, but to be paid on a royalty basis instead of a flat fee. The curt answer was that Her Majesty did not negotiate on such matters and always paid a flat fee. I accepted. Who argues with Her Majesty?

Langston Hughes / USA

New York was as fast and overwhelming as any great city I had visited. The pace was hectic, the traffic frantic. I would never drive in New York. My first impression was of abundance. For some reason I no longer remember, we were given lunch at the airport. Coming from Europe with its shortages and scarcities, the amount of food on my plate almost made me sick. The huge half chicken would have fed a family of four in Europe, with a large amount left over. There was a mountain of freshly cooked vegetables and a basket of rolls and butter. It was all too much and I found myself unable to eat. The waiter was upset, thought I did not like American food, offered alternatives. Then Mr. Jim Crow hit me and a stream of taxis ignored me till one with a black driver stopped.

I spent my first day in a hotel around the corner from Knopf's offices, and suffered the most terrible claustrophobia. High-rise concrete buildings hemmed me in. No trees, no green spaces, no sunlight between the tall buildings, no natural breezes: everything sealed in and air-conditioned. I moved into a smaller cheaper hotel near a park overlooking Harlem from where I could see the sky at night, feel the wind and see green trees.

Then I called Langston Hughes. We had been in touch off and on for years. I had reviewed his books whenever they were published in England. He wrote to tell me of his and his fellow black writers' appreciation of *Tell Freedom* and my references to black American writing. Now, at last, we were about to meet. Knopf had arranged a small gathering for me to meet some of the Harlem writers as well as a few others. I also wanted to meet them on their own ground, in their own setting.

The over-dressed, over-decorated doorkeeper of the grand-looking Harlem restaurant was tall and ramrod straight. He paraded with authority in front of his establishment. I checked the name of the place with him. He towered over me, making me feel small, insignificant. His booming voice was in keeping with his size, shape, air of authority. He recognised me as foreign by my speech.

'Mr Langston? You the brother from England?'

'Yes.'

'Table in the corner, left. Mr Langston's table. Can't miss it.'

The place was dim, its lights subdued. I paused just inside the door to get my bearings. A few seconds and I began to see people and things. I recognised the man at the far corner table who stood with both arms extended. He gave me a Latin hug.

'You don't look like your writing.' His voice was soft, disarming. He looked like his writing: warm, open, deceptively simple. Soon we were talking like old friends. Every now and then someone, male or female, would come to the table. Hughes would introduce me. They would chat for a while, then they would leave us. Some shared a drink with us, some just chatted and left. Most stayed only a few minutes; two stayed much longer, each talking earnestly and seriously with Hughes so that I could not hear. This, I found out, was where the man held court, received his information, kept in touch with his friends. It was the equivalent of the special Paris café table where you could always find a certain writer or artist. This was where Langston Hughes could be reached when he was in town and available. He wrote at nights and slept during the days. When he was not writing he met his friends at nights. I spent much of my short time in Harlem talking the nights away with Langston Hughes, meeting his friends and eating the 'soul food' that was so deliciously prepared.

He was nearing his sixties when I met him. He had, it seemed, come to terms with himself and America. His travels were behind him. He had been to many places in his youth, visiting Africa as a seaman and the Caribbean. He had travelled in the Soviet Union. All this, added to life in America, had been the stuff of his writing. Now he was content to live out his days in Harlem, 'the great dark city' he loved so dearly.

Langston Hughes fell in love in Paris. She was a beautiful young woman from Trinidad, sent to Paris as the finishing touch to a proper European education. Her family was well-known and wealthy. He was a poor young wandering writer with few prospects. They met in the city of romance and love happened. When the family got wind of it, the young woman was whisked away. He never saw her again. She later married one of the Caribbean's leading barristers and became a great social leader in her homeland. He never forgot her, never married. He told me about this unrecorded episode in his life shortly before I returned to Europe, after all the guests had left the small farewell party put on for me by Ruth Jett. He had not come to that party, so I went to his table in the left corner of his favourite nightspot in Harlem. Then, as dawn broke, we bade each other farewell and I walked through that little Harlem park to my hotel to prepare for the journey home. That was our first and last meeting. We parted as brothers. Come to think of it, those 'pure Coloureds' who visited us in Debden would have been proud to call him one of their own. He was light brown with a slight overlay of yellow to the pigment mix. He would have been taken for a light brown man in the pigmentocracy of the English-speaking Caribbean, a member of the élite in the French-speaking Caribbean, as just a man — as mixed as all the others — in Spanish-and Portuguese-speaking Latin America. Only in Europe and America was he a black, a Negro and, in many parts, even today, a nigger. We never talked directly about colour; there was no need. Our common experiences of prejudice and discrimination made that unnecessary. Richard Wright had to talk to me about colour, to compare, to check if it was really the same. With Hughes it was part of the baggage we carried, part of the obstacle we had to overcome. It made for an easier relationship. We did not upset and hurt each other unnecessarily.

Langston Hughes, the writer, seemed to me to have broken free of the dependence on the white literary establishment for survival and progress as a writer. We all, like it or not, write for white readers. They, after all, are the buyers of the books and magazines. The publishers cater to their needs and interests. If we did not take account of those needs and interests, they would not publish what we wrote. In the process we became interpreters, conveyors of the black reality to the world of white folk in the forms most acceptable to them. If we did not write what was acceptable to them, we would not be published. To be sure these same limitations apply to white writers, to all writers. You need approval to be published and to succeed and the buyer ultimately gives or withholds that approval. There is, however, a difference between seeking the approval of your own people and seeking the approval of those who view you as the outsider, the different one, the one they feel they have to hold in check. Not far below the surface there is the fear that the outsider may, if he had the chance, behave as badly toward them, as they had to him. If they had the power and opportunity, would blacks lynch whites? Would blacks do to whites what whites had done to blacks? These are not obvious, conscious concerns. This kind of anxiety, based on an historical sense of guilt, is usually suppressed, submerged below the surface of consciousness. To win approval, the black writer has to present even this reality in forms acceptable to his white publisher and reader, if he is to be published. This is where most of us who are black and who write, have experienced the most devastating emotional and intellectual ambivalence in dealing with DuBois' problem of the twentieth century. The message has to be dressed up to accommodate the sensibilities of the recipient. Tell the truth, but carefully measured, so that it does not upset, anger, overwhelm. If it is too harsh, too glaring, too devastating, the recipient will reject both message and messenger. Even your own reality, your own perception of that reality, has to be tailored to suit their reality. It was much easier, more convenient for them, if they themselves defined you, interpreted your needs, knew what was best for you. In our time the experts on Africa were usually not African. The few who were, were usually white Africans.

Langston Hughes was among the first to begin the change in the nature of this relationship. He wrote for his own black audience and in the process he helped to create that audience. By the time he died, in 1967, he was able to earn a living as a writer without having to earn the approval of white publishers or white readers. If they did approved, fine. If they did not, a pity. But there were enough black people buying and reading his work to keep him going. He did not make the kind of money Richard Wright had. But he could survive and continue writing, with or without white approval. He was, in his own words, 'a literary share-cropper'. He was also at peace with himself, one of the happiest and most generous human beings I have known. I have often wondered how he would have fared in a world as warm-hearted and free of prejudice as he was.

My travels in the United States were carefully managed. The 1950s was the time of the great civil rights struggles. The blacks were fighting racial segregation on all fronts; the whites, particularly the Southern whites, were resisting and fighting back. It turned violent and ugly at times. The brutal murder of a young black boy of fourteen, Emmett

Till, for supposedly flirting with a white woman, was a main news item. Fights and scuffles between black and white over the integration of lunch counters, against school segregation or segregation in buses, were going on all over the place. The fear at Knopf and among my Harlem friends was that I might get caught in one of these violent clashes. On the other hand, we all agreed I had to visit the South.

Raleigh, North Carolina, was chosen as a starting point. If I could reach there without incident, I would go further south. I would have liked to visit Spartanburg, South Carolina, the hometown of our friend Lyle from our Paris and Paley days. It would be good to see the background in which this enlightened white Southern Catholic grew up. The planners thought it not safe. The NAACP had a good organisation, good people, in Raleigh, so North Carolina was relatively 'safe'.

It was decided I would see more from the railway than if I travelled by air, though there was less risk of racial encounters by air than by road or rail. I travelled first-class and the railway porters along the way seemed to know of me and I was aware of a discreet protective aura. I had a compartment to myself for most of the time. Twice, well-dressed, affluent-looking black folk were ushered into the compartment by a black railroad official. They all travelled shorter distances. Once only, a white passenger shared the compartment with me for about half an hour. No word passed between us though the man seemed cordial enough. At last, we arrived at Raleigh, North Carolina. As the train slowed down the black official came and said:

'I see your people waiting for you. This way, please.' He took my travelling bag and led the way. I knew I was under special protection. I followed him down the passage and then down the three small portable steps.

A dozen people, half of them men, half women, dressed in their best, circled me. The railway official spoke briefly to a big brown man I assumed to be the leader of the group, touched his cap, and climbed back on the train. I had been safely delivered from one point to the next. Was this the modern-day version of the underground railway of slavery days and the great migration northwards? The train pulled out. Small clusters of people left the station. My reception committee had three cars. I was ushered into the second and introduced to the sister at whose home I would stay. She was the local secretary of the NAACP. She sounded more like the caring mother of a large family — which was what she turned out to be. I met the leaders of Raleigh's black community at her home. A meeting had been arranged for that evening. Then there would be a reception for the community to get to know me. The Mayor and the editor of the local newspaper, both white, would be introduced to me, then they would leave and the reception would continue for a while longer for us to have a chance to talk among ourselves about our people's problems. Then I was allowed something over an hour to bathe, refresh myself and rest for the evening's proceedings. It dawned on me that my visit was an important event for the black community of Raleigh, North Carolina. I was later shown that it had even made the local white paper before my arrival.

The only thing that spoiled that evening for me was the arrival at the reception of a genteel woman in her forties, very thin, obviously not poor, and white. She was a poet come to pay her respects to a fellow writer. She was turned away, politely but firmly. This, she was told, was 'our occasion to respect our own'. She left. I tried to hide my distress. I felt guilty; I also felt I could not interfere. There was a volatile atmosphere throughout the country, and the stranger had to walk with care. I mentioned my distress to my hostess at breakfast next morning. Her husband, a big silent man of few words, and an enormous love-filled authority over their five children, shook his head and grunted: 'It's all bad.' Then he shook my hand and left for work.

The woman fussed about the large breakfast table and saw the children off to school after checking that they were properly dressed and clean and had their lunch packs.

When we were alone at last, she explained with a hint of defensiveness. 'They do it to us,' she said. 'Then when one of our important people come, they try to take them over. She would have asked you to visit her and her friends but they have no time for us when we don't have people like you visiting. That's the only time they come to us. We must show them our pride.'

Later that morning, I resumed my journey further south. It was a different train and different officials, but again I had that sense of being watched over by the brotherhood of those who were the black part of the running of the American railroad system. Again I wondered, without surprise, at the smoothness of this protective system of travel for some of us in an otherwise hostile environment. My destination this time was the University of Atlanta, Georgia, the Deep South, where, a lifetime ago W.E.B. DuBois had thought through and written some of his most serious work on the key problem of this century. The land was vast, flat and drab, seemingly limitless as it flashed by. A strange austere kind of landscape; not the soft green of the British landscape, nor the rapidly changing one of Europe, nor even the ever present threat of wild forest and jungle, interspersed with the menace of desert, of the African landscape. Only the periodic human settlement flashing past, the occasional distant view of hill or mountain, only the whispering wheels of the speeding train, brought slight variations to the long monotonous journey. Then, suddenly, the landscape changed, became greener and darker. There were more human habitations, more trees, houses, hills, plantations in which shadowy human figures moved. Atlanta, Georgia, even back then in the 1950s, had the air of a great big city on the move.

Physically, the campus of Atlanta University was as I had come to envision it from my readings. But the mood and spirit with which I had invested it, the expectation that I would feel and sense the influence of DuBois, perhaps see tangible signs of the legacy of his work in this place, were sadly absent. The records said the man had been there. The reality said: so what? Perhaps I had expected too much. I found the place disappointingly detached from the racial turbulence taking place almost everywhere in urban America. It was an oasis of peaceful tranquillity. I knew I was being judgmental and unfair. Judging the attitude and behaviour of one generation by the standards of another is usually unjust. I am not my son; my wife is not her daughter. Seeing them as a continuum cannot be right. The connections — biological, genetic, physical, familial — do not add up to a continuity of emotion, vision and feeling. DuBois' scholastic and intellectual children were not reproductions of DuBois in another time. This is a hard lesson for older people to learn. I was forty years younger then and had not yet learned it, so I left with some sadness the university campus into which I had put Jacob Brown in *The iew From Coyaba* to learn from the wisdom of the great DuBois. The civil rights struggle, raging almost everywhere else in America, was now not noticeable there, not to me.

Back in Harlem, Ruth Jett who was herself born in the Deep South, took me on a tour of the homes of families being supported by social security. My own family had received help from the British welfare services when I had my eye troubles and we were in greatest need. The home we lived in Debden was a by-product of the British Welfare State. In France the welfare system was elaborate and benefited large poor families most. The rest of Europe was not far behind. The United States, too, I knew, had an elaborate, well-planned social security system. Ruth Jett's purpose was to show me the impact on black family life of one part of that system. All the homes on welfare she took me to were headed by women, often with two or three or more children. After the first few places, my first question was: where are your men? Where are the fathers of these children? It came out that the men had left their wives or women because that made it easier for them to collect welfare. A household without a man received more welfare assistance than a household headed by a man. Where a man headed the family and was unemployed, the assistance was less and the man was under constant pressure to take any low-paying job to which he was sent. Welfare inspectors made life difficult. When the man revolted against the pressure and left the home, the system became more benevolent to the woman and her now fatherless children. The family, without its unemployed male head, received better treatment from the social security system. When this reality sank in, it became the norm. When conditions turned bad, when a man lost his job, leaving home was a way of making things a little better for his family.

This, I am sure, was not the intention. No society, not even the most racist, would deliberately force a man to leave his family. In Southern Africa the system of migrant labour separates the man from his family, but only for a time, to earn money, part of which is sent back or is held until his return to his family. Long separation often undermines the family. But it is not this kind of forced separation which breaks up the urban black family in a place like Harlem. Even where the family bond is strong, reality dictates that the man sneaks in only when the social security official cannot see. What impact does this have on the children? On the man himself? On his relations with his woman? Sooner or later, unless by some miracle their economic circumstances change, the marriage or the common-law relationship falls apart. The nature of the family becomes distorted, a variation on the theme of Jamaican sociologist Edith Clarke's *My Mother Who Fathered Me.* Those who run the social security system of the United States must surely know what they are doing. To undermine and at times destroy the sense of family in the black ghetto male is to lay the grounds for serious social problems.

Those who try to prevent this undermining of black male family pride and responsibility, like the Garvey movement in the 1920s, 1930s and 1940s, and the black Muslims in the 1950s, 1960s and 1970s, were met with hostility by the American system. Yet these were the groups who were most strongly opposed to the drug culture which is so seriously undermining the stability of the entire American social fabric in these closing days of the twentieth century. Are these the seeds of its own destruction which the communists, before they themselves collapsed, ascribed to the nature of capitalism? Is racism part of capitalism and part of the seeds of its destruction? Then what of the collapse of the pre-racist, pre-capitalist empires of human history? One thing history makes clear: empires and any and all forms of injustice hasten historical change. What would change be like in a world free of capitalist exploitation? Free of racial discrimination? Free of empire? There would still be change because change is inherent in the whole process. But of what would that change consist in a just, free and equitable world? Perhaps the new century and its new technology will provide a pointer. Will the transnationals continue to dominate? Will they take over the new technology? Or will it undo them? Will my young black boy up in the hills of St Andrew, Jamaica, conspire with groups of young people in North America and Europe and other groups in the villages of Africa and Asia, all with control over the computer, to create a brave new world in which co-operation replaces competition and the well-being of people overshadows the profit motive? Or will the new technology inaugurate a new tyranny?

The night before I ended my first American visit, Ruth Jett and Langston Hughes arranged a farewell gathering, all black and an interesting mixture of Harlem's political and literary leaders. At the last moment Langston Hughes phoned to say he would not attend. Things would be more focused if he were not there; he knew what was on my mind and I would get the best out of these folk if he was not there to 'share the glory'.

We discussed the future of black Americans. They would, I suggested, always be a minority. The chances of them creating a black state of their own, either as a state of the Union or as independent, were so remote as to be impossible. They had to reconcile themselves to permanent minority status or to being absorbed and assimilated over time. In time, I suggested, the American black might disappear completely with only a slight tanning of the national American complexion. I sensed people bristling, getting angry, outraged, indignant. A fierce, at times angry, almost abusive argument ensued. After about an hour of heat and passion, the argument cooled down, became rational. Which was the choice? A permanent visible minority, or the disappearance of the blacks by assimilation? In the end, drained of all heat and passion, we agreed that there was no simple answer. No people want to see themselves fade into the nothingness of absorption into a larger dominant group. All groups want to retain the special qualities that make them distinctive. Then we talked about the distinct character of the black American contribution to American art and culture. And so, gradually, we arrived at the point where they were Americans, unhappy, angry, rebellious at the history of discrimination and exploitation dating back to their very beginnings and the arrival of black slaves in this land. The desire to see Africa free and flourishing and great was because they knew it would make a difference to how they themselves were seen and treated. If other blacks, in other parts of the world, flourished and were accorded the respect usually accorded to the strong and the successful, they, in America, would be seen in a different light. It did not mean they had to go to Africa — except perhaps as tourists and visitors.

These people had two things in common. They were all American; they were all, despite their varying shades of colour, their varying physical types — from thin tall near-European to short squarish Asiatic-Mongolian to hawk-like Amerindian to West African negroid to mixed mulatto brown — described as black Americans, as Negroes, by their fellow countrymen. What bound them together was not tribal, not ethnic. They were centuries removed from any tribal links, any ethnic connection. They were not even of the same colour. They were of the same culture, the same language, the same value system. Only the prevailing racism of the society forced them into togetherness. Remove that and they would be indistinguishable from all other Americans. If and when colour ceases to be a yardstick to measure a person's worth, the black American will become just an American, as committed to his native America as all other Americans. They have already begun to emerge as some of the finest pro-consuls and diplomats serving American interests in far-flung corners of the world. Yet the sense of the two-ness expressed by DuBois at the opening of this century persists. They have become great American soldiers and statesmen and diplomats, members of their Congress, advisors to their Presidents, leaders in their armies. Yet still that 'two-ness' American, and black, persists. What would they be, how would they behave, when that sense of 'two-ness' is finally dispelled?

The irony of it all is that this deeply entrenched racism of the twentieth century is only as old as colonialism, imperialism and capitalism. Slavery is almost as old as the story of man. Throughout human history man has enslaved his brother man for all sorts of reasons, white men enslaving white men and woman and even children; black men doing the same to their own black folk; yellow and brown men to their own yellow and brown people. Before imperialism, colonialism and capitalism the encounters of peoples and cultures took place in relative peace and harmony, with relative mutual respect. At times there were wars and clashes, of course. They were not invested with the notions of the right of one racial group or colour type to overlordship of the rest. Even the Roman Empire, because its expansionism was essentially confined to Europe and the Mediterranean, was not based on the difference in skin colour between the conqueror and the conquered. Slavery, in its earliest manifestations, was not based on skin colour. Varying forms of slavery existed within and between groups of the same colour. Africans had African slaves; Europeans European slaves; Asians Asian slaves. Racism was not the primary factor in slavery. Slavery predates racism. Racism, as we know it in our time, is of comparatively recent origin, the product of the combination of imperialism, colonialism and the massive trade in African slaves transported to the New World.

When scores of millions of black people were plucked from their African homelands and transported to foreign lands to labour as beasts of burden, producing goods and services for the whites of Europe and for the white settlers in Europe's colonies, this wholesale enslavement and exploitation had to be justified. Slavery on this scale was unprecedented. Europe was Christian, civilised. If Europeans could do this to one group of people, then why not to each other, why not among themselves? But they would not because Europe was civilised; its peoples were civilised and therefore would not and could not, be treated in this manner. The black slaves out of Africa were different, hardly human. They looked different from the civilised whites because they were different. They were lazy, immoral, promiscuous, incapable of abstract thought, unreliable, brutish, nearer animal than human; or, if human, at the very lowest rungs of the human level of evolution. There was nothing wrong or immoral in using such creatures as beasts of burden as you do other, nobler animals such as horses and oxen. In the nineteenth century, a whole body of literature to justify this view of the blacks came into being. There were 'scientific' studies 'proving' that blacks were not human in the same way whites were. More important, the fruit, the benefits of imperialism, colonialism and racism were tangible in the steady flow of wealth from the colonies to the "mother countries'. Gradually, between the birth and flowering of empire and our time, white racism was institutionalised as normal. Blacks were preordained inferior, whites superior. Empire and colonialism were *The White Man's Burden.* Civilising the blacks was the justification for grabbing their land and its resources. So the whites of Europe and North America, with rare exceptions, became accomplices in the perpetuation of twentieth-century racism.

When Adolf Hitler developed his racist, anti-Semitic theories to instigate and justify his genocide against German Jews in the 1930s, he depended heavily on the body of nineteenth-century writing which provided 'scientific' and philosophic justification for the notions of 'white Aryan superiority' over Jews, blacks, gypsies and all the lesser breed without the law. Among Hitler's most important sources was an English writer named Houston Stewart Chamberlain, whose philosophic racism was essentially anti-Semitic. Initially that racism was directed more against Jews than blacks. But in the 'age of reason', when men had to find 'good' justification for their wholesale exploitation of Africa and its peoples on a scale unknown in all previous empires of human history, the theories of race, buttressed by skin colour provided that justification. Hitler did not invent racism and colour prejudice. He just used them.

In the end most people, black and white, came to accept this value judgement that whites were superior and blacks inferior. It explained why things were as they were. It made for an uneasy but orderly relationship in places where black and white shared the same land space and amenities, as long as both accepted this order. The protest against this order of things, and its rejection, became, in the twentieth century, the primary preoccupation of the black intellect and black intelligence of our time. DuBois defined it early in the new century. Garvey, without the scholastic and intellectual tools of DuBois, assailed it head-on and was destroyed by it, but not before he awakened mass black consciousness. It is arguable that as many as those who died fighting against slavery died in the struggle against the racism that was spawned by imperialism and colonialism. It was the vastest, most sustained effort by one group of people of one colour to break free of the physical, emotional, psychological overlordship of another. It was, indeed, *the* problem of the twentieth century.

As with all such long and epic struggles, the nature of those engaged in it, as well as the nature of the struggle itself, undergoes change. The racists become confirmed in the rightness of their cause. They seek justification for it in any and all likely areas of scholarship. Blood becomes something racially special: white blood, black blood, brown blood, yellow blood. Those at the receiving end insist their blood is as good as, or better than, the dominant 'white' blood. Racism begets racism. My blood is better, purer, than your blood. Black racism becomes the counterpoint to white racism. Those who lead the whites say the white race first; so, those who lead the blacks say the black race first. No matter that the scientists tell us we humans are all of the same blood, common shareholders in the same half-dozen or so blood types of all humanity across all boundaries and barriers of origin, nationality, colour. A young black man from the ghettoes of Kingston recently sang to the world that we are all of One Blood:

> You could a' come from Libya or America
> You could a' come from Europe or from Africa
> You could a' come from Lebanon or from Iran
> You could a' come from China or from Japan
> One blood.

It is no accident that Junior Reid came from Marcus Garvey's Jamaica. Some day, some other young man or woman will sing of *One Race*. The white race and the black race and the yellow race and the brown race are as bereft of scientific truth as is the notion of the colour of blood.

One of the cruellest, most tragic, most disastrous of the foolishnesses of our century is this elaborate edifice of race and colour, built by whites to justify raw exploitation. The only things worse were the two world wars of this century in which they ritualistically destroyed the flower of their manhood in its prime and laid waste to each other's resources with a savagery unimagined in the most barbaric tribal killings. Was there a connection between this terrible self-

destruction of Europe and the way they dealt with the darker races of
mankind in the twentieth century? Is there a lesson in it for the darker
races? The Europeans and Americans slaughtered well over one
hundred million of their own in their two world wars. Since those
two wars we have had the Cold War with its 'proxy wars', in which
hundreds of thousands of Africans, Asians and Latin Americans
slaughtered each other with equal abandon. Do the darker races think
they can remain uninvolved if there were a third such world war?
What are we to do to help save ourselves and all of humanity?

Way back in the 1920s Langston Hughes, then a young man
starting out on his life sang

I, too, sing America

I am the darker brother
They send me to eat in the kitchen
When company comes,
But I laugh,
An' eat well
And grow strong.
Tomorrow,
I'll sit at table
When company comes,
Nobody'll dare
Say to me
'Eat in the kitchen'
Then.
Besides,
They'll see how beautiful I am
And be ashamed -
I, too, am America.

The Road to Coyaba

— 8 —

A Farewell to Debden

I arrived back from America with more money than I ever had before. I had American dollars in my trouser pockets, in my shirt pockets, all my jacket pockets — inside and out. And there were some in my suitcase as well. I had given a half a dozen lectures, arranged by my publishers, and the money was the proceeds from these. So I arrived home flush with greenbacks. Daphne, the children and the young woman friend who had stayed with them during my absence marvelled as I pulled the stuff out of my pockets. America, we agreed, was where writers could make most money, most quickly. This was not an unmixed blessing. That rarely gifted Welsh poet, Dylan Thomas, had discovered how easily and quickly money could be made by way of the American lecture tour. They are lavish affairs, where food and drink and idle rich women abound. Thomas' London boozing was held in bounds by the cost of booze. There was no such limitation on the American lecture circuit. So he died of alcoholism in New York before he was forty. Going after this quick money could be risky and dangerous. Someone who organised these things had suggested I spend three months of each year on such lecture tours.

For a small percentage they would take care of everything, all travel and subsistence costs. I would make very good money, more than enough to live on for the rest of each year. I decided against it and the organiser said I was a fool to do so. 'It's big money.'

I had a fortnight with the family before I had to take up the Jamaican commission. I went to London almost daily to work out plans for the coming trip with planners at the Colonial Office. I rarely saw George Padmore these days, and when I did, the old warmth and intimacy were there. He remained very much on top of political developments throughout the Third World. Whenever I invited him to Debden — I knew he loved children and would have enjoyed ours — he turned it down. I think he never forgave Daphne for, as he put it once, taking me away from the 'movement'. He refused to believe that it was my own choice, long before Daphne, to be the loving critic within the Pan-African family. If nobody looks at our faults and failures and talks about them, we may come to believe ourselves without fault. This is especially easy for those whose cause is just and who are greatly embattled. It becomes easiest to blame everything — our own failings included — on 'the enemy'. I had, long ago, tried to explain this to George and the others. They had tended to laugh it off as sentimental literary agonising. Gorky, George had once told me, had been just like that. When I asked if he had known Gorky, he clammed up, became the Comintern man. He had no problem with my agreeing to do the book on Jamaica for the Colonial Office: he knew it was what Manley wanted. How did he know? Comintern man.

Padmore, like DuBois, ended his life in Ghana, both dying before Nkrumah was overthrown. I am glad they did not live to see that first flush of Pan-African success dissipated. Both had struggled so long and hard, both were realistic enough, understood the ebb and flow of the historical process and the dynamics of change well enough, to know there would be setbacks. To know is one thing; to experience the bitterness of such setbacks, especially so late in life, is another. So I was glad they did not live to see the birth of the new colonialism which occupied no lands, was responsible for no peoples, yet dominated the world as completely as had the earlier, more directly brutal, empires which collapsed after the Second World War.

What a pity we know so little about the life and work of George Padmore. There are the few books he wrote, his record of informing the Third World, but very little else. I know he was born in Trinidad, but nothing about his background and family. I know he spent time in the United States; not how much or how he lived. I could never get him to talk about when he went to the Soviet Union and his experiences there. I got hints from older European communists who had been in the Soviet Union that he had been an important figure in the Moscow Soviet. I know his influence on the anti-imperialist and Pan-African movements of the first half of this century was pervasive. Yet when I check the records, when I open my computer and feed it my encyclopaedias and ask it to find George Padmore or Padmore, George, they come up with nothing.

What Miss Lou — Louise Bennett — called 'colonisation in reverse' was in full flow in the 1950s. West Indians flocked to Britain in their thousands. This was the mother country; now mother was expected to do something for her many children who could not find jobs back in the sunny Caribbean islands. Migration had always been a fact of West Indian life. When the Panama Canal was being built, West Indians formed the bulk of the unskilled and semi-skilled heavy-duty labour force. They went to work on the sugar plantations of Cuba and Central America. They went everywhere, did everything and always, when the jobs were over, some stayed behind. Those who returned brought back a cosmopolitan view of the world. They sometimes brought back Hispanic wives. They always sent back money to help the folks at home or to be held until they returned to set themselves up in business or on a farm or to build a home. After the war, it was Britain's turn to receive the West Indian migrants.

Migration in itself was nothing new to the British. Before and during the war, vast numbers of people on the march, homeless, ragged, hungry and frightened, carrying or pushing or pulling all they possessed, fleeing the Nazis or the fighting or both, became Europe's refugees. We saw them on our nightly cinema newsreel clips. Many had flocked to Britain for sanctuary. The British had coped with compassion. They set up shelters in their cities and found homes and schools and hostels for the refugees and their children in quiet peaceful rural British communities. The able-bodied men joined the British army and returned to fight against those who had made them 'refugees' — that special word of the war. These refugees looked like the British themselves. Only the language and their different folkways marked them out. As soon as they learned to speak English and adapted to British ways, they easily became part of the British community.

What was new to the British was to suddenly have large numbers of black people among them, seeking the same jobs they sought, wanting the same services they wanted, looking for homes in their communities. The first batch who did the menial jobs British people did not want or need — the collecting of garbage, the driving of buses, being conductors — posed few problems. The problems came later when more black migrants came and competed for the available amenities. There was little reaction when the European refugees did this. It was different when the West Indians did. Yet the West Indians, if anything, had a greater claim on Britain and its resources than did the European refugees. They were British subjects, citizens of Britain's colonial empire, entitled to all the rights and responsibilities that came with that citizenship. Historically, they had been the source of much of Britain's wealth. In the war many of them had died for Britain. There had been less resentment against a much larger influx of European refugees. And this resentment did not extend to those from the West Indies, or indeed, from anywhere else in the empire and Commonwealth who were white. White Australians, South Africans, East Africans, Canadians all flocked freely into post-war Britain with no objection or resentment. To be sure they came in smaller numbers and, being white, were from the privileged sectors of their societies. The white West Indians and Africans in Britain had no difficulty finding homes and jobs and trade union membership.

When there were only a few of us, Britain was extraordinarily tolerant. We had little experience of racial prejudice and almost none of discrimination. So we came to appreciate the country and its people. When the numbers changed, attitudes changed. The latent built-in prejudices on which the colonial relationship is founded, came to the fore. Many of the new West Indian migrants found coming to the mother country a shattering experience. Many were from the peasantry or working class, semi-literate, not as well-mannered or well-spoken as those the British had encountered earlier. They had come to the centre of their world; they spoke its language, however crudely, and had grown up with its history and culture as their own. The more educated spoke better English than the English majority and knew no other language. Indeed, they saw themselves as different from and better than the Africans. The Africans were 'monkey chasers', not as civilised as they were. They felt British, thought British, were British. I witnessed the devastation of their first encounters with colour prejudice and discrimination. The open warmth with which they arrived turned cold and withdrawn. The initial friendliness turned into angry, bitter disappointment. Many would have turned back immediately. They did not have the return fare and had all come on one-way tickets paid for through the 'throwing of pardner', the sale of a bit of land or a cow or two or through family borrowing. Besides, after the fuss and fanfare of the departure — days of partying as part of the farewell ceremony — going back would be the ultimate humiliation. You can't go home again — unless you can carry the trappings of success. All of which made for bitter anger and resentment in a cold country with hostile people of whom you had expected a better welcome. It was a sad thing to watch. The old hands who had enjoyed their minority status when there were so few of them, could do little to help or comfort the new-comers. So they, too, were resented. Indeed, the old hands often blamed the newcomers for the heightened prejudice and discrimination.

For the British, too, this must have been a disconcerting revelation. I do not think they ever expected to have this problem of the dark-skinned people of their empire coming in such large numbers to the mother country. They had been high-minded and moralistic about the American colour problem, usually siding with the black Americans, especially the black entertainers. Paul Robeson and the pair of Layton and Johnson were enormously popular. Now the problem was on them and they were no better at dealing with it, no less prejudiced than the Americans they had condemned. And the immigrant blacks, like all other people, resented being seen as 'a problem'.

I prepared for my trip to the West Indies in this unhappy climate of growing hostility among the white population against the black new immigrants. The Britain of easy tolerance, when the blacks among them were an almost invisible minority, was changing. There were too many blacks; too many of them poor; too many of them changing the faces and appearances of old settled working-class and lower middle-class communities for the whites to be comfortable with black next-door neighbours, often on both sides. When the Indians and the Pakistanis and the East African Indians joined the flood of dark faces into Britain, the children of the mother country were embattled. Increasingly, this was ceasing to be the Britain I came to at the height of war. Then, the struggle against Nazism brought us all together and the great Winston Churchill used the poetry of black Jamaican, Claude McKay, to rally the Commonwealth and the world: *If We Must Die...*

So, one mild September evening — 1 or 2 September 1955 — we had a small party to see me off to the West Indies. Most of the regulars to our home in Debden were there. It had been mild enough for the children to have spent the best part of the day on the beautiful green hill across the street. I remember, later that same day, Aron quietly polishing off a whole pound of apples our greengrocer neighbour had delivered earlier on his rounds. He had an almighty bellyache. I had also, earlier in the day, gone to our Polish family doctor for my vaccination shots and certificates. He had shared a rare drink with me. Then, abruptly, he had said:

'Wish I could go with you. I have always wanted to live in the sun.'

I was startled, not knowing how to answer.

'Perhaps you will.'

He shook his head. 'No, we Poles are dreamers. If you find a place, take it. Bear that in mind.'

The nurse looked in. Mrs So-and-so was in the waiting room. We shook hands solemnly. He looked at his glass; it was empty. He managed to get a drop from it to libate his carpeted floor. He had remembered this little African ritual from one of my books.

On a cool misty morning the great British Airways plane — I think it was called BOAC then — lifted me off on the first stage of the road to Coyaba and the reshaping of the way in which I saw my world. The details of that journey — my visit to all the main islands of the English-speaking Caribbean and what was then British Guiana, and how I literally walked the Jamaican landscape and got to know the Jamaican people — are set out in *Jamaica: An Island Mosaic,* published in 1957 in the Corona Library series.

After that journey, I returned to Debden, spent the best part of the next twelve months writing the book and, as soon as the manuscript was delivered, Daphne, the children and I said our farewell to Debden and started the long journey to Coyaba. The children did not want to go. All their friends were there; the large school playground backed onto our house and the children could get to school without crossing any street. Aron, thanks to that terrible drawn-out birth in Paley, was mildly spastic and he had an adoring and adored physiotherapist whom he shared with half-a-dozen more seriously impaired children. He was the leader of the gang, sometimes beating his drum and marching them up and down, as did the grand old Duke of York. He really did not want to go. The girls were much less resistant, more interested in the adventures ahead. Daphne was too busy packing to think of anything else. She had been happier in these last few years in England than she had been in her earlier years when her parents had sent her 'home' to ensure she did not go completely native Javanese. They thought of sending her to school in Australia, but her mother did not like the crude egalitarianism of Australia, so sending her to Britain was seen as the safer, though costlier, option. She was miserable at boarding school, miserable with kindly relatives who knew nothing about the place in which she spent her key formative years. She had been the outsider, the 'weirdo' who wanted to be an artist and moved like the native Javanese women did. It was this 'outsider' thing which attracted us to each other. Over the years the colds she caught with regularity each winter grew worse; they lasted longer, were heavier, drained her more. When summer came, she opened like a sunflower; with winter she shrivelled up, more drained each year. Our Polish family doctor checked her and found nothing wrong, just that her resistance to winter was weak. She was difficult about taking tonics but good about eating fruit. She needed the sun; she belonged in the sun. I had worried quietly. Now at last I was able to take her to the sun. Now all her energies were spent on packing our possessions.

On my first trip, a year earlier, I had met a Jamaican journalist who speculated in land on the side, so I let him know that I was looking for a piece of land. He had met many past visitors, journalists among them, who had been captivated by Jamaica and thought it a good idea to own a piece of this beautiful place. It had usually been a passing fancy, a nice idea. He had shown them pieces of land which he either owned or had arranged with the owners to sell. He collected small deposits from such interested would-be buyers. Usually they went away and nothing came of it and he pocketed their small deposits. It was honest, lucrative, harmed no one. There were worse and uglier ways of 'taking' visitors.

In my 'walking' Jamaica, I had come across this high hill a few miles out of the village of Red Hills, which was itself about a dozen miles out of Kingston. It had attracted me and I wanted to explore it, but it was densely forested and I did not know to whom it belonged. All Jamaican land belongs either to some person or to the Crown. One afternoon, my land speculator/journalist friend picked me up at the Press Club and drove me up into the hills, to a place called Rock Hall which was the next well-populated village after Red Hills going up into the hills. The road was relatively wide but rough, running through steep sloping land on one side, and land falling away on the other. When we passed what I had come to think of as my hill, I asked him if he knew its owner. We stopped and he got out and looked at the land. There was a narrow track into it. Swarms of mosquitoes, big and black, assailed us. My friend brought a half-full small bottle of kerosene corked with a piece of paper and lit it. In a few seconds the foul smell and smoke drove the mosquitoes away.

He pointed up. 'That?'

'Yes.'

'I'll show you a better, cleaner piece in Rock Hall. People nearby.'

'I want to see this piece.'

'Alright. Let's go to Rock Hall and if you still want to see this we'll get a couple of fellows to cut a path for us. It will cost you.'

'How much?'

'Ten shillings; five shillings each.'

'Alright.'

' Better give it to me.'

'I will pay them myself.' I had learned about Jamaican rates. As in many parts of Africa, you ask for double the going rate and pocket half.

His face took on a 'caught-out' expression. 'Give them two-and-six each.'

He put out the foul-smelling but effective repellent torch. We drove up to Rock Hall. The village square was on the edge of the road near the border between West Rural St Andrew and St Catherine. Rock Hall was to become the place where, for many years, we bought our weekly supply of fresh beef and pork and grapefruit and root vegetables. That first day, however, I felt I was entering hostile territory. The rum-shop was crowded; the noise was loud. Most of the men had just returned from their fields. The place ponged. My friend made space for us at the bar counter and ordered with ostentation. He recognised a young man and sent him to call somebody. He introduced me as the gentleman from England 'looking a piece of land'. There was a momentary hush, then bedlam broke loose. Everybody spoke at once at the top of their voices. They all, it seemed, had a piece of land to sell. My friend made notes in his reporter's pad; I tried to make sense out of the verbal chaos. A tiny black man, a few inches shorter than my five-six and thin as a rake, came in from the back of the place. He moved slowly and looked pickled. The young woman who served made room for him to face us across the small bar counter. He offered me his hand. The place grew silent.

'A.B.' he said, 'A.B. Ricketts.' He waved a tiny hand casually. 'Pay them no mind; give them no money; they will sell what does not belong to them. See a title paper before you pay a penny...' He stared at my journalist friend: 'even him.' Then he shoved a drink in a fresh clean glass to me and we toasted each other. This was the owner of the village bar, the community's scholar and intellectual, produce dealer, a man who had gone to one of the best schools down on the plains. For a while we all listened to 'A.B', silent and respectful, as he told me about Rock Hall. Then the men the journalist had sent for turned up and we went looking at land.

After nearly two hours of looking at pieces of land, none of which really interested me, we drove back to the square where the two men collected their long machetes, then down in the direction of Red Hills and the plains below. We stopped at the little track where we had stopped on the way up. My friend and the two men each lit their small paper-corked kerosene lamps. The smell and smoke made a safe area against the swarming mosquitoes. Then I saw the leaking standpipe tucked back on the edge of the track. A large pool of stagnant water surrounded it: the breeding place of the swarm. As though reading my mind, one of the men unstoppered his lamp and poured a few drops of kerosene on the stagnant water. Then we moved up the hill, the men slashing a way up for us. We reached the top of the hill nearly an hour later. The sun had moved to the horizon. Soon it would be gone and night would fall, suddenly, instantly, as it does in the tropics. A huge trumpet tree, struck dead by lightning, towered over the bush. Beyond it was the broad flat crest of the hill, a good five hundred feet or more higher than where we had parked the car.

The air up here had a cool edge to it. A gentle breeze stirred the air without quite driving the mosquitoes away. I borrowed the stink torch from one of the men. His companion built a small smoking fire of twigs and green leaves. I scrambled to the top of the flat ledge, grateful that the others stayed back by the little smoking fire. I sat on a large stone and looked at the world about me in the fading light. There was the Caribbean Sea far below, curving with the curve of the earth, flat, with the setting sun striking light off it. To the left, seeming to rise out of the sea, were the Blue Mountains, lit up by the setting sun. Above all this, a clear sky reflecting the light of the sun, with tiny patches of fleecy clouds suspended, apparently, between heaven and earth. I felt more at peace on that spot than I had ever felt in my life.

Something about this place, something about the mood and feel created by this piece of land made me sure that this was the place for us. This, I knew, Daphne would love. This was where we would build our home.

I rejoined the others and we made our way back down to the car. The way down in the near dark was more difficult than the way up. I slipped once, grazed an elbow, leaving skin scrapings on a bit of black marble rock.

Back at the car, I gave the senior of the two men ten shillings to share between them. We stopped in Red Hills, at Tiny's bar, where the two men said they would wait for Mas John's truck to take them back to Rock Hall. Tiny prepared a snack for us by shredding a piece of dried saltfish into small flakes, cutting a hot red pepper and an onion into it and dousing it all with pickapepper sauce. We ate this with door-step slices of hard-dough bread, washed down with overproof white rum laced with coconut water. The two Rock Hall men joined in the eating and drinking, no longer just hired hands. I remembered African folkways with their fluid flexibility between master or mistress and servant. The snack was hot, sustaining, nourishing and intoxicating. I liked the look of Tiny and arranged with him to return the next day. I was fascinated by Tiny's ability to fall asleep for a few seconds, standing up, between serving his customers in the bar or the slightly larger, partitioned-off grocery store next to it. He simply closed his eyes, turned off his 'lights' for a few seconds, then turned them back on instantly on call. When I asked him about it later, he said his grand-daddy had taught him how to take these catnaps. Using them a man could work all day and all night without getting too tired. If Tiny was representative of Red Hills and its people, then we would be in for an interesting experience. In my mind the die had been cast. Only the negotiating now remained.

I spent the next few days driving up to Red Hills every morning, using Tiny's bar as my base, and exploring the area and getting to know the people. My journalist friend was also busy. We met at Tiny's a few times, then, I do not know how or when, he got hold of 'the papers' for the piece of land I wanted. Now we could deal. We agreed to an acre of land for about three hundred pounds Sterling. I gave him a first deposit of fifty pounds and we signed a note of agreement to be converted into a registered title on completion of payment. As far as I was concerned, the land was now secured. I sent Daphne a telegram: *Bought you a hill.* She must have thought me touched by the sun. Then, the research for my assignment completed, I returned to Debden to complete the job. All that was a year earlier. I realise now that my journalist friend who had corresponded with me throughout that year, who had sent glowing reports of how the building of the roadway up to the top of the hill was progressing, and needed some extra money to pay the workers, really did not expect me to return. I had sent small amounts — twenty pounds at one time, ten or fifteen another, always gratefully acknowledged with assurances of the work in progress.

Now, a year later, after a long sea voyage, we were in Jamaica.

It would be ungracious, ungrateful, not to look back and thank Britain and its people for the good years we spent there, especially the five Debden years at 37 Jessel Drive, across from that beautiful green hill with its grand old trees under which our children spent so many happy days. I remember a pair of West African students, tennis fanatics, turning up on Sunday mornings and using our home and my name as a Debden tenant to gain access to our tennis courts. They played the mornings away, then returned to our house to change, have soft drinks and rush back to London. I do not remember their names. I remember endless streams of newly arrived South Africans, all sizes, shapes, genders, colours, coming to Debden for help to find their bearings in the 'world's greatest city'. Some, I remember, abused their sanctuary grossly. There was one particular slim, cold-faced, young Coloured man who took such advantage of young English women that I had to forbid his coming to our home when I discovered he had made two of them pregnant simultaneously and had no intention of taking responsibility for either. Most of the others were nicer, more thoughtful, people. For them, as for us, our home in Debden was a sanctuary of physical and spiritual warmth in a cold country.

The London County Council of the day made that possible for us. They helped me and my family when we needed help most. I have paid taxes wherever I have lived and worked, but never as willingly and happily as in Britain's Welfare State. My taxes there, in small measure, paid back what my family had received and helped make possible the same kind of support for other families in times of trouble. The Welfare State taught us concern for the welfare of our fellow beings.

On that last night in Debden, the children tucked up and asleep with their teddies, Daphne and I thought and talked about these things, about the people who had come to be with us for a time, or just for the warmth of the great fire in our very special hearth which warmed our entire home and our world on cold winter days and nights when all the world seemed bleak. These we would never forget. These we would always be grateful to Britain for. It was the best possible mood in which to leave one country and journey to another. It is a mood that is rarely sustained for long.

The sea journey, 'special tourist', was a nightmare which began before we reached the ship. We stayed overnight in London with our friend, Marjorie Nicholson who had been a witness at our marriage and was godmother to Naomi. The train to Southampton to join the ship left too early for us to join it from Debden. Late that night, Marjories's flat was thrown into turmoil by the discovery of the absence of one of our family teddy bears. I made the late-night journey back to Debden, woke our former next-door neighbours and found the teddy where the children had watched television earlier that day. It was after midnight when I got back to Marjorie's. Everybody was asleep, so I tucked the teddy into the arms of its owner. We were not done with teddy trouble. At Southampton station Aron's teddy, Lulupet, fell onto the rails as we came off the train. He would not budge until he had Lulupet back. A kindly railway official, obviously a father himself, went to a great deal of trouble to find a long piece of wood with a hook, then retrieved Lulupet while a growing audience watched. We all applauded when he handed Lulupet to Aron with a magician's flourish.

We boarded the ship and Daphne's troubles began. She was seasick most of the time. The children were miserable and ratty and harked back to how wonderful life had been in Debden with all their friends. The ship belonged to the brothers Grimaldi and the food was Italian — spaghetti and meat sauce and meat sauce and spaghetti. Daphne could not keep anything down, did not eat anything the first day at sea.

Our first and second stops, each a day long, to take on food and drink and cargo, were ports in Portugal and Spain; and to pick up people migrating to Latin America. These travelled steerage, as do most migrants the world over. They had the look of the kind of poverty I remembered from my childhood days in Vrededorp, only without the sunshine and laughter. Their appearances reflected the unending drabness of the quality of their poverty. Once into the dark holds of the ship, we did not see them again. When, three or four days out at sea, a delegation of us protested to the Purser over the food, he told us the Italian- and Spanish-speaking passengers found no fault with it. I could understand that. It would take time before the half-starved-looking people I watched boarding the ship would be fussy about quality. That comes when you have outlived historic memories of famine and hunger. When the English-speaking Caribbean folk were on the verge of revolt two weeks into the three-week voyage, I told them the Hispanic passengers would not join us. The ship's people tried to improve and vary the diet, but they did not know how to prepare food for the special Caribbean palate, which, essentially, had forgotten historic hunger.

Our third stop was Madeira, where everybody lived off the famous wine, tourism and the small cottage industries associated with tourism. I bought a sturdy pretty little wicker rocking chair for Naomi (which was stolen on the docks in Kingston). I felt uneasy at the sight of grown men and women ingratiating themselves with strangers in order to make a sale. The smiles never showed in their eyes; their gestures reminded me of beggars. Tourism can be a wonderful interaction between peoples and cultures where there is respect and self-respect, where there is no question about the dignity of those who serve and those who receive the service. It becomes degrading where the tourist is offered 'feelthy pictures' or 'come with me, my sister pretty'.

At Barbados, our first stop on the American side of the Atlantic, they took on fresh meat. I hired a taxi and took Daphne and the children on a 'tour' of the island. I took them to the hill from which, the year before, I had a view of the entire island. For Daphne, with her memories of Java, a different kind of island, Barbados seemed awfully small. 'Where can you go if you want to be alone? Really alone?'

Our next stop was La Guaira, Venezuela, an extraordinary seaport overshadowed by the sheerest and highest mountain I had ever seen rising almost straight up out of the sea. It looked like a slate mountain. The port and its surrounds seemed a place on the move, being built as you watched. A long wide road had been blasted through the high mountain, and big cars and trucks streaked along the wide highway into and out of the belly of the dug out mountain.

Most of the Hispanic passengers disembarked at La Guaira. The presence of military types loaded with firepower, which we had noticed in Spain where we saw heavily armed soldiers outside every large building, was outdone here. There were armed soldiers everywhere; not, as Daphne noticed in Spain, accompanied by priests; just soldiers by themselves, heavily armed, making us feel nervous, anxious, embattled. There is something unsettling about armed soldiers patrolling civilian areas in times of peace. Seeing armed police on beat patrol in France had taken some getting used to. Our norm was the unarmed British Bobby. Spain and Portugal, with armed soldiers in the streets, had been disturbing. The gun-toting soldiers of Latin America were frightening. I had to reassure Daphne that it was not like that in Jamaica. Had she seen any armed police in Barbados? She was reassured.

In Curaçao, our last stop before Jamaica, a passing worker from the oil-fields which dotted the waterfront seemed as struck as I was by the family likeness between us. He could have been a blood cousin of mine. He stopped and we struck up conversation, trying out the different languages we knew; first in Dutch, at which I was no good, then in English at which he was hopelessly bad, then in what sounded like South African Afrikaans, which made primitive communication possible. I told him I was from South Africa, my wife from Java, our children were born in Europe and we were on our way to Jamaica. Had I been to the Netherlands? Not really; I had only passed through once. He tried his Dutch on Daphne, but she had lost hers altogether. He was excited and invited us to go to his home and meet his family. I was worried about our getting back to the ship on time. His home was in walking distance. He would see us back to the ship; no need to worry. So we accompanied the oil-field worker to his home. A small typical tropical urban house: two, three rooms and a largish living room; outside toilet and cooking facilities; a little courtyard in the back, spotlessly clean. There was a small chicken house in the yard and the chickens wandered in and out of the house as we were introduced to the man's family. There was his mother, a typical African, Asian, Caribbean matriarch, mother to the whole family, including chickens, dogs and any other small stock and family pets. The wife was a shy busy young woman, olive brown and dumpy as a certain type of Dutch and Afrikaner woman tends to be. They gave us something to drink and we talked as best we could. He wanted to know everything about the world. What was happening in the British colonies? From Daphne what was happening in the Dutch colonies? I translated as best I could. When would we all be free? When would the change come? Would there have to be another war? His hunger for knowledge was moving.

Then it was time for the last leg of our journey. The ship's food was much better now; there was more of it and in greater variety. There were less than half the numbers with which we had crossed the Atlantic. Most had disembarked in Venezuela. With so many fewer mouths to feed, the ship's people could afford to feed us better, give us more of a Caribbean flavour. They tried their best and most of us were appeased. Walking on land at every stop seemed to restore us to more normal, rational beings, and the talk of drastic and dreadful legal action subsided. After stops in the Dutch Antilles, things became even more normal and settled. A few still talked of suing the company but it was half-hearted now. A Jamaican woman journalist on the trip threatened an exposé of conditions on the ship. Nothing came of it.

It was raining and damp when we came off the ship. My family were disgusted with me. Where was the sun I had promised them? They did not like what they saw of Jamaica; neither did I. This was not the Jamaica I had promised them. To make matters worse the friends who had promised to meet us were nowhere in sight.

Then two cars sped into the docking area. A group of people spilled out of the cars. I recognised them. My friends had just made it, Jamaica time. Things looked a little better, Jamaica a little more friendly, though still damp and drizzly. Douglas, Norman Manley's elder son, his wife Carmen, both friends from our London days, were there. So was Hal Glave, the government public relations officer who had 'walked' the island with me the year before. So too was Elsie Barsoe, editor of *Pepperpot*, one of the island's handful of annual magazines, in whose baby Austin I had travelled much of the island. Then there was Verona Goetz, Elsie's bosom friend; Olga Passmore, Verona's sister, a first-rate photographer who had trudged up the hill that was to be Coyaba to take the first pictures of that view in the setting sun. And there, too, was my journalist-land-speculator friend, looking dejected at the sight of me. He was supposed to have found a place for us. Now he told me the place he had reserved had suddenly become unavailable. I suspect that right up to the last moment he had hoped and expected I would not turn up.

Elsie Barsoe had sold her home in the Cross Roads-New Kingston area (not yet so named at that time); it would be empty for a few days, so she offered it to us till we found a place. The Manleys fed us at their university campus home. Douglas had been a Covent Garden porter when we met in London, supplementing the allowance from his father while he worked for his doctorate in sociology at London University. Now he was a lecturer at the fledgling University of the West Indies at Mona.

That first night at Elsie Barsoe's place on Haining Road was uncomfortable and unsettling for Daphne and the children. The order, stability and certainty of the Debden days were gone. They had been thrust into an unknown colonial world and did not like it. We did not have much money and there was no welfare state to help out.

Next day, I arranged for storage of our possessions till we found a home. The sight of a big dray cart, all our possessions stacked high and tied down on it, moving from the docks up King Street attracted no attention. The town was near on fifty years smaller than it is today, the traffic fifty years lighter and not made up of mainly 'pre-owned' Japanese motor vehicles which now clog King Street. Dray carts, donkey carts and handcarts were the common means of moving goods; walking the common means of moving people. The town, then, smelled of sea breeze, clean air, tinged by the not-unpleasant smells of the Coronation Market and the cooking from the many Chinese restaurants. The people reminded me of the populations of the great West African cities of Lagos, Accra, Kumasi, Freetown, transported to a more temperate climate and, after three centuries, all now speaking one common language. They were more united here than were the citizens of those great African cities because they spoke one common language — one with which I sometimes had trouble; but nowhere near the trouble I, and they themselves, had with the variety of languages and dialects among the citizens of those other cities. We take for granted this extraordinary unifying power of language.

After a few weeks of unsettled, unhappy settling-in, often with great help from friends and friends of friends, we rented a newly built three-bedroom house in the working-class area of Cockburn Pen. It was low land near the sea, parched and dry until our East Indian next-door neighbours worked their magic on it and grew the best lettuce, callaloo, escallion, cabbage and tomatoes, which their women then sold at the Cross Roads or Coronation markets. The Indian family had leased the land only and built their shacks on it. They had water but no other sanitary facilities. Our landlord was a big stocky dark brown man, who had returned from a spell abroad with enough money to buy up a big parcel of Cockburn Pen and develop it. He also operated a bar on the Spanish Town Road. He was interested in one of the young Indian women and we formed the impression that he used his powers as landlord to get his way. The family, two or three men, at least twice as many women and a host of children, seemed unable to do anything about his steady pressure.

Our other neighbours were mainly artisans. The most skilled made kegs for the thriving rum industry. Some built dray carts. Some were cabinet-makers, making exquisite furniture in small, drab workshops, usually using only a few essential tools: hand saw, hammer, chisel, plane. Some of the finest furniture in Jamaica's best homes came from these backyard workshops. Some were wheelwrights and coopers; some masons, carpenters, plumbers. This was a range of skilled artisans such as I had not met anywhere in Africa. I had met a few such skilled artisans only among South Africa's Cape Coloureds, and there they were a disappearing minority being pushed out by poor whites. Nowhere in the rest of Africa, at that time, and indeed nowhere in the developing world, did I find this skilled, clearly definable, artisan class. This, for me, was something strikingly new about Jamaica. The artisans, the black and brown professional class of doctors, lawyers, dentists and business people, headed a strong Jamaican middle class, predominantly brown, but even then becoming increasingly darker in complexion. These groups were the pillars of Jamaican stability as she shaped new relations and a place for herself in the world. The other, older, perhaps stronger, pillar was made up of the small farmers of Jamaica, the independent black land holders who had made possible the relatively stable transition from slavery to being free people in a free land.

The history of Jamaica's peasant farmers began when the slaves from the large plantations refused to be apprenticed to their former slave masters and withdrew, instead, into the mountainous hinterland to make a living off the land and to be their own masters. Over time they carried their surplus produce down to the plains to sell, and established tentative and uneasy contact with the government. Ownership of the land on which they lived was gradually formalised. Small services like roads and water were provided; small taxes were levied. Missionaries established churches and schools. Independent black churches flourished. With the Kikuyu in Kenya the colonial government had discouraged and tried to suppress the independent black churches and their independent black schools. This had been British colonial policy for most of South, Central and East Africa. In Jamaica, and the rest of the English-speaking Caribbean, the independent black churches and their schools were left alone, met only by the competition from the white missionaries, who, of course, had the support of the colonial government and the local plantocracy.

In Haiti, the land of the glorious Black Jacobins, the transition had led from one form of tyranny to another. A landless people makes for instability. The absence of a middle class leaves an unbridgeable gap between the landless peasant mass and an elite minority owning and controlling everything. Only in Jamaica, only in the English-speaking Caribbean, had emancipation been a relatively straightforward movement from tyranny to freedom. How an enslaved people come to be free, the institutions and patterns of association they fashion as part of the struggle for that freedom, usually determines the nature of that society. Where it requires great violence to attain freedom, violence may become part of the nature of that society in freedom. The absence of strong social institutions may result in a tendency toward chaos.

With my family settled in Cockburn Pen, I turned to the Coyaba enterprise. My speculator friend who had let us down so badly went up to Red Hills with me and admitted his glowing reports of the progress on the road had not been true. He blamed the man to whom he had entrusted the job and 'given the money'. Some sort of start had been made, but nothing much. And the experienced man who had made the start told me, to my friend's face, that he had not been paid the promised money, which was why he had not proceeded with the work. Later, when we went to my friend's lawyer to finalise the land deal, I insisted on deducting this money from the balance I still owed on the land. After much haggling I paid off the balance, less the advances I had sent for the road. I paid the money to the lawyer this time. The lawyer promised to let me have the title 'soon'. In the event, I had to get the help of another lawyer, nearly five years later, to get my title. But I was now free to get on with my plans to build while awaiting the title. My speculator friend now put it about that this African was trying to rob him of his land. This type of rumour in a small society is routinely used as a form of vengeance. But I, not my friend, had been the harmed party. At least one merchant would not sell me building material on 30-days credit until some of my friends quashed the rumour. Lying shamelessly then resenting being caught out was something I encountered again and again. It was, they said, the 'Anancy syndrome', a throwback to the deviousness developed to survive under slavery.

Money was running low, so I found a job on the weekly newspaper, *Public Opinion.* O.T. Fairclough, then treasurer of Norman Manley's People's National Party, was the managing director of the paper he had founded in 1937 in association with Headley Jacobs, an Englishman who came to Jamaica in the late 1920s to teach and who, like so many before and after him, fell in love with Jamaica, became Jamaican, and stayed. Fairclough was also managing director of City Printery. Job printing had a strong tradition in Jamaica. Marcus Garvey's first job had been in a Kingston printery. Fairclough was born in Westmoreland in 1904, when Garvey was seventeen and still in Jamaica. He went to Haiti in the 1920s and we find him working in the National Bank of Haiti between 1924 and 1932, during which time he rose from credit clerk to assistant manager. He was a black man and such opportunities were not open to him in Jamaica.

He returned to Jamaica in the turbulent 1930s, met Jacobs and Manley and was deeply involved in the formation of the People's National Party. On one rare pensive Friday night after we had put the paper to bed, he called me into his office and over a drink he remembered how it was at the start. For no reason I could explain, other perhaps than the way he treated them, I felt he was always impatient and judgmental of black people, especially those who worked for him in the printery and on the paper. I felt even that rare private drink was a special concession. Yet the man compelled respect. He was as black as could be. His personal trademark was the starched white linen suit he wore every day of his life. I never saw him in anything else. An austere, very black man in a very white linen suit, always starched, always without a crease out of place. His face seemed permanently sad, even when he smiled. He was a key man in the PNP and in the Jamaican national movement, and the one perhaps least rewarded and least honoured. Very Jamaican, but atypically so.

From his writings and speeches Garvey must have been somewhat like this. George Padmore had a similarly hard judgmental attitude toward black people who did not live up to his expectations. And the thing each of these men had in common was their blackness — no tinge of mulatto to it — and their enormous personal pride. It seemed they expected their people to perform above the normal and were hard on them when they did not. So Fairclough was feared and respected but not loved by his workers. How much had his Haitian experience to do with this? But Haiti was a place of abject poverty and exploitation for its black majority. Was it that some of us, the brightest among us, had acquired the same contempt the whites had for our perceived weaknesses — our 'laziness', 'indolence', 'irresponsibility'? Was it that their show of disapproval was to distance themselves from the rest of us? To show that they were different? A complex and subtle form of self-contempt?

So I worked for Fairclough at *Public Opinion* for a little over a year, starting in 1956, first as chief sub-editor, then as editor, when the Englishman who held the position left. He had been provided with a home and a car as part of the job. I received no such perks. My pay went from twenty pounds a week to twenty-five. My half-dozen reporters, some of the best in the business, received an average of twenty pounds a week.

Public Opinion was not the organ of the People's National Party. It was established as an independent nationalist paper to serve the cause of Jamaican nationalism. Fairclough himself was a nationalist, not a socialist, nor even vaguely left-wing. The party itself had an ambivalent relationship with the paper. Whenever we printed anything critical of any aspect of party policy or the performance of any government official or, indeed, of any business person who was a financial supporter of the party, I or Fairclough would sometimes get a telephone call of protest on behalf of this or that minister. I never had any such call from Norman Manley, even when we published matter I knew he did not approve of. Noel Nethersole, his Minister of Finance, was another one who never tried to influence or interfere. I recall one minister of government telephoning me to complain about an agricultural article; and another to demand a retraction of parts of an article about the Jewish-Arab conflict because an important Jewish friend had complained to him about its lack of 'balance' and 'fairness'. It was, I think, about the blowing up of the homes of Arab families whose relatives were arrested or killed or convicted of anti-Israeli activity. We had condemned the practice editorially. I refused to retract; Fairclough refused to interfere, though the Jewish gentleman in question was a friend of his who provided us with good advertising and printing jobs. In general, however, the politicians in power in Jamaica at that time showed a greater respect for press freedom — even over a paper they essentially owned — than I had witnessed in Africa, or anywhere else in the Third World except India.

There had been a bond of mutual respect between Norman Manley and me from our first meeting in London. He and his wife had received me at their home, Drumblair, on my first trip. He had, from time to time, invited me to find out how my research was progressing. His suggestions of who to meet or where to find some piece of information had been helpful. Our friendship had deepened, though we had both been delicately careful. He respected my determination to avoid any partisan influence. This was to be my book on Jamaica. During my stint at *Public Opinion* there were no such restraints and inhibitions. I got to know the man reasonably well. We shared a common passion for music, literature, the exploring of ideas, world affairs and the state of black people in the world. He also took a great liking to Daphne.

Norman Manley was of the mould of Jawaharlal Nehru. He was personally quiet and austere, a natural intellectual and genuinely tolerant of views with which he did not agree. He was what in South Africa would be called Coloured. His wife was an English woman who was distinctly white by South African standards, but was yet a distant cousin of both Norman Manley and Manley's cousin, William Alexander Clarke, later William Alexander Bustamante. Bustamante was to be Manley's great political rival in the shaping of what became the most stable two-party parliamentary democracy in the Caribbean and the Third World during the 1950s and 1960s, and which was almost destroyed in the 1970s when Jamaica was overwhelmed by the ferocious dogs of the Cold War. Both the elder Manley and Bustamante were no longer on the scene during the undeclared civil war of the 1970s and 1980s. While they were around, their understanding of the personal restraints and delicate balance required for multi-party democracy to survive ensured Jamaican political stability. In that climate economic progress was steady; education, the health system and other social services grew, and gradually but steadily the quality of life for most Jamaicans improved.

It was a particularly exciting time for me personally. At long last I could become involved in a positive way. All my life up to now had been spent in fighting against racism, against colour prejudice, against active discrimination, against political and economic exploitation: always against, always negative. Now, at last, Jamaica gave me the opportunity to work positively for change, for development, for social equity. I was becoming part of a process of building rather than of tearing down. In the South Africa of my childhood and youth, I had to be against the system as an affirmation of my humanity. In Europe I had to be anti-colonialist, anti-imperialist. In the Jamaica of my adoption I affirmed my humanity by becoming part of the process of the building of a nation. It was emotionally emancipating. I threw myself into working *for* Jamaica with a passion which had previously been used only to struggle *against* colonialism, empire and racism. Fighting for is much more liberating, much more exhilarating, than fighting against — even though it is only the other side of the same coin.

I remember the first time I took the family up to Red Hills to see the land that was to be our home. It was a Friday, the end of a particularly wet October. I had bought a small second-hand car and this was to be a family occasion: no friends, just the five of us with something to eat and drink. I had grown used to the winding, twisting drive up the hill, so we reached Tiny's bar in less than half an hour. It was early afternoon and men returning from their fields, some leading donkeys carrying hampers laden with produce, others with big bags on their shoulders or heads, congregated in the clearing outside the bar. They 'parked' their animals and goods and stood talking and sipping rum and water, rum and coconut water or rum and milk — cow's, evaporated, condensed — according to taste, fancy or state of pocket. Tiny scribbled the price of each round ordered on a bit of brown paper which he spiked on a piece of wire. The chat was lively, humorous, ribald, with sudden loud eruptions of laughter. I had grown familiar with these delightful after-work sessions on Friday afternoons and I knew many of the participants, so some invited me to join them until they saw the family. Women and children never took part in such 'street' events.

I introduced Daphne to Tiny and he in turn introduced her to his two brothers and sister who were at the shop next to the bar. The corner of Tiny's eyes crinkled, a warm smile lit up his face as he grasped Daphne's hand:

'This is Miss P!' he announced to everybody. Some of the men raised their glasses. Daphne has been Miss P ever since to the Red Hills community and the small satellite communities around. Then we drove the three miles to the foot of my hill and parked at the mosquito-breeding standpipe. I had forgotten to bring a stinking kerosene torch, so the swarms of mosquitoes assailed us mercilessly. Old Mr Markland, the wiry hermit who lived in a little hut behind our hill and who was the guardian of the standpipe, and sold four-gallon tins of water for a few pence to the people who lived in the bush, came out to meet us, swinging a broad banana leaf against the mosquitoes. He looked like the earth and it was hard to even guess at his age. He had travelled and lived in Central and South America in his early years. He once had a wife and family. He had once been a follower of Mr Garvey. Bad people who pretended they were Garveyites, had made collections on the promise of taking people back to Africa. They had taken everything he had. He had lost his family. So now he was alone up here in the hills. He told me Mr Patterson, the road builder, had cleared a walkway up to the top, and his men had started on the road itself. 'You will see it on the way up.' Then he gave Daphne a delicate little white orchid and turned back into the bush in the direction of his hut. We climbed the hill.

It was an easier climb compared with the first time, but not for my family. For them, this was the first time, and they all complained bitterly. It was so far from anywhere. The mosquitoes were biting all the time. Why had we left our nice home in Debden? They did not like Jamaica. Could we go back to Debden? I said somebody else was now living in our home. That only deepened the misery. We reached the top. I gathered twigs and made a smoky fire near the dead old trumpet tree. Aron was curious about how lightning had struck it dead.

'Like the derricles in Debden, daddy?' Derricles were thunderbolts.

'Yes.'

'But they never killed the trees on our hill?'

'We did not have the same kind of lightning.'

'Why not? Is it bad lightning?'

I was getting into deep water but the misery eased a little. The two older ones were suddenly excited by finding sea-shells and smooth round sea washed stones so high up and so far from the sea. How had they got there? Had the sea once been as high up? Their excitement grew as they hunted for, and found, more sea-shells and fossilised imprints of sea-shells in the white marl stone, and the smooth round black-and-white pebbles usually only found by the seashore or the banks of fast flowing rivers. They wandered off, forgetting the mosquitoes and the lightning, building fantasies around the sea-shells and pebbles so far from the sea. The little one, now two years old, grew tired. Daphne sat on a flat stone and adjusted her legs and clothes to make a cradle in which Naomi dozed off. I had watched Daphne closely all the while. If she really did not like this place, it would be a great disappointment and setback. I would not persuade, let alone try to force, her to accept it. She either wanted to be here or we would have to start all over again; find another place where she would be happy. The risks would be great. I would not, certainly not in the short term, recover the money put into this land. What remained of our pool of savings which had made possible this enterprise was now too small to re-launch anything similar. It was enough to clear the land and begin building; not enough to find new land and start afresh. I knew how precarious life could be in a Third-World country with no social security safety net. If I were to get ill and be unable to earn anything, it would not be as it had been in England. If anything were to happen to Daphne or any of the children requiring costly health care, there would be no National Health Service or child welfare support to fall back on.

I had thought of all this, but I did not want her to be influenced by these considerations into accepting what she really did not want. I knew her well enough to know that location, where she lived, was of cardinal importance. If there was harmony between her and her environment, there would be harmony between the two of us; and harmony between the two of us would make for harmony with and between our children. Whenever we had argued and disagreed and fought, as all families do, it had always affected the children. We could not quarrel without upsetting them. I think I realised that more sharply than she did. Sometimes, in my anger, I thought she exploited my desire to avoid a quarrel for the sake of the children. She would push harder to get her way. When her anger abated she realised this and tried to make amends. The damage usually lingered. We could both be hot tempered and stubborn. She cooled down more quickly. It took me much longer to regain my equilibrium. When we were cool, thinking beings, we always thought of what was best for the children. When we lost our cool we usually lost sight of that and upset them. In an unfriendly environment life would be trying for all of us. I would do everything in my power to avoid that. So I watched and waited for her reaction to the place.

I stoked the little fire. The smoke kept the mosquitoes at bay. The two older children were out of sight; only their excited squeals at new discoveries reached us. We were not worried. Jamaica's little creatures are not as dangerous as some of the small creatures I had known in Africa and she had known in Java. The little snakes here are harmless; scorpions can cause nasty painful swellings, nothing more. Our children knew they were to avoid troubling little creatures. The soothing tranquillity of the place was all about. I sensed that she was immersed in it and my spirits lifted. When she adjusted her position without disturbing the sleeping child, looked back at the hills looming behind and slightly above us, I felt it would be alright. The Blue Mountains rising high in the east; Kingston and the Liguanea Plain straight ahead, looking south, stretching away was the Caribbean Sea until it spilled over the horizon, and the Plain of St Catherine to the west, were all laid out before us in the damp misty October sun. She had taken it all in. Now she nodded.

'Yes, daddy. This is home. It won't be easy. We can make it.'

She stretched out her hand. We clasped hands.

It was the end of October 1956, when the decision was finally made. The work on the road had already started in a small way. The big work, the building of a house and turning it into a home, lay ahead. The greatest step of all had been taken. The long journey to Coyaba had been successfully made.

9

Norman Manley's Jamaica

The general election which Norman Manley's People's National Party won in 1955 was the third such held under adult suffrage. The first two had been won by Alexander Bustamante's Jamaica Labour Party. Bustamante had been Jamaica's Chief Minister between 1944 and 1955. During that time the Governor presided over the Executive Council, 'the principal instrument of policy' in the island. The pace and character of constitutional change and the day-to-day running of the country were still under Colonial Office control. The civil servants were still under the control of a Colonial Secretary sent from Britain.

When Manley gained political power, he set about changing this in a quiet methodical way. Between 1955 and 1957 he transferred the powers of the Executive Council to a Cabinet of Ministers. The way in which this great shift of power was made was so quiet that the Jamaican people hardly noticed it. The Governor, Manley's opposite number in the delicate game of the shift of power from colonial to native hands, was Sir Hugh Foot, one of a handful of very bright and enlightened Colonial Office pro-consuls coping with the problems of the wave of 'decolonisation' then breaking out all over the world of empire.

Jamaica's population at that time was approximately one-and-a-half million; and the majority were black and poor. Kingston was a comparatively small city then, with very few cars, and a small, but strong, white and near-white mercantile community The only outstanding black or dark brown people were the lawyers, doctors and dentists and, of course, the clergy, though even there shade of colour was a factor. Sugar was the single largest employer of labour and wages were low. The bauxite industry was in its infancy, and tourism was still a small-scale, elitist affair, depending mainly at that time on the wealthy of British and European high society. American mass tourism was still in the future.

Into this Jamaica, still largely owned and controlled by a white minority, Manley injected a sense of national pride. Jamaica Welfare had been one of the earliest community self-help efforts he had launched. When I first came to Jamaica, I observed the activities of Jamaica Welfare all over the island. Its most striking feature was, for me, its utterly apolitical nature. Party politics was rampant everywhere, arousing intense partisan passions. People were either PNP or JLP, 'comrades' or 'labourites'. The odd thing was that the 'labourites' in the Jamaican context were the conservatives, while the 'comrades' were, at that time, predominantly of the middle class. The symbolism, too, was odd. The clenched fist salute of the 'comrades' did not signify the hard radicalism it would in Europe. And the V sign of the 'labourites' came oddly from the poorest, blackest, most depressed sections of society.

In Jamaica Welfare these odd differences were subsumed by a wide range of community activities in small towns and villages up and down the country. For the women and young girls there were housecraft training sessions: from how to keep drinking water safe, to how to cook a balanced meal on a small budget, to sewing, dressmaking, keeping a kitchen garden and poultry rearing. For the men and young boys there were farming sessions on the growing of crops and the rearing of animals and good land use habits. Young men from poor homes went to youth camps to learn carpentry, masonry, plumbing, electrical work.

The Jamaica Agricultural Society, the oldest mass organisation of small farmers and peasants, the Four H clubs of young people, even the world famous Jamaica School of Agriculture, the government's agricultural extension services, all became part of the educational thrust of Jamaica Welfare. Manley's Jamaica spread a vision of pride in self and community, a willingness to work our troubles away, a spirit of fairness between each other. Those who caught Manley's spirit threw themselves into the effort, and it was visible all over the land.

The government itself set the example. It was small, frugal, unpretentious. Manley and his ministers lived in their own homes, drove their own cars, paid for utilities and domestic help out of their own salaries. Their pay and perks were modest and were made public in the annual *Handbook of Jamaica*. Manley and his ministers did not accept presents or gifts. It was a far cry from how it was in many of the newly independent states of Africa, where, with rare exceptions such as Julius Nyerere, politics and political power were avenues for personal enrichment. Manley's Jamaica, for me, was an example of how poor Third-World countries should set about working their troubles away.

At *Public Opinion*, when I took over the editorship, we tried to live up to the standards set by Norman Manley. The printery was old and prone to frequent breakdowns. Fairclough kept it going by a combination of faith and hard-nosed business effort. My small corps of half-a-dozen reporters included J.C. Proute, whom I had met in Barbados on my swing through the islands in 1955. He was an experienced journalist who had outgrown his tiny environment and felt hemmed in. I encouraged him to come to Jamaica. Then there was the young John Maxwell, twenty-three or -four at the time, brash, aggressive, brilliant. There was also the withdrawn and reclusive Derek Walcott from St Lucia. I cannot remember the number of times I had to talk Fairclough out of dismissing him. He rarely wrote, but when he did he always produced something special. Nash Herbert, a portly ageless character who always had his hat on, reminiscent of journalists in American pop movies, was our very reliable journeyman who could sniff out scandals faster than anyone else. Then there was our young features man, Jervis Anderson, quiet, reserved, intensely ambitious. Later, over the bitter objection of Fairclough, I got Consie Walters to join our group. He had lost his job at the *Gleaner* and was thinking of migrating. I knew he was a good journalist and persuaded him to stay. The artist, Carl Abrahams, became our cartoonist — and a good one, after he got the hang of the politics of drawing cartoons. Aston Rhoden and Charles Kincaid supplied our photographs, which at times achieved the level of fine art, especially in our weekly front-page pictures of beautiful black children.

For the little over a year I edited the paper, we turned it into an exciting weekly with first-rate features about Jamaica and Jamaicans. Our approach reflected Norman Manley's 'abiding faith in the good sense and goodness of the Jamaican people...' Our angle of vision, our perspective, was a challenge to the *Daily Gleaner*, Jamaica's grand old national daily which had been in existence since 1834. Other newspapers, dailies and weeklies, had come to challenge it, stayed a while, then collapsed. Only the *Gleaner* remained, flourished, became an institution in the life of the country. It was the paper of record, housing all the important details of Jamaican development and change over 165 years, seen from the angle of the descendants of the plantocracy and its rearguard resistance in a changing world. It had seen, reported and commented on the rise and fall of Marcus Garvey. The Garvey papers show how he saw and felt about the *Gleaner* and his passionate bitterness against its 'light-skinned' editor of the time.

It had been, as it has remained, the paper of the dominant economic, social and colour group in the society, though, by 1956 it had progressed to the point of having its first black editor in Theodore Sealy, a first-rate journalist in any context.

I liked and respected Sealy greatly, which made it that much more fun for our little weekly to 'scoop' the staid old lady two or three stories a week. John Maxwell, Consie Walters and J.C. Proute were the principal 'scoopers' on hard political and economic news. Herbert always had the juiciest bits of high-profile scandal long before they did. On Friday nights, after our paper was put to bed, the *Public Opinion* corps would swagger down to the Press Club on Water Lane, just off Harbour Street, take over the bar and play big about what would appear in tomorrow's issue of our paper. It usually got to Sealy and his people, which was the fun of it all. Our people often came back with exciting, though I was not sure always true, reports of Sealy's editorial conferences, our paper in hand, our scoops circled in red, 'tracing' his people for having missed these.

The *Gleaner* had the last laugh in the end. It is still there today: *Public Opinion* and at least two or three others since, including a couple of dailies, have vanished from the scene. It has new competition now which, for the moment, looks like lasting better than those others which had tried and failed. But the explosion in the electronic media — radio, television, satellite broadcasting, the internet — poses new challenges for Jamaica's oldest and most durable newspaper. How she copes with these will be as interesting and exciting in the twenty-first century as was her dominance and survival during the previous two centuries. The *Gleaner* will clearly still be here when the twenty-first century dawns. Whether she will survive for another century or two will depend very much on how she adapts to future change. The once dominant class whose interests she served so well for so long is dwindling. When she no longer needs to serve the interests of that class, whose interests will she serve? If she can transform herself into a truly mass-based Jamaican daily, serving the interests of the majority of the Jamaican people, she has as fair a chance as any newspaper in the world of surviving in the twenty-first century and beyond. Her greatest dangers may be her deep-seated class/colour biases and her confidence in her own ability to slow down, resist and, where necessary, hold back change.

The paper can survive; the ancient assumptions on which it was founded cannot. I remember, for instance, that when I first arrived in Jamaica on my assignment the paper could say I was a South African writer but not what kind of South African I was. Policy did not allow for the description of a person's colour except in the police 'wanted' notices for escaped prisoners and the like: John Thomas, alias Stale Bread, five foot-two, black complexion (or light black or dark brown; never white) scar on left cheek; murder convict; dangerous. So journalists had a problem letting their readers know I was not a white South African. It is easier today to talk and write about the colour of people's skin and about colour prejudice and discrimination. In those days nobody admitted to prejudice and discrimination based on colour. There were places black Jamaicans did not go to; a kind of 'gentlemen's agreement', not anything to talk about.

It began to change slowly in Norman Manley's Jamaica. One of the distressing symptoms of the attitude to colour by even black Jamaicans was the almost traditional denigration of everything black or African-looking. Black mothers told their black children they were ugly because their lips were thick. Their kinky hair was 'bad'. Brown was better than black; the paler the brown the better. White was best. So, as in America, everybody black tried to straighten their hair and bleach their skin. The results were disastrous at times: people got skin and scalp ailments. Blonde, hennaed hair on the head of a black woman can be embarrassing, disconcerting. Others denied being Jamaican. They were Panamanian, Cuban — any kind of Hispanic — so long as they were not Jamaican. And talk about colour was wrong, uncomfortable. The aspiring black artisans and lower middle-class groups — except those who had been to the United States — were embarrassed by Marcus Garvey and talk of the Garvey movement. Some made a mocking joke of it, others treated it as subversive. A small few said blacks were responsible for their own plight. White people treated blacks as they did because blacks deserved it. They were backward, lazy, ignorant, did not know any better. Nothing too black could mean any good. I met black domestic workers who refused to work in the homes of black families. I met black families who treated their domestic helpers atrociously, as, I suspect, they imagined whites did. Some had themselves worked as domestic helpers in the United States and earned enough to come home and have domestic helpers of their own. Had they really been treated as badly by their white employers? Or was it an attempt to put a distance between themselves and those from whose ranks they had risen? A variation of the harsh judgement on their own who fall short that I saw in Fairclough, in Padmore, in Garvey?

I was very ambivalent about domestic helpers in our home. Our children had visited the homes of their friends and seen their friends ordering their domestic helpers about: a child calling a grown woman by her first name, ordering her to fetch a glass of water without 'please' or 'thank you'. My mother had been a domestic worker. Had those little white children in Johannesburg treated her in this manner? I laid down some initially unpopular rules for how helpers were to be treated in our home. In the end the best helper we ever had, who came to us as a young woman from the Accompong Maroons, and did day work for us for about nineteen years, became part of our family while making and raising a family of her own up in Rock Hall. Daphne taught her to sew at the same time that she taught her own daughters; together they learned each other's ways of cooking and shared the household chores This kind of sharing came easily because of the strong African retentions of the Maroons. When Maisie finally left, Daphne's attempts to establish similar relationships with other helpers were disastrous. They mistook it for 'softness' and some robbed her of pots and pans and cups and plates and knives and forks and spoons. Some even swiped food and drink to take home to their families. It was their way of augmenting their miserably poor pay, of expressing their resentment against a system which held them in low esteem.

Without approving of it, we understood why Jamaican middle-class households locked up food and drink and everything else they could. With rare exceptions, the relations between employer and employee, especially at the personal and domestic level, were, in many respects, a throw-back to the relations between slave-master and slave: hostile, distrustful, dishonest, adversarial. And all this was overlaid by the hard, often intractable, matter of race and class and colour. When black people handle each other in this way, they become like those whose values and systems they say they oppose. 'I am become mine enemy'. So my trade unionist friend was one of the greatest resisters when Michael Manley, in the 1970s, introduced a national minimum wage of five shillings an hour for domestic helpers.

When will we get over this deep psychic and emotional damage done by the racial experience? When will the scars heal and disappear? What can we do to hasten the process?

I knew Norman Manley had experienced prejudice and discrimination. He and a brother went to war for Britain in the First World War. He returned, but his brother did not. Like most of the survivors who fought in the trenches in that war, he said little about it. I sensed the hurt — not all because of prejudice and discrimination, though that was there too — in much the same way as I sensed it in conversations with DuBois and Langston Hughes and all the others whose hurt and anger are not expressed in violent language or action.

How do you teach a people riddled with self-contempt, whose received history taught them they are worthless, whose environment taught them self-contempt, how do you instil pride and self-respect and respect for each other in such a people? We talked and thought about this and I thought that Norman Manley, a brown man grown up in a relatively privileged setting in post-emancipation colonial Jamaica, in which other brown men over the years, had thought and struggled, had with some reluctance, decided that being successful and wealthy, even being the most successful barrister in his island, would not compensate for the hard knot of hurt left by the white world's racism. Like all those others, like DuBois, that superlative scholar, he had to do something about it. I found Norman Manley the most reluctant of all the politicians I have met in a very long life. He was a wonderful family man, a lover of music and the arts, gregarious, interested in literature and oh, how he loved the hills and mountains of his beloved Jamaica. In a world free of empire and colour Norman Manley would not have become a politician, just as W.E.B. DuBois would not have left his scholar's environment to go into the harsh world of politics and protest. This was the common thread linking all those in Africa, Asia, Latin America and the islands of the seas who were compelled to confront DuBois' problem of the twentieth century. Norman Manley was in that tradition.

Manley's Jamaica made steady progress. Its budget was balanced each year. It recorded a small surplus each year. More children went to school. *Public Opinion* campaigned strongly for that very elusive target of spending 25 per cent of the national budget on education. At one stage we got as close as 20 per cent. Those were good days for environmental protection. The head of the British-owned West Indies Sugar Company, Harold Cahusac, was a native-born white Jamaican whom Manley put in charge of protecting the island's watersheds. Cahusac had enormous respect for Manley and they enjoyed a warm friendship; they also shared a common love of the land. Daphne and I went on several day-long watershed inspection trips led by Manley and Cahusac. The lush green protection areas were a joy to behold.

Watching and listening to these two men — Manley was older, born near the end of the nineteenth century, Cahusac was born in the second year of the next — I had my first experience of a white colonial who was more committed to the land of his birth than to his British 'mother country'. In South Africa the white Afrikaners after three centuries still invoked their European origin to justify their racist behaviour. In 'white' East and Central Africa the settlers justified their 'alienation' of all the best lands from the Africans on racial/colour grounds. Cahusac, the native Jamaican, a patriot in every sense, was a new kind of white man for me; the kind I had not met up to that point. I met others like Cahusac later: white Jamaicans willing to be simple serving citizens of the land of their birth without demanding special privileges based on colour, willing even to accept the black leadership of their country. It was not perfect but it was an important beginning in Manley's Jamaica of the 1950s.

In the politics of the time the contrasting personalities of Manley and Bustamante, and the public reaction to the two men, were both interesting. The white and upper-class Jamaicans were almost uniformly opposed to Manley and his party. Most of them supported Bustamante and his Jamaica Labour Party. The JLP was not seen as a threat to white and upper-class interests. Manley's PNP was. The brown and black middle class tended to give guarded support to Manley and the PNP, provided they did not sound too extreme and did not interfere with their hard-won rights and privileges. The working people were split down the middle. Roughly just under half of them were members of the trade union arm of the PNP, the National Workers' Union. The other slightly more than half were members of the Bustamante Industrial Trade Union, the trade union arm of the JLP. Bustamante himself was president of both the party and the union. Manley had no direct hand in the NWU. The leadership of the Jamaica Agricultural Society cut across party lines, with the supporters of the PNP outnumbering those of the JLP, but the majority of the rank-

and-file small farmers supported and had voted for Bustamante's party in the first two elections under adult suffrage. However, over the years, since 1938, the PNP had been spreading the message of nationalism and social justice and this, added to changing social and economic circumstances, increased the mass following of the PNP. It ceased to be a middle-class grouping of mainly brown people and became a nationalist movement, much like the Indian National Congress and South Africa's African National Congress.

Bustamante was by far the more popular of the two. He was a demagogue and people felt closer to him and could, at the same time, laugh at him and mock his shortcomings. The people held him in less awe than they did his cousin Norman. They made mocking jokes about Busta, never about Manley. Busta was not as well educated or as well-spoken as 'me cousin Narman'. His ways were more like those of the mass of the Jamaican people. Manley was 'different'. Busta was shrewd and a smarter political manipulator of situations than Manley. And he was not hampered by any body of principles. He also had the support, sometimes tacit, often overt, of the Gleaner and a business community frightened by the clenched-fist nationalism and the language of 'comrades' in Manley's PNP. These, and the ignorance of the electorate, had made Busta an easy winner in the first and second general elections. Bustamante's government did not disturb the relatively enlightened colonial policies or the dominant position of the local white establishment He did, as far as lay within his power, try to improve the harsh conditions under which the black majority lived. His union provided excellent bread-and-butter services: better though moderate pay increases, improved conditions of work, regular hours and, above all, a measure of security of job tenure. These, at the outset, were more important than political power or even education. Busta himself had said you can't eat education.

By the time of the third general election, the PNP's nationalist message had spread sufficiently for it to win power. The price the

PNP paid was to have to purge itself of the small radical pro-Marxist group within its leadership. Without that political purge it may not have won that third election and the process of national development might have been delayed, or taken a different form and direction. In the event, Manley gained power in 1955. Bustamante accepted defeat with grace. The roots of the two-party system were deepened. Henceforth the Jamaican electorate had choices; they could change their government freely, without the chaos which accompanied such change almost everywhere else in the region. A government could lose power without its former ministers being killed or locked up or driven into exile.

Political debate, when we first arrived in Jamaica, was part serious national business, part street theatre, and all great fun. Members of one party attended street corner meetings of the rival party to heckle, provoke, mock, scoff and ask hard questions. Audiences loved it. One of the mocking jokes against Bustamante concerned his ability to spell. According to the story, at one public meeting, Busta was in full flight on a list of demands and promises. At one point it came to the matter of bread.

'The people want bread!' he declared; then for emphasis he spelled it out: 'b-r-e-d!'

Someone on his platform whispered: ' "a" ', Chief, ' "a." '

Busta said: 'b-r-e-d-a.'

This was, of course, a PNP version of what was supposed to have happened. It is a fair reflection of the often gay and happy mood of the street-corner politics of the Manley-Bustamante era of the 1950s. We watched and enjoyed it at weekends, going from the meetings of one side to the other without fear.

On the trade union front, the rivalry could, and did, at times turn ugly. The battle for representational rights, for membership, was intense. Hugh Shearer was the Island Supervisor for the Bustamante Industrial Trade Union. Michael Manley, Norman Manley's younger son, was the Island Supervisor of the National Workers' Union. There were a number of other, smaller unions, but these were the big two: the affiliates of the two major political parties. The key areas of struggle in the 1950s were the old sugar industry, new import-substitution local manufacturing and the new bauxite industry, which Norman Manley's industrialisation policies had done so much to foster and encourage.

Both Shearer and the younger Manley were striking figures, both tall, good-looking, charismatic. Shearer, the black man, was the elder by about a year, outgoing, with a ready and sunny smile. Manley, the brown man, was shyer, more reclusive, more studious. They both had the gift of attracting great loyalty, and the young women of their parties found both irresistible. They acquired, among the legions of their supporters, the status of folk heroes. The union rivalry which both led with such vigour did harm to the Jamaican labour movement for a long time.

When I met them in 1955 and raised the matter of the harm their rivalry was doing, Shearer did not seem too interested. After he saw me having lunch with Michael Manley at the same restaurant where I had lunched with him two days earlier, his warm friendliness to me cooled. It seemed a case of for me or against me; you talk to my rival, I cannot trust you. Michael Manley, on the other hand, seemed more interested in my concerns and we talked at length on ways of resolving the problem. However, when Norman Manley found out about this line of my enquiries he was very disturbed. He warned that in the present circumstances Michael could lose his mass following in the union movement if the workers got the idea that he wanted to make common cause with Shearer and the BITU.

In both sugar and bauxite the memberships of the two unions were so evenly divided that the two leaders found themselves forced into joint negotiations. The bauxite companies and the sugar manufacturers did not like to make separate agreements, so, in their own interest, they became facilitators for joint negotiations. Once they got down to it, Shearer and Manley discovered they made a great negotiating team. The studious Manley usually came with a well-prepared brief. Shearer was brilliant at seizing the central point of the brief and running with it. The bauxite and sugar workers benefited greatly. But old habits die hard, and union rivalry persisted, though with decreasing intensity.

At the level of the people, Norman Manley's Jamaica made steady but slow progress. Housing, education, health services all improved. Kingston and St Andrew had a reasonably good public transport system provided by a British transport company on franchise. The railway provided an acceptable and cheap service, stopping at the many towns and villages on the way to linking the capital to Montego Bay. A stable, middle-level economy and society were taking shape. Incidents of racial discrimination popped up from time to time. Investors sometimes brought in white managers and supervisors not used to the Jamaican way of underplaying racial difference and prejudice. The government usually kept a close watch on these. Any overt act of discrimination was usually dealt with by the withdrawal of a work permit or some discreet pressure on the management concerned to repatriate the offending person. The more enlightened white Jamaicans ensured that the foreign staff they imported were made sensitive to Jamaican mores. So 'race relations' were made to seem better by the careful suppression of all their outward manifestations. That was, until a young Jamaican lawyer, recently returned from a long sojourn in Britain, opened the very sore point of the skin colour of all the people who served the Jamaican public in their banks and business offices.

Millard Johnson came back to Jamaica angry about his experiences as a black man in Britain studying law. When he saw, here at home, only whites and pale coloureds in all the front offices and at all the tellers' windows of our banks, his anger exploded. He re-launched the

People's Political Party, the party originally founded by Marcus Garvey. For a time, Millard Johnson's revived PPP flourished. He held huge public meetings in Kingston, at which he denounced the politics of 'The Two Cousins' in fiery language. The latent resentment of the blacks at their lowly status erupted into angry street marches and demonstrations in front of selected business places, which frightened the business community and the paler-skinned. The government dared not suppress Johnson and for nearly two years he dominated the political landscape. Because I did not denounce his racist rhetoric in my news commentaries, my sponsors at that time withdrew their sponsorship. Millard Johnson, on the other hand, assailed me from his platforms for not supporting his campaign. We had moved into an uncompleted Coyaba, so one day after I had just come home from a hard day and had gone to sleep, resting before going down for a night broadcast, he drove up and demanded to see me. Daphne explained that I had just come home dog-tired and gone to sleep, that I had to go back down in a couple of hours, that she would not wake me. An angry Millard Johnson waited a while, then made his way down. I got a threatening and abusive phone call late that night.

All my time was consumed between running the paper, doing the daily news commentaries and building our home up in the hills. The building was slow and difficult. Trying to lead normal lives with workmen all about was not easy. The road was not complete and all the material, as well as all our household needs, still had to be carried by head from the standpipe corner to the top of the hill. The builder hired scores of women from Rock Hall to carry the building blocks; masons and their helpers carried the steel, carpenters and their helpers the lumber. At first, water too, was carried in this way in four-gallon kerosene tins. Then I hit on the idea of getting half-a-dozen of the longest rolls of hose and a dozen 45-gallon drums. We connected the hoses to each other, running them uphill as the crow flies and filling the drums near the building site.

No matter how much I gave the builder for his weekly pay-bill, he was somehow always short, and every Friday evening I had to find extra cash to make up some shortfall. Every now and then the work stopped because the builder had not paid for some agreed portion of the material and the supplier would not release any more till the old bill was paid. In the end, I bypassed the builder, paid the supplier directly, and the material flowed more steadily. The builder saw this as questioning his honesty and integrity and brought the work to a halt. I could not find him for a week. Just as I was about to arrange with the senior mason to supervise the work, the builder arrived at the site by taxi all the way from Kingston. He was in jacket and tie despite the hot Friday afternoon sun, a trilby squarely on his head and a spanking new leather briefcase tucked under his arm. His anger of the week before had vanished. He greeted me with warmth. He had settled some problem on the north coast and the work would not be interrupted again. He lived up to that assurance. I continued to pay my suppliers directly and nothing further came of the matter. Up in Rock Hall, the rumour spread that I had brought a keg of African gold to build my home. In reality, money was running low and we were anxious to complete the floor tiling, put in as many doors and windows as possible, then close down the job and do the rest of the work ourselves, in our own time, at our own pace.

The gregarious social life of Kingston was time-consuming. When we were at Henderson Avenue friends who did not normally come so far downtown dropped in uninvited, unexpected, almost every evening. Sugar Mill rum, a favourite at the time, was under ten shillings a case. Food, too, was inexpensive. The cost of entertaining our friends was no problem. Time was. There was no hope of doing what I had to do to earn a living and still find time to write. The distance to Coyaba made a world of difference.

About this time the ongoing debate about a federation of the West Indies came to the fore once more. This time it looked as though the regional leaders were in earnest. Both Manley and Bustamante met with the other regional leaders in Montego Bay. A timetable was set and the British government encouraged the setting up of the Federation of the West Indies. Committees of civil servants, of planning groups, of specialists on this, that and the other, travelled between the islands and federation took on the air of reality.

To earn more money, I had begun, in 1958, to broadcast a daily five-minute news commentary on Radio Jamaica, part of the British-owned region-wide Broadcast Relay Group in England. As I remember, I was paid two guineas for each broadcast. What started as a small side job became, for the next forty years, one of the important public education tools in the country. Many people, especially at the lower levels of society, came to look forward to the daily five-minute review and explanation of the most important events of that day, locally and internationally. It was somewhat similar to the lectures I had delivered in Britain for the Workers' Educational Association — only by radio this time, and condensed into a tight five-minute time frame. I finally ceased doing these news commentaries this year, 1999, at the age of eighty. The commentaries themselves are continuing, having become part of the Jamaican radio landscape. But radio, and later television, broadcasting, became part of the party political struggle for power and I often found myself caught in the middle of it all.

In the beginning, Radio Jamaica was little more than a vehicle for canned music, potted news bulletins provided by the *Gleaner* and advertising. Its Board of Directors was made up of local businessmen. We tended to have an overlapping listing of the same names of businessmen and corporate lawyers on the Boards of Directors of all the island's major companies. Someone at the University of the West Indies at Mona once described them as the 'Twenty-One Families' who controlled Jamaica's wealth. Radio Jamaica's managers, imported at first, local later, were servants of the British parent company. This was how it was throughout the islands; this, indeed, was how it was throughout the empire. Rediffusion, like Cable and Wireless, was part of the commercial business extensions of empire.

This was one of the things Norman Manley was not happy about. He thought that not all of a nation's means of communication should be vested in foreign hands. He was not opposed to foreign ownership, but to *only* foreign ownership. So he set about organising a Jamaican-owned radio, and later, television service. He tabled a Bill in Parliament in 1958, setting up the Jamaica Broadcasting Corporation as a publicly-owned national entity. JBC went on the air in June of 1959. Manley was angry with me for not applying for a job at the new station. I knew what he wanted for the station. I wanted to see whether the managers of the station had the same vision for it, and above all, I wanted to see whether the party politics of the time would allow for a truly free publicly-owned media house. His criticism of my attitude was that I had to help make the freedom I expected. But I was, after all, an outsider, not even a West Indian by birth, so I held back. I did not want to become what I had always criticised: the smart-ass expatriate coming in to tell and show the natives how to run their affairs. If, one day, I earned their acceptance and acquired citizenship in an independent Jamaica, I would have the right to that kind of involvement. He said nothing; I do not know whether or not he agreed with me. I suspected not. However, I did get deeply involved in the great debate on the West Indies Federation when Radio Jamaica launched a weekly *Forum on Federation*, of which I was moderator. It ran between 1958 and 1961. I also became Controller of a regional daily radio news hook-up between the islands of the Federation, which lasted until the collapse of the Federation after the Jamaican referendum of 1961.

At the height of the federal period, during 1958-1962, Eddie Young, a fiercely patriotic Chinese-Jamaican and a former teacher turned successful insurance executive, offered to finance a regional monthly magazine and invited me to edit it. The *West Indian Economist* was born and Arthur Lewis gladly lent his name to the enterprise. Leaders and intellectuals of the region welcomed the magazine, contributed to it and helped turn it into an influential organ of information and opinion on the West Indies Federation.

Eddie Young was a strong supporter of Bustamante's Labour Party, but such was the general atmosphere of tolerance in Norman Manley's Jamaica that I could take Eddie Young to one of the annual Manley parties at Drumblair to raise money for good social causes without any fear that PNP die-hards might turn on him or the hosts might embarrass him. Manley's Jamaica was more tolerant of dissent and disagreement than I have found anywhere else in the developing world. I remember Eddie Young coming away from that particular party bemused by the warmth of his reception by the great man himself. For him the myth of the cold, aloof intellectual, so forbiddingly different from warm, down-to-earth Bustamante, was dispelled forever. He did not change over to the PNP. He simply became a better Jamaican patriot and I often teased him over his new vision of a 'greater Jamaica' in line with the Athenian culture he studied as a schoolboy.

Millard Johnson's undoing finally came when his party fielded candidates for the general elections of 1962 and they were roundly defeated. They polled less than one per cent of the votes cast and all lost their deposits, as third parties and most independents had been doing with increasing frequency since adult suffrage. In the first general elections of 1944, independent candidates had polled thirty per cent of the votes compared to the PNP's 23.5 per cent. The winning JLP had polled 41.4 per cent. All the other parties between them had polled a total of 5.1 per cent. In the second general elections of 1949, the PNP polled 43.5 per cent of the votes; the JLP 42.7 per cent, and independents got 12.6 per cent; two other parties between them shared 1.2 per cent of the votes. But though the PNP won most of the popular votes, the JLP gained more seats, reminiscent of Britain's Labour Party gaining big popular majorities and losing elections. In the 1955 elections, the PNP gained 50.5 per cent of the vote to the JLP's 39.03 per cent, but won only 19 of the 32 seats with the JLP winning the other 13. Independents were down to 4.95 per cent. There were three so-called 'third parties who between them polled just a little over four per cent of the popular vote — less than the independents. In 1959, the PNP won 54.8 per cent, the JLP 44.3 per cent, four 'third parties' combined received less than one per cent of the popular vote; there were no independents. In 1962, after the Federation disaster, the JLP won 50.04 per cent of the vote and a return to power. The PNP received 48.59 per cent and became Her Majesty's Loyal Opposition. Millard Johnson's People's Political Party fielded candidates in 16 of the now 45 constituencies and polled 0.86 per cent of the votes; independents in 8 constituencies received 0.51 per cent and, like all Millard Johnson's candidates, lost their deposits. The Jamaican electorate, not fully enfranchised then, had rejected Garvey's 'race politics' in the 1920s; they rejected Millard Johnson's version of it in 1962. They also rejected independents and entrenched the two-party system.

But Millard Johnson had made his major point back in 1957/8 when his agitation brought the black masses out on the streets and forced a change in employment policies and practices in banks and front offices throughout the country. The over 90 per cent of black Jamaicans began to see black faces in front offices and at the teller windows of the country's foreign-owned banks. The whites, Jamaican and expatriate, and the brown Jamaicans had panicked at the perceived threat of a black uprising and did, out of fear, what they would not do out of reason or decency.

Why did the black majority embrace Millard Johnson's strident demands for opportunities for blacks while rejecting him at the polls? Was it a highly developed political sophistication, or a cynicism born of the long survival struggles during and after slavery, when the rebellious leader was often sacrificed in the interest of the group? He had opened a door that needed to be opened. What else could he offer them? His own party was divided. He had no money backing. The story was that his father had given him a few thousand pounds to make his bid. If he failed, he was on his own. It was safer to go with the two major parties and the 'benefits' — the little road work, the housing, the 'tickets' to get farm work in America or Canada — they could provide. Millard could offer none of these, even if all sixteen of his candidates had won. The two major parties had shown signs of closing ranks against him. The big people with money backed the two parties, contributed to both to hedge their bets. So they were grateful to Millard but did not give him their votes. Only the few who were not realists did, and they were not important in the scheme of things. Experience had taught them the safety of always siding with the strong, or, where that is not clear-cut, with those most likely to win. This, it struck me, was the combination which undid Millard Johnson. There is an acute awareness of the problems of colour. There is also awareness of its complexities. And there is a strong in-built self-contempt. To have been in slavery is to have been degraded; to have been less than human; a beast of burden like any animal — an ass, an ox, a horse — is deeply damaging to a sense of self-worth. That is how it was until just over one hundred and fifty years ago. The scars — visible and invisible — ran deep.

After 1962 a bitterly disillusioned Millard Johnson left Jamaica. Unlike Garvey, he did not have to go to England. He was a trained lawyer and there were many independent black African countries where a black lawyer from Jamaica was welcome and could make a good living.

At the personal level, we had moved up to Coyaba by July of 1957. A few months after we started the *West Indian Economist* I gave up my work at *Public Opinion*. As the paper flourished, Fairclough and I seemed to find more issues on which to disagree. In the end the sheer weight of my workload — at the paper, the daily radio news commentaries, the *West Indian Economist* — settled the issue and I decided to give up the paper. When I told Fairclough, he seemed genuinely horrified, and for a week or so he and the City Printery Board of Directors tried to persuade me to stay on. In his usual discreet and careful manner, Norman Manley only asked whether I might change my mind. When I said no, he left it at that. *Public Opinion* had survived a history of fall-outs between Fairclough and the paper's many former editors. It would and did survive this one.

With one job less I could spend a little more time with my family. I could spend the weekends at home and take more of a part in the road-building, which Daphne had largely managed on her own with the help of Enos, alias Norwegian because somewhere in his antecedents an unknown Norwegian had planted his seed in the high hills of St Andrew, and this stocky, wiry, pale brown peasant young man with hazel eyes was the result. His dear friend and partner was Miss Euphie, big and black as the African night. She could have come straight out of today's Nigerian hinterland. She sometimes brought him a hot cooked meal, walking all the way from Rock Hall. She did not want him to eat only the heavy boiled 'spinners', little fingers of rolled up dough dropped into boiling water, which was staple among rural work gangs. She said it upset his belly. Enos oversaw the four or five men who gouged the driveway out of the marl bank which led the way up our hill. Daphne drove the old Land Rover hauling rock and stone and fine marl up and down the hill. When there was need to blast a piece of rock which obstructed the way up, I became the dynamiter. Enos drilled the holes; I got the permit and the required sticks of dynamite and lengths of fuse from the City Engineer on the order of the Town Clerk — both of whom knew Enos and his ability to do such dangerous work. Thus we gradually blew obstructions out of the way and moved up the hill.

While this work was going on, everything we needed for the house was carried up on human heads and shoulders. All our furniture and household utensils had been brought up thus. John Maxwell, J.C. Proute, Terry Smith and others, workers and friends, helped carry all our stuff up the hill. It was as things were done in the ancient days before money and motor vehicles and smooth driveways. Tiny talked some of my drinking buddies from Red Hills into joining in the 'hauling of Miss P's goods' up to her house. After the weekend shopping we carried blocks of ice to keep the refrigerator and the food and drink cold.

Hal Glave the government public relations officer when I first came, was now the public relations manager for the then Canadian-owned Jamaica Public Service Company, the electricity company. With his help and the paying of the cost of an electricity post we received electric power three months after we moved in, just in time for Christmas of 1957. About three months after electricity was connected, and after buying a small number of telephone shares I did not want, we received a radio telephone service. We could now drive up our steep road. We had light and telephone — all the amenities for 'civilised living' as the advertisement said! In retrospect, 1957 was a good year for us. At the time it was hard, difficult and trying; it was also our first Christmas at Coyaba. That made all the effort and stress and hard work worthwhile. Our children, it seemed, had adjusted to Jamaica. Daphne was absorbed in the land: she had started planting fruit trees, shrubs, flowers. I watched the bond between her and the land develop and grow deep to the point where she became so possessive of it that she would not let me plant anything because there was either no space for it or she could not take care of it. I felt excluded but did not mind it all that much. It made her happy and that, for me, was most important.

I had come to recognise this intense possessiveness of Daphne's over people and things she cared deeply about as the obverse side of an equally intense generosity which at times gave away precious possessions with little thought. I had only been seriously angry when she had 'lent' or given away books of mine without asking me. I had lost several very precious books this way: one, an especially inscribed first printing of the autobiography of Langston Hughes, the other Nehru's *Glimpses of World History*. My partner could be fiercely possessive about some things, like land and trees and plants and children, and even her drawings and paintings. She could also be dangerously, almost carelessly generous, with books and papers — things which are precious to me. Coming to terms with this has been a point of conflict and friction between us throughout the more than half a century we have been together in love and friendship. There was no question about her staunch support in times of trouble; we had shared much.

Up here, on Coyaba's long verandah, with the small swimming pool attached, facing out and down to the Caribbean Sea, the higher Blue Mountains to the left, the wide Catherine Plain to the right, we have over the past near on fifty years, sat with our children, watched them swim in the pool made for them for free as a 'morning sport' by our male friends from Red Hills, and watched them grow up and change; go to school and college and university, and leave home as rebellious young adults. On this verandah, for two decades and more, we entertained our friends at our Sunday morning 'Open House' of food and drink and talk and talk and talk. And always, after the children had gone to bed, after the friends had gone down to the city, when the world was far away and quiet, we, just the two of us, sat on the long verandah drinking chilled freshly squeezed orange or grapefruit juice, or, in their season, soursop or cherry or pineapple juice and we talked; half a century of sharing our thoughts and feelings and impressions and judgements of our world and its problems. In the process we changed, became the creatures of this place and the peace and tranquillity and clarity of vision it generated. Over the years it became, for us, a place of light in a sea of darkness; not investing us with any greater wisdom, just giving us a balance and perspective we had not known before.

I often had the sense, up here, of being in communion with other people and creatures who had inhabited this place in other centuries; a sense that they too had sought and found sanctuary and peace of mind on this hilltop and the gently sloping land which we have walked with generations of dogs as beloved companions — joyfully playing games when they, and we, were young; more sedately now that we are old and they — the fifth or sixth generation of Coyaba dogs — are growing old. There were times, in the still of a clear moonlit night, or in a storm with charged bolts of lightning piercing the dark, sometimes striking the earth, when it seemed that those spirits and presences were very close, very real. The past, the present, the future all came together here on those rare moments. We are, always, silently grateful that Jamaica and those who inherited it have allowed us to come here, welcomed us as no other place or people have, made us feel at home and then left us alone to make our lives on this piece of earth. I can think of no other place on earth where we could have received this kind of welcome.

Many, many years ago, back in the 1920s when he was a young radical, Langston Hughes wrote a poem which was really about a search for spiritual and emotional sanctuary. It began with: 'I am looking for a place in the world/where the white shadows will not fall', and ended: 'No such place, dark brother/ No such place at all.' Coyaba was a place where the 'white shadows' did not fall. It was also a place where no 'black shadows' would be allowed to fall — at least while we are the keepers of Coyaba. I tried once to persuade Langston Hughes to come and spend a Christmas with us here. He found the idea appealing, but somehow it just never happened. I am sure he would have been enchanted by Coyaba.

The one thing Daphne never needed was any sort of perspective on race and colour. She knew about it, of course; she had to face and deal with her own family about it. It just was never a factor in her own dealings with people. If I had been in China at the time when I had this great need for a woman to be my partner and the mother of my children, and if that Chinese young woman had been like Daphne, with her characteristics, then my wife and the partner of my life would have been Chinese. If I had been in India at that time, she would have been an Indian Daphne. If I had been in Africa, she would have been an African Daphne. It had nothing to do with race or colour; everything to do with time and place and need and person. She had to be a certain kind of person in a certain place at a certain point in time. When a young woman once asked me why 'successful black men' turn to white women for partners, I tried to explain what happened in my case. She wanted to make it a colour issue, so she did not believe me. I think the natural impulse among most people, no matter of what colour, is to stay within their own group; to marry the girl next door, or one like the girl next door, out of the same environment. So the majority of whites will fall in love and marry some person from their own white group. The majority of blacks will marry blacks; the majority of Chinese or Indian or whatever other group, will want to marry into their own group. This is how it has been throughout human history. Equally, throughout human history, there have been the minorities who have found themselves in faraway places in different cultures and who have met and fallen in love and married men and women outside their own group. It goes all the way back to the Old Testament, where the woman of one such says: Wither thou goest I will go; thy people shall be my people. These minority exceptions to the norm are as old as the story of human migration. All we have done in our time was to put a peculiar new twist to an ancient human love song.

When a Russian woman marries an Englishman, it is as much a mixed marriage as when a West African man marries an East African woman. There are the same differences of language and folkways, yet such marriages are rarely, if ever, called 'mixed'. If, on the other hand, that same Russian woman were to marry a black or dark-skinned, or Asian-looking Russian, that would be labelled 'mixed', even though they speak the same language, have the same schooling, grew up in the same environment and have the same cultural background. The argument that any marriage between human beings of different colours is 'racial mixing' is bedded in the genetic fallacy that there is more than one human race. The fact that in our century highly qualified intellectuals have indulged in this genetic foolishness shows the extremes to which we humans will go in pursuit of gain and power over others.

This is the dark side of our nature which makes possible colonisation and empire and the cynical manipulation of human societies in the narrow interest of this or that special ideology, this or that special class, this or that special race, or, in the closing days of our century, the so-called 'global village' under the control of the new ideology of 'market forces'. This is what made possible the rise to power of such human horrors as Hitler, Stalin and their brutal cohorts; which in turn made possible the terrible wars of our century in which vast armies of humans were slaughtered. Notions of race, class and colour have led our species into a blind alley. It has ceased to be the problem as posed by DuBois at the dawn of the twentieth century. It has become, on the eve of the twenty-first, the problem of how humanity must push aside all this overblown intellectual garbage built up over the past three hundred years to come together to save itself in the present. If we are not very careful, the very clever hairless monkey, with all his very clever technology, will turn the twenty-first century into a new technological, self-destructive barbarism, in which race and colour and 'the market' will be part of the irrelevances which bring us down.

These were some of the explorations of the mind we shared on the quiet nights on the long verandah here at Coyaba. Coyaba helped us to see and think more clearly about the human condition than we had been able to anywhere else.

Over these past near-on-fifty-years people from all over the world have come to sit with us on the long verandah and talk about the problems and visions for our world. Jim Gale and his family came from Australia to brood about justice for the Aborigines and how to make that part of the world a nuclear-free zone. South Africans, in their numbers, came to talk the language of Anti-Apartheid. A white Namibian journalist, who had for years suffered the persecution of the Apartheid state, sat on the steps of the long verandah and dreamed of how they would eliminate all forms of racism. She was startled but not surprised when I worried about the tribal differences which I feared might follow the end of racism. There were signs of it in many places in Southern Africa: the Zulu-Xhosa conflict under the surface in South Africa; the Ndabele-Shona thing in Zimbabwe; the Kikuyu-Luo-and others, in Kenya where the 'tribe that won the war' also wanted to dominate the peace. Only in Tanzania, where Nyerere, as deliberate policy, had worked and planned against it, was there no underlying threat of future tribal conflict. The white Namibian woman journalist said she would raise the issue with the black majority leaders when she got back. She had earned the right to raise hard questions; the right, even, to criticise with love. We both understood the power seekers would not hesitate to exploit tribal differences.

Others who came to Coyaba were some of the black Americans I had met on my two visits to New York with side-trips to other places. We had converted a most inappropriately placed carport at the side of the house into a small flat of one bedroom, toilet and shower, sitting room, and its own tiny kitchen. It could comfortably house one couple or up to four single people, using mattresses on the sitting room floor. It had its own small lawn, commanding the same view we enjoyed from the long verandah. The Americans were among the first to stay in the flat. Many others also did. Notably, our friend Hannah from our Paris and Paley days; Marjorie Nicholson of the Fabian Colonial Bureau and the British Trade Union Congress, godmother to our children and one of the two witnesses at our London Registry wedding and a dear intellectual battling companion over Britain's right to Empire. Oden Meeker and his wife slept in the flat. So did John Hatch and his wife before he became a Labour Peer. The Americans used the flat as a base from which to explore, first Kingston, then Norman Manley's Jamaica. Many of them came to love it and those who could afford to do so, turned it into the place to which to run in the cold winter months, or to have a few weeks of ease from the racial pressures of being black in America.

John Akar from Sierra Leone who had been a suave young rising diplomat when he visited us at Debden, and later his country's representative at the United Nations till he backed a coup that failed, turned up in Jamaica and visited us at Coyaba. He was still the same tall, dark and handsome charmer who, as some Jamaicans would say, could 'magnetise' the women with his witty charm and elegant grace. Many fell for him. He stayed in Jamaica for some years, doing freelance work for *The Gleaner* and, when it came, for our television station. He died here in Jamaica in the early 1970s and his body was flown back to Sierra Leone for burial. The leader he had betrayed did not carry the grudge to the grave.

Two white South Africans from our Debden days used the flat for a fortnight's visit to Jamaica and ended up spending six weeks with us, except for a few days on the north coast. When they visited us in Debden, Arnold Klopper had been a young Afrikaner physician still learning his surgical skills. He came from a poor white background. His father was a policeman. His wife, Mary, had been the one with money and her support had made possible his studies. Klopper was committed to his Afrikaner people but not to their Apartheid ideology, which made life complex and difficult. When they came to Jamaica, the difficulties and complexities seemed resolved. He was now a highly respected professor in his field. Success had bred a hint of arrogance and replaced his tentative air of the Debden days. Mary had changed less, was as we remembered her. Jamaica was a revelation for them. They saw black — and for them 'Coloured' — people in charge everywhere. It was possible for black people to govern themselves democratically; not with one big chief, one big leader, one big king deciding everything and handing down orders. They had been to Uganda where, even after the Kabaka and Idi Amin and Milton Obote, decisions were still made at the top and handed down. They found a press and radio that was not afraid of the politicians; a police force of civility compared with what obtained in Africa; a society of law, governed by the rule of law. And Arnold seemed a little more than confused by the recognition and respect I was accorded in all the places we went together. I had been in Jamaica a long time, I spoke daily to Jamaicans on radio. I had become part of the Jamaican landscape. Because he was still the South African in exile, he expected me to also be a South African still in exile. He found it hard to accept that I had long ceased to be in exile. I had sunk new roots; I was accepted as Jamaican; became only 'that damn South African' when my enemies wanted to curse me. They realised this was home for us and it seemed to unsettle my friend. He was still waiting to go home. He expected me to have the same mindset. I sensed a hint of let-down, of being betrayed.

I realised then how strong the mindset of exile can be; how people in exile can spend all their lives waiting to go home. It can influence the way you see your world, everything you do, and the way in which you act and react. At its extreme, waiting to go home can limit your capacity to go forward. Miriam Makeba, too, came to Coyaba to relax. We shared memories of the long ago when we were both young and filled with dreams in the dark pulsating life of the black slums of Johannesburg few whites had ever seen. She seemed to understand that Jamaica had become our home.

In June 1959 Norman Manley's Jamaica Broadcasting Corporation — the JBC — finally came on air and electrified Jamaica. For the first time in the history of Jamaican broadcasting Jamaicans spoke to other Jamaicans in the language and accent of Jamaica. Hitherto, the stories on Radio Jamaica had been canned stuff, produced elsewhere. The voices on air were British or American or imitations of the two. The JBC gave Jamaicans their own folk tales, in the Jamaican way. Louise Bennett and Ranny Williams entertained us with Jamaican folklore and we discovered how richly gifted we really were. Jamaican folk music compared favourably with the best of the world's folk music, and it was young enough to incorporate new songs like the hauntingly beautiful Evening Time by Barbara Ferland, an English woman who was a British Council worker in the 1950s and who fell under the spell of Jamaican folk music and contributed to it.

Radio plays, local as well as the best of the overseas classics, became regular fare. And how Jamaicans talked to each other through radio! The style and quality and character were distinctly Jamaican. Freedom to think your thoughts, to speak your mind, were limited only by the requirements of good taste, good manners, and doing no harm to others. For me personally, the period between the establishing of the JBC in June 1959 and its emasculation after 1962, was the high-point in the unfolding and flowering of Norman Manley's social and cultural vision for Jamaica. It was the high-point of Jamaican freedom of expression in all its many facets. We discussed, argued, debated, disagreed with each other on all the issues of the moment without fear.

Perhaps I was wrong. Perhaps I should have joined this exciting enterprise at its very start. But the lingering doubt persisted. Was all this happening because this is how Jamaica was? Was this what Jamaica wanted? Or was it happening because of Norman Manley's vision and wish for Jamaica?

Throughout this period the debate on a federal West Indies continued. It was nothing new. Talk of regional integration had been a constant feature of West Indian development over many years. At times it had seemed that the idea had been abandoned — only for it to resurface at one place or the other. There were points in the past when the smaller islands of the Lesser Antilles had been the primary movers toward regional unity. In the 1950s the larger territories — Jamaica, Trinidad-Tobago, Barbados, Guyana on the South American mainland — were the main movers. Norman Manley and Alexander Bustamante of Jamaica, Grantley Adams of Barbados, Eric Williams of Trinidad and Forbes Burnham of Guyana, were the key players. Before Eric Williams, an assortment of always-changing leaders, like a pack of continuously shuffled cards, had spoken for Trinidad. After the emergence of Eric Williams there was stable regional leadership, permitting for stable and reliable forward planning. Manley and Bustamante worked together on Jamaica's stand in the discussions. Errol Barrow, then leading the kind of intimidated opposition I recognised from my African experiences, was not consulted by Grantley Adams. Trinidad's opposition parties were in disarray and too numerous for meaningful consultation; Eric Williams was the sole voice of Trinidad and his People's National Movement held overwhelming power in Parliament.

And there was the extraordinary spectacle of the type of non-intervention in each other's internal affairs which allowed the rest to watch in silence as Forbes Burnham shamelessly manipulated Guyana's electoral system to keep Cheddi Jagan in the political wilderness. This was the one thing on which both Norman Manley and later, his son, Michael, disappointed me. Burnham used race and colour politics, fanned racial discord, between Guyana's people of African descent and her people of East Indian descent; and the leaders of the West Indies Federation in the making saw nothing, said nothing and did nothing about it. Burnham was an honoured member of this group which brought West Indies federation to the fore. The British and Americans had, for ideological reasons, supported and facilitated Mr Burnham. Jagan was an avowed Marxist, Burnham a devout political opportunist. I tried to raise this matter on our weekly *Forum on Federation* programme on Radio Jamaica. Nobody took me up. They cited the principle of non-interference in the internal affairs of member states. So the Federation of the West Indies came into being with the blessing of Britain, the mother country, on 3 January, 1958, with Norman Manley as leader of the group of broadly socialist parties holding the majority of seats. The opposition parties were not as clearly defined. There had to be an opposition for electoral purposes, so those who did not support the governing parties came together as a loosely based opposition. Bustamante became the *de facto* leader of the opposition after the federal elections held in July 1959.

Between 1958 and 1962, the politics of federation dominated Jamaican and West Indian affairs almost to the exclusion of everything else. There were heated debates about where the capital should be sited. Manley had decided not to go forward as the Prime Minister of the Federation, so someone else had to be chosen. There was argument about the wisdom or lack of it in Manley's decision. Many observers thought that was the beginning of the end of the Federation. The Governor-General of the Federation, a movie-star handsome Englishman, became, for a time, the dominant personality. Port-of-Spain, Trinidad, had been chosen as the federal capital. She had the resources to build a fitting capital. Bustamante had decided he would not leave Jamaica. Many felt Manley did not want to leave Busta at large in Jamaica while he went to live in Trinidad, a thousand miles away. So Grantley Adams became Prime Minister. He was near enough to oversee his home base from Port-of-Spain and could hop over by air within the hour should the need arise. It was a matter of protecting turf. I thought Eric Williams, the youngest of the senior political leaders, would have been the best choice in those early days. He, however, did not seem interested. He seemed to want the power of control that went with the provision of the money, without the responsibility of seeing things work. The leaders from the smaller islands, like the federal Finance Minister, the dandy Robert Bradshaw, from St Kitts-Nevis, and Grenada's eccentric Eric Gairy, were more interested in the bigger stage on which to play their roles. So, apart from Grantley Adams, none of the major leaders — Manley, Bustamante, Eric Williams — assumed direct federal leadership.

The Federation staggered along amid confusion and controversy for two years, and some of us hoped that it would, in time, settle down and become a regionally accepted reality. We hoped that in time the major leaders would find the courage to go forward and assume leadership. The civil servants were doing a first-class job; regional institutions were being established and run efficiently. Grantley Adams put his foot in it a couple of times, once by wanting to levy federal taxes without the approval of the units; another time he talked of the powers of the federal Prime Minister superseding the powers of the heads of government in the units of the Federation. All this made for suspicion and distrust.

Then, in 1960, Bustamante abruptly announced his party's about-face. He recalled his party's federal Members of Parliament from Port-of-Spain and called on the Manley government to hold a referendum on whether Jamaica should continue in the Federation or withdraw from it. His party launched a clever, carefully planned and orchestrated anti-Federation campaign which caught Manley's PNP completely off-guard. They had not anticipated Bustamante's about-turn. They had no way of nullifying its impact. Manley was forced to agree to the referendum. He delayed it for the best part of a year to give the electorate a chance to be informed on the issues involved.

A period of intense public education ensued. The PNP used all the resources at its command to spell out the long-term benefits of a federated West Indies in a fast changing world. The JLP countered with a combination which highlighted the failures and shortcomings of the Federation thus far: the attempts of Grantley Adams, 'the man from Barbados', to impose taxes and other laws on Jamaica, how Jamaicans with two cows would have to give one to the people of the small islands. Federation came out as a plot to take over Jamaica. They played on fears, some valid, some manufactured, to whip up anger at what those 'small-island people' would do to us if they got the chance. The PNP's campaign of fact and reason was no match for the JLP's whipping up of fear and prejudice, exploiting of ignorance. On the day of the referendum, out of a total eligible electorate of 774,787, 473,580 cast their votes. 256,261 voted to leave the Federation; 217,319 voted to stay in. Manley lost the referendum vote by 38,942. More than 300,000 eligible Jamaicans did not bother to cast their votes.

Down in Trinidad Eric Williams declared the new political arithmetic: eleven minus one equalled nought, and Trinidad withdrew from the Federation.

I remember a group of us, mainly journalists, were monitoring the results of that referendum of 19 September 1961 on Coyaba's long verandah. Some were hoping against hope that the Jamaican people would support the Federation. We had carried out our jobs professionally, presenting both sides of the story as impartially as we could. A few journalists were against the Federation; most were for it. Most saw unity as in the best interest of the region. We were critical of how the process had been handled, not of the process itself. So when the results were announced, there was despair that night. J.C. Proute, the Bajan, looked sick. Terry Smith and Aston Rhoden left abruptly. When we saw Rhoden the next day his face was scratched and scarred. He had fallen on his face as they ran down our steep rough road that night. Despair and anger, anger and despair at what the majority of the Jamaican people had been led to do to themselves and to a dream many generations of West Indians up and down this chain of sun-kissed, former slave islands had nurtured for so long. It had started to happen; now it was over. For how long? Another century of dreaming and hoping and struggling? That was a night without comfort.

A handful of disappointed intellectuals, mostly from the Mona campus of the University of the West Indies, were bitter in their criticism. One or two questioned this 'Westminster way' of doing things. It was possible to juggle the numbers to show that the outcome was not a fair reflection of the will of the majority: the huge rate of abstention and the smallness of the gap between the pros and the cons. In the end we all accepted that this was the will of the majority. This was the democratic way. The power to make the choices — wrong or right — belonged to the people. As long as that was so, the people could correct their mistakes, make new choices to reverse old mistakes. Or make mistakes, learn from them, then correct them.

I did not see Manley for nearly a month after the referendum. I had heard and felt the hurt in his statement accepting the results. He said then that new arrangements and decisions would flow from those results. There was confusion and a sense of drift. When I finally met Manley, the hurt and shock had eased, but the disappointment was still there. He said it had all turned out a costly waste of time. We had now to turn to the business in hand: independence for Jamaica on her own within the Commonwealth. We knew Britain would not resist that. We also knew that the chances, now, were that Bustamante and the JLP would inherit the power to lead that final transition.

Between the referendum of September 1961 and the general elections of April 1962, Jamaica was on hold. The Manley government behaved as a caretaker, the JLP opposition as a government-in-waiting. Those who had forced the collapse of the Federation were aggressively jubilant. They were everywhere, at street meetings, on the radio, sure that they would form the next government which would lead Jamaica into independence. The clear, focused Manley vision of what Jamaica should be became blurred. For the first time since 1955, Jamaica was not sure of where it was going or how it would get there. The period of Norman Manley's Jamaica was coming to a close. The freedoms we had come to take for granted — press freedom, the freedom to mock and guy our leaders, to poke fun at them and at each other, in affection; to hold views from the extreme left to the extreme right without fear of being punished; the freedom to have and to read 'subversive' literature, the right to a passport and to freedom of movement inside and across borders — all came under threat. Because of the kind of person he was, because of the character and quality of his leadership, we had been secure in our right to these freedoms.

I had, after the referendum, in association with the likes of Mickey Hendricks and Merrick Needham, moved from the commercially oriented Radio Jamaica to the Jamaica Broadcasting Corporation. Hendricks had become JBC's General Manager, Needham its Programme Director. I did my regular daily news commentaries in the same way as before, in the same time slot; only the station was different; I took part in the exciting JBC discussion programmes. There were pressures from the cocky JLP government-in-waiting. We felt sure we could contain them. We had taken over the lead in popular ratings and audience numbers. We had dislodged Radio Jamaica from its dominant position. Any new government would surely recognise this reality and leave us alone to continue doing what we were doing so well. The tolerance of Norman Manley's government had lulled us into a false sense of security. It did not last for long after he lost power.

The general elections returned the Jamaica Labour Party to power with 26 seats to the People's National Party's 19. In 1959 the PNP had won 54.8 per cent of the popular vote to the JLP's 44.3 per cent. This time the JLP won 50.04 per cent to the PNP's 48.59 per cent. The collapse of the Federation undid Norman Manley's hopes of leading Jamaica into independence. I knew privately how deeply this had hurt but he never criticised the Jamaican people. The choice was theirs and he accepted their choice without question. Manley, in defeat, commanded my deepest respect.

10

Bustamante / Seaga

The elections were in April 1962. Within four months, on 6 August 1962, Jamaica became independent and chose, as most of the other former British colonies had, to remain within the Commonwealth. William Alexander Bustamante, well over six feet tall and with a shock of white hair standing up as though electrified, was a striking and towering figure at the London talks preceding independence. Bustamante was 78 in 1962. His cousin, Norman Manley, was nine years younger. Busta was flamboyant, larger than life, the air of a Spanish Grandee about him. The popular British press loved him. Manley, beside him, the man who had presided over the drafting of the independence Constitution, went almost unnoticed until some important constitutional or political point arose. Then Bustamante turned to 'me cousin, Norman' to supply the answer. Bustamante showed affection and deep respect for Manley, Manley kept his feelings about his cousin to himself. I knew he detested Busta's autocratic style of politics. With few exceptions, those around Bustamante tended to fawn and flatter, saying what they thought 'The Chief' wanted to hear, doing what they thought 'The Chief' wanted done. Among the exceptions were his political right-hand man, Donald Sangster, and his trade union right-hand men, Hugh Shearer and Linden Newland. Robert Lightbourne, the brilliant author of Jamaica's industrialisation effort, was a respected senior advisor who did not need to flatter or ingratiate himself. The youngest member of this group of Bustamante insiders was Edward Seaga.

Sangster became Bustamante's Deputy Prime Minister and Minister of Finance. Lightbourne was made Minister of Trade and Industry. Edwin Allen, a teacher from rural Jamaica, became Minister of Education. And Seaga, at 32, became the youngest Cabinet Minister with the portfolios of Development and Welfare. The trade union leaders had no formal Cabinet posts but their influence on all decisions affecting labour matters was clear. John Gyles, from a white Jamaican farming family, became Minister of Agriculture. Under his watch, the world-famous Jamaica Hope breed of cattle nurtured by T.P Lecky was almost wiped out. Edwin Allen, on the other hand, did a great job of expanding education and educational opportunities for the poor. Manley and Glasspole's efforts under the PNP were improved on by Edwin Allen under the JLP, despite Bustamante's electioneering scoffing that 'you caan eat education.'

Industrial development, under Lightbourne, became more sharply focused than it had been under the PNP. Lightbourne had been a successful dye and tool manufacturer in the British Midlands. His expertise and experience promised to transform Jamaica into a First-World industrial producer. His trouble was that our local manufacturers of the time were 'screwdriver operators', importers of parts to be assembled in Jamaica, not real manufacturers. And they flourished on margins, subsidies, tax holidays and all other available concessions.

On the social development scene, Edward Seaga set about changing and re-naming the institutions the JLP inherited. Jamaica Welfare became the Social Development Commission. People were replaced for no reason other than they had been associated with the previous government. Partisan loyalty became an issue in voluntary social work as much as in paid work. The new government was putting its own stamp on the face of Jamaica, and to do so it had to remove or change the imprint of what had been Norman Manley's Jamaica.

Jamaicans of left-wing views returning from abroad had their passports seized and their radical books and papers — especially those dealing with either communism or black power — confiscated. The freedom of movement of some was severely restricted. The political climate took on much of the mood of fear and suspicion I had seen in places like Kenya and parts of West Africa.

Shortly after independence the news media came under active government scrutiny. *Public Opinion's* advertising from the government was cut drastically. Opinion journalism came under fire, first at the JBC then at RJR. Sponsors were put under pressure to drop certain types of programmes. My own news commentaries came under special examination and attack. Not long after 1962, the head of the firm which sponsored my commentaries was put under heavy pressure to stop the sponsorship because of my alleged bias against the government party. The pressure was so great that the man ordered an audit of all the commentaries they had sponsored. The auditors came up with a careful, detailed analysis which showed that I had been neither for not against either of our two main parties, neither for nor against our main political leaders. He presented the results of the audit to the people concerned and news commentary was left alone for a time.

On the straight party political front, events took a new turn. West Kingston, the constituency won by Edward Seaga in 1962, was one of the most depressed areas in all Jamaica. I had visited it often with Odel Fleming when he was the government's Chief Probation Officer back in 1955 and I had visited it many times since. It was a place of poverty and degradation which reminded me of the brute poverty of the Cape Flats of my young manhood in South Africa. The big difference was that there, though near the sea, the place was all desert sand. Here, at Back O' Wall, the earth was red dirt; things could still be made to grow on it. As with the Cape Flats, it was a place of shanty dwellings of bits of wood and zinc nailed and tied together. In party terms, it was almost evenly divided, with the PNP having perhaps a slight edge when it came to bringing out the votes. In the post-Federation election, the JLP had won a sweeping victory and Seaga became its Member of Parliament.

The new government and the new MP then proceeded to bulldoze Back O'Wall out of existence. Jamaicans were stunned; they had never experienced anything like it. Resistance to the bulldozing was brutally suppressed. A cowed news media reported the event without serious outrage. A few, like John Maxwell, wrote and spoke in horrified anger. The bulldozing proceeded till all the poor and dispossessed were driven out of their shacks. Then, in surprisingly quick time, new, tall, high-rise concrete buildings went up. New people, carefully scrutinised and selected, became the new tenants of the new buildings. Thus, Tivoli Gardens, Edward Seaga's own political power base, came into being. It was Jamaica's first closed political enclave. This was the prototype of the urban political garrison.

I remember Norman Manley being horrified by it. He was even angry with Dudley Thompson, who stood for the PNP against Seaga, for responding with violence to the violence against his supporters. But Anthony Spaulding, a brilliant young lawyer and PNP political firebrand, matched Seaga's garrison with one of his own in South St Andrew. Willy-nilly, the new politics was on us. The gun, as an instrument of electoral campaigning, was introduced during that election. Norman Manley was sure we had taken a bad turn in the road. We talked, then, about the fragility of the democratic process and of the dilemma of dealing with deliberate violence as part of the political process of a democracy. I tried to comfort him by telling him how Kwame Nkrumah had locked up his plotting opponents without ever hurting or killing any one of them. He would not be comforted. He saw, more clearly than most, where garrison and gun politics would lead Jamaica, even if we succeeded in bringing it under control in the end. In later years people like Lightbourne, Edwin Allen and many others came to recognise what Norman Manley had feared so much about garrison and gun politics from the outset.

Inevitably, the PNP responded by creating garrison constituencies of their own. But the first, and still the strongest and most tightly organised, on the eve of the new century, is Edward Seaga's Tivoli Gardens. It is a model community in many respects. The houses are good, the infrastructure is well-cared-for. It has good schools, good sportsmen and women and good sporting and social activities; it produces good community citizens. It is also a law unto itself — at times a group who see themselves as outside the Jamaican rule of law. It has protectors, enforcers and Dons to ensure that everybody within the community puts loyalty to the community above everything else. It resists paying rent and for utilities used. As a community, it has taken more from the public purse, and returned less to the public purse, than any other community in all Jamaica. At one point, a JLP minister of government, Wilton Hill, had to protest at the resources poured into Tivoli Gardens at the expense of other communities. It has ensured the safety of Edward Seaga's seat in Parliament in every election since 1962.

I am one of those who agree with Norman Manley's conviction that Jamaican democracy cannot co-exist indefinitely with closed garrison communities within it, functioning as autonomous fiefdoms of political Dons. For Manley, the threat to democracy inherent in the political garrison goes beyond which party sets up the garrison. A PNP garrison, ultimately, is as great a threat to democracy as is a JLP or any other garrison. It divides and segments a people, sets them against each other, undermines and distorts national unity and makes impossible serious long-term effort at nation-building. The interests of the garrison, the new kind of 'tribe', become more important than the interests of the nation. On this one point, Norman Manley's party has not always kept faith with his high ideals for Jamaican democracy.

But how do you deal with the reality of garrison politics?

Norman Manley had been angry and disappointed that Dudley Thompson did not stop his supporters from fighting back when they came under attack by Edward Seaga's supporters. If Thompson had stopped his supporters, they would have been sitting ducks; they would either have deserted him and his party's ranks or stayed home to avoid being beaten and blasted off the streets. Once election campaigns are turned into violent street battles, once firearms are brought into play, the old rules fall by the way. Free and fair elections are predicated on all contestants accepting the same set of rules, abiding by those rules, and persuading their supporters to do the same. If any one set of supporters, with or without the approval of their candidates, operate outside the rules, the whole thing falls apart. There were three options. First, the two party leaders, Bustamante and Manley, could have jointly decided and announced that they would not accept this form of campaigning. The two candidates would then either have agreed to peaceful campaigning or been replaced by other candidates. This course was not adopted. Second, Seaga and Thompson could have met and tried to agree on peaceful campaigning. This did not happen. Third, one could have withdrawn, ceding the election to the other and thus stopping the violence. This, too, did not happen. What was untenable was for one side to use violence, to kill and maim the supporters of the other side, while the other side tried to play clean, non-violent politics. So the campaign was violent and people were killed.

There had always been an element of skirmishing during street meetings and marches at election time; stones and bottles had been flung, a stick or fist fight here and there. There had never been the kind of deliberate, planned, violence as in the run-up to the 1962 elections. That was something new to Jamaica. The political gun, the 'Molotov cocktail', fire and terror became our new 'cultural weapons'.

It is easy to arm people — to put a gun into a man's hand — but difficult to take back that gun from that man. So the unlawful arming of poor Jamaicans began in the closely controlled political garrison. It became part of our new politics. And it developed and grew and spread as Norman Manley feared it would. It has been the curse of all our elections since, culminating in the bitter Cold War, civil-war, class-war elections of 1980. By then Norman Manley was dead. His dream and vision of an open, caring, creative, hard-working, self-respecting, free Jamaica was put aside.

I first met Edward Seaga in the 1950s at the home of M.G. Smith on Retirement Crescent in the Cross Roads area. He was leaving as I was entering. M.G. Smith introduced us and that was it. I did not know anything about him. He just looked like a white Jamaican to me. M.G. Smith, a close friend of both Norman and Edna Manley, was a pale, but clearly coloured, Jamaican. Seaga was unmistakably white. Smith and his wife Mary were brilliant social anthropologists. Smith was also an outstanding Jamaican poet, one of the voices of the national cultural awakening following the upheavals of 1938. Smith told me Seaga was trying to get a job at the Mona campus of the University, but there was some problem of which I never got the hang. My own first impressions were of a very serious, very ambitious, very focused young man. I usually smile politely at introductions. His hand was limp, no answering smile on his face. Cold eyes examined me and seemed not to like what they saw.

The next time I heard of him he was an officer of the Jamaica Labour Party and a protégé of Bustamante's. I had met Bustamante several times: first when I came to write the book and afterwards when we settled here. I had visited him at his Tucker Avenue home in Kingston and spent the best part of a day with him on his farm in St

Thomas. Bustamante always had people around him — political subordinates and supporters who always hung on his every word. He was a good storyteller with a novelist's gift for evoking atmosphere. He was immensely charming, with a strong streak of the autocrat and the bully. He genuinely liked Shearer, whom he treated like a son; he depended on Sangster to manage the details of his political office; and he respected Lightbourne's opinions and advice. Lightbourne could 'sell' an awkward or difficult plan or idea to 'The Chief'. I remember Lightbourne saying: 'Look at it this way, Chief...', and most times Busta listened and ended seeing it Lightbourne's way. All the rest, it seemed to me, were people to be used to suit Busta's purposes. I tried to, but could never pin down any idea or belief Bustamante had. Yet he was a shrewd judge of human character and I once saw him play the fool to bring out the fool in a very clever legal luminary. He also had a great capacity to make people feel he cared about them, that they were important. At Tucker Avenue, I watched Busta listen to his advisors, then, when they had all done talking, he would decide on the matter in hand: and that was that. He brooked no question once he had made up his mind. Those around him knew the unwisdom of talking back.

What made him choose Seaga as a protégé? And what kind of man wanted to be the political protégé of William Alexander Bustamante? A man who either respected and admired Bustamante, or a man who admired and desired the great power he had. I think with Seaga it was a combination of both. Busta had the great power he wanted to inherit; Busta was the kind of man he wanted to be.

Bustamante, like Manley, was a brown man in an overwhelmingly black country. A complex and subtle contest between brown and white for control and influence over the minds of the black majority was the backdrop to much of Jamaica's post-emancipation history. The more far-sighted among the whites and browns had always seen unity of action by the two groups as the safest way forward, with the co-opting, whenever necessary and wherever possible, of the brightest and best brains to emerge from the black majority. This they saw as the safest, most stable and predictable way forward.

In addition, they had over the years come to recognise the importance of structures and institutions as organs of social stability: the church, the community social groups, the thrift associations and the political parties. Anyone wanting to launch out on a political career had to join either the PNP or JLP to have any reasonable hope of succeeding. These two parties had proved themselves by surviving and forming the elected government of the country in turn. They were known and established entities. The day of the independents was done. New political parties had to show the ability to survive electoral defeats and setbacks before the electorate would entrust them with their votes. To get anywhere, at any level, you had to belong to some party, some association, some grouping which had its claim to attention by surviving as part of the fabric of society. It was so in business, in the professions — everybody who wanted to succeed had to belong to some recognised institution.

For Edward Seaga, or anyone else, to succeed in politics they had to be members of one or the other of the two parties. Many had tried other ways; all had failed. The politically ambitious with nationalist and socialist inclinations joined the PNP. Those with non-socialist, pragmatic or capitalist inclinations found their political home in the JLP. So the young brown and black intellectuals and doctors and lawyers and teachers tended to be in the PNP. The young businessmen, white, brown and black, as well as the doctors and lawyers, mainly black but against socialism, found their way to the JLP. The mass support of the PNP was largely the educated and the skilled — the black and brown middle class, the skilled artisans and the educated and unionised blacks.

The base of JLP mass support was made up of the poor, unskilled, illiterate or semi-literate black urban dwellers and rural agricultural workers, whose pay was still measured in two or three or four or five shillings a day when we arrived in Jamaica.

Thus, to have a successful political career, Edward Seaga had to join either the PNP or the JLP. The PNP was rich in the intellectual skills and talent Seaga had to offer. But there was no room for starting at the top, near the leader. Party structures and the path to advancement were clear; no shortcuts to the top by getting close to the leader. Personal advancement in an open, democratic party of freely contending ideas is much more difficult than in a party where the leader, by himself, with or without consulting others, can raise you up or pull you down. Edward Seaga rose fast in the JLP under Bustamante. He leap-frogged over many who had served the party longer. Bustamante nominated him to the Legislative Council in 1959, making him the youngest member ever. Busta named him to the committee of Parliament drafting the Constitution under which Jamaica would move into independence. He was elected assistant secretary of the Jamaica Labour Party. The man had, in a short time, moved to the centre of Jamaican political power, close to Bustamante.

With the dedicated help of an efficient public service, Sangster was running the government, Lightbourne was running the economy, Shearer was running the powerful Bustamante Industrial Trade Union. Seaga, who became Minister of Development and Welfare after 1962, was taking control of the party machine and quietly reshaping its image from the easy-going, pro-union, pro-*laissez faire* capitalism stance to something wholly new to Jamaica.

The strike at the government-owned Jamaica Broadcasting Corporation had been in the making almost from the time the JLP came to power in 1962. Commentators at the station had begun receiving notes from the Prime Minister himself any time they said something the government disapproved of. I received one or two such.

The people in the newsroom received phone calls; some were summoned to either the office of the General Manager, Mickey Hendricks, my friend from our Radio Jamaica days, or sometimes, from the new JLP-appointed chairman of the board — it was invariably over some complaint from the government. When I received a summons from Mickey Hendricks and heard the nature of the complaint against one of my broadcasts, that doubt I had felt at the start of the JBC was settled. The freedom the JBC had enjoyed under Norman Manley was a thing of Norman Manley's creation, of Norman Manley's vision for Jamaica. It was not inherent in the Jamaican political culture. It was a dream, a hope, an aspiration. And now, under Bustamante/Seaga, that dream was about to be put on hold. Norman Manley's great experiment of a genuinely free and independent government-owned media house of the highest quality was starting to come unstuck.

I comforted myself with the thought that Jamaicans had, between 1959 and 1962, witnessed and experienced for themselves the kind and quality of freedom of speech, of artistic expression, found in very few places anywhere in the world, and nowhere else in the so-called developing world. Things remembered do not die as long as memory lasts. Things remembered can always be revived.

A year or so later, a strike at the JBC obliterated what was left of Manley's vision. It began over whether the station should or should not have carried a minor news item about the desire of the workers to seek trade union representation. The government thought the item should not have been carried. The report was correct in every detail, but the two journalists responsible for its broadcast were sacked. The union to which the workers had turned, the National Workers' Union, was an affiliate of the PNP. Its Island Supervisor was Michael Manley. The Prime Minister was, nominally, in charge of information, but Seaga was effectively 'the minister responsible' and Seaga was not about to allow a PNP-affiliated trade union to represent workers at the government-owned JBC. At the very least, he would give them a very hard time about it. The result was one of the bitterest and most protracted strikes in the history of Jamaican labour relations.

When it was over, nearly a hundred days later, the original JBC, as I had known it, ceased to exist. The station remained on air, the name remained. A few of the corps of dedicated and talented workers, those considered 'not political' were kept on; the rest were made redundant and paid off. Most found other work, mainly in advertising and public relations. A few migrated. There were the inevitable human tragedies. A few young couples could not take the stress and the strains and pressure of unemployment and dislocation and their marriages collapsed. Many other types of relationships broke up.

The JBC became for all practical purposes the propaganda arm of the party in power. Its nightly news content, especially on television, was now dominated by government ministers making speeches, signing agreements, handing out 'benefits', by filmed speeches at business luncheons, banquets, dinners. For a time there were no discussion programmes, no commentaries, nothing controversial on air.

Edward Seaga's power and influence seemed pervasive. He changed things, renamed things, launched things. Up in Red Hills, our old community centre and the local Citizens' Association, which had run it for as long as we had been there, were split down the middle. Mr Seaga's people were on a new '100 Villages Campaign', which succeeded in dividing old and stable community groups of long standing along party political lines. Community elders had, in the past, settled problems between farmers, or young men, or boundary disputes, in the old traditional ways I remembered from the past. They dealt with and controlled praedial larceny by at times making the thief work for the one he had robbed — with or without a few lashes, depending on the nature of the offence. Crime was minimal and peace was the norm where communities were not divided. All this broke down under the new changes. Tiny and Biggy Hamilton and all the elders who had kept our Red Hills community united and peaceful withdrew from community affairs when the government's '100 Villages' came. New people the community did not know took over; the community split, order and control declined until there was need for a police station to keep the peace in the area. This was the pattern everywhere.

People who were neighbours and who knew that this or that neighbour voted for Bustamante's party and the other for Manley's party, were able to live side-by-side in peace and harmony. For me this was one of the great things about Jamaica. People accepted and respected each other's differences. Indeed, so strong was the spirit of tolerance, they were able to joke about each other's leaders and beliefs. It was common, at Tiny's rum bar for 'comrade' Joe and 'Labourite' Tom to play one of those 'party tracing' games for the entertainment of the rest of us.

Comrade Joe: 'Labourite foolish you see. Busta say you caan eat education!'

Labourite Tom: 'But Teacher Allen build more schools than Glassy.'

Joe: 'Cause Glassy caan beg.'

Tom: 'What good is a Minister who caan beg from foreign?!'

Joe: 'Don't change the subject... Busta...'

Tom: 'Is who change subject? Answer: What use Minister who caan beg?'

The consensus is that Labourite Tom wins this one, so Comrade Joe buys the next round.

When grim-faced politics entered, this kind of banter became impossible. Arguments and disagreements increasingly became strident, angry, bitter and finally violent. The old politics of peace and goodwill, with its occasional flinging of stones, was replaced by the politics of anger and hate.

In the slums of Kingston, neighbours who had lived side by side on the same street or lane for years turned on each other. If Labourites predominated, they drove out the Comrades; if the PNP predominated, they drove out the Labourites. We began, on a miniature scale, what has become known as 'ethnic cleansing'. Only there was no 'ethnicity' involved. The people who drove each other out of their homes, who burned each other's homes, who later killed each other, were all black, all poor, all struggling to survive. Instead of Serbs and Croats and Albanians, instead of Jews and Arabs, instead of Zulus and Xhosas, Shona and Ndabele, our house was divided between JLP and PNP, between 'Comrades' and 'Labourites'. By some extraordinary twist of fate, an element not part of its history, not part of anything in its unfolding story, turned Jamaica into a battlefield similar to the battlefields of the Balkans and the Middle East and Southern Africa; on a lesser scale, to be sure, but at its zenith quite as bloody and brutal as any of those others. A combination of our own garrison-style politics and the intensification of the Cold War brought Jamaica to the brink of chaos.

Norman Manley retired from politics in 1969 at the age of 76. His son, Michael, stood for the PNP presidency and won over his good friend, Vivian Blake, a brilliant legal protégé of Norman Manley's. The change in the party leadership was easy and democratic. Norman Manley died that same year.

Two years earlier, in 1967, on the eve of the general elections for that year, Bustamante announced that he would retire after the elections. The JLP won those elections and Bustamante retired from active politics at 83, though he remained titular head of both the JLP and the union which bore his name. Donald Sangster, the man who had carried the work as Busta's Deputy Prime Minister and Minister of Foreign Affairs, became Prime Minister. He died within two months of taking office. Hugh Shearer, whom many in and outside the JLP saw as Bustamante's primary political and trade union heir, became Jamaica's next Prime Minister.

Shearer was the first black Jamaican to become Prime Minister and Jamaican reaction to him was largely negative. Jamaica's whites, browns, and even blacks of the middle class did not think he was qualified for the job. A member of a prominent Jewish business family who had been an appointed member of Bustamante's Cabinet made it known that he would not serve under somebody with whom he had negotiated on labour matters. Others were more discreet. But some said outright that this black man was not fit to be Prime Minister of Jamaica. All sorts of ugly stories about the man went from gossip verandah to cocktail circuit back to gossip verandah. Even some PNP 'brownings' indulged in these smear tactics. They had scoffed and mocked at the first black native Governor-General. His ridiculous uniform, which had been accepted as normal for a white Governor of Jamaica, became a point of mocking and sneering on our black Governor-General. Even Bustamante had boasted of his ability to remove the Governor-General. Institutions we had respected in the control of whites became things to mock under black control. And the workman and the house-maid and the gardener, all of whom had always taken their cue from 'bucky massa' and his lady, followed suit in this inculcation of open or veiled contempt for all things black, people and institutions alike.

I found this the most difficult aspect of colour to deal with. Someone would make some remark laden with contempt about some black person we both knew. We would both know it had racist undertones. The moment I questioned it, I was too sensitive, I was reading unintended meaning into the remark, it was because of my background; in any case, what was said was true and they would say the same about some white person should the need arise. The point that the need never arose had nothing to do with anything. Anyhow (this at the lower, blunter social level) people who are too black could never be trusted.

We had adopted and applied to ourselves the judgements and values whites had used to justify the way they treated blacks. We had, to a greater extent than I had seen elsewhere, become the frontline of black self-contempt.

11

The Rastafari

They came out of the bush immediately below Coyaba in the late afternoon, There were more than six of them — eight or ten. They looked as though they had walked all the way up to us in a straight line across hills and valleys. Most of the men working on the road had gone; only Enos and Maisie were still with us, but ready to go to Rock Hall. The men were bearded, their long braided hair covered by bulging tams. The two elder ones were like people out of the Old Testament, dressed in flowing white robes. The others were more conventionally dressed. One or two of the younger ones seemed hard put to grow the appropriate profusion of 'dreadlocks' and thick beards. Most had rods and staffs; those of the two elders were the most elaborately carved. They emerged directly from the bush onto our rough road.

Daphne called Delilah to heel. She was the big beautiful yellow Labrador who had adopted us and followed us all the way up from Henderson Avenue. After the first week of refusing to feed her at Henderson Avenue, hoping she would go back to her own home, she had turned up with a huge block of processed cheese, then a whole chicken as if saying, 'If you cannot feed me, I can feed us.' Daphne had collapsed between tears and laughter and Delilah had joined the family. She came to heel at Daphne's command. The elder raised his staff. I waved them to come.

They were hot and sweating. I invited them to the long verandah. They preferred to sit on the steps and boulders just below it.

'We will have water, please,' the elder said.

I signalled to Daphne and Maisie, and they went for cool spring water from our old-time water cooler. The men nearly emptied the cooler.

'You the brother from Africa?' His speech was soft and clear. Behind the thick beard was the lean face of a man between forty and fifty. His dark brown face glowed with good health.

'Yes.'

'They say you from Ethiopia?'

'No. My father was.'

'But you are one of us; Rastafari?' It was a challenge.

'No.'

'Why? You join Babylon?' A hint of anger.

'No.'

'You're not with us and you're not with them?'

'That's right.'

'He's no Rasta,' one of the others said. The elder silenced him with a wave of the hand without turning his head.

'Then what are you doing here? Why are you here? Not in Africa?'

Enos and Maisie decided it was safe for them to leave us alone with the Rastas. They helped Daphne bring fresh orange juice for the visitors, then started the long walk to Rock Hall.

'House slaves,' one of the Rastas said softly.

'They are our friends,' I said. 'You do not have to be a slave to work for a person.'

'Stop that nonsense!' The elder was impatient. 'So why are you here, Mr Abrahams?' He looked into my eyes and a polite smile touched his lips.

I told them about my travels and experiences and about South Africa and our search for, in Langston Hughes' words 'a house in the world where the white shadows will not fall'. Some of the younger ones made their 'spliffs' and lit up and the smell of ganja was strong in the still atmosphere. We talked for more than an hour and the idea of a black man not finding a place of peace in his own continent shocked them. Africa, by their folk myth, was the home of all black people, the one place on earth where all black people could be free of Babylon and in control of their own lives. For most it was a land of milk and honey as in the Bible. Ethiopia, the land of my father, was free and independent and its ruler was the reincarnation of the living God.

They had rejected Babylon and this slave culture to which they had been brought against their will. All they wanted from Babylon was to be repatriated, to be returned to the Africa from which they had been snatched. Repatriation and reparation: that was their right. The Germans were paying the Jews reparation for slaughtering six million Jews. More than twenty million Africans perished on the Middle Passage and still no reparations more than one hundred years later. And this Babylon government here did not have the guts to stand up for black people's rights in the world. Only Marcus Mosiah Garvey did, and see what they did to him. So Rasta makes his own life and raises his children to be pure and clean and his women to be modest and cover themselves as women should. And for this they are hunted and humiliated and their locks cut off. But Rasta will survive Babylon and Africa will be free and all her children from all the four corners of the earth will return to the motherland.

When the sun began to dip, we stopped talking. They had refused food and the bottle of white rum I had brought out. I could see that but for the authority of the two elders, some of the younger ones would have gone for the rum. The authority of the elders was quite as strong as anything I had seen in Africa. I had suggested that wherever Africans and people of African descent formed the majority, that place should be seen as a part of Africa.

The elder whispered: 'Africa is its people.' Then he shook his head.

It had not turned out a good encounter. I could see they had expected something better from our meeting. I had no 'good' answers for them. They could not dismiss me as a 'liard' because I had been born there and despite their wishful dreaming they recognised the truth of what I told them. But how they wanted Africa to be their Zion, their land of milk and honey, the place where all the pain and anguish of generations of black visionaries would be put to ease. How deeply must you hurt to escape into such dreams?

They gathered themselves together for the long journey to where they had come from; somewhere in Western Kingston, I suspected. There were places there and in the Wareika hills and other remote corners of the land where the Rastas could still worship their black God, beat their drums, make their music, teach their offspring Jah's ways, smoke their sacred herb, and defy Babylon.

Already their cultural contribution to the world far exceeds the contribution of any other comparably small, discriminated against minority anywhere in the world in our time. And their salutation is: peace and love, brother; peace and love, sister.

At the moment of departure the elder asked:

'The woman?'

'The mother of my children.'

'From where? Not here?'

'No. Born far away in Java.'

'Sees like you?'

'Yes.'

'Call her, please.'

I called her and she came. The elder took her hand.

'Thank you for receiving us. I wish he was one of us; and you. Take care; peace and love.'

Then he led his group back down into the bush, as though they would make the same straight line down to the plain as they had made on the way up.

I went in and made notes of the encounter. I would want to write about it some day.

In Red Hills next day the talk was all about the Rastas' visit to Mr P's place. Their progress up the hill through the bush had been observed by men and women working their fields; word of their presence and long stay at Coyaba had circulated. Tiny confronted me; the onlookers waited eagerly.

'You have Rasta visitors last night, Mr P. I hear they stay long. What happen?'

'We talked; they wanted to know about Africa.'

'You not afraid? Me 'fraid of them!'

'Why? They're just people.'

'Not like us,' somebody said.

'Them bad,' somebody else chipped in.

'Them smoke the weed and turn mad,' another voice said.

'They smoke it at your yard?' another voice asked.

I ignored that one. It was against the law.

'Miss P not 'fraid of them?' Tiny pressed.

'No reason to be,' I suggested.

'You don't know them,' someone else said.

'I'm 'fraid of them bad,' Tiny insisted. 'Don't like them in my shop.'

'Why?' I asked.

After much discussion it boiled down to: 'they not like us' and 'they are dirty, don't wash their hair'. I told them the men we had seen had been scrupulously clean, even after the long sweaty climb up the hill. Their hair and beards were clean. For a time after that, a section of our village community condemned me as a friend of the Rastas. They were tolerant of strangers of all kinds, white or black, foreign or native, but not of native-born Rastas. The Rastas were indeed different and I suspect it was the nature of their difference that made other Jamaicans of all classes fear and distrust them. They rejected what all the others had accepted. It showed in the way they walked and talked and looked at you. They were the mirror-image of what you would have been if you had dared to reject Babylon. Seeing yourself thus can be unsettling, frightening. We hate being reminded of our weaknesses.

Jamaicans, until very recently, did not want to recognise the centrality of colour and colour prejudice in almost every aspect of their lives. They tried to forget slavery and resented those who reminded them of it. They played Anancy with the shade game. Unless they had 'good' hair, male Jamaicans either covered their heads with hats or caps, or cut their hair so short they looked almost bald. Only two men I knew, beside the Rastas, in those early Jamaican days, allowed their kinky hair to grow long, or, as the Jamaicans say, 'to grow tall'. Theodore Sealy, the first black editor of the Gleaner was one, Alva Ramsay, editor of the *West Indian Sportsman*, was the other. I later found a third in harbour pilot Roderick Francis.

The Rastas, the Garveyites, the supporters of the American-based black power movement which was shaking the United States in the 1950s, were the only people I found who supported Hugh Shearer as Prime Minister. Most of the rest of Jamaica had difficulty accepting a black man as their Prime Minister. Within the Jamaica Labour Party itself there were those who thought they were better qualified for the job. Seaga, whom Shearer had re-appointed Minister of Finance, was one of those. During his very short-lived period as Prime Minister, Sangster had appointed Seaga to Finance. When Sangster died, Shearer kept him there.

During this period Jamaican politics entered a new phase. The black power movement reached the young intellectuals at the University of the West Indies. Black power, the Rasta movement and the discontent of the young people from Kingston's burgeoning urban ghettoes converged, and there was chaos on the streets. There were demonstrations and marches. Fiery speeches were made. White and brown people were abused on the streets. Our son, who was at the University at the time, told us with distress of the reverse racism which seemed to have taken over on campus. We explained that change often came in extreme forms. Society went into panic. The police cracked down on the 'subversives'.

In its early phase the University of the West Indies had been as elitist as any small conservative British regional university. Its colonial and post-colonial objectives were to produce the people who would manage and run the administrations of the region: the Financial Secretaries, the Central Planners, the Permanent Secretaries, the doctors and teachers and nurses and the senior heads of departments who would take over from the British civil servants. But by the 1960s, the place was becoming radicalised by a first generation of black West Indian scholars replacing the expatriate teachers and lecturers. Many Jamaicans saw the Mona campus as a revolutionary hotbed. A neighbour living on the hill above us, the charming wife of a senior local government official from the colonial era, swore that the people down at Mona were all bent on making Jamaica communist. She would not allow her son to go to that university.

One of a large number of young radicals at the Mona campus in the 1960s was a young man from Guyana named Walter Rodney, whose political activism either frightened the daylights out of Hugh Shearer's government, or was used as an excuse to clamp down on the radicalism spreading from Mona. Rodney had been on a brief trip out of the island. On his return, he was stopped at the airport and ordered expelled as an undesirable.

When the news broke there was pandemonium on the streets. University students, some of their lecturers, Rastafari, ghetto youth, Garveyites, the unemployed, all took to the streets in angry protest. The police and the military came out in force. Helicopters flew overhead. Tear-gas was used to disperse crowds. There were a few violent skirmishes. Shearer, the trade unionist turned Prime Minister, told his police not to recite the Beatitudes to the protesters. The 'Rodney riots' were put down forcibly within the week. Hugh Shearer lost that special aura as the first ever black Prime Minister of Jamaica. He was, they said on the streets, just another one of 'them'

Yet I found Hugh Shearer not 'one of them'. He remained the same as he was before becoming Prime Minister. He had no circle of influence-seeking businessmen around him; no old boys' network from shared schooling in one of the island's handful of prestige colleges; no connection by membership in any of the recognised clubs. Both Manleys, father and son, had such connections. So did Sangster. So, later, when he became Prime Minister, did Seaga. Bustamante had been the first outsider in terms of the Jamaican social establishment. When he became Prime Minister, the establishment had to meet and deal with him on his terms. Busta was a light brown man, which made it easier for the high and the mighty to swallow their pride and deal with him on his terms. Black Hugh Shearer, like brown Bustamante, was also related to the Manleys, though more distantly; he came from the darker side and had not been to any of the elitist colleges. So they found him hard to take and he was not about to change to suit them. Shortly after taking office, Shearer invited a group of us, the senior journalists, for an informal Sunday morning chat at Jamaica House, then the official residence of the Prime Minister. Among the things I remember was his insistence that he would not allow any of the household staff to polish his shoes. It was traditional, as in some better old-time hotels, to put out your shoes the night before and get them back highly polished the next morning. 'I don't ever want to forget where I came from and how to polish my own shoes.' He was the most modest, least pretentious Prime Minister of Jamaica I knew — without a hint of the arrogance that office nearly always seemed to engender.

In 1968 Alexander Bustamante was 84 and in retirement. His cousin and great political rival, Norman Manley, had died the year before. Busta was going blind. His grip on both his party and his trade union was loosening. The times were changing. The two cousins had, between 1938 and 1968, held Jamaica together as a stable, flourishing two-party parliamentary democracy. They had done it by keeping their rivalry within bounds. When it was the turn of one to govern, the other stood back, allowed him to do so, held a watching brief as Her Majesty's Loyal Opposition. Whenever Manley's people went too far in their opposition, which was almost never, he would pull them back; whenever Busta's people did so, Busta too would pull them back. Busta, in particular, made sure that his followers showed respect for 'me cousin, Norman' at all times. So it seemed that parliamentary democracy and the adversarial two-party system were secure. In times of trouble the two parties always worked together. The interests of the nation always superseded the interests of the parties and of the special interest groups. Jamaica, under Bustamante and Manley, flourished. The first hint of trouble had been the violence of the West Kingston elections in which political opponents traded gunfire. That, on the surface, had been brought under a measure of control by behind-the-scenes pressure from the two cousins. They induced their followers to accept a set of basic rules for peaceful co-existence. They worked out a formula for the sharing of public works jobs and 'scarce benefits'. They avoided the politics of 'winner take all, loser suck salt', by agreeing to forty per cent of available public works jobs going to PNP supporters, forty per cent to JLP supporters, and twenty per cent to those of neither party. This had worked throughout the Manley-Bustamante years. In the run-up to his brief period in office Sangster had been the first to break this compact. The younger Manley and Seaga, later, quietly let it slide. Now, with one dead and the other incapacitated, with their steadying influence no longer there, Jamaica drifted into the 'war politics' of the Cold War. Up to this point, that Cold War happened elsewhere, not in Jamaica. It happened in Africa, Asia, Latin America, not in Jamaica. As with the limitation of press freedom, free speech and freedom of movement, we said those things cannot happen here. They did.

The Cold War
and the
Third World

—— 12 ——

The Dreamers & the Armageddon Boys

Cuba is Jamaica's nearest neighbour, just ninety miles to the north. So when the 'Cuban Missile crisis' erupted in 1962, and the world seemed on the brink of war, Jamaica was near the eye of the storm. We watched the nightly American television reports of the unfolding crisis, replete with clips from the White House as the Kennedy brothers and their advisors discussed the situation; we saw clips of Nikita Khruschev banging his shoe at the United Nations; and we watched montages of marching armies and exploding nuclear devices. The Cuban missile crisis took our minds off our internecine struggles. If a nuclear war broke out between the United States and the Soviet Union with Cuba as the battlefield, Jamaica was bound to feel the effects. On one television discussion programme somebody mentioned the possibility of a nuclear missile going astray and exploding near or on Jamaican soil. The shock of the thought was sobering.

Jamaica has had a small fringe communist movement over the years. In the wake of the Cuban revolution, it had become more active and, with the Cuban crisis, grew into a full-fledged political party, the Workers' Party of Jamaica. It tried to use the Cuban crisis to radicalise Jamaican politics. Those at the other extreme of the political spectrum inevitably declared their anti-communism. The house, now, was dividing on ideological as well as traditional party lines. There were rightist factions within the governing JLP and leftist factions within the opposition PNP; not for the first time, only more clearly defined now. Only the fear of a possible nuclear accident involving Jamaica held us together in our insistent call for the de-escalating of the crisis. I am not sure that either the Americans or the Soviets noticed our protests. We, on the other hand, had come to the stark realisation of our vulnerability. These things could happen to us — even if only by accident, no matter how well and peacefully we behaved. The sudden proximity of the Cold War was unsettling.

Fidel Castro's revolution of 1959 had been, for the radically inclined young of Jamaica and the world, charged with romance. The fact of a small band of 800 brave men taking on and beating a professional army of 30,000 is the stuff of high drama and romance. For a time there were those among us who wanted to take to our own hills to emulate what Castro and his followers had done. Never mind that we were under no dictatorship, that we could change our government by the ballot rather than the bullet. That was too dull, too staid for the young and angry among us. The inculcated self-contempt, the traditional belittling of each other and the inability to fulfil the wilder dreams and promises associated with political independence, all fed into the romanticising of the Cuban revolution, which our local communists exploited to the full.

In Iran, Mohammad Mosaddeq, a nationalist leader, had been elected to power on the promise that he would nationalise the Anglo-Iranian Oil Company. When he did so in 1951, the British withdrew from Iran. Mosaddeq's enemies, headed by the Shah and supported by the British and Americans, mounted one of the earliest campaigns of 'destabilisation' in the unfolding tactics of Cold War politics. Mosaddeq was a highly educated man, with a Doctor of Law degree from the University of Lausanne, but the Western news media portrayed him as a fool and a buffoon. They called him 'fainting Mosaddeq'; they scoffed at him; mocked him; ridiculed him. Few of us who read those Western accounts about this 'foolish old man' were left without a sense of shame. When a handful of operatives of the then fledgling Central Intelligence Agency of the United States stage-managed his overthrow in 1953, at what one of them described as a ridiculously small cost, most of us reacted with mixed feelings. Only George Padmore, back then, understood and told us what this was all about.

Nearly a decade after the overthrow of Mosaddeq, when I saw that last picture of Patrice Lumumba on the steps of an aeroplane, surrounded by a bunch of white Americans who handed him over to his enemies to be killed, I remembered Mosaddeq and how he was destroyed. One of the things these two had in common was their desire to nationalise the rich resources of their two countries. The other, the unseen hand of the CIA.

Fidel Castro, like Mohammad Mosaddeq, like Patrice Lumumba, nationalised his country's resources and expropriated the massive holdings of non-Cubans — mainly Americans. So he, too, became a target of the CIA. He, too, was ridiculed; there were lurid stories about his life-style, horror stories about his brutality and cruelty. There were attempts to destabilise his government and to assassinate him. There were also attempts to invade Cuba from the American mainland. When these failed, an economic embargo was placed on trade with the island, and calls and threats were issued to all other countries not to do business with Cuba on pain of being punished themselves. Inevitably, Cuba turned to the Soviet Union, received the needed economic assistance and became the first communist state in the Americas. Cuban short wave radio described it as the first free state of the Americas. In fact it was the first Soviet satellite state of the Americas. Is this what Cuba wanted?

When Castro first made his revolution he was no communist. He was a nationalist. He wanted Cuba to belong to the Cubans rather than the Americans. He wanted an end to gambling and prostitution, an end to his country being in the pockets of either American gangsters or the American government. If the American government had accepted and helped an independent Cuba to find its way in the world, would Cuba have turned to the Soviet Union? I think not. When, in the 1970s I visited Cuba as part of the group of journalists who accompanied Prime Minister Michael Manley on a state visit, I met the man and watched him closely. Later, when he came to Jamaica on a return visit, I watched the wonder of Castro's interaction on the Catherine Plains with free black Jamaicans who received him with warmth and friendliness, yet spoke their minds and asked the hard questions his own people dared not. I got the impression then that if he had a choice, this man would have preferred to go our way rather than the Soviet way. Instead the Americans offered the option of doing it their way, being their client, bending to their wishes or being the outcast of the Americas. Perhaps the Cubans thought the Soviet option would be different, though I suspect not. In any case, if you have to be a client state, dependent on the protection and aid of a greater power, it is preferable to be the client of somebody far away. A distant overlordship is usually less overbearing than one close at hand. There is more space for doing your own thing. The very far-flung nature of the British empire made for its greater liberality in those places where it did not have large concentrations of its own people. In South and East Africa, where there were large British settler populations, they were less liberal than in West Africa, the 'white man's grave', where British or white settlement did not exist. America was close to Cuba, Soviet Russia a long, long way away. I felt convinced that in the case of Cuba, the Americans, reacting like a spurned/rejected lover, forced her into the arms of the Soviet Union.

Today, with the Cold War ended almost everywhere else in the world, the Americans are still having this difficult rejection complex about Cuba. For over thirty years they have tried and failed to bring tiny Cuba to heel. So Cuba still remains the bone in America's throat. This inability to swallow 'small bones of failure and defeat' on the way to greater glory is one of America's major problems in her role as the sole superpower in today's world. She had this same difficulty with China and, later, with Vietnam. All the great powers of the past have had the capacity to accept setback, defection and defeat, then at the end of the day, forgive, or appear to, and make friends with former enemies and move on to fulfil their 'manifest destiny'. Without this historical flexibility, a nation, no matter how powerful, forfeits any claim to greatness. History is impatient of petty spite in powerful nations aspiring to greatness.

Jamaica was ambivalent about the Cuban-American problem. It has a long history of giving asylum to Latin American and other regional leaders fallen on bad times. The great Simón Bolívar found sanctuary in Jamaica. So did many others, including people from Cuba and Haiti. In their turn, many Jamaicans went to work in Cuba, Central America and elsewhere in the region. There was a constant coming and going between Jamaica and her neighbours. Many Jamaicans settled in those places and raised families. Many Jamaicans, too, had over the years travelled to the United States where they found work and settled down, always with the dream of returning home. Some did; some did not. Today, there are at least as many Jamaicans settled in other countries of the world as there are Jamaicans in Jamaica. The largest number are found in the United States. Some are American citizens; Jamaican law allows such to retain their right to Jamaicans citizenship. Others are 'Green Card' holders, which allows them residential rights and, most cherished by most Jamaicans, the freedom to come and go to the United States without let or hindrance.

All this went into making the Jamaican ambivalence over the Cuban-American fall-out. Those who wanted to travel to America were, or pretended to be, against Castro's Cuba. The business community and the upper and middle classes were anti-Castro. The Jamaican government, however, under both PNP and JLP, insisted on retaining relations with Cuba even when most of the rest of Latin America was coerced into severing relations. The Jamaican 'man-in-the-street' had a sympathetic open mind. He approved of and wanted for Jamaicans the good things Castro had brought, like free education for all to university level, free health services, full employment, no income taxes — but all without a communist dictatorship.

The general elections of 1972 resulted in a sweeping victory for Michael Manley's PNP and a crushing defeat for Hugh Shearer's JLP. Shearer's period in office had been beset by serious economic problems in the country, and debilitating internal problems within his party. Seaga, the Finance Minister, now had a firm grip on the party machine. To be sure, Shearer still controlled the Bustamante Industrial Trade Union. Seaga, however, gained the loyalty of three of the key BITU leaders under Shearer, he outflanked Robert Lightbourne, and then made his successful bid to wrest the leadership of the party from Hugh Shearer, who was blamed for losing the election. I got the impression at the time that if Hugh Shearer had really wanted to fight off the Seaga challenge, he could have done so and won. He did not and Seaga won easily.

Jamaica now had a new Prime Minister, aged 48, dynamic, eloquent, as charismatic as Bustamante in his prime and as educated and sophisticated as the great Norman Manley. For Leader of the Opposition Jamaica had Edward Seaga, six years younger than Manley, as well educated, a first-rate planner and manipulator, intensely ambitious and with a streak of tough ruthlessness. He was the first 'white' Jamaican — of Middle Eastern background — to aspire to the highest elective political office in an overwhelmingly black country.

Seaga was now as firmly in control of the JLP as Bustamante had ever been, Michael Manley as firmly in control of his party as his father had ever been. But there were profound differences in the internal structures and dynamics of the two parties. The PNP was open and democratic with everything up for debate from the lowest to the highest levels of the party. It was modelled on the British Labour Party and the socialist parties of Western Europe. The JLP had been Bustamante's party and he, after advice from a chosen circle, had the final say on party policy. He was 'The Chief', whose word was law within the party and within his union. One was an 'open' party, the other a 'closed' party. Busta was 88 in 1972 when effective control of his party passed into Seaga's hands. Seaga, in his turn, ran the party as Bustamante had. Some of those who had been close to Bustamante, like Lightbourne, the young lawyer Ian Ramsay, and others who fell foul of Seaga, had to leave the party. Toward the closing years of his career, when the JLP was reduced to a shadow of its former state by splits and divisions, Seaga once declared of those who opposed him that it was 'my way or the highway'. But back in 1972 he was a strong young leader who engaged Michael Manley in the terrible Cold War politics of the 1970s and 1980s.

Jamaica was broke when Michael Manley took power. His party's ideological stand on Cuba and on socialism worried the Americans as well as the Jamaican élite. The fear was that Manley was taking Jamaica toward communism. The local communist group, the tiny Workers' Party of Jamaica, made matters worse by pushing the line that socialism and communism were really the same thing, and, if not quite the same, that socialism was simply the first step on the road to communism. Anti-communist Jamaicans bought this line and the fear of communism assumed panic proportions. One result was a marked slowdown in America's aid programme to Jamaica. Manley's 'politics of participation', with its heavy emphasis on equality for the poor, further frightened the local élite. His education programme, in which the children of employers and their employees would go to the same schools, sit side-by-side in the same classes, unsettled many middle-class parents who had spent a life-time working to separate themselves from the lower classes and move up to the upper classes.

The National Minimum Wage compelled employers of domestic workers to observe set base rates and hours and conditions of work. Before that law, domestic helpers were at the mercy of employers. A good employer might pay her household help reasonably well and allow for an eight-hour day, with every other weekend off on full pay. A bad employer might pay very little and insist on a twelve- or fourteen- or even sixteen-hour day with no weekends off. It was all up to the employer. Since most employers of domestic helpers were themselves office workers or shop assistants who paid their helpers out of their own earnings, pay was low, conditions of work bad. One ironic consequence was that some of the better paid unionised workers and their trade unions objected to the National Minimum Wage because they would not be able to afford domestic help under its conditions. The minimum set was not outrageously high: it began at fifty cents an hour. One prominent trade union leader warned the Prime Minister of mass unemployment among domestic workers. He was, this union leader insisted, pricing them out of jobs. It did not happen. But Michael Manley lost some support.

Unemployment in the wider economy was another hard problem Manley faced. The bureaucracy was top-heavy, the civil service was one of the larger employers. Once 'established', a civil servant's job was his or hers for life, short of some terrible misdemeanour. Every year, a number of school leavers who had successfully passed their examinations entered the civil service; every year, the civil service numbers grew; every year, the cost of running it grew; the cost of the perks kept growing; the cost of the pensions for those who reached retirement age kept growing. Maintaining the civil service became one of the costliest items in the national budget. It was only later, during and after the IMF-World Bank years, that debt and debt-servicing, would become a greater drain on the national budget. When Michael Manley tried to impose some discipline on this ballooning problem, he encountered stubborn resistance. Resources which should have gone into new job creation went instead into supporting the bureaucracy.

I was particularly interested because in his other, earlier, role as one of the two key trade union negotiators, he and Hugh Shearer had successfully advanced the view that a worker's job was as much his property as was an employer's factory or real estate or capital. They argued that, as such, a worker was as entitled to the rights and protections that went with such ownership as was an employer. If your labour is your property, the equivalent of the businessman's money investment in the job, then you have the same ownership right to the job without which the business cannot function, as the investor of money. He invests his money, you invest your labour, therefore your rights are equal to his. It follows that it is unjust, unfair and unlawful to separate the worker from his job without the level and quality of compensation an investor could claim in the event of expropriation. Shearer and Manley had won many victories on the battlefield of labour negotiations with this approach. Shearer, as Prime Minister and, later, Manley as Prime Minister, were often stopped in their tracks when their own arguments of another time were used against them when they tried to cut the bloated bureaucracy and move the national economy forward. Neither of them, in their time in office, got over this one. Others, not inhibited by this millstone from the past, have succeeded partially in making the civil service more efficient, more responsive to the taxpayers it serves, and more accountable for the resources it controls. But it is still set in its ways, still top heavy, still subject to vast cost and time over-runs on contracts and projects under its control and supervision. Far too much of the nation's resources are still wasted without anybody going to jail or losing their work. This is part of the reason why Jamaica is poorer than she need be, why she is still 'developing' rather than 'developed'.

When Manley launched a works 'impact' programme to provide day's work for unemployed women from the inner-city areas, he fell foul of an outraged, heavily taxed middle class. These impact workers were sent into middle-class housing areas to sweep the streets, trim the hedges and verges and gather up the rubbish for the public cleansing system to collect and remove. The women were big and heavy, as people fed on a mainly starch diet usually are. Manley had explained the programme in Parliament. It was to afford these women, usually household heads of families without fathers, a way of earning a little money to feed their families. It was an alternative to social welfare hand-outs and of women trying to live off men by 'having pickney for him'. Women who had never worked would, the hope was, acquire work habits and go on to find or make proper jobs for themselves. When the middle classes saw these women preparing their starchy lunches over small fires on the pavements outside their quiet suburban homes, their reactions were strong. They phoned the radio call-in programmes, wrote letters to *The Gleaner,* denouncing the waste of tax-payers' money and the intrusion of these loud, lazy, aggressive types into their quiet peaceful areas. The anger vented on an essentially intelligent social welfare make-work programme was surprising.

Some of Manley's other social programmes were less controversial. People accepted the elimination of the distinction in the recording of the births of legitimate and illegitimate children. The vast majority of Jamaicans were born out of wedlock. Only employers and their organisations quarrelled, though not all that fiercely, with the maternity leave law under which women received three months' paid leave after the birth of a child. The principle of equal pay for equal work between men and women and many other social laws came into being. Indeed, the Michael Manley government of 1972 inaugurated a social revolution in the relations between the classes in Jamaica. It manifested itself in some interesting ways.

When we arrived in Jamaica, the lower classes, the black Jamaicans, those who lived in the ghettoes, were self-effacing and drab as people who want to avoid being noticed. The clothes were of quiet colours, nothing striking, nothing to draw attention. From 1972 on, all that changed. We saw a riot of bright colours: reds and yellows and blues and bright greens. Women dressed as though to say: Look at me! The pretty young black and brown women on the streets of Kingston compelled attention by the new freedom with which they used their bright colours. Jamaicans began to show the radiance of glowing smiles in dark faces; gleaming white teeth against a dark setting. Manley's slogan was 'The word is love'. This was a Prime Minister who moved freely among his people. Everybody seemed a few inches taller, backs straighter, heads held higher. The Rastas seemed more evident, more sure of themselves, more assertive in this new climate of social freedom and peace. The young were empowered. Student Councils helped set standards in schools. Domestic workers saw their children win scholarships to old established high schools, where once only the children of their employers could go. We all wanted, as the saying on the street was, to 'live loving'. Freedom of speech, association, assembly, movement were all back. No passports or travel documents were seized. There were attempts to restore the JBC to what it had been in Norman Manley's time.

Jamaica, under Michael Manley, became a leader in Third-World affairs, in the Non-Aligned Movement, in the Socialist International. Students from many parts of Africa came to the University of the West Indies, some under scholarships from the Jamaican government. Famous leaders from many countries came visiting Jamaica, affirming her importance in world affairs. It seemed that under Michael Manley and democratic socialism Jamaica had finally found the way forward. Now, all we had to do was to set about working our troubles away.

Then, in 1973 the Organisation of Petroleum Exporting Countries triggered the international oil crisis by raising the price of a barrel of crude oil from around US$3 to over US$12 and plunged the world into an energy crisis. Jamaica imports all its oil and the OPEC move was a crippling blow. Jamaica's friends among the oil producers — Nigeria, Venezuela and Mexico — helped by making concessionary arrangements. But these could not offset entirely the crippling energy price increases.

Up to this point, the multinational oil companies were in control of Jamaica's oil refining and distribution. They ran the industry under government licence and they determined scope, size and price. They had largely co-operated with successive Jamaican governments in the setting of prices and margins. The other two big multinationals were the sugar industry, headed by Britain's Tate &Lyle, and the bauxite industry under Canadian and American control.

All these multinational companies were doing good profitable business in Jamaica. Jamaica and Jamaicans benefited greatly from their presence. Sugar was a particularly large employer of labour. It paid huge taxes and it helped serve the national economy in many other ways. One example was Harold Cahusac's contribution to the island's Watershed Protection Programme. The bauxite industry contributed equally massively in taxes; and among its other ways of serving were research, cattle-breeding and large-scale citrus production. The more prosperous and profitable the companies were, the more they contributed to Jamaica's well-being. High profits meant generous wage settlements, which, in part at least, was why Shearer and Manley, as the chief negotiators for their two unions at the time, could extract such generous 'landmark' contracts. When things turned difficult, when markets slumped and companies experienced decline in profitability or loss, the generosity ceased. Layoffs and cutbacks were introduced. New, less attractive wage contracts replaced the 'sweet' earlier ones. The world of work changed from a comfortable to an unsettled one. All this and more, such as a reduction in tourist earnings and in investments, turned the OPEC oil crisis into a disaster for Jamaica. Add to all this Michael Manley's determination to continue on his democratic socialist direction, and all the elements of a political-economic crisis were in place.

Edward Seaga was now Leader of the Opposition in Parliament. He was a former Minister of Finance, whose supporters said he was the best such Jamaica had ever had. They credited him with creating Jamaica's modern financial structures. Those who knew that Noel Nethersole, the Finance Minister in Norman Manley's government of the 1950s, was the true architect of those institutions, held their peace and the word-of-mouth myth became the reality. Seaga's reputation as a financial genius was affirmed by repeated declaration of it. He also had a very high reputation as a planner and a no-nonsense manager. Most important, Seaga took up his job as Leader of the Opposition with the support of most employers, manufacturers, commission agents, the upper and middle classes and all those others who felt threatened by Michael Manley's democratic socialism. The media, too, gave Seaga full and sympathetic coverage. His style was in sharp contrast to Manley's. Where Manley was open, forthcoming, almost anxious to show his hand and argue his case, Seaga was reserved, cautious, watchful, aloof, almost non-committal until he was ready to act. As Seaga's power and influence grew, those around him seemed to develop a fear of him. When they called Bustamante 'Chief', it was tinged with affection. When they spoke of Seaga as 'The Leader', it was affirmation of his power in the party, the one not to be crossed.

Some of us in the media who had watched Seaga's rise, who had witnessed his handling of the JBC strike, were concerned about the man's attitude to the democratic process. The 1962 election campaign in West Kingston was a brutal and savage contest in which the bullet was used to influence the outcome of the ballot. When it was over and Dudley Thompson and his supporters had been routed, the PNP, as a political party was completely wiped out in West Kingston. There was no room for it to regroup and rebuild. More than thirty years on, there is still no viable two-party system functioning in that constituency. The PNP — in or out of office — has fielded token candidates who have routinely been trounced by staggering majorities. The place had been turned into a closed, solid and permanent power base for one man. Our concern was whether anyone who did this in one constituency would want to do the same thing nationally if he became Prime Minister. Could democracy itself be used to undo its own foundations? It was nothing new in history. Electoral means had been used by the Nazis, by the South African whites, to legally re-order their societies and subvert democracy itself. The road to Apartheid had been a legal and constitutional step-by-step process, carried out in a democratically elected parliament. The trick there was to so re-order the franchise to deprive the country's non-whites from taking part in national elections. Where some kind of limited franchise was allowed, it was so restrictive that it could not influence national decisions taken in parliament. Could the creation of a series of closed constituencies, based on the West Kingston model, spread throughout the country until one party finally captured and controlled a majority of such closed constituencies? If this happened, that party would ensure its permanence in office.

Certainly, the West Kingston 'political garrison' had resulted in the PNP, after Norman Manley, building its own 'garrison constituencies'. If the whole national house were to be divided into two contending groups of 'garrison constituencies', and if one group were ultimately to gain the upper hand, would it matter which party was dominant? Would a PNP 'garrison' government be less repressive than a JLP 'garrison' government? There would have been a systemic change and the very nature of it would ensure a new politics of imposition, coercion, repression and, ultimately, the distortion and destruction of democracy itself. But this concern was drowned in the tidal wave of anti-Manley, anti-communist sentiment washing over the island.

Violence became an everyday event all over Jamaica. Large quantities of firearms were coming in. It was hard to decide where criminal violence began and political violence ended. The happy mood of 'The word is love' and the bright and sunny colours on the streets, dissipated. A new angry sullenness came upon us. Basic foods like rice and sugar and corned beef and saltfish went into short supply; some vanished from supermarket shelves for long periods. Unofficial rationing came in. Middle-class housewives who knew the supermarket managers and owners, went to special doors and came out with brown paper bags stuffed with what they needed. Poor people looking for food staged minor demonstrations and were told to ask Mr. Manley for what they wanted. When, later, the Manley government turned to the IMF for help, the JLP slogan was: 'It's Manley's Fault'. IMF – It's Manley's Fault, stuck powerfully, reinforced by the violence, the atmosphere of instability, and the onslaught of the local and foreign press. The *Gleaner* almost daily reproduced some article or editorial from the foreign press harshly critical of the Manley government. It ran a corps of columnists who sneered and jeered and ridiculed almost everything Michael Manley did. My friend the novelist, John Hearne, tried to recruit me to this group. I refused. I also refused when Dudley Thompson approached me to write a column reflecting the PNP slant, or at least one less sharply hostile. They had worked out an understanding with the *Gleaner*. A respected researcher from the university campus later wrote such a column. It was good and ran for several years. I just did not like the idea of the journalist as a political mercenary, in any context; certainly not in the context of the current harsh and bitter Cold War politics.

When Michael Manley introduced the Bauxite Levy in 1974 and a year later delivered his 'going to the mountaintop with Castro' speech in Havana, he confirmed all the worst fears of his enemies, at home and abroad. The multinationals operating in Jamaica, other foreign investors, Jamaican business people, the Jamaican upper and middle classes were now confirmed in their fears that Manley intended to bring Castro-style communism to Jamaica. Why did he do this? Why provide his enemies with the excuse and justification for wanting to drive him from office?

I was in the massive audience in Havana that clear moonlit night. The crowd was excited, the atmosphere charged. Michael Manley at his best was one of the most charismatic speakers I have listened to. He used reason and passion to work an audience into a frenzy. In the process he worked himself up as well. He became at once both the instigator and the prime participant in the emotional frenzy he aroused. The interaction between the man and his audience could be breathtaking. This was easy with Jamaican and West Indian audiences, with whom he shared a common language and culture. Could this be done with people who did not share the same language and cultural background? I thought not. Yet I think Manley achieved it that night — but at a very high price. Castro, a great wordsmith and mover of peoples himself, was on the platform as Manley's host. Manley opened quietly and rationally enough and the translator seemed to reflect his mood. At some point, the vast audience burst into spontaneous applause — and Manley took off! He had broken through the barrier of language and culture. This might as well have been his own beloved Jamaican audience. At one point Castro got to his feet as a wave of applause and shouts of approval rose from the crowd. Manley and his audience were as one, interacting with each other. The voice of the translator became Manley's voice. He was speaking now directly to the people; they were responding directly to him. So the words about going to the mountaintop together, hand-in-hand, came out as a natural climax to a great exercise in oratory.

Looking at the man enveloped in the glow and passion of the moment, I did not think he realised what the impact of those words would be elsewhere. I knew him well enough to know that he was not a communist, not even an intellectual Marxist. He was a Fabian-style socialist with a strong populist streak and the dangerous capacity, in a political leader, of being carried away by a responsive audience and his own words. When he tried to explain away those words later, his enemies did not believe him. For him it had just been the language of solidarity. The Cubans were our friends pursuing their own path to socialism; we would pursue our own path, in our own democratic way. Nobody believed him. Cuban-style communism was now a clear and present threat to Jamaica. His enemies mobilised against that threat.

Employers' groups came together and talked of an employers' strike. Housewives took a leaf out of Chile's book and there was talk of a housewives' strike. Food shortages got worse. So did demonstrations demanding food. The tourist areas were disrupted. Roads were damaged. It seemed that one half of Jamaica was bent on tearing down whatever the other half was putting up. The destruction and the destructive impulse was as I had not seen it in any other Third-World country. We were, it seemed, prepared to reduce Jamaica to rubble and ruin if that was what it took to get rid of Michael Manley and the communist threat with which his government was now firmly associated. We were in a mess. Poor black Jamaicans were killing other poor black Jamaicans on an unprecedented scale in what was supposed to be a peaceful, democratic country not at war with anyone. The police had a hard time trying to contain the violence. Every now and then, after some particularly nasty outbreak, the soldiers had to be called out to help the police. If things continued, it would be a matter of time before the soldiers were permanently on the streets.

The options for the government were getting fewer. It was only a matter of time before the government would have to turn to the International Monetary Fund for help. There was a great debate in the PNP about whether or not to go to the IMF. The radicals were opposed; those who knew the details of the state of the economy prevailed. Going to the IMF meant, inevitably, the introduction of harsh austerity measures: wage freezes, spending cuts, ending subsidies on basic food, relaxing the controls on prices and profits where there were such. Any government which undertook such a programme and then had to face the electorate within twelve months, was sure to lose the next election. So the PNP decided to hold an election a year earlier than it was due. I think most of us thought the JLP would win the 1976 elections. The JLP itself seemed sure it was going to win. It had the overt or covert support of investors and business people and all those who had been frightened into a state of non-think by the communist scare. And things were bad out on the streets. On top of the violence and the food shortages, we had almost daily electricity power cuts and water shortages. Life was ugly and becoming uglier. The country was under a State of Emergency to try and control the violence. This mitigated it marginally, though violence continued throughout the campaign itself. It seemed to me then that the forces of the opposition JLP were out-gunning those of the governing PNP. And I remember wondering what would happen to Jamaican democracy after the JLP won this election.

Polling day, 15 December 1976, was a relatively quiet, but worrying, day. I thought the JLP would surely win. The PNP had run out of steam and would have a bad time at the hands of the IMF. The JLP might fare better. The Americans had quietly shown their support for Seaga and the JLP. So when the results were announced that night and the PNP was returned to power with a massive forty-seven out of sixty seats and 56.8 per cent of the popular vote, I was completely surprised.

Daphne and I spent that night on the long verandah trying to make sense of this unexpected turn of events. The only reasonable conclusion we reached was that the Jamaican majority was sending a strong message of support to Michael Manley the man. They had all been witness to the bitter, strident campaign against him personally. Among many the perception was that this was because of his — to use one of his own favourite phrases — 'unswerving commitment' to the cause of poor black people. There was a widespread conviction that he cared personally and deeply about the problems of the poor black majority. So they gave him their love and their adulation. He had given them back a measure of their pride; made it possible for their children to aspire to and attain a quality of education once reserved for the 'high ups' only, in much the same way as it was in South Africa. They understood the forces that were opposed to Manley; they were the same forces they themselves had contended with all their lives. They called him 'Michael' in affectionate familiarity when he moved among them, and 'Joshua' when he inveighed against his, and their, enemies. He had developed an intensely personal relationship with the mass of ordinary Jamaicans. This was something few in his own party understood and none among his enemies seemed to.

The JLP opposition had, to a large extent, taken its cue from the anti-Manley propaganda in the 'foreign press' and mocked and scoffed and sneered and jeered at him. They ridiculed him in much the same way they had Mosaddeq of Iran. Despite strong denials, the more experienced observers had seen the 'fine Italian hand' of the CIA in aspects of the anti-Manley campaign. A majority of ordinary Jamaicans must also have concluded that the hand was being set against him. They rallied to his 'defence' while some of his own party people wavered, distanced themselves from him, even deserted him. Poor black Jamaicans saw him as the only champion of their cause since the days of Bustamante and the elder Manley. I do not think many believed he could overcome his enemies. They hoped he would. In any case, they wanted him to give them a good fight; they would be there for him as long as he was prepared to fight. Time longer than rope, and victory, however remote, was possible. That 1976 electoral victory was, we thought, a giving back to Michael Manley the love and confidence he had given to Jamaica's poor and dispossessed who were black. There was no other way to explain that electoral victory. And if we were correct, if this was no more than showing their love and giving the man another chance to resist his enemies, then the show-down was only being delayed. The forces against Manley had shown that they were not prepared to accept the will of the majority and allow him to govern in peace and stability.

Wise old Norman Manley, at the end of the 1950s and the start of the 1960s, had been gravely disturbed by what he sensed as the new type of politics the young Edward Seaga was bringing into Jamaican life. It was, he said, a departure from the old tradition of accepting and abiding by the will of the people until your turn came. The great virtue of the Bustamante-Manley version of democracy was its foundation of the right of the people to make the choices, right or wrong, good or bad; and if they came to regret any choice, they had the right to reverse themselves and choose again. As long as that process of peaceful choice prevailed, change and progress and development would be stable and orderly; not dramatic, as in violent upheavals, but slow and steady. Disturb this process and peaceful democratic change is put under threat. When the young man angrily threatened 'blood for blood and fire for fire' back then, Norman Manley was worried. By 1976 his fears were confirmed. The politics of peaceful change was under the threat of violence; the social fabric was being destroyed; there was no progress; no stability; little development. The Armageddon boys had come among us, and, in the language of the urban ghettoes 'the corner was dark', literally and figuratively. Remembering how it had been when we first came to Jamaica, and remembering the slow but steady change and development we had watched over the years, we too felt dark and bleak as we took stock on that 15 December 1976.

There was a short scheduled power cut in parts of the Red Hills area that night. There were no friends on the long verandah to share our thoughts and concerns this time. Far down on the plain the city of Kingston looked deceptively peaceful. We watched as one patch of lights came on and another went off in the now familiar game of the rationing of our electricity by residential blocks.

13

Radio Jamaica / The Media in the Third World

few months after the 1962 JBC strike, the chairman of the station's board of directors, Ivan Levy, telephoned me and asked me to resume working for the station as anchor for some of its talk programmes. I refused. He thought it was political. I said it was not. I told him that from what had transpired I did not think any government of Jamaica, after Norman Manley, could be trusted to own and control any media house without wanting to use it. We argued the point for the best part of an hour. Was there anything wrong with a government which had set up a publicly-owned media house giving direction to it? I said no, what was wrong was for the government to use it as an instrument of policy, to use it in the service of the party in power. How do you separate the national interest from the interest of the party in power? Are not the two inter-changeable? Norman Manley did it by giving it what amounted to a charter and then leaving it alone. But his early appointees to its board were mainly from his own party and his friends. The JLP government was doing nothing different. The great difference, I suggested, was that neither the government nor the board appointed by Norman Manley interfered in the daily running of the affairs of the station. What if the workers at the station were all either members or supporters of the opposition party? Was the party in power supposed to just let them use the station to undermine the government? Good professional journalists would not do that. Were all the journalists at the JBC before the strike 'good professionals'? I said yes; he said no. I said in any case that was not a judgment to be made by political partisans. So you would not take direction from a minister in charge of information? If I am working for the Ministry of Information, or some department of it, yes. You would not expect me to do so as a *Gleaner* or Radio Jamaica reporter, so why as a JBC reporter? Because you see it as a propaganda arm of the government? Norman Manley never did. The conversation ended. I never worked for the JBC again, not even when the PNP was returned to office after 1972.

For many years after the JBC strike, 'opinion journalism' disappeared from the radio and television landscape. The political climate was such that Radio Jamaica censored itself, broadcast no news commentaries. Radio Jamaica was foreign-owned, operated under government licence, depended on the goodwill of the government for its continued operation. Only the *Daily Gleaner* published opinion columns and freely exercised the right to criticise.

In a predominantly oral society the absence of political and opinion talk on radio and television was like imposing a rule of silence on ninety per cent of the Jamaican people. The only talk on radio and television were the speeches of ministers at this or that opening ceremony, or banquet or receiving some foreign dignitary. Our open society became semi-closed; the rich, educated part of it had access to the *Gleaner* and its subsidiaries, to short-wave radio (the 'dish' had not yet arrived) and to foreign newspapers and magazines. The poor, especially the rural poor, had only the dreary drone of ministerial chat about what they needed to know. It was a bleak period in Jamaican life. People who had been a part of the long history of voluntary social services quietly withdrew from doing their good works. The young, the poor, the weak, the old suffered. The business community was less charitable. We all withdrew, became impersonal. Towards the end of the 1960s, I think even the government recognised the sense of withdrawal which enveloped the nation. They did not know what the people were thinking. The interaction between leaders and led was confined to the faithful within the ruling party, or to the few outside that circle who still hoped for a little 'scarce benefits'; and to the business people who had to deal with government ministers and the departments from whom they needed licences and permits for the necessary imports. For the rest, the people were more withdrawn from their government than I had seen them in all my years in Jamaica.

So after a time, there came something of a relaxation and a few safe radio and television talk shows came back on the air. Radio Jamaica called me back to resume news commentaries. My scripts, now, were carefully vetted well before broadcast time. I usually recorded in good time for the station's lawyers to go over what I said. A few others were brought in. The JBC, however, did not resume news commentaries for a good while longer, though it did have some safe discussion programmes. But it was not as it had been before. The verve and élan had gone out of our journalism. With the exception of the ever-defiant John Maxwell, who had the proud reputation of being the most sacked journalist in Jamaica. A few other journalists, especially the veterans with family responsibilities, went back to the JBC, but handled their jobs with delicate care. The media managers were on guard. The minister in charge of information had built a reputation as a dangerous man to cross. I had spent most of this time writing a couple of books, *A Night of Their Own*, set in the South African anti-Apartheid struggle, and *This Island Now*, set on a Caribbean island that could be Jamaica. The basic themes were surprisingly similar. To help make ends meet,

Daphne taught art for two days a week at St Hugh's, a well-known girls' school, and two days a week at Priory, a co-educational school then independent of state support and catering mainly to the children of diplomats, expatriates and Jamaican children whose parents could afford the cost of an independent school. Most, if not all, of the small group of independent schools have since come under the umbrella of the state school system.

By the time of the 1972 elections, it was clear that the JLP was on its way out. There were deep divisions in the party and, as almost everywhere in the country, so many in the governing party were unhappy and withdrawn. The overwhelming Manley win of 1972 was, for me at least, more a rejection of the JLP than any enthusiastic recalling of the PNP. Many people were worried about what might follow the PNP's return to power. History proved them right. The Cold War turned very hot in Jamaica. Not as hot as in Nicaragua, where they had a full-fledged civil war with thinly veiled American involvement. But hot enough for little Jamaica to be deeply damaged.

In September 1977, the Prime Minister summoned me to Jamaica House. I knew what it was all about, so I went with mixed feelings. The government had decided to buy out and nationalise Radio Jamaica. Claude Robinson, his press secretary, had asked me for my suggestions on how they should proceed. It would, I knew, be one set of suggestions among many from people with more power and influence. My note suggested that if they bought Radio Jamaica, they should immediately divest it into as widespread a Jamaican ownership as possible: to the Jamaica Council of Churches, the Jamaica Agricultural Society, the Jamaica Teachers' Association, the business community, the trade union movement, the co-operative societies — all the so-called people-based organisations. The workers of the station should be the only people with individual share-holdings. When I met him, Manley liked the idea. It coincided with his own views. The question was how to execute it. What about a service contract with the former owners of Radio Jamaica? He was not sure we had the technical skills in Jamaica to run the station without their help. I knew the source of this advice. If it was accepted, huge service fees would go to Britain every year. I had worked at the station long enough to know that the engineering and technical people on the spot had been doing the work with minimal overseas technical help. To be sure, the chief engineer had come from Britain a long time ago. He, like so many of us from elsewhere, had fallen in love with Jamaica. He had become a Jamaican citizen after independence, married a Jamaican woman and decided to live out the rest of his life here. I was sure he would continue to work for a Jamaican-owned Radio Jamaica. There was no need to pay a massive annual service charge to any firm in Britain. The Prime Minister was still worried; those who had advised him of the importance of such a technical service contract had done a good job. He was almost sold on it. Then he said:

'I want you to chair the board that will oversee the change.'

I did not want to. I knew the JLP propaganda would put me through the wringer even before I started. I was concerned about the political ramifications. Ideally, the take-over of a radio station was important enough to be a bipartisan matter. In the Norman Manley-Bustamante days it would have been. But the two parties were so caught up in the ideological Cold War that bipartisan action on any issue was out of the question: the one proposed; the other opposed. I also thought a person with legal training should undertake this complex task. I said so to Michael Manley.

'That's why we're appointing Howard Hamilton as your Deputy Chairman. Your hands will not be tied. Put the station into Jamaican hands; that's all.'

'No behind the scenes directions?'

He bristled. 'You know me better than that!'

He was true to his word, though others among his inner circle did try a little influencing.

As I expected, all hell broke loose when Manley announced my appointment and, a day later, the names of a distinguished group of Jamaicans who would sit on the board. The JLP went to work immediately. As I drove home that evening the graffiti was already writ large on the walls I passed. The mildest slogan I remember said: HANDS OFF RJR. NO PETER ABRAHAMS! Others were more strident, some even personally abusive. Before the new board of directors held its first meeting, the Leader of the Opposition issued a declaration of 'no confidence' in the board and its chairman. I was, now, in the direct line of fire of our partisan 'war politics'. At the little official appointment ceremony, I told the Prime Minister, the media and the country that under my chairmanship Radio Jamaica would be neither an arm of the government nor an enemy of the government, no matter which party formed that government. It made no difference to the JLP. They wanted me to fail; they wanted the take-over to fail; they wanted the PNP to fail. If pulling me down personally would help bring down the PNP, they would do it; if pulling down RJR would help bring down the PNP, they would do it. The propaganda campaign was harsh and sustained. It began around 21 September 1977, when I was appointed, and continued until 11 June 1980, when I could write to the Prime Minister and tell him that the divestment had been completed, that the new ownership structure was in place, that Radio Jamaica now belonged to the people of Jamaica.

I was physically and emotionally drained and exhausted. What had started as a one-year assignment had taken the best part of three years to complete. It had proven more complex than we had thought. None of the directors had been given the traditional directors' fees. They were all people with other jobs and I insisted on no directors' fees. Not everybody liked it, but it prevailed. I continued my job as news commentator and accepted no other fees or perks. When it realised I would not be driven into quitting by its propaganda, the

JLP tried another line. The chairman of the board of directors of a company should not also be a worker of that company. So they called for me to either resign as chairman or resign as the station's news commentator. On this, too, the house was divided. For working journalists the important thing was the symbolism of my position. If a working journalist could become chairman of the board of a media house, it opened new possibilities for all journalists, set new horizons. Others, notably the print media, were not impressed; they played on the conflict of interest line. The latent self-contempt of others made them hostile to the notion of journalists running any major media house. We had two of the station's workers, elected by their peers, sitting on the board and sharing in the making of policy. One of them was a union delegate, the other the programme director. They faced periodic elections by the rest of the workers. If they did not serve the best interests of the workers, they risked replacement by other workers. This was one of the earliest worker participation exercises. We had regular departmental meetings and monthly staff meetings where management and workers discussed matters of concern.

Under its old structure, Radio Jamaica had been a successful vehicle for selling advertising, its primary concern the ensuring of a healthy profit for its overseas principals. Its board of directors, local businessmen and lawyers, were rewarded for their services, so my 'no directors' fee' policy was not popular. The staff was apolitical in the main. The few who were politically inclined, kept their views to themselves. They had been, generally, hostile to the take-over and the new structure. A few left; most stayed, watchful, on guard, ready to make trouble if their jobs were threatened. One or two ingratiated themselves with key people in the party in power; one or two others carried tales to the opposition. There were also some nasty little internecine battles by way of letters to the new chairman from one head of department about the performance and attitude of another, followed by some equally nasty petty response. Some resented me in my new position.

The Press Association and Theodore Sealy, the doyen of Jamaican journalists, now in retirement as *Gleaner* editor, supported me strongly. This helped greatly in that Cold War climate. Gradually attitudes changed. The station's workers shifted focus from serving foreign owners to serving Jamaican owners and the interest of the Jamaican people. When they arrived at the point of seeing me as 'the buffer' against political interests from all sides, distrust turned into co-operation. Staff members brought in small advertisements for a small commission. The big advertisers and the agencies continued to give us their advertisements. The sales staff began to realise that good quality radio could sell as well as the lowest common denominator stuff. Radio Jamaica, in Jamaican hands, was doing as well, or better, than in foreign hands.

It was possible at that point to do something about the equipment we used. Profits did not have to be sent abroad, so I had a talk with our chief engineer, the Englishman who had chosen Jamaica, and I discovered how rundown the equipment was. The former owners had spent little on new equipment. We were running on stuff ten years old and older. I got the board's agreement to release a million dollars for new equipment. The chief engineer's joy was beautiful to behold. Then I tackled a delicate and tricky one. The person doing the work of the company secretary was also functioning as secretary to the general manager. She was the Jamaican wife of the chief engineer. Her salary was less than the job was worth and when I enquired, I was told that if she were paid any more, the combined salaries of her husband and herself would be greater than the salary of the general manager. So she had to be paid as a secretary while doing the work of a company secretary. It was the only time during my entire stint there that I blew my top. The lady was formally installed as company secretary and paid the salary the job commanded. The rate for the job, regardless of gender, was applied across the board. At home that night Daphne's appreciation of the principle made this one of the sweetest of my small victories.

I often thought of how much easier the job would have been without the constant harassment from the opposition party. Radio Jamaica was being run as a much more socially aware entity now. We were supporting a basic school in our area, running a citizens' advice bureau, supporting a cluster of old people's homes after the government's old folks' home in Anthony Spaulding's garrison constituency was burned down with heavy loss of life — part of our ugly 'war politics'. In other circumstances, I might have gone to the leader of the JLP, told him what we were doing and where we were going and asked for his co-operation in what was clearly in the interest of the country. I could not. The new politics decreed that there were only two sides and who was not on the one side had to be on the other. Any approach would have to be a capitulation, a choosing of sides. You are either for or against: no middle ground.

Many people from other countries came to look at what had become known as the 'Radio Jamaica model' or the 'Radio Jamaica experiment'. They came mainly from Third-World countries where the preoccupation with press freedom was great. The Africans were interested in the details. How did we pay for the take-over? The government used taxpayers' money for the buy-out. We then worked out a share structure and the price for blocks of shares. A government entity held these shares until they were paid for in full. The churches and other large bodies had little difficulty paying for their blocks of shares. Some, like the agricultural society, arranged loans from the government. The station's workers, the only individual shareholders, paid for their shares by monthly deductions from their salaries. In this way we repaid the money the government had advanced within two years. All profits after that went to the shareholders. Because the take-over had been smooth, despite the political attacks, the station had been profitable throughout the transition. We had been able to improve the quality of the product out of earnings and build up a special reserve fund against libel when insurance became difficult. When they saw the picture clearly, most of the Africans wanted to adopt the model. The problem was whether their political leaders would accept a media entity that was independent of their influence and control. On that one we could not help. That was one between the media house of the country concerned and its political leaders. I realised then that even in the context of our bitter Cold War we were, in some ways, still better off than most other Third-World countries.

The Minister of Information from Guyana was interested, but doubted whether the President of the day, Forbes Burnham, would be. Mrs Phyllis Coard, the Jamaican-born Minister of Information in Maurice Bishop's revolutionary government in Grenada, spent the best part of a day examining the details of our model. At the end of it she exclaimed in disbelief that this really made the station a law unto itself. Accountable to the people by way of its broad-based ownership, I suggested. But this did not satisfy her. How could any government acquire something like this and then give away its power of control? They would not do that in Grenada. We even had a visit of exploration from two TASS operatives based in Mexico. They asked questions and listened, stony-faced. They made no comment after getting all the information they could. The important thing for most of our visitors was the question of whether poor Third-World countries could own one or more media houses that were independent of foreign money or narrowly-based local capital, and at the same time be independent of political control.

The Radio Jamaica model had shown that it was possible, but in the context of a relatively free and open society in which the government and the national leadership were prepared to facilitate the process. Of course, it can be undermined, as it was in the case of the JBC. But we had chosen another route. Instead of government ownership, we had gone for mass people-based ownership. We had so carefully planned the share-ownership that it would be almost impossible for any small group to stage a take-over. The test would come when another government, not as committed to a free press, came to power. What we had done was to ensure that it could not easily dismantle the new structure. To do so, it would have to invade Company Law, since our Articles of Association were bedded in Company Law and by this route Radio Jamaica acquired all the rights and immunities hitherto enjoyed only by the *Gleaner.* We sought and got an end to the business of licensing to broadcast. In any case, to suspend or take away the broadcast rights of an entity of such widespread national ownership would put any government which tried it into serious trouble with its own people. The greatest point of weakness, the greatest risk, now, was with the people at the station who had inherited this great new power. If they kept faith with the Jamaican people and did not undermine the process from within, Radio Jamaica would survive any external threat. If they broke faith, then, in time, what we had worked for so hard could be undone. Always, in the end, it comes down to the quality of those who manage and run the system. There is no protection against people and the ambitions of people.

During 1979 the country's 'war politics' became worse. The violence took on a random, unfocused appearance, no longer confined to the political garrisons. It hit the uptown areas which up to that point had been considered safe. It spread to the tourist areas, the whole country. The nation was caught in the grip of lawlessness and senseless violence. Our news reports, on both the electronic and print media, became daily and nightly catalogues of horror upon horror. The country was being methodically ripped apart. The government was losing control. As soon as it brought one crisis under control, another erupted. At the party level the JLP was on the offensive; it out-politicked, out-gunned, out-talked the PNP. The PNP itself was in confusion. It did not seem to know what was hitting it from all sides. Every time it failed some IMF test, it was thrown into turmoil. Those who had always been opposed to going to the IMF were almost as critical of the government as was the opposition.

For its part, the opposition seized on every IMF test failure to attack the government. The graffiti on hoardings, lamp posts, sides of buildings screamed: IMF - It's Manley's Fault. The shortages in the shops and supermarkets were Manley's fault. The high prices were Manley's fault. The electric power failures were Manley's fault. Jamaica was being made ungovernable and it was Manley's fault. Manley was scoffed at, caricatured as an idiot figure unable to do anything right — the Mosaddeq, Lumumba, Castro stuff. It was psychological warfare at its best. I did not think Manley or his party knew how to cope with this mocking kind of personal attack on a country's Prime Minister. But what damaged him and his party most with the mass of the Jamaican people was the feeling that they could not cope. Once or twice Manley had himself come under threat of harm. Once a group of soldiers of the Jamaica Defence Force had surrounded him, pointing their guns at him and he had to face them down. Another time the pilot of the helicopter in which he travelled lost consciousness and the helicopter nearly crashed. Manley himself wrote about these two incidents. In the prevailing climate of terror and intrigue they appeared sinister. One leading opposition politician had told a businessmen's gathering that the Manley government had to be removed by 'overthrow or underthrow'.

At the height of the anti-Manley campaign, when it seemed that some sort of coup was impending, a well-known figure in local banking telephoned me one evening to find out where I stood should something happen. It was a careful, guarded conversation but the implication was clear. I was shocked. I had not thought it had gone that far. I said I was against the unlawful change of any government. I said once you start changing governments that way, you opened the door to government by *coups d'état* and the end of democracy. I begged him and his friends to think seriously. That telephone call was a fair reflection of the mood among Jamaica's upper classes. They wanted to get rid of Manley at almost any price.

Among the mass of the ordinary people a mood of resignation had set in. It was clear by 1980 that Manley and the PNP could not prevail over the combined pressures of the internal political and economic opposition, the IMF, the US State Department and a generally hostile world press. And the ordinary people were bearing the brunt of the hardship.

In June 1980, the Chief of Staff of the Jamaica Defence Force announced that three officers and twenty-three 'other ranks' of the JDF: 'were detained on my orders... The facts are that within the past few weeks I received information that contact had been made by a civilian with a member of the JDF with a view to the implementation of a plan designed to overthrow the constitutionally elected government of Jamaica...' That one was nipped in the bud, but not the factors and forces behind it.

I had, soon after our arrival, developed the habit of spending part of my weekends wandering among the rural communities of Jamaica. I enjoyed the free, friendly warmth and generosity of the little village communities and it also gave me a good feel of the mood of the country. That mood, toward the end of 1980, was one of apprehension tinged with concern for the safety of Michael Manley. In one little rum shop an old man said: 'them waan kill him.' The mood was the same in Tiny's little bar in Red Hills square, though there they did not say it out loud. It was in one of the PNP strongholds, not too far from Radio Jamaica, that I first picked up the idea that if 'they' wanted the power so badly, if they were ready to kill him for it, then give it to them and save Michael.

When I told Michael Manley this after his bitter electoral defeat of 30 October 1980, he did not seem to take it in. He was shattered. His people had deserted him. His enemies had prevailed.

For me, the worst thing was not the defeat of Michael Manley. It was the destruction, for the time being, I hoped, of the Bustamante-Norman Manley way of conducting our politics. The door had been kicked wide open by the 'new politics' of destabilisation with outside assistance, terror and violence and economic sabotage internally. From here on, stable parliamentary democracy would be at the mercy of any strong ambitious politician who captured the leadership of either of our two major political parties, and for whom all means justified the ends. Democracy, everywhere, has always been vulnerable to such attacks. So how to safeguard against them?

First is the need for those who lead, or aspire to lead, to understand the limits of democracy. It is not only an awkward, costly and clumsy system to operate. It is also the most delicate yet devised by man. All sides must be committed to its rules, the most cardinal of which is that power resides in the people, not in the parties or their leaders; that the only way of access to that power is by free, peaceful and fairly conducted elections at regular intervals, with the outcome accepted as binding on all participants. Have this and it becomes possible to change and change again in peace, harmony and relative stability. Challenge, undermine, any facet of this and the system becomes corrupt, subject to abuse and manipulation and ultimately no longer a true reflection of the freely expressed will of the majority of the people. This process cannot be turned on and off. You cannot have 'a little democracy' until it becomes difficult; you cannot replace it by 'a little dictatorship' until the difficulty passes. If you do, the restored democracy will be a sick, distorted version of the real thing. It is too delicate for careless handling or the manipulation of it we have seen here in Jamaica and throughout the Third World in the age of decolonisation.

The miracle is that this delicate flower has survived. For this, I think, we must thank the will to freedom of the ordinary peoples of the Third World much more than their leaders. Leaders, freedom fighters, dreamers and visionaries have turned tyrant after achieving power; they have betrayed the trust of their people; not all but many; the people have been constant. I lean to that view of history which sees the broad movement of peoples, groping, searching, evolving, growing, as more important than the larger-than-life heroic figure who, it seems, makes things happen: history as social movement instead of history as the story of kings and queens and princes and powerful individuals. Of course, both views of history are valid. It is a matter of the priorities. Which came first: the people or the leader? You can have the people without leaders; you cannot have leaders without the people. Usually leaders emerge from among a people.

Edward Seaga was unique in Jamaican politics because he did not, like Alexander Bustamante, Norman Manley, Donald Sangster, Hugh Shearer and Michael Manley, emerge from the Jamaican people. His taproots, his origins, his historical and cultural past, did not come out of the evolving Jamaican story. He does not even have the same colour, or anything near it, of the mass of the Jamaican people. Bustamante, Sangster, Michael Manley were clearly 'Jamaica Browns' — light coloured Jamaicans, Norman Manley was rather dark 'Cape Coloured'. Shearer was black — no question; like 98 or so per cent of the Jamaican people. Seaga's ancestry was Middle Eastern, Lebanese, white, with no historical Jamaican linkages. There are white Jamaicans, whose roots and social historical background are as Jamaican as those of the blackest Jamaican. The point is not colour, though some from outside — especially blacks from Africa and the US — have made the point of the extraordinary phenomenon of a white man being elected to the highest political office in an overwhelmingly black society. It is not as simple as that. The man who leads the party becomes the Prime Minister when his party wins an election. The party makes the Prime Minister — when it wins. That is part of the institutionalised strength which has made for Jamaican stability. This man had to win, gain, capture the leadership of the party to have any hope of becoming

Prime Minister. If Mr De Klerk of South Africa had been a member of the ANC, become its deputy leader instead of Mr Thabo Mbeki, would he have become President of South Africa after Mandela retired? Most unlikely. Yet the ANC is as non-racial as any Jamaican political party. Joe Slovo, the white South African communist, was a leading member of the ANC and very close to Mandela. Yet nobody, certainly not Slovo before his death, aspired to being the non-black political leader of a black country.

In part, this is because of the tacitly accepted universal notion that leaders should be and should look like those they lead. The vast majority of Americans are white. Will the American majority be the first to elect and accept a black President? Certainly, Britain, the cradle of democracy, is never likely to accept a black Prime Minister. It has the unique distinction of having had a Jewish Prime Minister, but that was in another century, and he had been baptised as a Christian, thus overcoming the rule that Jews could not be members of the British Parliament. That rule was abolished in 1858. Britain's first Jewish Prime Minister was one of ueen Victoria's greatest empire builders. But Jews look like all other Europeans, which is what makes anti-Semitism the dangerous aberration which was the forerunner to racism and ethnic cleansing in our time. After Disraeli, a Jew as Prime Minister of any European country was feasible; you can even imagine a Jewish US President one day. The deep-seated notion of 'looking like one of us' precludes a black Prime Minister or President in any predominantly white society. So a white Prime Minister in black Jamaica was incongruous. What made for it? Could it happen anywhere in Africa?

Nowhere in Africa have I found the same deep-seated contempt for their blackness that I found among Jamaicans. It led to self-contempt and contempt for others like them. You hate what you are, you hate what you look like, you hate those who look like you. You want to be what you are not. What you are not is good, beautiful, wholesome, trustworthy. 'They' are everything you are not: 'they' are beautiful; 'they' are decent; 'they' are honourable. You trust them more than you trust your own. If 'they' ill-treat you, it is your fault, it is because of something you have done. Are these psychological wounds a hangover from the slave past everybody wants you to forget? Why is it better for them to lead than for your own? Where does it come from? Why this unique black country, with its unique white Prime Minister?

In the tourist trade the front line of discrimination is manned by its black workers. They are the ones who stop their fellow black Jamaicans at the entrances to the properties and make it difficult for them to get in. Or, when they get in, do not serve them for a long time, or until all the white customers have been served. It is not uncommon for black Jamaicans and black Americans to be made to wait until everybody else, even late arrivals, have been served before they are attended to. Then, as if to underscore that black is unwelcome, the service is bad and off-hand. In contrast, when I was first booked into Washington D C's Mayflower Hotel in the Kennedy days of the 1960s, the black taxi driver, the black door-keeper in his general's uniform, the black porters and the black waiters and maids who looked after the rooms, all went out of their way to make me feel welcome and looked-after in a place where hitherto few, if any, blacks had been received as guests. A smile, a small gesture, an eye contact, told me they were glad that I had made it and so opened the door a little for others like us. The taxi driver at the airport had been particularly concerned that I was not going to the wrong address, risking some public rebuff. I had to show him the telegram of confirmation of my booking by a famous publisher. Once that was clear, he was proud to take me and showed it with the flourish with which he opened the cab door and saw to my luggage at the great hotel's entrance. I had similar experiences in East and South Africa where the blacks always took care of their own. Only in Jamaica was this not always so. Here, in the service of the interests of their masters, black Jamaicans, like the drivers of slavery days, were harder on their fellow blacks than were *Bucky Massa* and his lady. This is part of the problem still to be overcome. Having a white Prime Minister in a black country indicates the dimensions of that problem.

14

Into the Jaws of Debt

One of the first small signs of the change of government after 30 October 1980 was the fading of the bright colours from the streets. Drabness, shortages, increasing poverty and unemployment had resurfaced sharply in the latter part of the 1970s. But the colourful dress chosen by many people had remained. With the assumption of political power by Edward Seaga, Jamaicans reverted to self-effacement; muted, colourless, almost invisible. The police once again became almost the repressive force of colonial days. Black youth in uptown areas were stopped and searched and 'draped'. The police described the new dispensation as the turn of the 'high ups'. I remember being told of a group of young white drunk American tourists in an open car on the Spanish Town Road hurling insults at all the blacks they passed. This was not Edward Seaga's fault. The man himself was free of any hint of racism. It was a consequence of the political changes of 1980. Jamaica had taken a dramatic swing to the right. The left was almost wiped out. The social manifestations were the resurgence of the old class and colour arrogance.

At a more serious level, key social programmes were dismantled or had their focus shifted. Housing was one such. There is a chronic housing shortage in all Third-World countries. In Jamaica the brilliant young British-trained barrister, Anthony Spaulding, PNP MP for the South St Andrew garrison constituency, and an American Jesuit priest, Father Gerald McLaughlin, co-operated in launching what they named a 'Sites and Services' programme. Spaulding was the Minister of Housing in Michael Manley's government of the 1970s, McLaughlin was his key adviser. Sites and Services allocated basic housing units at the cheapest cost to the poor in greatest need of housing. Each plot had the bare essentials: one room, toilet, light and water. The person buying this basic unit was then helped to complete the rest of the house. Buyers did the rest of the building or hired help to do it; they were responsible, while the Sites and Services people supervised. Those seeking homes became part of the process of providing homes. The money they paid for their homes went into providing more homes. In the period leading up to the change of government, Anthony Spaulding's Housing Ministry built, helped build and supervised the building of more homes than had all the previous governments combined since self-government. Sites and Services was at the heart of this massive building programme. When the new government came in, its supporters pounced on the Sites and Services houses. They abandoned the eligibility requirements and the self-help group structure on which the programme was based. Completed, but not yet paid off, units were taken over by middle-class party activists — for their own use or as investments from which to collect rent. A programme which had produced upwards of a quarter of a million housing units annually for the poor and needy quietly collapsed.

When Edward Seaga was sworn in at King's House by Governor-General Sir Florizelle Glasspole, a former protégé of the great Norman Manley, there was not-so-veiled mockery of ex-Prime Minister Michael Manley. The new Prime Minister called for an end to political violence.

There was, he said, no longer any need for it. Could the genie really be returned to its lamp that easily?

The most important problem facing the country and the new Prime Minister was, as it had been throughout the 1970s, the economy and Jamaica's critical foreign exchange problems. The Michael Manley government had had bitter experience with the conditions attached to IMF loans. The hope was that Seaga, free of any leftist political taint, no friend of Castro, no big voice in the Non-Aligned Movement, would do better with the IMF and the Americans. The Americans welcomed Seaga's victory and showed it with a quick inflow of aid. Corn flakes assumed symbolic importance; the supermarkets were full of huge boxes and shoppers showed their boxes on loaded trolleys. Imported meats and fruit and vegetables and wines and cheeses were everywhere. 'Eddie' was bringing in the goodies. Everybody seemed happy. Many Jamaicans who had left the country at the peak of the Manley years when the threat of 'communism' was seen as real, now came back. Not all; some had sold their homes at give-away prices to upwardly mobile 'socialists' and 'comrades'. They were the ones who had believed the propaganda; they were the ones who could not come home again. The 'realists' who had left but kept their homes and ran their businesses from Miami or South Florida or Atlanta or even further afield, were the ones who could, and did, come home again.

All the new goodies, the food and drink, as well as the essential oil and raw materials 'Eddie' brought in, had to be paid for, just as under 'Michael'. There would be continued borrowing from the IMF. We all knew it; some hoped the conditions for the borrowing would be less harsh on Seaga's Jamaica. After all, Jamaica had become a first-class member of the IMF back in 1963 when Donald Sangster, Bustamante's Finance Minister, once boasted in my presence of Jamaica's high credit-worthiness. In his eyes, the ability to borrow was a virtue, an affirmation of the high esteem in which the world at large held the country. That may have been true back then when we occasionally borrowed small sums of foreign exchange to tide us over some particular short-term exchange problem and when we could pay back the low interest loan on time. First-class membership had given us a special standing then, when we had the financial appearance of a developed country.

By 1976, world economic conditions had changed so much, and Jamaica, in common with the rest of the Third World, was in such a bad state of indebtedness that there were no classes of credit-worthiness. We were all flat broke, up to our ears in debt, and the IMF had become the world's loan shark, acting for the rich at the expense of the poor. Yet this was not what it was originally intended to be. Its primary objective back at its founding in 1944 was to secure international monetary co-operation and stabilise exchange liquidity. Membership was by subscription in accordance with the financial and trade standing of member countries. In return, they were afforded the facility to buy needed foreign exchange in their own currencies and so get over their temporary foreign exchange problems. It was only later, when the former colonies gained independence, that the IMF was transformed into the international moneylender of first resort, imposing its harsh economic prescriptions on the world's poor. So when Michael Manley sought a loan from the IMF in the 1970s, it demanded a massive devaluation of the Jamaican currency, a freeze on wages, cuts in government spending, an end to price controls and subsidies on basic foods, and no restraints on prices and profits. It was the beginning of a struggle with the IMF which increasingly occupied more of the government's time than managing the nation's affairs. Every quarterly IMF test became a battle of wits to fulfil IMF conditions and to persuade the IMF that the tests had been passed. It seemed the IMF could, at will, using its own sometimes movable targets, declare any test or any part of a test failed. A failed test meant the withholding of the credit tranche and the setting of new and harsher conditions. This played no small part in the failures and the final defeat of Michael Manley's government of the 1970s. Would Seaga fare any better under the IMF?

He did. Three months after Seaga became Prime Minister of Jamaica, Ronald Reagan took over the presidency of the United States from Jimmy Carter. Seaga was one of the first foreign heads of government invited to the Reagan White House. With the Prime Minister of little Jamaica an early honoured guest at the White House, the propaganda impact was region-wide. Jamaica, now, through Edward Seaga, was a respected friend of the United States. The feared 'Cuban connection' was dead. Aid flowed in. The IMF quickly signed an agreement with the new Jamaican government. The terms were better than those Manley had to accept, not so much in the letter as in the spirit. The quarterly tests and failures, so highly publicised in the Manley years, faded into the background. Jamaica became America's strategic Caribbean ally in the Cold War as the political pendulum swung from left to right almost everywhere in the world.

The attitude to Cuba had been part of Jamaica's politics from the first day of the Cuban revolution. In the Bustamante-Manley days the attitude had been largely bipartisan: respect for the rights of the Cubans to choose their own form of government and their own leaders; the right to be left alone to sort out their own problems. When Cuba declared itself communist, not everybody approved, but it remained their right to decide and it did not affect Jamaican diplomatic relations with Cuba. The Bay of Pigs was seen as an attempt by external forces to overthrow a sovereign government. This had been the attitude through the years under JLP and PNP governments. In the 1980s, with the political pendulum at its farthest point to the right, the Cold War at the point of visualising Star Wars, the traditional Jamaican-Cuban relationship was changed. Jamaica, under Seaga, expelled the Cuban Ambassador and severed relations. The attitude of the Cuban Ambassador, a very black and self-assertive man, the presence of a large number of Cubans in Jamaica, had all been turned into a party political issue as part of the wider Cold War conflict. The building of a school on the Catherine Plains by Cubans as a gift to Jamaica had been turned into a bone of contention. The training of young Jamaicans in Cuba as *Brigadistas*, construction work brigades, caused bitter political rows and fuelled the charges of Jamaica going communist. Cuban doctors had come and the quality of their services in the rural areas won them wide acceptance and popularity among the Jamaica people, so when the government severed diplomatic relations with Cuba in 1981, it announced that the Cuban doctors were free to stay and continue their work. The Cubans chose not to. Jamaica had placed itself in the forefront of the anti-Castro, anti-communist forces in the Caribbean and Latin America.

Jamaica became one of the major recipients of US aid. The economy looked good; future prospects were promising. But unemployment and poverty persisted. The government's spending cuts on social services allowed schools and hospitals and clinics to run down. In pursuit of eliminating waste in the public sector there was a general scaling down of such free services as pap smears for women at the one end and drastic cuts in spending on school and hospital maintenance at the other. The quality of life, ranked among the highest in the world in the 1970s, quietly began to decline in the 1980s. Jamaica borrowed more in the first three years of the 1980s than in all the rest of her borrowing put together since independence. Seaga's very high approval ratings from Reagan in Washington and Mrs Thatcher in London made it that much easier for Seaga to take Jamaica further into the jaws of debt than the 'socialist' Michael Manley was ever allowed to go. This one is, and will remain, the millstone around Jamaica's neck for as far into the twenty-first century as you care to look — unless the world economic order is radically reformed and Third-World debt is cancelled.

A small sign of the times for journalists was when President Reagan visited Jamaica in April 1982. The usual small army of advisors, security people and news people travelling with the President outnumbered the local journalists who covered the visit. At the Hope Road entrance to Jamaica House, the Prime Minister's official residence, the Americans went in without let or hindrance. The Jamaican journalists were stopped and searched. Even Ken Chaplin, the Prime Minister's Press Secretary, had to resist the indignity of a body search from American security. The local journalists were made to wait on the grounds outside Jamaica House while some American security person asked, 'Who are all these black people?' Only after that question was answered to his satisfaction were the Jamaican journalists allowed in.

In terms of the Cold War, however, Jamaica in the 1980s was a key player in the Reagan anti-communist thrust. This was made manifestly clear by her role in the sorry events in Grenada in 1983.

Grenada, 'The Isle of Spice', is the southernmost of the Lesser Antilles. It is 21 miles long, 12 miles wide, and in 1983 it had a population of between 90,000-95,000, of whom 85 per cent were black, 11 per cent mixed or coloured, three per cent of Indian origin, and the remaining one per cent of European and American origin. Two-thirds of the population lived in rural areas, one-third in the urban areas. After the collapse of the Federation of the West Indies, it became an independent member of the British Commonwealth. Its elected Prime Minister was trade unionist turned politician Eric Gairy, who turned out to be a 'boss politician' of the worst order. Though Grenada was a constitutional democracy, Gairy's 'goon squads' routinely beat up opposition politicians and broke up their meetings. He nonetheless had a strong following among the rural poor. Among the opponents killed by Gairy's 'Mongoose Gang' was the father of a young man named Maurice Bishop. The young Bishop, in association with others formed the New Jewel Movement and in 1979, while the now knighted Sir Eric Gairy was out of the country, Bishop's NJM staged a bloodless coup and established the first Marxist revolutionary government in the English-speaking Caribbean.

Most leftists in the region, especially the fledgling communist Workers' Party of Jamaica, saw this as the start of the shape of things to come. Bishop, as charismatic as Michael Manley, but at a quieter level, established strong relations with Cuba, visited the Soviet Union, and was on his way home from one of his overseas trips, when a group of hard-liners within his revolutionary government, seized power. They confined him to house arrest on his return. Then, in one of those murky political power plays only possible where there is no open democracy, they kept him away from his beloved 'masses'; and when he did not bend to their demands to endorse rule by some faceless party committee, they killed him and those loyal to him. As so often in history, a revolution had consumed the finest of its own. The terrible and tragic implications of this piece of political self-destructive foolishness came starkly home to Jamaicans as they listened on their radios to General Austin ordering all Grenadians to stay home or be shot on sight.

A week later, the United States staged a full-scale invasion of little Grenada with all the might and power of the world's ascendant superpower. Jamaica's Defence Force sent Jamaican soldiers as part of that invasion. One or two other Caribbean countries which had been lobbied by Seaga and the US State Department operatives, sent token supporting police. Trinidad was opposed to the invasion, asserting that there could have been a Caribbean solution to the Grenada problem. Mrs Thatcher's government, it emerged, had not even been informed. Michael Manley, not yet recovered from his terrible electoral defeat, warned quietly that the entire region would live to regret taking part in that invasion. The leaders of the Workers' Party of Jamaica urged Cuba to intervene. The Cuban government, however, was not about to put its own revolution at risk by going to the aid of dangerously reckless political adventurists. The Cubans had lost some of their best workers who had been building a new international airport for Grenada. They did not want to risk losing Cuba itself in a head-on confrontation with Reagan's armies. The Cubans rejected the WPJ efforts. The WPJ itself would not condemn the group that had seized power and killed Maurice Bishop and those loyal to him. A particularly ugly feature of the Bishop killing was the ensuring that his remains would not be found. This was a throwback to the darkest days of the Soviet communist purges, a mirror of the Argentine 'disappearances' in our day.

Grenada was occupied in a week. The prospects for socialism of any kind — democratic or Marxist — in the Caribbean were set back for as far into the future as you care to look. The Caribbean house was now as divided against itself as was the Jamaican house. Some were part of the American invasion of little Grenada, some were opposed. Jamaican soldiers were shown on television as part of the occupation forces. Enthusiasm for victory in the short run overshadowed any doubts and questions ordinary Jamaicans had. Seaga, and the Americans, had defeated the forces of communism in the Caribbean; he was hailed as a hero. He seized the opportunity to call a snap election.

One of the few matters on which the two major political parties worked together was electoral reform. Parliament had agreed on an advisory committee to oversee all the details necessary for the conduct of free and fair elections; the periodic updating and revising of the voters' lists, ensuring that the physical plant and personnel were in place. The advisory committee worked with a full-time director of elections who supervised a well-trained staff of professionals. After the last elections, Prime Minister Seaga had promised the Leader of the Opposition, Manley, from the floor of the House that no further elections would be held until the electoral lists were brought up to date. The lists, in 1983, were more than three years old. The opposition PNP reminded Parliament and the country of the Prime Minister's promise. The Prime Minister refused to back down and what became known as the 'Nicodemus' election was called for December 1983.

Michael Manley persuaded his party to boycott that election. Many did so unwillingly but none defied the party's decision. Jamaica became, for the first time in its modern political history, a one-party state. All sixty parliamentary seats went to the governing JLP. The country was plunged into confusion. Nobody expected this turn of events. Editorials and pressure groups tried to persuade Manley to reconsider. For Manley, it was a matter of principle. The Prime Minister had made a promise in Parliament and the Prime Minister had broken that promise. To participate would be to condone that violation of a solemn pledge. I formed the impression that Seaga himself had been caught off-guard by this development. But like Britain's Margaret Thatcher, the gentleman was not for turning. Between 1983 and 1989 Jamaica had a one-party parliament and was, for all practical purposes, a one-party state.

Many people within the governing party were not happy. The Prime Minister's control over his party by now was such that they either held their peace or left the party. It had reached the point, as he described it in later years, of 'my way or the highway'. Even Hugh Shearer dared not speak out publicly. So the party, its trade union affiliate, all the organs of the 'high ups' — the chambers of commerce, the manufacturers' association — quietly accepted the fact of the one-party parliament. Whenever Parliament met, the constituents from the Prime Minister's West Kingston packed the public galleries, often participating loudly in the proceedings. Radio and television were commandeered to provide full coverage of important events, and the government determined what those were. Society appeared intimidated and submissive. Political patronage was more pervasive than ever. Old institutions were given new names and served partisan ends. The young who were politically 'correct' went to academies for a few weeks or a few months and then, in neat two-piece dark suits, 'graduated' and received certificates. It was a bad time for the old-style Jamaican education of proficiency in reading, writing and arithmetic.

The old-style independent civil service was brought under direct political control at the upper levels. The lower levels quietly resisted the politicisation. The quality of the service deteriorated. Unemployment and poverty deepened and the guns which had been introduced as tools in the 'war politics' of the 1970s, now became tools of crime and apolitical violence. As crime escalated, the police became more repressive towards the young men of the inner-city ghetto areas. The sight of jeeps full of police with long guns racing through the streets became commonplace. Motorists and pedestrians hurried past or looked away as police tumbled out of jeeps to pounce on young men and 'drape' them. It happened on the highways, around the supermarkets, in business districts, even in some quiet residential neighbourhoods. Again, as when times are not seen as right, the house became quiet, sullen, withdrawn. The government tried to counter this by inviting non-elected groups to come to the bar of Parliament and speak to the nation's problems. The PNP opposition maintained its boycott. A few groups came forward; nothing came of them.

The Prime Minister's friendship with the American President made it easier to get aid, but it did not affect the relations with the IMF as much as had been hoped. The conditions were as stern and harsh for Jamaica as for all Third-World countries: the same wage freezes, the same cuts in social spending, the same deregulation, freeing up of profits and opening up of markets. By 1985, the after-glow of the Grenada adventure had faded. Unemployment was rife; the social fabric was falling apart; a coalescence of discontent resulted in the general strike of 1985. The Prime Minister's handling of that general strike was every bit as tough and unyielding as had been Thatcher's of the British miners' strike and Reagan's of the American air traffic controllers. It developed into a showdown between the Prime Minister and the organised trade union movement. The Prime Minister won; trade unionism in Jamaica has not fully recovered from that defeat.

The local government system had been one of the greatest victims of the one-party parliament. Its annual budget of the time was withdrawn and re-allocated in equal amounts to each of the sixty members of parliament to spend in their constituencies. They would not receive direct cash, but would identify projects and once these were approved the money would be released. Final approval was with the Prime Minister as Minister of Finance. The local government system was allowed a few minor responsibilities, such as looking after cemeteries. This, more than anything else, galvanised the PNP opposition into campaigning for local government elections which were long overdue. The government was forced to call local government elections in 1986. The outcome was a devastating defeat for the governing party. A rejuvenated PNP, now in charge of all but one or two of the largely powerless local authorities, declared this clear proof of the people's disapproval of the Seaga government. They called for new national elections. But then nature intervened to put Jamaica's party politics 'on hold'.

15

Wild Gilbert!

On 12 September 1988, Hurricane Gilbert struck Jamaica. It was a Monday. Jamaica had been preparing for Gilbert since the Thursday before, when it became clear there was no way the storm would not strike. It was coming straight at us with no other land in its path. Forecasts from the weather centre in Miami and from our own local centre brought televised images of a storm of vast proportions. Its area was several times the size of Jamaica, and it would cover the entire island. In the past, storms had threatened, then passed on, touching some point of the island, never the whole island. We had had near misses so often, had been side-swiped so often, that many believed it would happen again. Some believed devoutly that the Almighty was especially protective of Jamaica. Why else had it been spared so often? We talked of the time when one hurricane had hovered over neighbouring Cuba, moving back and forth, back and forth, smashing her again and again. The damage was awful, the loss of life minimal. The loss of human lives in these storms provides a fair measure of the social state of a country. In the more developed, the French-, Dutch- and English-speaking Caribbean and

Cuba, loss of life was low. In Haiti and parts of Central America, it was heavy. Some Jamaicans were sure that hovering storm over Cuba was a sign of anti-communist disapproval from On High. If He took sides in wars and battles, why not in where and how storms struck? God had been on our side in most of the previous storms of this century. We had had a few bad ones, of course, but others had had worse. This time all the signs said it was our turn. Still some hoped for a miracle.

At Coyaba, an exposed house on a hill, Daphne and I were alone with our four Labradors, two of them descendants of dogs inherited from Aron when he left home in 1972 to go to England. Our eldest daughter, Anne, had left home earlier, in 1966, and was in Milan, Italy. Our youngest daughter, Naomi, was in England. The family was scattered and we were alone.

We had built two cottages not far from our house in the 1970s as part of our pension plan for old-age. Jamaica was no welfare state; social security was rudimentary. Daphne recalled the difficulties we had faced as a young couple with small children and decided to rent to such young couples with small children at nominal rentals as a way of helping out at a difficult point in life. We ran into problems when we refused to rent to people without children. The housing shortage was widespread and rents unreasonably high; some thought it unfair that we, with our low rent, discriminated in favour of young families. Singles, couples without children, older folk also needed help. We agreed, but we could not help everybody — we had chosen our way to help.

There were problems. A young man came and told us he had two small children so we let him a cottage. It turned out the children and their mother were not with him and he moved in with a 'fiancée'. They both worked down in Kingston, left the place locked up all day and came home very late at nights. One day the place was broken into and robbed. They left after four months. Another man came with his wife and three small children. In the course of a careful interview it came out that he wanted to rent the cottage as a form of investment; they would move into one room and sublet the rest for two or three times the rent he would pay. They were indignant when we turned them down and threatened legal action on grounds of discrimination. Another time, a 'mother's boy' lied to us about his family and brought in a beautiful young half-Chinese wife who had her first baby at Coyaba. He tried to keep her in virtual isolation while he spent his nights out. When he brought one of his ladies to the cottage and the wife objected so loudly that we heard it all from about one hundred yards away, we decided it was time for a change.

Our original idea was that as soon as tenants were secure and able to, they would leave and make room for other young couples more in need. It was the idea of the 'halfway house' of the British Welfare State that was bound to come unstuck when taken out of context. And it was. Anybody, any couple, letting a modern steel and concrete house of three bedrooms, two bathrooms, large 15 by 19 feet living-room, kitchen and spacious verandah, all tiled and situated in half an acre of garden space for one hundred and twenty Jamaican dollars a month, had to be either rotten rich, stupid or weird, or a combination of all three. Many of those who became our tenants thought we were. One of the cruellest things about colonial and post-colonial societies, especially among the middle classes is their indifference to the social conditions in which their neighbours live. So we were seen as odd, even by those who sought to rent our 'cheap' cottages. These were all young middle-class people who came as the result of either word-of-mouth recommendation or by way of advertisements in the paper. The people we wanted to help most, who needed the help most, were not the ones who came until many years later. After a series of bad encounters with middle-class tenants, we decided to stop having tenants for a while. So we were without tenants in 1988 when Hurricane Gilbert came.

Miss Maisie, who had worked with us for nearly twenty years, had, in 1983, decided it was time for a change. She had been Daphne's help and companion and shared in the transforming of Coyaba from just a place in the wilderness into a warm and friendly place in the wilderness. They had built stone walls and footpaths together. She had helped with the building of the cottages. They had painted walls and ceilings together, planted and nursed trees together, learned to mix mortar together. Daphne had taught her how to make patterns, how to sew. They exchanged cooking knowledge. She had discovered how much a person could do for themselves and started doing it at their own little house in Rock Hall. Her children had grown up, received free secondary schooling during the Manley years and got good jobs, but her husband was ailing. So she gave up the day's work, but not the warm friendship. In 1988, she too was gone and we prepared for the coming storm on our own.

On the Friday Daphne began taking down all the pictures, wrapping the manuscripts in plastic and covering the books. On the Saturday we began to batten down the house. A carpenter from Rock Hall known only as 'Shorty' had, in the early days of the building of Coyaba, spent weeks building and hanging folding storm shutters. They had not been needed till now. They were pretty things in natural mahogany for which I remembered paying a pretty price at the time. We opened and tested the shutters on the Saturday and they seemed fine. I wondered in passing whether they were not too delicate, too artistic to withstand any serious storm. But they were all we had and they gave us a sense of security.

Then we checked all the basic things: kerosene, tins of bully beef, sardines, milk powder, flour, and hundreds of bottles of drinking water and drums of water for household purposes. We had seven fifty-gallon drums placed strategically to catch rainwater from the slightly sloping roof. We did not think to take up Daphne's most expensive piece of sitting-room furniture, her 17-feet by 12-feet carpet. That one we would live to regret. The house was now prepared.

On Sunday morning I prepared a draft of the news commentary for broadcast on the Monday evening. Daphne and the dogs spent the morning and most of the rest of the day picking fruit. The dogs competed to retrieve the fruit that had rolled down the hill. I helped heaving large baskets of fruit and laying them out on the table tennis board in the huge living room. Hundreds and hundreds of oranges and grapefruit and ortaniques and limes; vast quantities of avocado pears, with larger numbers left on the trees; some too high to reach, others not fit. Daphne had a favourite lime tree, not too far from the kitchen, which she fed constantly with waste and which returned the favour by bearing most profusely nearly all year round.

The wind began on Sunday evening. The electricity company warned early that light and power would be cut during the storm, so we prepared our lamps and candles. The wind grew stronger, took on a steady high pitch. The shutters began to shake. The television, the lights, suddenly went out. We lit our lamps and candles, checked our preparations again. I had put fresh batteries into the radio, so the sound of Radio Jamaica was loud and clear. The telephone, too, stayed with us. Darkness fell over all Jamaica that Sunday night; darkness and the steady howl of the wind.

On Monday morning I finished my commentary early. I telephoned the radio station and arranged an early booking. The line was starting to break up. The wind now brought gusts of rain with it. Trees were swaying wildly everywhere you looked. Some were being blown over. Our stretch of the main road between Red Hills and Rock Hall had a sharp rise on one side and a steep drop on the other. There was the danger of rocks rolling onto the road from the top and of vehicles and animals dropping down the sharp fall. In the blinding wind-driven rain it would be easy to go off the road. I drove slowly, carefully, down to Kingston. The road was deserted. Red Hills square was empty. I passed one or two cars on the way down. Usually the traffic is heavy. At Havendale the road in front of the gas station was already flooded. All the way to Radio Jamaica it seemed like a deserted town. A few people at the supermarket on Red Hills Road, which is not part of our Red Hills up in the hills, were doing last-minute shopping. The Constant Spring Road was wet and empty. Kingston was fast turning into a ghost town. On radio, the disaster preparedness people had taken over and were telling people what to do and where to go in case of need. There were lists of shelters for the various communities, mainly church buildings; instructions on where to go and what to do if you were flooded out. It was all businesslike, efficient, professional. In times of trouble Jamaica is at it best, Jamaicans are at their best. The cantankerous divisiveness disappears and they become a strong, flexible united force. Daphne and I had agreed, a long time ago, that if we had to face any serious natural disaster we would prefer to be in Jamaica, among Jamaicans. Why can't they be like that without the threat of disaster? Britain, too, had been a good place to be in times of trouble. The only difference, for both of us, was that in Jamaica we had no sense of being outsiders.

Radio Jamaica was at its embattled professional best, all small-minded pettiness buried under the imperatives of the day. I recorded quickly and left, knowing they would stay on air, whatever Hurricane Gilbert threw at us. Then I made my way back to Coyaba where I knew Daphne and the dogs waited anxiously. For their sakes as much as mine, I had to get home quickly and safely. The radio reported land slippages and fallen trees in many parts of the country. The wind was now wild, the rain heavy, the beginnings of thunder and lightning. I encountered rocks and boulders on the way up. The rushing water made it difficult to see the road surface; there was the danger of small, submerged sharp obstacles cutting tyres. I did not want to be immobilised on the road today. I was able to work my way past two big fallen boulders on the road near Red Hills. If one or two more rolled down, the road would be blocked. My first fallen tree was past Red Hills Square, past the school, past what was known as Feurtardo's Corner. It was small enough for me to drag to the side of the road. I reached home near on twelve with Hurricane Gilbert now on us. The strong house with its solid slab roof was shaking as though some invisible giant was trying to uproot it. The two younger dogs were a bit hysterical; the elders, like Daphne, tried to contain their alarm, stayed close to her. The radio said the storm was blanketing Jamaica. The two international airports were closed. All fishermen were ordered back to land. We were at the mercy of a storm which had travelled all the way from the West African coast to come here and take little Jamaica by the scruff of its neck and shake the daylights out of it.

We heard a sharp crash. One of 'Shorty's' shutters had been ripped open, smack against the wall then swung inward shattering one of the windows. Wind and water poured into the sitting room in a huge torrent. We struggled to seal off the opening with hard board backed up by chairs. We were now ankle-deep in water. One of the younger dogs looked at all the water, looked at us struggling with it, then squatted and peed in it. It eased the tension, made us feel better. Somehow we stemmed the rushing in of the water. It still came in, but more slowly now. I worked my way to the verandah by way of the bedroom door which was more protected from the driving wind. I clung to the wall while trying to secure the swinging shutter. Every now and then a gust of wind threatened to lift me bodily from what we had always seen as a most sheltered verandah. Once I had to drop flat on the ground and hang on to the verandah railings not to be swept away.

Then the steel arm on top of our roof which carried electric current to the cottages in normal times, snapped from its mooring and swung wildly in the wind, and smashed into our bedroom window. I was glad the power had been turned off. We would have been in worse trouble with an unmoored live wire violently swinging in the wind. Daphne had noticed a rhythm to the storm. The wild gusts built up to a crescendo, tapered down, then built up again, in a circular motion. Once we got the timing of it, I could dash out at the 'quieter' points and anchor anything loose. I managed to 'rope' the piece of swinging steel during one such 'quiet' point and anchored it to a strong young Pouis tree. It was then that I saw that the two large picture windows Daphne had put in the little guest flat beside the house were no longer there. They had been removed so completely and neatly that I did not notice it at first. Gilbert had simply taken Daphne's picture windows.

In the quiet, when we were in the 'eye' of the storm, we went out to look at what Gilbert had done. It was eerie. The Jamaican landscape had been transformed. There were no trees anywhere on the hills surrounding us. Daphne wept for the first time when there was no sign of her favourite lime tree; it was gone as though it had never been. The hundred or so avocado pear trees she and Maisie had planted over many years on the western slope below the house were knocked down, broken, or gone. Down in the valley where old Ernest Williams had worked the land and grown all manner of vegetables, it was a bleak and barren moonscape. In every direction we saw a ravaged land. Roofs of houses on odd spots of barren land; smaller wooden houses themselves lifted up and planted in most unlikely spots. The only living things, two cows walking sedately up the parochial road from which I had first approached Coyaba all those many years ago. Then the storm returned in force. The eye had passed over us and Coyaba had taken and withstood its first battering. We went in, fed ourselves, and braced ourselves for the next phase.

The lull lasted for about fifteen minutes. I was securing 'Shorty's' shutters on the western side of the house when the storm returned with sudden ferocity. It whipped the shutter out of my grasp. I felt a blow to the side of my head but managed to grab it again and secure it. Inside, Daphne suddenly cried out. Blood was streaming down the side of my face. I was unaware of it, felt nothing.

The wind now hammered so furiously that we thought it would smash down the most exposed of the two doors leading to the verandah. Water poured in from everywhere. Our sealed house was one big sieve. We were soaked to the skin, ankle-deep in water, minimally dressed. Everything was sodden. I fretted about the books which had not been cellophane-wrapped. We moved the driest of our clothing and bedding into the driest small bedroom, wedged between two larger ones. Then, with our lamps primed, the dry tack we would eat, our dogs, and vast piles of old newspapers for their bedding, and of course our reliable radio, we retreated into the small bedroom, turned on the radio, and waited out the storm. It was a long night of thunder and lightning. For all man's vaunted technological advances, one violent eruption of nature could show us up for the puny creatures we are in the cosmological scheme of things.

I turned to Daphne on the single bed in the tiny room. For all the roar and thunder and lightning and lashing rain, she was out like a light switched off, exhausted, worn-down, but a tranquil look on her face. The dogs were littered about the little room, as relaxed now as their sleeping mistress. They had been good throughout the harsh ordeal, always trying to please.

I made sure the torch was within reach; slipped the box of matches into a plastic bag, then I blew out the lamp. I remembered our youngest daughter's disappointment at not having experienced what she called 'a real hurricane' in all her years in Jamaica. I was glad she and her brother and sister were not here to experience Wild Gilbert with us. It would have been that much more difficult to cope; I would have worried more. Then I drifted off to the sound and fury of Wild Gilbert.

At some point in the early hours of the morning I was awakened by the silence that had come over my world. The sound and the fury and the thunder and lightning were gone; the world was unnaturally, disturbingly quiet. The door from the bedroom to the verandah had swollen tight and could not be opened. I went round to the sitting room. The wall clock had stopped. I tried the two doors from the inside; neither would open. The kitchen door would not open. I tried the door of the little storeroom facing north. It opened. I went out to a strange world, bleak and barren, as it might be at the end of man's time on earth, after everything had been destroyed. The light of the moon made a barren moonscape of all I could see. I felt alone and depressed. I went back in and woke Daphne.

'Is it over?'

I said: 'Yes.'

'Terrible?'

'Yes.'

She got into damp clothes and we went out again, followed by the dogs.

'Oh Lord...' she whispered.

This was not our world. Not the world of our Coyaba, of flowers and trees and the endless sounds of birds on wing, sometimes so close they whizzed past our ears and noses, so tame that we expected them to land on us. We saw a few dead bodies on the ground, no living birds at all. The birdbath was nowhere to be seen. After a while we saw a few bees, low on the ground, trying to suck nectar from the trefoils close to the ground. All the rest was a lifeless landscape of barren and broken things: snapped trees, transplanted roofs, downed power lines, trees across roadways and pathways, the television dishes of the rich and well-to-do perched on bare hillsides. When the sun came up, the unnatural quiet remained: no sound of traffic, no people on the road where it passed the foot of our hill. We were alone in the world. Our own long driveway was blocked with boulders and fallen trees.

We brought out the small power generator I had bought a few weeks earlier, read up on how to start it, and began a new daily chore which would last for at least three months. Shortly after I started our generator and got the power going to keep the food in our refrigerator cool, we heard the first sounds of life from across the hill: another generator starting; then there was another and another. It was the new sound that would be with us until light and power were restored. Radio Jamaica's first major morning news bulletin was the beginning of the long catalogue of the damage caused by Wild Gilbert. Roads, bridges, homes all over the land were destroyed or seriously damaged. Agriculture was wiped out. At least half a million people were homeless. Nationally and individually, we were counting our losses and beginning the long process of rebuilding. We were learning fast that the worst part of any disaster is the huge restoration effort that comes after.

When the airports opened within a few days, help from all over the world began pouring in. Without it, people would have starved and many would have died. Unfortunately, this type of help, on this large scale, also encourages the 'freeness mentality'. There were adults in the urban ghettoes of Kingston who have not held a job in their lives. Give them a job and they would work for an hour or two then leave because they got tired or bored — or just did not want to do it. They did not have the habit of steady work. These were the 'unemployables', incapable of holding down a job. Then there were the 'scufflers', usually small-built, energetic, very bright. They had spent a lifetime surviving on their wits by petty theft and petty 'conmanship'. They stole, robbed — on a small scale which made it not worth the victims' while to have them arrested. Oddly, few 'scufflers' went on to become bigger criminals. Lying by bending the truth in favour of self-interest is widespread throughout society, as is an enormous natural charm. Petty sessions court cases in which contending parties try to out-lie each other can be as entertaining as the best comic theatre. The aftermath of Gilbert was a golden opportunity for these. Some went from help centre to help centre, collecting bedding, clothing, household utensils, even furniture. This was small beer compared with some of the bigger stealing from the help that came in.

Gilbert had lifted roofs from homes all over the country. Millions of sheets of zinc came in to help restore the nation's roofs. Vast quantities of the zinc simply vanished on landing. There was a roaring black market trade in zinc. Those who needed the zinc most often did not get any. Speculators hoarded large quantities for later sale. It became the Zinc Scandal, which resulted in a later Zinc Enquiry. With corruption at the top and corruption at the bottom, it made the headlines. As usual, the overwhelming majority of Jamaicans, who are decent, honest, hardworking, uncorrupt, were tainted. Jamaicans, our own media said, copied by the 'foreign press', are a corrupt and thieving bunch. Jamaicans are violent; Jamaicans are aggressive. The Jamaican stereotype reaches out even to our friends in the smaller islands of the Caribbean who are convinced that Jamaicans are the most violent and dangerous people on earth. Living with all this, seeing it close on, we found it a microcosm of the human condition. Gilbert threw it into stark relief.

A small nation getting its light and power by individual families running their own generators is costly and polluting. The smell of raw petrol was everywhere: the homes on the hills and in the suburbs, the shops and plazas, the business offices. The steady hum of the motors became as constant as was the hum of Johannesburg near the mine dumps in the days of my youth. The minister responsible for public utilities in the Seaga government took the large number of the little generators as an indicator of how much hidden money there was in society. A middle-class professional woman with no 'man a yard', who had to start her little machine every morning, was not impressed and vowed to switch her vote. Our musicians turned the Gilbert disaster into the stuff of good entertaining songs: a memorable one was about how a man in a shack acquired a satellite dish.

The way the land recovered was a miracle. Within a few weeks the grey deadness turned to living green; no trees, of course; but green shrub and weed replaced the lifelessness. It was still a bleak land, but a living land now. Daphne saw a small flock of dazed birds among the dropped and rotting fruit. They were so desperately hungry they did not seem to notice her presence, even when she went close up to put down water for them. Life was returning to a desolate land. We made a new birdbath. Daphne waited for her beloved little hummingbirds. They did not return.

People who had bought insurance for just such a disaster discovered their insurers did not have the money to pay the full value they had insured for. They had to accept less, often after protracted negotiations. Among the more religious the extent of their damage was seen as punishment for hidden sins. People went into withdrawal. The trauma was pervasive, especially among the elderly, many of whom simply lost the will to life. We ourselves had not insured Coyaba. Instead, we had earmarked a portion of our annual savings for such a contingency. We spent about forty thousand Jamaican dollars on re-flooring the worst damaged bedroom, restoring the blown-out flat windows — not with picture-glass this time; replacing Daphne's ruined carpet. It would have cost much more if we had not done most of the work ourselves.

We were without electricity and running water for three months. Others were more fortunate. Those lower down the hills and in Kingston had light and power and piped water within weeks. Some, more remote and isolated than us, had to wait longer. Life gradually returned to normal. The wait for the return of the hummingbirds lasted three years. Friends had comforted us with reports of seeing a few in quieter parts of Kingston. A surprisingly large number of our fallen trees sprouted anew. Daphne and I now felt like seasoned Caribbean man and woman. We had encountered one of the major hurricanes of our century, endured its onslaught, experienced life in the eye of the storm. We had survived to think and talk about it. We had shared the experience and it had further strengthened and deepened the bond between us, between us and Coyaba, between us and the creatures who share it with us. The day the first hummingbird turned up outside the kitchen, Daphne went into a radiant glow. We had a party.

---- 16 ----

The Face of the New Order

J amaica gradually returned to normal. Our farmers had not
immediately replanted their lost crops: there had been no handing
out of seed or plant suckers, so three weeks and more passed
with no replanting. We lived off an abundance of gifts of food. One
of the most dubious gifts of all was a very large supply of small chain-
saws, ostensibly to clear our roads of fallen trees. They turned out to
be quick and efficient means of further deforestation. Charcoal was
in great demand where there was no cooking gas and electricity. A
thriving charcoal business sprang up. We forgot how long it took to
grow a tree and cut them down with abandon, so in the months after
Gilbert we decimated our tree population all over the island. Future
generations will suffer the consequences. If the population experts
are correct, then Jamaica's population, now an estimated two-and-a-
half million, will double to five-million-plus by the year 2038. Same
land space, same water stock, same arable acreage, fewer trees to
support twice the number of people. What of the Jamaicans abroad,
estimated to be as many again as those at home? What if they wished
to, or were forced, to come back? Another huge tribe in need of land?

The Africans say land is the life of a people. Where will the Jamaicans go? Only the Rastafari still hanker after Africa; the rest will not even settle in the vast empty spaces of Guyana. They want what is available in the great cities of North America and Great Britain. If they were forced back to Jamaica, we would face a crisis of living space. Norman Manley, many years ago, was the last person I remember talking about this spectre. It seemed not to arise for succeeding generations of Jamaican political leaders.

In the Seaga years, we lived increasingly from crisis to crisis, preoccupied with quarterly IMF tests. At one point, the Prime Minister boasted that he was ahead of the IMF in implementing its policies. Jamaicans bound their bellies till it hurt. The silence of withdrawal again descended on the land. When some indiscreet American political operative in Washington described Jamaica's Prime Minister as 'our man in the Caribbean', the silence and the withdrawal became more complete. In this atmosphere, in February 1989, general elections were held and Edward Seaga and the Jamaica Labour Party suffered a massive electoral defeat from which, ten years later, they have not yet recovered. From controlling all 60 parliamentary seats, they went down to 15 seats to the PNP's 45. They have since lost two general elections and one local government election. In 1993, they went down to 8 seats to the PNP's 52; in 1997, they had 10 seats to the PNP's 50. There is a widespread view that the JLP will not win another election as long as Edward Seaga remains its leader.

Michael Manley's return to power was anti-climatic. Those who had hoped for the old fire and passion were soon disillusioned. Occasional flashes of the old flair and passion were still there, but muted and more controlled now. The masses on the streets wanted a return to the old love affair with an angry Joshua lashing out at their enemies, giving voice to their feelings with the passionate anger of his early years. They found instead a subdued, sobered man. I think he had been more bitterly hurt by his rejection in the 1980 election than was realised. He still cared, he was still their man, still willing to fight for them, but aware now, that they could and would, if they saw the need, vote him out of office. Only his party had stuck with him through everything. So that passionate, unconditional commitment was transferred from the people to the party which, in his eyes in any case served the interest of the people. Bitter experience of the fickleness of an electorate had turned the great populist into a pragmatic party man. The subtle difference was shown in his dramatic increase in the pay and conditions of parliamentarians early in his second term. The old Joshua would have held parliamentary pay at prevailing levels because the mass of the people were so poor; the new Joshua had to reward the loyalty of his party which controlled the overwhelming majority of the seats. The old Joshua would have dismantled the Seaga system of allocating the former local government money to the sitting members of parliament to spend in their constituencies; the new Joshua kept it. New money, new taxes, had to be found for local government. The old Joshua had promised to do away with Seaga's taxation on the interest on small savings; the new Joshua went back on that promise. He had watched Seaga, who had fought him in the 1970s on the cry that the people had reached their 'taxable limit', impose more and harsher taxes, so he, too, increased the tax burden. The new Joshua worked more harmoniously with the IMF and the foreign lending agencies. But he did not raise the kind of loans Seaga had, since world economic conditions had changed and that kind of money was no longer available. The nation's debt had more than doubled in the Seaga years.

Reagan left office in 1989 and so did Seaga. Thatcher was forced to resign a year later. The three great symbols of right-wing political extremism in the United States, the United Kingdom and the Caribbean during the 1980s moved off the political centre stage about the same time. The political pendulum swung back to the centre. A year before he left office, Reagan signed a treaty with Mikhail

Gorbachev which was the forerunner to the end of the Cold War. Star Wars was placed on hold. The hard-liners had gone, even if the fallout from their policies lingered on.

Michael Manley's second term was cut short by ill health. In 1992 he handed over power to Percival James Patterson, his deputy and chairman of the PNP. It was done in the normal democratic PNP manner at the 54th annual conference of the party. Portia Simpson, the formidable member of parliament for one of the 'garrison' communities of Kingston, and as shrewd and tough a political operator as any of the notable women in the history of the politics of the left, challenged Patterson for the leadership. Both were black, young, gifted, so the issue of colour did not arise. Patterson, a successful barrister, had been Norman Manley's protégé from his college days. He had committed himself to the service of the party after completing his law studies and worked his way up the party ranks. When the party gained office, he moved up the government ranks by dint of skill and hard work. He knew the ins and outs of the party and its workings, knew the key people in its vast group structure. He was the better educated of the two, the more prepared to be Prime Minister. He had been the Minister of Foreign Affairs who played a pivotal role in the shaping of the African, Caribbean and Pacific group and the various sugar and banana agreements between the ACP and the European Union. So, with much affection for Portia Simpson, the delegates voted for Patterson. Portia got the message and immediately went on to part-time studies to improve her education while holding down a senior and demanding government ministry, and continuing to serve her constituents with the dedication which had made her, in every public opinion poll, the most popular government minister and member of parliament in the country. She earned her degree within a year.

P.J. Patterson's assumption of the leadership of the PNP was a double transition: the Manley dynasty had ended and the complexion of the party leader had changed from brown to black. Most Jamaicans pretended it did not matter. We are, after all, a multi-racial, multi-cultural society with a national motto: 'Out of many one people'. Beneath the surface it mattered enough for the very pale brown chairman of the opposition party to describe Patterson's ascendancy to his party's leadership and thus the office of Prime Minister as choosing 'a boy to do a man's job'. The same mindset which had made it difficult for Hugh Shearer as Prime Minister in the late 1960s and early 1970s was still at work. However, the mindset of a significant minority in the 95 per cent-plus black majority had changed. They were no longer prepared to either join the covert and overt sneering and jeering at an 'uppity black' who did not know his place, or to remain silent about it. This time the latent anti-black bias was forced back into the dark recesses from which it came. A year after inheriting the leadership of the party and the Prime Ministership, P.J. Patterson called national elections and was overwhelmingly confirmed in his own right. Now he was not 'Michael's successor', but was Prime Minister in his own right. Somebody said 'Black man time!' and the whole elitist establishment cried 'Racism!'

The accumulated problems of the past thirty years now fell on the shoulders of P.J. Patterson, 57, Jamaica's seventh elected head of government. He was the PNP's third leader, not a Manley, its first black leader. He was, in training, length of service and experience, the best prepared of all Jamaican Prime Ministers. He was from the poorer classes — hence that 'boy to do a man's job' which many in the power élite secretly believed and endorsed. You had to be from a certain class, be of a certain colour to be 'a man'. This was his invisible handicap.

The country was deep in debt, its economy in shambles, its social services run down. It had developed, over the years, a 'tear down' political culture in which those in opposition did everything in their power to ensure that the government of the day failed. The destruction of property, the oiling of roads, the frightening away of tourists, the plotting of subversion, terrorist tactics, the 'war politics' of the Cold War with its covert CIA intervention, were part of our power game. So was the burning down of large residential and commercial areas and even an old people's home so that, as one politician put it, he could stand at a spot in Half Way Tree and see all the way down to the ghettoes near the waterfront. It was the politics in which we were prepared to turn Jamaica into a wasteland to achieve political power. If Michael Manley had followed that same line, had taken to the streets and wreaked havoc, as a few of the more extremist of his followers wanted, Jamaica would indeed have been a wasteland today. This was what Norman Manley had dreaded all those years ago. It was this Michael Manley had failed to contain but refused to emulate during the one-party parliament; it was this that Edward Seaga had later found unmanageable. It was this Patterson inherited in 1992, and won in his own right in 1993. It was not the Jamaica of peaceful steady progress envisioned by the 'Two Cousins' in the 1930s and 1940s; not the Jamaica in which Donald Sangster boasted of our credit-worthiness as if it wrapped us in a cloak of high moral virtue; not the peaceful stable, law-abiding Christian Jamaica Hugh Shearer wanted; not the inspired socialist utopia of Michael Manley's dreams; not even the three-piece-suited free-market imitation of the American dream Seaga wanted Jamaica to be.

The Jamaica Patterson inherited had lost its innocence. The decent ones were quiet. Those who had given voluntary social and community service had withdrawn in face of the pressures of the hard-line political manipulators of both right and left. Downtown business leaders had paid scufflers to scrape up the poor and homeless from the streets, put them on push-carts and dump them at Bellevue, the under-funded Kingston mental health facility in spacious grounds on the waterfront, where female inmates were routinely molested and raped because security was poor. We had, among the growing poor, regressed to the kind of abject hunger I had witnessed in the urban slums of African cities in my young manhood. Prostitution was common; so was the use of drugs; so was the gun as a tool for extorting tribute from business houses; so was begging by strong men, strapping women, undernourished marasmic children The upper and middle classes were back at minding their own business and making money, even if it meant exploiting the poor, cutting corners, evading and avoiding taxes and 'doing a thing' about customs and import duties. We had become a society in which all means justified the ends, in which the only wrong was to be caught.

This was P.J.'s inheritance and into it he tried to re-introduce the values and attitudes — good manners, honesty, decency, pride and self-respect — Daphne and I had found so beautiful when we first came to Jamaica. The media pundits laughed him to scorn and reminded their followers of his own flaws and errors, real and imagined, over a very long political apprenticeship dating back to the days of Norman Manley. Indeed, even Norman Manley's memory was not above being besmirched by some of these latter-day 'tear-down' political pundits. One in particular reminded his audience of Willy Lynch, the West Indian planter of slavery days who told the American slave-owners how to keep their slaves under control by dividing them against each other, by injecting contempt and self-contempt into how they saw and dealt with each other. It was popular stuff among a small influential minority. So was the daily ritual of mocking the elected politicians as idiots, thieves, crooks and liars.

In this climate a group of men, most of whom had benefited from Michael Manley's programme of free higher education of the 1970s, came to the fore. Some had gone to Cuba, the Soviet Union and Eastern Europe for training. Most had gone to the University of the West Indies. They had become doctors, lawyers, economists, scientists, accountants, graduates of business studies. This new class of trained professionals was predominantly black, from poor economic backgrounds and, in the main, committed to the service of Jamaica. Out of this lot came the new breed of black Jamaican bankers. some of them had been second- or third-string officials in the country's old established banking and financial houses. The skills and the expertise were there. The Patterson era created the opening. Some became bank managers. Some formed their own banks: commercial banks, merchant banks, 'near banks', and all manner of financial institutions. New banks, each with its own constellation of subsidiaries, sprouted all over the place. At one point, little Jamaica had nearly a score of banks, near-banks, building societies, insurance companies which took in money — mainly poor people's money.

A young man from Rock Hall, one of the beneficiaries of Manley's 'free education' whom Daphne had from time to time given a lift off the hill to his school, now grown-up and prosperous, formed his own bank. So did others, all mostly black, though there were one or two Chinese-Jamaicans. Money became the big game. They collected people's money, offering and, for a time, paying attractive rates of interest. The poor put their lives' savings into the hands of this new breed of bankers. It was possible now, as never before, for a small farmer from the remote hills, to walk into a spanking bank, be received by a beautiful young black miss in neat uniform, be ushered into the office of the manager — or someone looking as important — and be offered a seat and something to drink before getting to the business of depositing the fifty- or seventy- or eighty-thousand dollars he had kept at home until he learned how that money could be made to work for him at the bank.

The new bankers took vast sums of money from small savers. They grew rapidly, spent lavishly on advertising, new buildings, fancy furnishing and high-life entertaining. They invested poor people's savings in land, in housing, in personal business ventures, in fancy cars and in generous loans to their families and friends. Because they offered higher interest rates than the older more traditional banks, more poor people put their lives' savings into the hands of this new breed of swinging, enterprising, young black bankers. Some savers withdrew what they had in the less friendly, less generous old-style banks, and lodged them with this bright new breed, 'our own people treating us with respect and paying good interest'.

A good friend of mine, a big strong proud country man, gathered together all the savings he had put in a number of different places as precaution — between $70,000 and $80,000 — and put it into the bank of the man from Rock Hall whom he knew personally. The bank had grown rapidly and was by that time the second or third largest deposit-taking institution in the land. My friend lost every penny of his savings when that bank collapsed. I met him for the last time at our post office a few months after the bank's collapse. I was shocked by the change in the man. The so-called stuffing — the self-confidence, self-assurance, the 'I am my own man' air — had been knocked out of him. He was traumatised by the loss, humiliated at having been played for a fool by someone he trusted. I knew now what they meant by a 'broken' man. He died two months after our last meeting. The banker relocated to the US. This is one simple version of the complex story of how the first generation of black Jamaican bankers let us down and brought ruin, suffering and grief to thousand upon thousands of their fellow Jamaicans. They blew the first great opportunity to build an honest, reliable and trustworthy locally-owned and controlled banking system. They were greedy, self-centred, as socially and morally irresponsible as any traitor to a great cause. It was a great betrayal of trust. I am particularly angry about the death of my friend. He might still be alive, but for the loss of his life's savings and his sense of bitter shame at having allowed himself to be robbed. Others have lost much more. I feel this one particularly because he was a good and honourable friend, a good man.

P.J. Patterson's government had to step in and take over a number of these failed and failing banks. His Minister of Finance, Omar

Davies, established a special body to deal with the problem. It has been a running political headache for the Patterson government. Those who lost their money blamed the government for not protecting their interests and demanded the return of their money from the government. The banking laws, basically what they had always been here and all over the world, are being updated to provide for closer supervision and to make it more difficult for any smart Johnny-come-lately to call himself a banker and play merry hell with poor peoples' savings. But the old system under the old laws had worked reasonably well until the world-wide financial crises of the last two decades. The change was in the people who operated under the same old laws. The new generation of black Jamaican bankers was, it seemed, doing what bankers were able to do everywhere else. That bankers elsewhere did not, in the main, do what our bankers did under the same banking laws, was a matter of personal integrity and corporate responsibility. Our new breed of black bankers used the old banking laws to enrich themselves and impoverish their clients. New banking laws may inhibit this brand of fiscal mischief in future; the hard challenges are the social attitudes and personal value systems these men brought to banking.

For those of us who were part of the long struggle of the dark folk of the earth to be, and to be seen, and to be acknowledged as capable of running their own affairs with honour and integrity, it was more than just a betrayal of financial trust. It was a betrayal of the long political dream of being able to entrust what we have to our own people, just as all other peoples do. That is part of the dream for which Garvey, DuBois, Manley and the legions of other black folk have struggled over the centuries. It was sad that the first generation of black bankers who had the opportunity, betrayed that dream, traded it in for fancy homes and cars, an opulent lifestyle, and the fawning approval of fair-weather friends. They did immeasurable harm to the long struggle of black folk to emancipate themselves from financial, as well as, mental slavery.

In the general mood of depression following the banking collapse Jamaicans missed the point of the creative way in which the government went about salvaging the situation. Elsewhere, the world-wide economic decline had resulted in large-scale business and personal failures with the loss of businesses, homes, pension rights, suicides; there was no government help, no bail-outs. In Jamaica the government established a Financial Sector Adjustment Company to help failed and struggling businesses. The government itself helped with arrangements to assist depositors of failed banks and this way the pain and grief were eased. The angry ones who wanted all their money back 'now!' were not satisfied. Nothing but full restitution with interest would satisfy them. This became a political football for many months — until the finance ministry threatened to wash its hands of the whole matter. The people suddenly became reasonable. We can be a very pushing people.

The Patterson style of government — subdued, quiet, self-effacing — was condemned as no government. From the late 1960s through the 1970s and 1980s and the start of the 1990s Jamaicans had grown used to a loud, strident style of politics and government. The political leaders and the government, Manley and Seaga, were all over the place, making the daily headlines and looming larger than life. There was no escaping or forgetting them. Suddenly, under Patterson, people could forget politics and get on with their own lives, think and talk about other things. This man did not frighten anybody, did not demand everybody's attention all the time. The tension eased and people relaxed. But after thirty years and more of living at political fever pitch, many found the new relaxed climate unsettling. Media pundits complained that the man was neither seen nor heard. They said he had gone to sleep. They reacted like people addicted to noise who could not bear the silence; there was, they said, something wrong. The captain was allowing the ship to drift.

An extraordinary people, these Jamaicans. They had managed what no country in Africa, and few anywhere else in the world had.

They had controlled their democracy so effectively that even when we had a one-party parliament, the traditional stepping-stone to dictatorship, they had kept democracy alive. I confess I had been deeply worried by the one-party parliament and feared for the future of Jamaican democracy. I spoke of my worries in some of my news commentaries which were closely monitored by the government. Out in the bush Jamaicans reassured me with a gruff: 'Dem naa go do w'at we doan want' or 'We know how fe 'top dem'. And somehow this mood of watching and warning reached those in power and inhibited them. Seaga, as Prime Minister, wanted to change some national symbol at one point. The objection was muted but strong, so the symbol was not changed. It was nothing tangible, but the sense of 'a fe we control' was strong, strong enough to inhibit, to instil a sense of caution in political leaders. It was something I had not seen anywhere in Africa. To be sure, there were pockets of organised opinion, sometimes strong and cohesive, as in black trade unions, or tribal associations engaged in specific struggles, but never this pervasive sense of 'we decide' I found in Jamaica. The black Americans come nearest to it, but theirs is essentially the defensive unity of an embattled minority. The Jamaican thing is of a majority which knows that if it has to, it can enforce its will.

So Jamaica could come out of the one-party parliament, the one-party state, without violent political upheaval. Is this why Michael Manley did not unleash terror and civil strife on the streets under the one-party parliament? Why Seaga, in control of all the instruments of state power, returned to parliamentary elections and accepted the will of the people, however grudgingly? This, for me, is something extraordinarily new in the recent politics of the black experience. There was a coup in Trinidad a few years ago. It failed because it had no focus, no organised follow-up. Nothing like that can happen in Jamaica except with the approval or, at the very least, the tacit consent of that wide mood of what is or is not acceptable to the majority of Jamaicans.

In this sense, it is the Jamaican people, not the constitution, not the politicians, not the political power-brokers, who are the primary guardians of Jamaican democracy. How else explain the terrible shocks and shake-ups and testings — the violence, the destruction of physical resources, the partisan political warfare, the one-party government, the excesses of the Cold War, the political adventurism, the burning and looting, the loss of a sense of direction — she has experienced and survived over these past 37 odd years with her democracy intact?

What the people, what their will to freedom could not do on their own was to produce goods and services and enlarge the wealth of the nation. They needed leadership for that. Their political leaders, after the Bustamante-Manley era, had no common vision or purpose on which to move the country forward economically. Indeed, the political opposition of the 1970s developed a vested interest in the failure of the Michael Manley government. It was not a very big step from wanting his policies to fail to ensuring that they did. Arson, destruction, disruption became part of normal day-to-day political activity. In the crowded ghetto areas of Kingston and St Andrew the supporters of one party drove the supporters of the other from their homes. Those who resisted were shot up and burned out. In the end, there was the same kind of forced movement of people associated with wars. It reached the point where a well-built house which straddled the divide between two party political areas became a national issue. Since it was neither wholly in the PNP area nor wholly in the JLP area, the leader of the opposition demanded that it be demolished. It was not, but that was an indication of the destructive mood. I remember a very angry Jamaican woman, middle-class-sounding, declaring on a radio call-in programme: 'They are out to rule or ruin.' And ruin they did. For more than thirty years, under both PNP and JLP, Jamaica's economy stagnated and declined. The bitterly divided house stood, but only just. Now, as we approach the turn of a new century, Jamaica is still trying to shake free of the legacy of the war politics of the 1960s, 1970s and 1980s. The burden of debt is an additional handicap. So is the growing population of the young who are unemployed and not educated enough to become part of the new technological age. So is an absence of the guiding values and attitudes P.J. Patterson is now trying to bring back. The bad habits of more than thirty years have gone deep.

When I was young, poverty meant not having enough to eat, not having adequate shelter, not knowing where the money would come from to pay for basic needs, for rent, for the next meal. The poor who are young in today's Jamaica have a different yardstick. The young unemployed demonstrating on Jamaica's streets often wear designer jeans, high-priced brand name sneakers, rings on several fingers and gold chains around their necks. The young women usually have expensive hairdos and are as bejewelled as their menfolk. For the dances which abound they wear special costly outfits. No young woman is seen in the same dress or pant-suit at the dancehall twice in any one week. They get their fried or jerked chicken, pork, beef or fish from the multitude of fast-food and usually franchised outlets found all over the Corporate Area. The prices are high and paying is 'no problem'. But they protest bitterly about paying the token 'school fees' to help defray the cost of books and materials for their children; they object to paying small charges for services at clinics or hospitals; they resist or stall paying their light and water bills. They have been acculturated into 'the freeness mentality' in which, in exchange for their votes, the political 'garrison' Dons ensure they are not troubled with having to pay rent or utility bills. There are areas in which people have not paid rent, or for light and water, for decades, where the only work they do is the occasional 'job', legal or illegal — petty theft, break-ins, ganja deals, beatings-up, gang fights, extortion, the rare elimination of someone — ordered by the Don. In exchange, they live 'free' and 'a money is dropped' for their expenses. Those who are not own-account mechanics, masons, welders, carpenters or electricians do casual day's work inside and outside their communities. At nights, when not on a 'job', they hang out in their beer and soft-drink joints or on their 'corners' in small groups, chatting, watching the world go by, 'checking the chicks'. They do not go in for hard liquor as did their fathers and grandfathers. Instead of gut-rotting over-proof white rum, they drink Red Stripe and puff on ganja spliffs.

There are many small children in these closed communities. Some go to school; some do not. There was a time when all went to school. Most still do. Many do not. And the 'street children', the homeless and abandoned ones from these communities are increasing. When a boy and girl of thirteen and fourteen and fifteen make a baby for which they are not ready, the women of the 'yard' help out. If there is no granny, either in town or back in the country where one or the other or their parents came from, then the child is likely to be either abandoned, or raised by the yard community in which the two youngsters live, or be cared for by some kindly neighbour or, when it is a little older, be dropped at the children's home. If it is a man-child, it is likely to end up on the streets. The girls are a little luckier; they are usually taken in by some woman without a child of her own, or a couple unable to make their own. The wonder is that so many children from this background still grow up, gain a reasonable education and become relatively normal decent law-abiding citizens. They are part of the age-old story of the human will to self-improvement and self-advancement under fearful handicaps. The question persists: do the odds still have to be as stacked against them as they are? Now, at the end of the twentieth century? I have watched street children in Jamaica who reminded me of my own days as a street child in Johannesburg three-quarters of a century ago. So little has changed over such a great time span.

The urban violence and lawlessness bred by the ghetto life of the great urban cities of Africa, Asia, Europe and the Americas, threatens but has not yet overtaken Jamaica and all the smaller islands of our world. There is, though, great cause for concern as the new economic order, the debt burden and the new face of global capitalism make life for the poor more difficult and unstable everywhere on earth.

Just the other day — 16 April 1999 — Jamaica was plunged into yet another of its paroxysms of self-destructive arson, violence and looting. In its last revenue budget presented in Parliament the day before, the government imposed a series of new taxes, with that on petroleum and its by-products almost doubling the price of petrol. Over the next few days, all hell broke loose from one end of Jamaica to the other. All the other details of the revenue budget were buried under the rage and fury of the 'gas price protests'. Kingston was brought to a standstill as roads were blocked. Strong young men, aided by women and children, set tyres on fire, burning road surfaces, and blocked roads with car-shells, huge boulders, all manner of rubbish. Venerable old trees were felled by chain-saw to block roads. Businesses and supermarkets and food outlets shut down; public transport came to a halt. The country was paralysed for three days. In the later stages, hooligans and gangsters took over; shops and stores were broken into and looted. The military had to be called out in force to help stem the lawlessness. The political opposition got into the act and tried to take over what looked like a popular uprising — but they were careful to distance themselves from the looting and violence. Power, the opposition leader said, had been transferred to his hands. That sobered many who had seen this as a non-political popular protest against one specific tax. In a broadcast to the nation the Prime Minister promised a committee to review the gas price hike and said he would announce the result within a week. The uprising ended. The estimated cost of the damage done during the three days of rioting was put in the region of between ten thousand million and fourteen thousand million Jamaican dollars.

Again, as so often in the past, Jamaicans had wreaked havoc on themselves. A week later the proposed increase was rolled back by nearly half, but now the cost of the damage was an additional burden on Jamaican taxpayers. This was Jamaica's third such 'gas price strike'. The first two were as destructive and costly as this last: one during the time of Michael Manley, the other during the time of Edward Seaga. Each time Jamaicans tore their country apart, setting back progress and development by years. Until they come to understand this, they will repeat this seasonal orgy of self-inflicted damage and destruction. Then, in their sober moments, they will continue to wonder why there is no growth. There can be no growth where you have this cyclical pattern of continuously building up then tearing down, no matter how well you plan, no matter how hard you work. This is the Jamaican dilemma today. Until Jamaica finds its way back to that spirit of national unity which transcends all sectional and factional interests, it will continue, in Michael Manley's apt simile, marching up the down escalator. He saw it in the context of the relations between the rich and powerful countries of the North and the poor and exploited countries of the South. It also applies within the South itself. The self-destruction symbolised by our 'gas price strikes' is prevalent all over the developing world.

In Trinidad in the Eastern Caribbean, and Guyana on the north-western coast of South America we have our own versions of ethnic conflicts holding back progress. These two former British colonies have almost evenly balanced numbers of Trinidadians and Guyanese of African and East Indian descent. They are as divided against each other as are Jews and Arabs in the Middle East, black and white in East, Central and Southern Africa, Catholics and Protestants in Northern Ireland, Serbs and Kosovars in Yugoslavia, black and white in the United States and Europe. Until recently, political control, and all the 'benefits' that went with it — staffing the civil service, getting the choice contracts — were in the hands of the black Trinidadians and the black Guyanese. Those of East Indian descent were the 'outsiders', the second-class citizens. In Guyana, for as long a time as Nelson Mandela was a political prisoner, Cheddi Jagan was kept in the political wilderness by Forbes Burham's manipulation and abuse of the electoral system. In the beginning Burnham and Jagan, the African and the Indian leaders, were united and built up the nationalist movement to struggle jointly for independence. Jagan, the Indian, was a communist, Burnham, the black man, was a pragmatist. Britain, the colonial power, and the United States, the regional super-power, were not about to accept the emergence of a communist state on the coast of Latin America. In the way these things can be managed, the unity between Jagan and Burnham was broken. Burnham's party became the party of the blacks, Jagan's that of the Indians. The house was divided. The voting system and everything else was rigged to ensure black control.

It was not quite as Machiavellian in Trinidad. The twin-island state was not as geo-politically important, but the seeds of ethnic division were there as well. Browns — the 'creoles' — and blacks ran the state apparatus. The Indians were the merchants, the small farmers, the people who worked for themselves and others. As long as the blacks controlled political power, as long as they could outvote the Indians, democracy was fine, the first-past-the-post system was acceptable. When the world changed and even the British and Americans could no longer acquiesce in the Burnham way of doing things, when international observers became part of the electoral scene, Jagan was finally elected in Guyana. Basdeo Panday became the first Trinidadian Prime Minister of Indian descent. Suddenly the blacks and their leaders found the old democratic system unfair and wanted shared governments, governments of national unity, proportional representation. In Guyana the opposition party seems set on a campaign to make Guyana ungovernable under Jagan's PPP. Jagan, like Burnham, is no longer on the scene. His party, now led by his widow, Janet Jagan, won the last election and she is now the President. Burnham's political heirs appear to be following the 'rule or ruin' route. In Trinidad the Prime Minister often gives the impression of wanting to do to the blacks what the blacks had done to the Indians. Ethnic tensions are at times exacerbated where there is no need. So blacks call Indians 'coolies', knowing it upsets, while Indians declare they would not allow 'my daughter to marry a black', knowing that upsets.

In any event, those who are determined to marry or cohabit across ethnic lines do not usually ask — hence the large numbers of beautiful doogla women and strikingly handsome men. I personally find the black-Indian mixture much more attractive than the more traditional black-white mixture. Both can be breathtakingly beautiful, the darker one just more aesthetically so for me, which is perhaps why I find the women of the East African coast with their African-Arab-Indian mixture the most attractive in the world, with the women of Northern Nigeria on the fringe of the great Sahara and its ancient trade routes a close second. One of the joys of the wanderings of my youth was to look on beautiful women. No need to turn them into causes for ethnic conflict and colour wars. They usually know what they do or do not want and have ancient ways of making it known. The sexist side of the ethnic hang-ups of Caribbean man — black, white, Indian, brown — will be brushed aside by Caribbean woman whenever it suits her. The Caribbean has produced some of the strongest, most balanced, most resilient, most tough-minded women I have encountered in a long life. They may yet take over and reshape what is now a confused and unfocused male-dominated region. Not everything wrong with us must be blamed on the whites and their relations with the darker races of man. We are ourselves responsible for much that is wrong with us. We have made wrong choices, pursued wrong objectives, chosen wrong directions; made more difficult the problems we inherited from the past.

We have turned Africa into a house divided against itself. Sierra Leoneans against Sierra Leoneans, Nigerians against Nigerians, Liberians against Liberians — Africans everywhere against their fellow Africans. Jonas Savimbi bleeds Angola's potentially great future into economic anaemia. We have learned how to destroy, but we have forgotten how to build and create and sustain. The Cold Warriors who taught us these destructive skills have, for now, withdrawn and gone home. We continue to savage ourselves, unable, it seems, to stop the self-destruction.

Only out of South Africa does there now appear to be some signs of hope. When Mandela was released from a third of a lifetime of political imprisonment, the dark folk of the earth celebrated as a united force, across barriers of location, tribe, and language. They accepted without reservation or question the sincerity of the whites who celebrated with them. Indeed, toward the end of his long imprisonment the movement for Mandela's, and therefore South Africa's, release from the bondage of Apartheid had taken on the proportions of an international crusade transcending colour, regional, social, cultural, religious and ethnic barriers. The movement to free Mandela was a triumphant moment after more than a quarter century of shameful indifference.

In earlier years, his and the ANC's struggle had been blurred by the attitudes and requirements of Cold War politics. Anti-colonialism and the struggle for national independence were associated with the pro-communist, anti-capitalist positions of the Soviet Union. The ANC admitted avowed communists like Joe Slovo to its ranks; therefore, the ANC and all its leaders were communists, crypto-communists or communist-front persons and organisations and therefore not entitled to the rights and freedoms and decencies inherent in the standards accepted for democracy. The Cold War had to be ended before Mandela could be freed. The slow, drawn-out and painful collapse of the Soviet Union, starting with Gorbachev's internal reforms in 1989/1990, and his relaxing of the Soviet iron grip on Eastern Europe, led, inevitably, to that collapse, and the end of the Cold War. Mandela was freed in 1990. Coincidence? I think not.

The long history of the Cold War is a story of nations and peoples and individuals being used as pawns in the great ideological power game which dominated twentieth-century international relations for the best part of the past seventy-five years. It began long before it was so named by Bernard Baruch in the US Congress in 1947; it started almost immediately after the Russian Revolution of October 1917 and lasted until the Soviet collapse of 1991. The communists always sought to spread their communism, proclaiming it the way of the future. At the height of its popularity, shortly after the establishment of the Soviet Union, its adherents proclaimed it the new solution to all the ills of humanity. It would inaugurate the brave new world of the equality of nations and the brotherhood of mankind: no more poverty and unemployment, an end to imperialism and the domination of the weak by the strong, an end to capitalist exploitation, from each according to his/her ability to each according to his/her needs. Its theoretical foundation was Karl Marx's monumental *Das Kapital*, its clarion call the *Communist Manifesto* by Marx and Engels with its electrifying: 'A spectre is haunting Europe — the spectre of communism... Workers of the world unite! You have nothing to lose but your chains.' Western capitalism, Western imperialism, were threatened by this new ideology and fought back. Communism and communists were opposed and resisted everywhere, by any means. As the tactics of communism were refined, so were the responses of capitalism. The Stalinist 'show trials' were matched by the US Congressional McCarthy 'witch hunts'. Means and ends coincided across the ideological divide. There were quiet periods in the conflict, times so quiet there seemed no conflict. It went underground at times and each side built elaborate systems of spying, undermining, sabotaging each other's efforts even to the point of killing. The unholy art of 'disinformation', 'character assassination', bearing 'false witness', were among its by-products.

Increasingly, as the world changed and the Soviet Union grew into one of the two dominant world power groupings, Russian Soviet communism heading the one, American capitalism the other, the conflict deepened until it engulfed the whole world, dominated all decisions. So Mandela was not freed until it could be done without threatening the geo-political interests of Western capitalism in Africa. This aspect of how and when Nelson Mandela was freed is glossed over. Would he have been freed if the Cold War were still raging? Was it coincidence that the change of US Congressional attitudes came after the American victory in the Cold War? If there is no thought and talk about this contextual background, the Mandela release takes on the appearance of a romantic fairy tale. In geo-political terms the winning of the Cold War was the pre-condition for the United States and its Western allies accepting a power shift from white to black in Southern Africa. With no communist threat, Mandela could be freed, South Africa could become as subject to the will of the majority as are all Western-style democracies. What if there were not this coincidence between the anti-Apartheid struggle and the collapse of Soviet Communism? What if the Soviet Union had held its own and the balance of terror remained as evenly poised as it seemed up to the end of the 1980s? What real change in the relations between the lighter and darker races of mankind of which DuBois wrote so long ago? Against which Garvey fought all his life? Are they any healthier now than at the beginning of the twentieth century? Is mankind itself, across colour lines, any better off?

— 17 —

A Century of Fear

I have always taken family birthdays seriously. It was something
with which I grew up, an inculcated family habit going back to
first consciousness — like our youngest daughter saying she never
learned to read, for her books and reading were natural, a habit. In
the Vrededorp of my childhood my mother and Aunt Mattie always
remembered everybody's birthday. There was always a small celebration
to mark this annual rite of passage: in good days it could be a special
meal, a few essential presents — shirt or dress or pair of trousers —
and a birthday cake; in not so good days it might be some hand-made
toy wrapped in bright coloured paper; in bad days it might be words
of reminder of the day and a session of telling of tall tales. I carried
this ritual over to my own family. Birthdays became an integral part
of our 'high days and holidays' at Coyaba.

11 February was our eldest daughter Anne's birthday. Nelson
Mandela was released on 11 February 1990. So that birthday
celebration was very special up at Coyaba. The family was dispersed;
our children were in faraway Europe, and most of the friends who
had shared these 'high days and holidays' with us in the past had

passed from the scene. Still, it was one of the greatest, happiest days of our lives. When the day was ending and everybody had gone, Daphne and I sat on the long verandah with the dogs lying about, chins resting on the lowest rail, watching the twinkling world far below.

I had not expected Mandela's release to come in this way. I had an idea about the ongoing talks. I knew the racist government did not want him to die while still a prisoner in their hands. The tacit alliance between Buthelezi's forces and those of the Nationalist Party suggested some sort of last-ditch effort to neutralise the ANC and Balkanise South Africa along ethnic/colour lines. I feared that if Mandela were released, it could be under circumstances which made things worse, not better. So the televised pictures of a healthy-looking, though gaunt, man and his first statement, set my mind at ease. I could, at last, let go of the inner tension and turmoil. I could let go of a lifetime's preoccupation with South African racism. That had been the backdrop to everything I had done all my life. It had been the invisible load on my back no matter where I was, what I was doing. I had shed as much of its ugliness as I could, tried to live as whole and healed a life as I could. But the knowledge of all those millions of black folk under Apartheid, of my having to live out my life and die with that monstrous system still intact, had been the burden of my life. Mandela's release, with its implicit promise of the end of institutionalised state racism, lifted that burden from me. I had been personally free of South African racism for the past sixty years. But for all that time the knowledge that it existed and was the controlling force over millions of black folk had made it impossible for me to let go. Now at last I could let go.

I took a long draft of the chilled grapefruit-orange-tangerine mixture — my heavenly nectar — and it seemed I had never been as aware of the delicacy of the blending.

'It's over at last.' I looked at Daphne.

'Yes.' Then, after a long pause: 'You can let go now.'

We lapsed into another long silence of shared emotions. Then she turned her head and looked at me.

'What do you want to do?'

'We've been here too long; our roots have gone too deep.'

'Want to go for a visit?'

'No. I know what it's like. I don't have to see it to know.'

'I know that. A short visit perhaps; to test the feel.'

'I'm over seventy, darling.'

'I sometimes forget... Let's have some music.'

So I put Beethoven's Fifth Symphony on the turntable and the majestic affirmation of the best in the human spirit swept down over our dark valley.

Mandela arrived in Jamaica, as part of his 'thank you' tour, on another family birthday. Daphne's this time, 23 July 1991. Jamaica did him proud. The day was beautifully clear; the way from the airport into Kingston was spotlessly clean. All the way, on both sides of the roads. Jamaicans in their thousands lined the streets to pay homage to the man. Many carried small versions of the flag of the ANC. Monitoring the great procession from the feeds of the two television stations, I was struck by the orderliness of the spectators and how well dressed, well turned-out, they all were. Such things normally tend to be a bit wild, with a hint of carnival about them; this was joyous, serious, orderly. This man, clearly, was very special to Jamaicans. By extension, I was waved at, warmly saluted by strangers pushing their heads out of car windows. Mandela day evoked the kind of responses associated with Marcus Garvey's expectation of how black people should behave among themselves and to each other. There was exhilaration in the air. For Jamaica's women, the black and brown middle-class women who increasingly run things, the presence of Winnie Mandela was special. She had, for all the years of Nelson

Mandela's imprisonment, been the great symbol of resistance to Apartheid, the front line fighter keeping the struggle alive.

Someone asked me on a radio programme whether I would see the man personally. I doubted it. Their schedule was tight and short of pushing, I did not see how I could meet them personally. Immediately a message was relayed to me that Miss Portia Simpson was having a special gathering for Jamaican women to meet Mrs Mandela; I was invited. Then Michael Manley's press secretary, Hartley Neita, tracked me down to say that the Prime Minister expected me at the great public ceremony at the national stadium the next evening. Michael Manley and Portia Simpson were determined that I should meet the Mandelas personally.

We celebrated Daphne's birthday and the arrival of the Mandelas in Jamaica with our friends up in the hills that night. The following night, Neita came for me and drove me down to a national stadium where even his official sticker did not help much in getting into the jam-packed place. The stadium was full to capacity, the milling overflow crowd outside at least as big again. The orderly, well-mannered behaviour of the day before was less evident; there was pushing, shoving, jumping of fences and some screaming and shouting. At one stage some jumpy policeman let off his firearm to stop stampeding fence-jumpers, hitting and killing an innocent spectator sitting in the stands. The Rastafarians were strongly represented. All Jamaica's top musicians were on hand and the grand concert had already started when we finally reached the seating area for the VIPs. The Prime Minister and his entire Cabinet were there; the news media — from the region and from the world — was in heavy attendance. There was no way I could have got anywhere near the place without Michael Manley's personal intervention. That was one of the man's special touches; in the midst of big things he could pay attention to small things. He had once visited the Half Way Tree lock-up and been so appalled by the conditions that he summoned the Minister of Justice and had something done on the spot. Not always the best way of conducting national affairs, but it endeared him to the Jamaican people. Manley personally introduced me to Mandela and we sat near each other throughout the ceremony — and we remembered our last meeting nearly forty years earlier in Johannesburg, shortly before his long imprisonment.

I was surprised at how clearly he remembered that last encounter. It was during my 1955 visit to South and East Africa as a journalist who was himself a story covered by other journalists. I was travelling on a British passport. I never had a South African passport, as their records did not recognise my existence. Perhaps I was not registered at birth, or if I was, perhaps the records went astray. All things were possible under Apartheid. So I was a British journalist on assignment from the London *Observer* and the BBC. How would the South African regime react to the presence of this former black South African subversive? They were having a bad world press at the time, so they left me alone. I was allowed to move about freely, reconnect with my family, spend time with the new black magazine *Drum* and meet old friends like Henry Nxumalo and all sorts of other people. I filed my stories without trouble and did not, myself, make a story.

At one of the receptions for me a group of men, the high command of the ANC I thought, attended. Mandela headed them. It was a dressy affair, open to men with their women. But this group was comprised of men without their women. I was angry, partly because I was there without my own woman, but more because the struggle for freedom could not be a thing of men without women. In my little speech I asked them where their women were. Were they not doing to their women what Apartheid was doing to them? They were angry and upset. My host told me afterwards that some had said I had changed and was no longer 'one of us'.

On that night in the national stadium, Mandela's first act after Manley presented me to him was to lead me to the other end of the platform where Winnie Mandela sat with the Chief Justice of Jamaica and his lady, and introduce me to his wife. Winnie Mandela embraced me and a huge roar went up from the vast throng.

Then Jimmy Cliff's pure voice exploded over the clear moonlit night. The vast stadium throng hushed; Mandela tensed to a familiar evocative sound, releasing memories. *Many rivers to cross...* Suddenly Mandela was somewhere else — not in Jamaica's national stadium. I wondered where; then, even before the song ended, it was over and he was among us again. *Many rivers to cross, but I can't find my way over...*

When they asked me to introduce him, I referred in passing to that event back in 1955 and spoke of the great role women have played in the freedom struggle. Then I told him, and the audience, about the decision of Norman Manley and his small band of men, to become the second nation in the world, after India, to impose economic sanctions on racist South Africa, even though Jamaica was not then in control of its foreign relations. When the South African government protested, Whitehall said nothing to Jamaica. Then I told them of my own decision to stay in Jamaica. The change had come too late for me personally, our Jamaican roots had grown deep and strong over the years. Jamaica had been good to us, had made it possible for me to help build positively instead of always being against. I had long ceased to be someone in exile, mental suitcase packed, waiting for the day to go home; this, now, was home.

There was a great outpouring of love and hope and confidence that night. In his speech Mandela thanked Jamaica for her support throughout the struggle. He banished the lingering fears that the forces of Apartheid might yet stage a comeback. Apartheid was finished; the struggle now was for equity, justice, an economic place in the sun for the poor, the homeless, the dispossessed who happened to be black. That was the hard road ahead.

But it was not only the black who were the poor and the dispossessed, and that was part of the problem. In 'mixed' societies like

South Africa, where the whites were a sizeable minority, there were large numbers of 'poor whites'. As in Jamaica, as elsewhere in the world, the drift from the rural areas to the great urban centres was a movement of the poor and the dispossessed. The complicating factor, going as far back as my own childhood days, was that the whites were not supposed to be poor. The overlords, the superior beings who held dominion over the blacks were supposed to be seen by the blacks as a breed apart. Yet there they were, white, the master 'race', yet poor. They were an embarrassment to their fellow whites, an embarrassment even to the white missionaries who, with rare exceptions, seemed to need to convince little tribal black boys and girls that emulating the ways of white folk was the road to salvation. The white government which enforced its racist policies on the grounds of whites being superior to blacks, more civilised than blacks, had problems explaining poor whites. In rural South Africa the poor whites were not as noticeable as in the great urban centres. But, rural or urban, blacks knew that poor whites were to be avoided. They were angrier than other whites and they took out that anger on any blacks they encountered. They resented blacks more fiercely than did any other group of whites; they dealt more harshly with blacks who came under their control. And they were the ones who became, on the farms, the overseers or the assistants to the managers, the farm-foremen, the supervisors, the prison guards, in effect, the 'drivers' of slavery days. In the towns and cities, in the factories, they were the unionised workers who ensured that blacks did not do the same 'skilled' work they did, that blacks would never acquire the skills to do that work. They excluded blacks from their trade unions. Long before Apartheid got its name, white workers and their white trade unions used organised white labour's 'muscle' to ensure that black and brown workers would never be their equal in the job market and on the shop floor.

The poor whites staffed the lower ranks of the nation's police force, the nation's army; the literate or barely so, the nation's civil service. They were the prison wardens and supervised the gangs of prisoners breaking rocks in quarries. They were always white, the prisoners always black. When I visited my brother at Diepkloof reformatory and saw him breaking rock on a hillside, all the prisoners were black and brown, all their armed guards white. When I showed my pass to see my brother to a strapping young white guard, I realised he could hardly read, certainly not as well as I could. He had to spell out aloud the words on the pass to get their sense and feel. Then he bellowed my brother's name. The gang, all dressed in the same faded white two-piece canvas shirt and shorts, stopped working briefly, my brother detached himself from the line and came running. Another armed warder bellowed for the rest to get on with their work. Lolly looked shame-faced as our eyes met. He did not want his little brother to see him thus. He was in for twenty-one days for smoking *dagga*, the South African version of ganja. I held out the parcel of food Aunt Mattie and Tibby had prepared the night before. The young warder grabbed it from me, opened and inspected it. He took out the biggest piece of meat, chicken I think, then handed the rest to Lolly.

'Better eat it here, Hotnot; those kaffirs will take it all from you.'

'Thank you, my *baasie*,' Lolly said, ingratiating voice, angry blazing eyes.

The young Boer turned his back, munching the juicy piece of meat.

'Five minutes!' He moved out of earshot so we could talk.

I still remember Lolly's bitter under-his-breath cursing all those years ago, and the ravenous manner in which he attacked the remains of the food. Prison fare was meatless, meagre, lousy; this Boer bastard had taken the best his Mattie had especially prepared for him.

The depth of the anger against each other of the poor who are white and the poor who are black has been one of the cruellest factors in the relations between the lighter and darker peoples of the earth. The prevailing value system says white is not supposed to be poor, not supposed to compete against black for available jobs, housing, schooling, services. Under slavery they resolved it by turning humans into property. After slavery, as in South Africa and, until very recently, the United States, they used the force of law to ensure this inequity. Everywhere else in the world they did so by convention. In empires whites go to their colonies and get the choicest available jobs; black who go to the 'mother country' get only the jobs whites do not want — the most menial, the lowest paying. This has not changed with the end of empire. The whites of the former colonies still enjoy job privileges because economic control still rests largely in the hands of the transnationals of the former empire. Only in the top echelons of the governments and government services has there been real change. Ministers, Permanent Secretaries, heads of statutory bodies reflect the political changes. Trade, commerce, industry, manufacturing, mining are still largely run and managed by whites.

Achieving Kwame Nkrumah's political kingdom has not changed the economic landscape and the relations between the poor who are white and the poor who are black. They still compete as bitterly as ever, and the tilt is still as firmly in favour of white and against black as it was at the birth of this century. Then, the white South African workers had a general strike in which they urged their fellow workers to unite and fight for a white South Africa. It took the best part of fifty years after that before the Reverend Martin Luther King and the Reverend Jesse Jackson, both black Americans, put forward the notion of a rainbow coalition of black and white who are poor. If that day ever comes when the poor who are black and the poor who are white really come together to struggle in unity, they will transform the nature and the terms of the struggle for justice, equity and an economic place in the sun. Mandela spoke to aspects of this at the national stadium in Kingston on that July night in 1991. How possible, how feasible is that unity of the poor across colour lines? That may be one of the critical issues of the next century. For it to have any hope of succeeding, we must come to terms with the many-faceted complex of fear of each other between black and white who are poor which was spawned in this most violent of centuries.

Before this century the story of mankind was told by those in control. It was their story of how things had developed. Empire builders told the story of empire; slavers told the story of slavery; the victors told the story of wars; the rich told the story of the poor. The perspective, always, was of those in control. That was the accepted orthodoxy. Those who could not read and write, preferably in the languages of Europe, had no history and were dismissed as savage. And savages did not have the same rights as the civilised. This justified conquest, slaughter, the seizure and occupation of land, the turning of humans into 'property'. In modern times Europe was the world and the story of Europe was the story of the world. Not all that different from the story of China in the distant times when she was the Middle Kingdom and the centre of the civilised world. Always, those in control define the world; history is what they say it is. They determine what is right from what is wrong, what is good from what is evil.

In October 1917 this orthodoxy was challenged by the Russian Revolution with its assertion of a new body of values, with the poor and the dispossessed at its centre. The world, according to communism, was divided into two classes, the working class and the ruling class; the one the victim of the other — which was the basis of the class struggle. But again, even in this revolutionary clarion call, Europe was the world. The history of Europe was the history of the world. Workingmen of all countries were the workingmen of Europe. When the Soviet Union came into being, the entire world was, for the next 75 years, plunged into a bitter conflict of ideas which, at times, assumed the proportions of a 'Holy War', at other times the appearance of a latter-day Spanish Inquisition with its show-trials, purges and 'liquidations'. It was a time of bloodshed, civil wars, of nations and peoples and even families rent apart. Europe, it seemed, had taken a sharp turn into an historical *cul-de-sac* and the rest of the world followed.

Before it was over, the Soviet Union and the United States of America, became the nuclear-armed superpowers and led the world into a state of universal fear unprecedented in human history. The Cold War, with its ever-present threat of nuclear Armageddon, lasted for the best part of this century. Communism has collapsed, yet the nuclear arms race and the terrible weapons it spawned are still here. The fear, now, is of the technology falling into the 'wrong' hands of what are called 'rogue' states, Islamic extremists, international terrorists. The men who dreamt dreams of Star Wars are still seen as heroes. The prospects of the good earth turned into the bleak, barren, empty post-nuclear winter landscape is part of the cultural baggage of twentieth-century man, woman and child. Never in human history has the possibility of the total annihilation of life on earth been so stark. As a species we have learned to live with fear and still remain creative. No mean achievement that.

Among the good things to come out of this great political-ideological schism of our age was the breaking of the 'one view' of the nature of things. In place of one orthodoxy there were now two: that of the communist East and that of the capitalist West. History could now be interpreted from a capitalist or a communist point of view; and since capitalism and communism were equally powerful then, and power confers authority, each view of history carried equal value. History could henceforth be viewed from the perspective of the poor and the dispossessed, not only as the story of great kings and their conquering armies, but also as the story of those who resisted the kings and their armies. And if two, why not three or four or more views of history? On the surface, Marxist communism challenged and ended the European monopoly on the defining and interpreting of the world for us. There can be more than just the European view of history. The interesting irony is that Marxism-communism was part of the European political evolutionary process — a heresy if you like, as were the reformers and Protestants against the Church of Rome — not the great new vision it was sold as. Its greatest contribution was the opening of windows of perception, of new ways of looking at old things. Its short history as a world power showed that it was essentially European in nature; its philosophical and historical ideas were bedded in the evolutionary history of European thought. And, in good European fashion, it knew that its truth was the only truth and best for all mankind. So we had Soviet imperialism, anti-Semitic, racist, non-capitalist; a European heresy — but European for all that.

Soviet man and Soviet woman were supposed to be superman and his supermate: square-jawed, heroic builders of a new world, marching with the red flag and the inspiring strains of the *Internationale*. The proletarian art was wonderfully uplifting, but there were no small people, no dark-skinned people, no people with small receding chins. When the Nazis came later their new superman, superwoman and superchild were the blond, blue-eyed Aryan prototypes of their notions of a master race. This matter of race and colour was a twentieth-century European sickness transcending ideology. Only the will to power was stronger than their racism.

In the two great wars of this century – the First World War between 1914 and 1918 and the second, between 1939 and 1945, — the will to power of the Europeans resulted in the stylised slaughter of an estimated one hundred million-plus human beings in each of the two wars. Casualties were restricted to mainly military personnel in the first war. Arguably as many civilians as soldiers died in the second. These estimated numbers do not include the peoples of Asia who were dragged into, or, like Japan, involved themselves in these European world wars. There are no casualty lists for them; a reasonable assumption could number their casualties as at least the same as the 6 million Jews who died at the hands of the Nazis. Estimates show that the human damage of the Second World War was greatest in Eastern Europe. Poland lost twenty per cent of its pre-war population, the Soviet Union and Yugoslavia ten per cent each. The movement of that great new class of humanity — the refugees — across the battle-scarred face of Europe was a sickening spectacle on nightly newsreel pictures and, later, television reports from the war fronts.

In our century more people were uprooted and made homeless by war than in any previous century. With the exception of the slave trade and its terrible Middle Passage in which twenty million Africans were transported to the Americas and the Caribbean, no other period in human history has seen such a vast forced movement of peoples. From Europe to Asia to Africa to the islands of the seas, peoples, in vast numbers, were forced to leave their homes, their dearest possessions, their businesses, their farms, the land of their birth — usually at short notice and without any form of identity — and seek safety and shelter in foreign lands. They were often met with hostility and often did not speak the language of the host-country. The numbers of men, women and children turned into 'stateless' persons — refugees — were legion. Estimates vary from between 45 million to 50 million. The latest wave are the people of Kosovo in the traditionally volatile Balkans. We enter the new century on a note of 'ethnic cleansing' and the now familiar bombing by the powerful and strong, led by the surviving superpower which once attempted to bomb Vietnam 'back into the dark ages'.

The Nazi occupation of Europe turned its vast industrial capacity into one massive productive slave camp to service the German army and the German state. The working men and women of Europe became the slave workers of the German war machine. Those of Eastern Europe were handled particularly brutally. In faraway Asia, the Japanese, allies of the Nazis, treated their prisoners of war in like manner. There, the whites and the 'Eurasians' — those of mixed European-Asian parentage — suffered the greatest cruelty, brutality, human indignities. Colour was a factor here; humiliate those who had humiliated you. Mussolini's Italian Fascists added the delicately cruel refinement of forcing the enemies of Fascism to take large doses of castor oil, lose control and foul themselves.

For their part, the Western Alliance, the forces fighting against the Nazis and their allies, undertook what they described as precision bombing of German industrial centres, great cities and what was left of Nazi-ravaged Europe. Great and ancient European cities like Dresden and Cologne were reduced to rubble. The Nazis did it to Coventry and London.

We lived through the German *blitz* on London; we shared the daily sense of the possibility of the end of time at any moment, which is the nature of life in times of war. Fear was a constant companion. What happened to us happened to the villagers in hamlets in faraway Asia. Only they did not have powerful anti-aircraft guns and planes of their own to force the enemy planes to keep their distance. In Asia those planes, usually American, could swoop as low as they liked to let loose their bombs with pinpoint accuracy. Nobody knows the numbers of the Asian dead, or those who died of starvation and the diseases born of the famines of the scorched earth, the poisoned land, the chemical and biological weapons of war.

Europe itself was pauperised by the two world wars. The consequences of the first were not as dramatic as those of the second. The British empire hung on after the first but collapsed after the second. Western Europe ceased to be the centre of the world. A new bipolar hegemony of superpowers replaced the more delicately handled, but failed, power balance imposed by the Western Europeans. The newness of the new world order, the lack of a sense of history of its new masters, their strutting determination to outdo each other in 'chucking badness', were some of the dangers. The British and French empires, as well as the other lesser European empires, had been around for more than a century and had, through experience and trial and error in quieter times, acquired the diplomatic skills and political polish and wisdom to adjust to the needs and pressures of the times, to give way on the lesser to secure the greater. Both the Russians and Americans were new to the complexities associated with the world they had come to dominate. Each had to 'score' every time, to win every point, to concede nothing. Europe had bled itself into economic, political and ideological impotence. It had lost its imperialist vision of itself as master of the world, too lacking in will to help show the new boys how to play the power game at its highest level. Besides, the Europeans' own two world wars were clear proof of their own failure to enforce the peace of the world. The Americans and Russians, heirs to a world they were ill-prepared to manage, compounded the mess.

So we had to live on the edge of disaster during the Cold War years while these two dangerous 'little boys' with little or no sense of history, little or no sense of the imperatives of the responsibility that comes with power, played their fearful power games which took humanity to the brink of perdition. Could anybody other than Mikhail Gorbachev, influenced by the woman at his side, have had the vision and the wisdom to back off from the Cold War and cede victory to Ronald Reagan and the Americans? If it had been Brezhnev, how would the Cold War have ended? Would the world be moving into the twenty-first century in this mood of relative peace and muted hope? There are special times in human history, as Lenin, Hitler, Gandhi, Churchill, Roosevelt and Mandela have shown, when, for good or ill, the individual, in the right place at the right time, can determine and re-order the course of events. Individuals can and do, on rare occasions, influence the course of history. The process is more flexible than most ideologues of the theory of history would have us believe. So Mikhail Gorbachev helped ensure the Cold War did not end in nuclear Armageddon followed by a bleak nuclear winter of death and desolation. We owe him for that. We have come face to face with that possibility. The fear of it is out in the open. The genie cannot be forced back into the bottle. Its existence cannot be denied. The consciousness of our fear can never be made to go away. We have lost our innocence, our capacity to dream of human immortality. How do we live with this reality?

18

Frederick Douglass:
What Vision for a New Age?

F irst we must seek out the truth, then we must strive to live by it.

Frederick Douglass was born a slave in 1817. He died in 1895 — five years short of the dawn of this century. When he died, he was the most famous and influential black American of his age. He had been a member of the US government, a friend and adviser of the great Abraham Lincoln and, in the last years of his life he was appointed US minister and consul-general to the black Republic of Haiti. His was the single most important black voice against slavery during the early and mid-nineteenth century. His autobiography, *My Bondage and My Freedom*, is the most vivid and compelling account of the day-to-day details of slavery I have read. His style reminds me of Charles Dickens, his descriptive skills of those of Mark Twain. His consuming passion was his fight against slavery. By the time of his death, W.E.B. DuBois was a young man of 17; Jamaica's William Alexander Bustamante was 11; Marcus Garvey was a boy of 8; Norman

Manley a two-year-old. The young DuBois would almost certainly have known about Douglass, would perhaps have read the paper he published and attended one or more of his public lectures. I suspect Bustamante might have heard of him; Garvey certainly knew enough of him to later want to name one of the ships of his Black Star Line the *Frederick Douglass*. A photograph of Frederick Douglass taken in the last years of his life is of a big strong black patriarch, head crowned with a shock of white hair, looking for all the world as the real brown-skinned Moses of the Old Testament might have — before his European Anglo-Saxon whitewash. Frederick Douglass was the historical, intellectual and spiritual link bridging the nineteenth and twentieth centuries in the struggles of the dark folk of the earth.

This man born into slavery, who at an early age literally began reasoning his way out of 'mental slavery' while still in physical bondage, possessed an extraordinary capacity for seeing things as they were despite the mores and value systems of his age. He saw cruelty as cruelty, whether perpetrated by black or white, slave or free. He saw human nature in all its many facets — modest, vain, kind, cruel, generous, greedy, corrupt, honourable — for the basic human attributes they were across colour lines. He refused stubbornly to allow anyone to control his mind. In 1834 he was hired out for one year to a man, Edward Covey, known for his capacity for 'breaking in' slaves. Stubborn, lazy, violent slaves were routinely sent to Mr Covey to have their spirits broken, to be turned into obedient and docile beasts of burden. Covey was a poor man, owning only one or two slaves and a small piece of land. This 'breaking in' of slaves for others was part of his job of advancing his fortune. Mr Covey dealt with Frederick Douglass as he had with other slaves: he beat him, worked him to exhaustion and fed him as little as possible. It was not economic to starve a beast of burden to death; if it needed to be broken-in you did not feed it well. After the first six months, young Douglass, 17 at the time, big and strapping, was almost broken in spirit. Covey had done his work well. But then, like all brutes and bullies, he went too far. One day he sent Douglass to the stable to prepare a horse and sneaked after him and attacked him inside the stable, bent on giving Douglass another flogging. Douglas had already been beaten and battered until he feared for his life. This time he thought Covey might kill him and this time he resisted. He fended off Covey's blows and attempts to 'rope' him but did not, for a long time, try to strike back. This only infuriated Covey more and he pressed his attack more furiously. At last Douglass struck back. A slave striking a slave-master! He knew that he could be killed for this. Others had been. But he also knew that if he survived, he would not be struck or whipped again — except with extreme justification. He forgot that he was a black slave and Covey a white slave master. This was one man brutalising another man unjustly. When it was over, Douglass knew he had frightened Covey; the slave had seen fear in the eyes of the slave-master. There was no later vengeance. Covey never laid hands on Douglass again. In the presence of others he often threatened to repeat the flogging he gave Douglass in the stable, but he knew, and Douglass and two other slaves who had witnessed the event and refused to go to Covey's help, knew what had happened.

His personal story is the story of slavery itself. He was born into slavery, his mother some anonymous female slave forcibly used by some unknown white man to slake his lust and move on, leaving the woman with child. No name, no responsibility. The woman was somebody's property, like a cow, horse or any other yard animal. Provided the owner consented, any passing white stranger could use the woman. Indeed, the bringing forth of a child added one more head to the owner's stock, increased his wealth. The little brown boy was brought up by his granny. Was she really his granny? Really the mother of his mother? No matter, she brought him up with a large number of other little children, all of whom called her grandmamma, all of whom she loved in the old African way in which the old women in the tribe bring up the young whose parents are not with them. Unlike the African tribal granny, though, this one only had charge of the little children for a short time before they were taken over by their slave master. Frederick Douglass lays bare the details of the system with great skill. It is a great temptation to retell his story, but the man has done it so well and the book is there for all who care to make the effort. My concern is with the man as a link in the continuum of struggle, of the handing over from generation to generation, from century to century, the human will to freedom and dignity and hope even when the prospects look most bleak.

On 9 January 1894, a year before he died, Frederick Douglass spoke at the Metropolitan A.M.E. Church in Washington DC. His subject was 'the so-called but misplaced Negro problem'.

In a sweeping, authoritative survey of the condition of America's black folk in the closing decade of the nineteenth century Douglass discussed the key problems of the times. First, he dealt with lynching, then reaching its peak. By that time somewhere in the region of over 4,000 Americans had been lynched, one-quarter of them white. Douglass said:

> I have waited patiently but anxiously to see the end of the epidemic of mob law now prevailing in the South. But the indications are not hopeful, great and terrible as have been its ravages in the past, it now seems to be increasing not only in the number of its victims, but in its frantic rage and savage extravagance. Lawless vengeance is beginning to be visited upon white men as well as black. Our newspapers are daily disfigured by its ghastly horrors. It is no longer local, but national; no longer confined to the South, but has invaded the North. The contagion spreading, extending and over-leaping geographical lines and state boundaries, and if permitted to go on it threatens to destroy all respect for law and order not only in the South, but in all parts of our country — North as well as South. For certain it is, that crime allowed to go on unresisted and unarrested will breed crime. When the poison of anarchy

is once in the air, like the pestilence that walketh in the darkness, the winds of heaven will take it up and favour its diffusion. Though it may strike down the weak today, it will strike down the strong tomorrow.

Douglass spoke of 'our' country, 'our' newspapers, an American talking about the American problem of lynching. Always, even when he was a slave, Frederick Douglass saw himself as an American. He was born in America, Maryland was his birthplace. When he met some slaves newly brought from the Guinea Coast, the first lesson he learned was that some blacks had once been free before they were stolen from their homeland and brought to America. It settled one question: all black folk were not born slaves, but some were stolen and made slaves. They were also different from him; not all black people were the same; some spoke differently before losing their language to slavery.

Unlike DuBois Frederick Douglass never had that sense of 'twoness: Negro and American'. Always, throughout his life, as slave, as runaway slave, as free man, as a great soldier in the emancipation struggle, as respected statesman and leading spokesman of his people, Frederick Douglass was an American — clearly, firmly, unequivocally American. There was no hyphenated identity for him, just American. America was where his was born; a man's home is the place where he was born.

He dealt with the 'Back to Africa' movement in that same speech and his position was clear:

I come now to another proposition held up just now as a solution of the race problem, and this I consider equally unworthy with the one just disposed of (the lynching matter). The two belong to the same low-bred family of ideas.

This proposition is to colonise the coloured people of America in Africa, or somewhere else. Happily this scheme will be defeated, both by its impolicy and its impracticability. It is all nonsense to talk about the removal of eight millions of American people from their homes in America to Africa. The expense and hardships to say nothing of the cruelty of such a measure, would make success to such a measure impossible. The American people are wicked, but they are not fools, they will hardly be disposed to incur the expense, to say nothing of the injustice which this measure demands. Nevertheless, this colonising scheme, unworthy as it is, of American statesmanship and American honour, and though full of mischief to the coloured people, seems to have a strong hold on the public mind and at times has shown much life and vigour.

The bad thing about it is that it has now begun to be advocated by coloured men of acknowledged ability and learning, and every little while some white statesman becomes its advocate. Those gentlemen will doubtless have their opinion of me; I certainly have mine of them. My opinion of them is that if they are sensible, they are insincere, and if they are sincere they are not sensible. They know, or they ought to know, that it would take more money than the cost of the late war, to transport even one-half of the coloured people of the United States to Africa. Whether intentionally or not they are, as I think, simply trifling with an afflicted people. They urge them to look for relief, where they ought to know that relief is impossible. The only excuse they can make is that there is no hope for the negro here and that the coloured people in America owe something to Africa.

This last sentimental idea makes colonisation very fascinating to dreamers of both colours. But there is really for it no foundation.

They tell us that we owe something to our native land. But when the fact is brought to view, which should never be forgotten, that a man can only have one native land, and that is the land in which he was born, the bottom falls entirely out of this sentimental argument.

What is Africa to me:
Copper sun or scarlet sea,
Jungle star or jungle track,
Strong bronzed men, or regal black
Women from whose loins I sprang
When the birds of Eden sang?

One three centuries removed
From the scenes his fathers loved,
Spicy grove, cinnamon tree,
What is Africa to me?

Countee Cullen, poet of the Harlem Renaissance, and friend of Langston Hughes, gave voice to the nagging ambivalence of black American intellectuals. Frederick Douglass had the answer long before the dawn of the twentieth century.

Africa is the mother continent, the place from which all dark folk stemmed. But you are a native of where you are born; home is the land of your birth. There should be no ambivalence about that. If you are born in Britain, you are British, whatever your historical antecedents, however much other British may want to deny you. Nationality, domicile, are not conferred by colour. You cannot be born in one place and be regarded and treated as the native of another without grievous injustice. A person of Indian ancestry born in Guyana is a Guyanese, no hyphenation needed; one born in Kenya or Uganda or Tanzania — or anywhere else on the African continent — is a native of the land of his birth; a Kenyan, Tanzanian, a Ugandan, a Fijian, a Trinidadian, a South African, a Frenchman, a German, a Jamaican. Post-Apartheid South Africans, and Jamaicans, seem clearer on this point than most others. Frederick Douglass saw and understood it at a time when most around him did not. So he scoffed at the 'Back to Africa' movement for the distraction it was. His criticism was harsh and dismissive. It need not have been. The escapism of 'Back to Africa' was as much an emotional and psychic support system as were the otherworldly spirituals of the black slaves. To dream of freedom, to sing of freedom, to conjure up a land of freedom, is part of the holding on to that human will to be free. It is part of the Old Testament promised land, part of the great movements of peoples throughout human history in search of the freedom to shape themselves in the ways and images they find most fulfilling. Escapism is sentimental, of course, but is also, used with some awareness, a great survival tool. Anancy, whose roots and origins Douglass so clearly understood, was the embodiment of how the weak and defenceless survived against the strong and the cruel. But 'Back to Africa' was a distraction as long as it diverted attention from the struggle for justice at home, wherever home was.

The Indians and the Chinese of the Diaspora never developed a 'Back to India' or a 'Back to China' movement. Why? There were steady flows of Indians and Chinese to other parts of the world. They maintained contact with the homeland, and those who prospered sent money to families back home and, wherever possible, arranged for family members and close connections to join them. A similar link exists between the people of the Caribbean and their families who have migrated. Remittances from relatives in Britain, Canada and the United States are important contributions to the economies of the islands. The separation is much more recent, not 'three centuries removed', and the intent of the expatriate West Indian migrant is to return to the islands after earning enough to live on in retirement. Only the children, born in Britain, America, Canada and educated in schools there, are likely to be more natives of the land of their birth than their parents or grandparents who continue living with the psychologically 'packed suitcase', waiting to go home. For the youngsters born there, home is Britain or Canada or the United States. These, and their white and other school mates of Asian and African ancestry, will make up the citizenry of the new century for whom there will be little or no ambivalence about being British, Canadian or American. For them, fighting for a fair chance in the land of their birth will take precedence over dreams of going 'back to Africa', 'back to Asia', 'back to the Caribbean'. And just as well. Elsewhere I have mentioned what a numbers problem we would face if all expatriate Jamaicans were to return to Jamaica. We already have a numbers problem without that.

The Frederick Douglass view of how it should be, as he enunciated it in that speech back in January 1894, looks very much how it will be in coming years. But what of the resistance? What of those who today want to circumvent the rights of these dark British, Americans, Canadians, Europeans to full citizenship in the lands of their birth? All sorts of efforts are being made in that direction, including redefining citizenship. Douglass deals with these things too.

He reminds of how the rights of blacks gained during the Reconstruction period were systematically whittled away until adult franchise, that greatest of victories for citizenship after the Civil War, was turned into a hollow mockery of itself, which had to be struggled for all over again. The struggle against these setbacks darkened the last years of Douglass' life. But the struggle continued and in our time, we have witnessed the reclamation of all those rights. From Mrs Rosa Parks' refusal to sit in the back of a bus, to the sit-ins and marches against segregation, and the brutal attacks on non-violent protesters, to the young militants of the black power movement, ready, willing and able to take up arms in self-defence; it did not cease and it will not cease until the vision of Frederick Douglass is turned into the American reality. You are American — or British, or anything else — because you are born there. As a citizen, you are entitled to all the rights and responsibilities of citizenship unconditionally. Colour, class, status are irrelevant to this reality. Douglass said:

> We have a fight on our hands right here, a fight for the whole race, and a blow struck for the negro in America is a blow struck for the negro in Africa. For until the negro is respected in America, he need not expect consideration elsewhere. All this native land talk is nonsense. The native land of the American negro is America. His bones, his muscles, his sinews, are all American. His ancestors for two hundred and seventy years have lived, and laboured, and died on American soil, and millions of his posterity have inherited Caucasian blood.

It is competent, therefore, to ask, in view of this admixture, as well as in view of other facts, where the people of this mixed race are to go. For their ancestors are white and black, and it will be difficult to find their native land anywhere outside of the United States...

The struggle, for Douglass, was clear. You strive for freedom and justice wherever you are. The indivisibility of the black struggle — the Pan African notion — was at work even in his time. But not as a great movement of black people going back to Africa. Those of 'mixed blood' were part of the black struggle, not a race apart, as they were sometimes duped into believing, or as a form of divide-and-rule, as in South Africa and elsewhere. Where would you send them if Africa were for the Africans, Europe for the Europeans, Asia for the Asians? Frederick Douglass, the 'Coloured' man, was Frederick Douglass the black fighter against slavery, the great abolitionist, the fighter against all forms of discrimination; he was a fighter for women's rights long before that cause became popular. He was, ultimately, the great American, committed to the American ideal laid out in its Constitution. The struggle was political and politics shapes a nation's destiny. Douglass was a political realist who urged President Lincoln to make the American Civil War a direct confrontation between the forces of freedom and the forces of slavery. He, however, opposed the 1859 assault on Harper's Ferry by fellow abolitionist John Brown and his band of 16 white and 5 black followers. It was not so much that he was against violence, I think, as that he saw the action at Harper's Ferry as unrealistic and doomed to failure.

Frederick Douglass' great speech ends on the note that if Americans of all classes, creeds and colours were true to the commitments and promises of their Constitution, all their problems could be solved. No great new revolutionary solutions; just live up to the principles on which the great republic was founded. Throughout the Reconstruction period, between 1865 and 1877, he campaigned for full civil rights and prospects looked good until the defeated South fought back and many of the gains of the Reconstruction period were rolled back. That was the background to his last great speech.

After the death of Frederick Douglass, Booker T. Washington became the next great spokesman for black American interests. Like Douglass, he was born into slavery but nearly forty years later, in 1856. Lincoln had proclaimed Emancipation in 1863 when Booker T. Washington was seven. His personal experience of slavery was brief; his family became part of the vast army of poor landless peasants with no work, no land and nowhere to go. The young Washington was eager to learn, but poverty forced him into an early life as a worker, doing any job he could get — in a salt furnace at nine, then in a coal mine. The will to get an education remained strong. An interesting intellectual experience is to read Booker T. Washington's *Up From Slavery* and Frederick Douglass' *My Bondage and My Freedom* side-by-side. In my childhood, *Up From Slavery* was a standard text for most young black boys fortunate enough to get places in missionary schools and colleges. We never heard about Frederick Douglass and we never saw his autobiography. The reason why becomes plain when the two books are read side-by-side. It explains as nothing else I know, the colonisation of the minds of generations of young black boys.

Washington believed the best interests of black people would be served by education in the crafts and industrial skills, and through the virtues of being patient, hard-working and thrifty. He urged blacks to abandon the struggle for civil rights, to forget about seeking political power or social equality, and strive instead to attain economic security by becoming good farmers and industrial workers. Accept segregation and discrimination until you pull yourself up to the point of economic prosperity where the whites will respect you. This, said Washington, would in the end lead to equal citizenship for blacks.

Washington practised what he preached. His Tuskegee Institute, with its emphasis on vocational training, flourished and quickly became a leading black American training college. White business people showed their approval by big funding grants. His influence among whites grew to the point where whites consulted him on which black individuals and which black institutions were worthy of their support. Government patronage and white corporate philanthropic support depended on the say-so of Booker T. Washington. Throughout his period as the spokesman for black America, the position of the black American was methodically brought down from the high-point it had achieved during Reconstruction and the leadership of Frederick Douglass. Rigid patterns of discrimination and segregation came back; blacks were deprived of the right to vote in the South; they were generally excluded from the political life and decision-making process of their country. Much of what had been gained had to be struggled for all over again after Booker T. Washington's death in 1915. In fairness to Washington, he bridged an important gap. The blacks of the post-slavery South from which he emerged needed the skills he urged and taught, for without those skills Southern blacks would remain in a state of peonage. The approval and active money support of corporate white America and the American government were essential. The poor, illiterate blacks of the South trusted him. The Tuskegee contribution to black American education remains of great value to this day. But, politically, Booker T. Washington put a long pause on the struggle for the full rights of citizenship. And pause, in the natural scheme of things, ends up as backward movement.

To counter this backward move, W.E.B. DuBois, then a young man of 37, called together a group of 29 prominent blacks to a secret meeting at Niagara Falls and drew up a manifesto demanding full civil rights, the abolition of racial discrimination and the recognition of 'human brotherhood'. The Niagara Movement lasted only five years but during that time it shaped a vision that would lead black Americans away from the Booker T. Washington view of things, back to the Frederick Douglass vision and into the civil rights movement of our time. The National Association for the Advancement of Coloured People, founded in 1909 by DuBois and his Niagara Movement associates as well as a group of whites who were against discrimination, became the new instrument of the struggle against racial discrimination and for equal rights and justice. The black American struggle entered a new phase. Instead of depending on the leadership of individuals, black Americans now had an organisation to speak for them. To be sure, the abolitionist movement during slavery was organised, but around a few powerful white personalities like William Lloyd Garrison who, incidentally, disapproved of Frederick Douglass' insistence on political action as part of the struggle, as well as the need for a separate, black-controlled newspaper. Douglass broke with Garrison and allied himself with a more politically-oriented faction of the abolitionist movement led by James G. Birney.

The NAACP was qualitatively different. Its membership was mixed, of black and white, its leadership predominantly 'black' by the American yardstick of colour, predominantly 'brown' by Jamaican Marcus Garvey's yardstick. In the Caribbean the lines were more finely drawn, the grades and shades more sharply observed and used to divide and rule. Coloureds, in the Caribbean, were buffers between black and white; white, black and brown had become partners in the subtle complexities of the 'shade game', somewhat similar to how it was in South Africa and among the 'Eurasians' of the Far East. The sharp American colour line allowed no room for 'wee droppers' unless they could get away with 'passing'. The effect was a sharper, more united concentration on issues of colour. You were either one or the other, no in-between, therefore relatively free of the psychological hang-ups with which the shade game reinforced the black inferiority complex. For all that, the complexes ran deep, as shown by the obsession with hair straightening and skin bleaching, though it is not as deep-seated as in South Africa and the Caribbean.

The NAACP united all shades of black — from the blue-eyed, white-skinned Walter White who went into the deep South to investigate lynchings because he could 'pass', to the brown-skinned middle-class intellectual DuBois, to the blackest railroad workers and household helpers — into a united force in its struggle for an end to discrimination. Over the years it developed a most effective legal arm to use the American Constitution and American law to fight for the constitutional rights of all Americans. To have their country's Constitution as a weapon in their struggle against racism was the unique advantage black Americans had over black South Africans. Once they hit on using the American Constitution and the law in their service, the Walls of Jericho came tumbling down. After three centuries and more, the struggle of black Americans assumed the moral high ground. This was cold comfort to those who had to fight the bitter, and often bloody, battles on the streets and in the sit-ins and marches which were day-to-day features of post-Second World War American life for the best part of three decades. Rights were conceded in law and denied in practice.

It was the opposite in South Africa in particular, and in what was then known as 'White Africa' — East and Central Africa with their settled white minorities. There, laws and constitutions invested racial discrimination with a moral, religious and legal authority. The African National Congress began its life as the South African Native National Congress in 1912, three years after the forming of the NAACP. The British were the colonial power of the time. The Boers or Afrikaners as they called themselves later, resisted British rule, as they, too, wanted to be free of colonialism and have a state of their own. In the Cape Colony, Coloureds and blacks enjoyed a limited franchise but there were those who wanted to take away that right. The main platform of the South African Native National Congress was the maintaining of the voting rights of the Coloureds and blacks of the Cape. The Coloureds, even then, had been sold, and bought, the notion of their 'difference' from the blacks. Still, the black organisation fought to retain their voting rights. In 1923 the organisation changed its name to the African National Congress. Membership was non-racial, but few Colorueds and fewer whites joined. In the late 1920s when communism was seen as the face of the future, a strong, predominantly white South African Communist Party sought to form an alliance with the ANC. The ANC leadership split over the issue with the majority voting against such an alliance. The split resulted in a long period of decline during which a number of other organisations came into being and challenged for the leadership of the black people. The ANC somehow survived all these challenges, possibly because it was the oldest political body in the country and Africans put a premium on the old. It never opposed ideological diversity and some of its members were known communists. At one point the conflict between Stalinist and Trotskyites even reached the platform of an ANC conference, but it was quickly overshadowed by the imperatives of the struggle against racism.

In the 1940s, under a new group of emerging young leaders — Mandela, Tambo, Sisulu, Govan Mbeki, — the ANC became more militant. It formed an alliance with the communists and began its series of non-violent protests. The government's response was violent, brutal, aggressive. The conflict escalated till the posture of non-violence became untenable. You either fight back or you capitulate. The ANC fought back and was branded a terrorist pro-communist organisation by the South African government and most of the Western world. The Cold War made South Africa a valued American ally. Only the black Americans called for the release of the imprisoned ANC leaders, and they could not succeed in persuading their government to turn against the racist South African government as long as the Cold War continued. The Soviet Union had to collapse, communism as a challenging world ideology had to be defeated before black Americans and others of goodwill could successfully persuade

Western governments to call for the dismantling of Apartheid. There had, of course, been strong forces in Europe opposed to South Africa's racism and calling for the freeing of Mandela. There could be no movement on this until the Cubans helped defeat the racist army in Angola, the Cold War was won, and the geo-political interests of the United States demanded the existence of a democratic South Africa.

What if the Cold War had not ended? What if the Cubans had not been prepared to fight and die for Angolan freedom? Black American and Caribbean influence, riding this tide of unfolding events, for the first time in five hundred years, played a critical part as shapers of history. Till now, others had shaped history for them, their own history as well as the world's history. Now, at last, black people were ceasing to be the victims of history. They were now becoming the co-shapers of their own and, therefore, of the world's history. The story of man, from here on, will not be told from one perspective only, will not be recorded, judged and evaluated as seen from Europe only. It will be, like Joseph's coat of many colours, a human mosaic of infinite and rich variety.

I do not think the end of racism will result in the kind of homogeneous, uniform, one 'global village', conjured up by the transnational New World Order visionaries. For one thing, it ignores almost all the lessons of history in its pursuit of endless 'growth', of profit as end in itself. It reduces the human person to an economic unit of production, of value only to the extent of its ability to produce. If this view, which now seems so pervasive, were to prevail, then the new century may run into serious social and economic problems in its very first quarter. People are more than units of production, more than tools to be manipulated for profit across frontiers and cultures and colours.

For Africans, for instance, land will always be more special than for most other people: land is their life, given by God in trust to sustain the tribe and the community. Man cannot own land in the way Europeans see ownership. If it mothers all who depend on it for life, how can anyone see it in terms of exclusive ownership. This will not suddenly change because the transnationals and the world regulatory bodies which do their bidding want land to be open and accessible to all in the pursuit of profit. For those who have not been separated from it too long, the relationship with the land and the things which grow on it still has deep religious spiritual and social overtones and undertones. All life, all living things — animals, plants, trees, rocks, man — have this in common: they are born of the earth, the land. They are therefore related to each other. The missionaries called this animism and sought to end this relationship in which the African accepted the earth as mother and all things on it as living relatives. Africans are not the only ones with such a view of life. In other cultures and other religions there are similar, though sometimes different and differing, versions of the sacredness and unity of all life, not only human life. This is in direct conflict with the materialism of the New World Order. How this is reconciled is one hard question. Conquest, occupation, slavery, capitalism, imperialism, communism, have failed to eradicate these deep-seated psycho-spiritual value systems. Why should an essentially amoral globalisation which accepts no moral responsibility for the consequences of its actions fare any better? Self-interest made the slave-owner feed and clothe and house his 'property', colonisers protected their colonies, provided essential services and, later, attempted to prepare them for eventual self-government; they accepted the responsibility implicit in power. Do the transnational creators of the New World Order?

DuBois' problem of the twentieth century, Marcus Garvey's struggle for African redemption and the return to the mother continent, and all the legions of others who had to struggle simply to affirm themselves as human, like all other humans: all this reached its high-point in our century when we could begin to influence the outcome of what happens to us, and how it happens to us. It ended the centuries of blacks as 'property', or other people's tenants even in their own lands, as 'victims of circumstances' created by others. Now, at last, as the Jamaican poet George Campbell wrote, we are tenants at will no longer. The land, the house, the thoughts, visions, dreams are our own now; no longer reflections and echoes of the reality of others. But is this all? Is this what black folk struggled and suffered for throughout the long and bitter history of their contact with whites? Fighting for too long, to the point of near-exhaustion, doing anything for too long, without respite, is debilitating, denies the effort its maximum result, distorts the vision, numbs the mind, blurs the end in view. Whatever qualitative difference there may have been in the beginning is eroded over time; and five hundred years is time enough to reshape a culture of tolerance to diversity into one of hostility; a culture of peacefulness into one of aggression; of trust into distrust. The stranger becomes the enemy who would seize what is yours; you in turn would, if you were strong enough, seize what is his. Might becomes right and the world belongs to the strong. Being weak, being overpowered, occupied, imposed upon, does not make for decency, pride, self-respect. Without decency, without pride, without self-respect you become, as little children so aptly put it, 'a not nice' person, a not so nice nation, a not so nice 'race'. You become the obverse of your enemy; what he would be if he were you; what you would be if you were him.

There is nothing noble or ennobling about oppression and exploitation; it only teaches how to oppress and exploit, just as beating only teaches how to beat, bullying how to bully, robbing how to rob. Does it matter who exploits whom if that is all there is to it? If the strong have licence to oppress and exploit the weak; if the transnationals of the New World Order and their World Trade Organisation can legitimise the exploitation of the poor nations of the South — what is the point? Let the South strive to become as strong and rich and powerful as the North now is, then do to the North what it has done to the South over the past five hundred years? To what point? To what purpose? There are signs of black and brown business tycoons moving in this direction, amassing vast fortunes at the expense of their own people and then branching out to create economic empires elsewhere. The unity of the transnationals, across national and colour boundaries, to create a new form of economic imperialism without the moral and social responsibilities of the old imperialism is a disturbing new development. Black businessmen are becoming the biggest union-busters in the countries of the South. They want longer working weeks and big pay cuts. Because they function in environments of greater poverty, they are more oppressive towards their workers than is possible in the North.

These black and brown bosses are not like the 'drivers' of slavery days, or the overseers of the post-emancipation plantation days. They are either owners or partners or top managers in the enterprises. The nature of the exploitation has changed, not the exploitation. Is not this a mere variation of the age-old struggle for justice and equity but without colour as its base? Is this the shape of things for the future? The 'market' which is now supposed to regulate everything, is a faceless mechanism with no humanity, no compassion informing its so-called laws. The new marketeers seem to have forgotten the wisdom of Adam Smith who knew that the wealth of nations resides in its working *people* — not in bloodless units of production. If the South, if DuBois' darker races of mankind follow the direction now charted by these new free-marketeers they will replace one form of oppression and exploitation by another, more ruthless form. But what are we to do? Another five hundred years of struggle?

The story of mankind, indeed of all life, is the story of struggle; it is in the dialectics of nature: the struggle to emerge from the womb of the woman to enter the world; then the endless struggle of the woman and, in relatively normal societies, her mate to nurture and protect the babe, young child, the teenager until he/she is prepared to go forth and continue the struggle on its own; finds a mate to share the struggle; they, in turn reproduce themselves and a new life struggles into the world to repeat the cycle. These are the dynamics of the process, how the species perpetuates itself. To be free of struggle is to be free of life, which is death — and that comes in the end anyway. The problem is not the struggle — that comes with the territory — but what it is, its nature, the way it is conducted, to what purpose. One of the wisest and gentlest teachers in human history described the purpose of the struggle as *that ye might have life and have it more abundantly.* The struggle, for all people, in all cultures, all nations, of all colours is summed up in this. Another of the wisest teachers in human history urged that whatever we do, we *do no harm.* To have life and to have it more abundantly and to do no harm — these are surely ideals which, if attained, would invest all life with a new and special and gentler quality. That is worth struggling for.

The impulse towards this level of struggle is the story of human evolutionary change and development and progress. Life today is richer for more people than ever before. Which makes the poverty and deprivation suffered by the poor more stark. The North enjoys the abundant life, yet within it there are pockets of poverty similar to the pervasive poverty of the South. And in the poor South there are pockets of opulent wealth greater than anything found in the North. In the rich North the pockets of extreme poverty are a minority. In the poor South the pockets of extreme wealth are a tiny minority. At its best and most creative, the struggle in both North and South is to ensure that the extremes of poverty are checked and held within bounds. In a good society no human being should be allowed to drop below a defined level of existence. The British Welfare State and European social security systems largely serve this purpose. In the developing world there are no such social security systems. There should be. If the New World Order of the free market is to begin to justify itself, and to survive longer than Soviet communism did, it will have to address the problem of minimum social security wherever it operates. The economic imperialism of the transnational bottom-line with no social responsibility to the people and resources it exploits is as assured of long-term failure as was communism without a human face. This is the challenge facing the ideologues of the New World Order in which 'the market' replaces God and morality and Adam Smith's compassionate concern for working people. It may well take all the efforts of all people in all countries committed to enhancing life and doing no harm, to struggle together to change the face of the new economic order, to make it more human, more compassionate.

In a world where such a vision prevails across boundaries of nationality and colour, the rich and opulent may be shamed into using their riches to help good causes — education, health, the nurturing of young minds. Here, too, there are hopeful pointers. The magic of the new technology can be harnessed to make life more abundant for more people, and to do less harm to more people. We may not, in the new century, succeed in the high hope to *do no harm*. We can minimise the harm. Those with very great wealth should use some of that wealth socially. A few of the very rich have set examples. Others should be persuaded, pressured, induced to follow suit.

There are obstacles and confusions in the way. Most of those concerned with colour are on the way out and are not likely to survive for very much longer. Indeed, the colour problem has already become largely the involuntary death-spasm of a dangerous dying beast. The profiteers see less profit in it; the social bigots get diminishing mileage from it; racists have to find other names for their racism; the fear on which it flourished is dying. No one group of people is threatening the identity of another by absorption. The blacks of South Africa are no more heeding George Bernard Shaw's advice, more than three-quarters of a century ago, to 'miscegenate' their problems out of existence than did the frightened whites of the time. Groups and communities prefer to stick with their own. It is easier, more comfortable, the way human societies have evolved. People do not go out of their way to look for husbands or wives or lovers or friends in other groups. The impulse is to stay within the group; the girl or boy next door or nearby are the usually chosen life partners. Circumstances have to be exceptional to depart from this norm. People have to be transported from their normal habitat, to be without men and women of their own communities; they have to be engaged in wars or great migrations or be a long way from home for a long time, for the mixtures between black and white and brown and yellow to take place.

In a settled, orderly world such mixing and intermingling will always be restricted to unconventional, nonconformist minorities. The Boers of South Africa, like the whites of the Southern United States need not fear being swallowed up by black majorities, with only a slight darkening of the general complexion. All the mixing that took place in the Caribbean, resulting in some of the most beautiful female 'brownings' in the world, was not caused by black men running after or raping white women. It was white slave owners, their white estate managers, white overseers, white tradesmen and craftsmen all of whom often came without their women, who did the mixing. The idea of the black man lusting after every white woman in sight, was and remains a self-serving myth made up of a combination of a sense of fear, inadequacy and guilt: if this is what we did to and with their women, they will do the same with ours; and what if our women found them more satisfying, ended up preferring them? That sexual fear feeds much white male prejudice. The notion of the 'black stud' is as false as the notion of the 'master race'. Women, regardless of colour, tend to have a more realistic view of the situation; they know the origins of these attitudes; they know these attitudes reduce them to one-dimensional sex objects without sense or choice; they suppress their outrage and anger; they resent being 'fair game' in anybody's racial hang-ups; which is why they have at times, in the

US, South Africa and the Caribbean, manipulated the situation and the men to their own purposes. All that is coming to an end. It will remain a minority who will make marriages and families across colour lines. There will be no sexual swamping of any group by any other group. That contrived cause of fear and fantasy, as part of the cultural rubbish of the past three centuries and more, is on its way out. It is not part of the problem of the twenty-first century.

I pause from writing this, look up through my open study door across the large living-room to where Daphne sits at her sewing machine; a few dogs lie at her feet; the rest are with me, littered on the floor of the study, one under my desk, one under the card-table on which my ancient, now useless, typewriter rests, the third one close beside me under the shelf of reams of paper. There is a convention among the dogs that only three at a time, usually the three young females, share the study with me at work. When Daphne is with me, all six of them insist on turning my study into an overcrowded dog place. It is a cool fresh room, especially designed as my workplace by Daphne. It has two large windows facing each other north and south, allowing for good light and a through draught. The soft tapping on my machine and the low steady hum of the fan always tranquillises the dogs, making them the best company for an essentially solitary occupation. Daphne looks up briefly and smiles. It is the first of June, fifty-one years after we entered into our partnership.

19

Tomorrow's People — With Love

The Rastafari of Jamaica have used music as an instrument of mental and emotional liberation. In the early days of their struggles the songs had some of the other-worldly qualities of the American slave songs of which Frederick Douglass wrote with such feeling. The Rastafari dream of Africa was

> By the rivers of Babylon
> Where we lay down
> And there we wept
> When we remembered Zion
> When we remembered Zion
And Jimmy Cliff's:
> Many rivers to cross
> But I can't find my way over...

which moved Nelson Mandela so deeply that night in 1994 at Jamaica's national stadium. But in our time, and over the years, the Rasta songs have undergone profound change, led at first by Bob

Marley, Bunny Wailer and Peter Tosh who questioned and challenged the prevailing value systems of the Jamaican establishment. They ended up its modern-day cultural icons, who have carried Jamaican music and, with it, Jamaica's name, to every corner of the earth. And today a new generation of young Rastas, with a new vision in a changed and changing world, has emerged to sing, like Junior Reid, of *One Blood*.

> You could a' come from Europe or from Africa…One blood
> You could a' come from Libya or America…One blood
> You could a' come from Lebanon or Iran…One blood
> You could a' come from China or Japan…One blood
> You could a be a Catholic or an Anglican…One blood
> You could a be a black man or a white man…One blood

So the young people of traditionalist and culturally conservative Japan have become camp followers of Rasta Reggae, have accepted the new Rasta vision of a common humanity of peace and love, at times in a haze of ganja smoke, and do their best to grow dread-locks. We are all of *One Blood*. Urban, and even some tribal Africans, sport the Rasta dreadlocks these days. I have even seen a few white-skinned dreads at those modern-day replacements of the ancient Roman arenas — the great soccer fields and tennis stadiums. Instead of mortal combat between man and man or man and beast, the combat is in kicking big balls or beating small ones. And in America they have transformed the age-old children's games of rounders and basketball into big multi-million dollar enterprises in which 'professional' young men, and now young women too, can earn huge fortunes. It is easier to become a sports millionaire than to become a millionaire as a great doctor or research scientist or teacher or writer or artist. There are notable exceptions to this rule; the developers of the computer come to mind. Generally speaking, though, entertainment is more richly rewarded than most creative or socially more valuable undertakings. If those who saved lives and those who nurtured and opened human minds to the wonders and glories of life and knowledge were rewarded half as well as the 'stars' of entertainment, what a wonderful world this would be.

The communists began to offer a new value system of apportioning reward according to quality of contribution but then blew it with their own *Nomenklatura*, the special privileged ones who became a new class, the new élite, with special access to all the good things of life in a supposedly classless egalitarian society. In his time, my friend George Padmore had been a very highly placed member of the Moscow *Nomenklatura*. So the question of whether the big money and the fame generated by Rasta music will work to change the nature of Rastafarianism and its unique vision is very real. All sorts of visionary movements have been changed by success and institutionalisation.

For now, the unfolding vision, especially among the young, is toward the acceptance of our common humanity; there is an impatience with old barriers and sick old platitudes about what does and does not confer grace and virtue. One trouble with this healthy attitude is its tendency to dismiss past experience as of no relevance to the future. Our present is based on what happened in our past. If we do not learn from that past, we are doomed to repeat its failures and mistakes. One danger with the wonderfully useful computer is that it could, unless we are careful, marginalise the written word, the printed document, the book, the habit of reading. There are bright young people, highly computer literate, able to browse the Internet and download information from anywhere, who do not read books; who do not know the extraordinary experience of sitting or lying down with a book, preferably out in the open under a shady tree, with a sandwich, some fruit, something to drink, and read a Sunday morning or afternoon away in glorious happiness and tranquillity. This kind of sharing of human experience by way of the printed word is something no computer can replace. There is no need to replace the one by the other; both are of inestimable worth. The true learning process, the process of human experience is inclusive, not exclusive; selective to be sure, but never exclusive. I wonder how many of India's very bright and brilliant computer programmers have read Jawaharlal Nehru's *Glimpses of World History* and *The Discovery of India*? How many in the Indian Diaspora? How many in the African Diaspora have read DuBois' *Souls of Black Folk* and Garvey's *Philosophy and Opinions*? And Frederick Douglass' *My Bondage and My Freedom*? Or the poetry and novels and scholarly works of their own black writers? How many have missed the wonder and the glory of the discovery of themselves and their world through books written by people like themselves?

The ideal is the unity of the arts and the sciences, not the excluding of one for the other. The scientist who is culturally literate, reads poetry, history, philosophy, fiction, listens to music, is usually a better scientist than the one involved in his/her subject only. The more rounded and whole, the better a person usually is at his/her chosen speciality. You need to know and understand and have a feel for good language, good English or French or Hindi or Chinese before you can be a good dialect poet. Exclusive specialisation endangers this wholeness. This is one of the great dangers of our time, especially in traditionally oral societies. It can lead to an intelligent and all-knowing ignorance about who we are, where we came from and how we got to where we are. All this rich body of knowledge and information is stored in books. When we do not read, all this is lost to us. I knew a journalist once who had not read a novel in his life and who boasted that he could not waste his time on such stuff; all he read were the 'How To' manuals. I was appalled. If we do not read, if we do not know who we are and how we came to where we are, any demagogue, any false messiah, can use the new technology to bend our minds in the service of false gods and a new barbarism. We have seen the beginnings of this in the recent past. We witnessed the mass suicides in the wilds of Guyana led by Jim Jones. We have seen the televangelist miracle-mongers swoop down in droves on tropical lands whenever winter hits the United States. It is something to guard against in the new century. That guarding begins with the creating or reawakening of the habit of reading. That is the irreducible minimal survival skill with which to go into the future with any hope of doing better than we did in the past.

For that the people must all be literate. Ignorance has been and remains the greatest enemy to human progress and harmony among peoples. It is the handmaiden to fear, prejudice, and all the false notions about the nature of things. It is to our shame that we move into the new century with so many millions of people still unable to read and write, still without the tools to help reason things through for themselves, still prey to the manipulation of the greedy and power-hungry who turned the twentieth century into the century of two world wars, countless local wars, the most violent displacement of peoples in human history, and the threat of nuclear Armageddon. In our ignorance we have become accomplices in the massive pollution of the environment to a point of near-fatal danger.

This last is perhaps the single greatest danger to the continuation of life here on earth. It does not matter who you are, where you are, what you believe, what your shape or size or colour, if your world is steadily polluted to the point where it can no longer sustain human life. Once that critical point is reached, nothing else will matter. The difference between black and white, rich and poor, the powerful and the weak, North and South, will all become irrelevant. The idea of escaping the mess by colonising space, by travelling to other planets is, for the foreseeable future, not on. Which makes the problem of human survival in the twenty-first century and beyond the critical one. DuBois's problem of the relations between the darker and lighter races of mankind is fast being replaced by the *twenty-first-century problem of the relations*

*between humans and the physical environment within which they have to
live and survive.* If they continue, in the new century, to abuse and
degrade and pollute the environment as they have done in this century,
then the future for human life on earth will be bleak, increasingly brutish,
with the prospects of a lingering end.

That morning after Hurricane Gilbert when I stepped out of our
back door and looked out on a bleak dead moonscape, I thought: 'This
is how it would look at the end of time; barren and lifeless, nothing
green.' Then, a mere three weeks later, the land was green again, life
had returned. Nature had performed its miracle. This is what makes us
behave as though we are immortal; as though we can do any damage
we like and still survive because nature performs miracles for us. Do
not be too sure. The most terrible hurricane you care to imagine cannot
do the long-term damage done by human pollution of land, oceans
and the atmosphere. There is a limit beyond which not even nature can
repair the damage and restore life. We humans test that limit at our
peril. The hope is to learn that lesson before it is too late.

A century and more of bad old habits stands between us and the
learning of the lesson for human survival on earth. The balance sheet
has to be drawn up, the profits and losses spelled out. This has been a
century of the widening and deepening of our humanity. More people
know more about their world than ever before. In relative terms, fewer
people live in the ignorance and mental darkness which were so
prevalent up to the early years of this century. Science and technology
have made yesterday's miracle today's commonplace. We live longer
and better; we multiply in greater numbers. World population
numbers have passed the six thousand million mark as the century
draws to its close. But a new dread disease threatens, the sexually
transmitted AIDS, for which, up to this point, science and technology
and human skill have not found a cure. This is our new plague,
different from all earlier plagues in that we know what causes it but
some of us persist in misreading its message and so perpetuate it. Like

all real plagues, it is impersonal, afflicting the good and bad and even innocent babes sucking their mothers' milk. Nature's simple message is: there are things you cannot do without paying a bitter price. Promiscuity is one of them, sexual deviance from nature's norms another. Extreme self-indulgence, a modern-day variation on the Biblical Sodom and Gomorrah, comes with the price tag: premature death. Nature says: 'You are free to do these things; you will die before your time if you do them.' This is why, in earlier times, when the survival of human life was more precariously uncertain, taboos and inhibitions evolved as forms of protection for the species. To do this thing — eating pork, incest, homosexuality, promiscuous heterosexuality — leads to premature death, so you do not do them: they are *taboo*, not to be done.

The price of survival is to observe these taboos. This lesson needs to be re-learned. Is it an accident that nature's teeming armies of viruses and retroviruses rarely overcome the body's immune system where people live within the inhibitions imposed by taboos about what is clean, what is unclean? When pork, with its special worm, could not be properly sterilised, the eating of pork became taboo in many societies. Orthodox Jews and practising Muslims have this taboo in common to this day. Accident or survival tool? Nature's version of acceptable sexual behaviour is to make pleasurable the reproductive process between male and female; perpetuating the species is the primary purpose; the high moment of joy is the sweetener. Modern man's 'right to be different, to do as I please' is tolerated as long as it does not go counter to this primary purpose. Where it does, nature can be clinically destructive. And nature will win every time, no matter how smart we think we are. Tribal folk everywhere, across barriers of language and culture, and those still close to the earth, understand this and do nothing to cross nature and the forces of death and destruction it can unleash. It is safer by far to respect nature's rules and abide by them. Are we too smart, too far gone to take this imperative seriously? It is, ultimately, the option between the destruction or survival of the species.

Another ancient human hang-up, older even than anti-Semitism and colour prejudice, is the systemic suppression and exploitation of the female of our species. Men are born of women and without them there can be no species: no kings, princes, popes, presidents, prime ministers. Yet, as age-old habit, the male of the species has decided woman's place in the scheme of things. A bishop born of woman decrees that no woman shall rise above a certain position in the Church. Rome uses women, but no woman can be Pope. For twenty centuries and more, man has made of woman a creature akin to his property, just short of being his slave. Until this century, women took little or no part in the deciding of public affairs: they could not vote, own property in their own names, needed male approval to conduct business. In this century the relations between man and woman have undergone greater change than in any previous age. In our time woman has increasingly been accepted as a person in her own right, not the appendage to some male. She is into the professions and the arts; she is among the most important public servants at both national and international levels. Yet old habits die hard, and the career woman who goes out to work still comes home to cope with the housework and the taking care of children and serving the man of the house. The notions of partnership, a sharing of responsibilities, a fair division of labour, are still observed more in theory than practice. So the women carry a disproportionate share of the burden of making life good and comfortable for the family. The old hunter-gatherer habits of another, more precarious age, when she took care of everything at home while he went out to find food and returned to be pampered, served and spoiled, still persist despite the enlightenment of our times.

The options have begun to define themselves. The male of the species either accepts that his female is an equal partner in all respects and builds a new, more honest, more honourable and worthy relationship with her or risks a future in which she increasingly sees and fights him as her exploiter and oppressor. The notion of *The Female Eunoch* is a warning signal. Somewhere along the way we seem to have lost the essential point of the relationship between a man and a woman. It does not consist of one strong and dominant and another weak and submissive partner, but of two humans who, in nature's scheme of things, are complementary, the two halves of one socio-biological whole for the primary purpose of perpetuating the species. Neither can do it without the other. The one nurtures, the other provides and protects. Within that basic framework nature allows for change, variety and even a measure of power-play between the partners. But the basics for survival are as constant as nature itself. Mess about with these and you have no future. Through all the evolutionary changes of the millennia the way of human reproduction has remained the same; man and woman coming together to reproduce with the process being rewarded by shared pleasure and a built-in desire to repeat the pleasure. There is an interaction between society and the male/female biological unit. Societal change leads to individual change; individual change, in turn, influences societal change. Men become more or less caring about the needs and wants of their women, women more or less resentful depending on the responses of men and society to their needs and wants.

So we had the changes in this century in the struggles and status of women. Nature is not hostile to change which falls within its basic rules. If women break any of those basic rules, nature will strike back. Prostitution and female circumcision are brutal and ugly, not socially desirable, but they do not violate the basic rules, any more than putting women behind the veil. Nature has tolerated the suppression and exploitation of woman, as it has slavery and anti-Semitism because these do not violate its basic rules. The using of women in slavery as both beasts of burden and for forced reproduction, barbaric as it was, violated no rule of nature. Nature is no progressive egalitarian. It is indifferent to human cruelty, exploitation, discrimination and injustice which do not violate its rules. It is harsh, practical in its desire for the survival of any species. You live up to its requirements or you are discarded. It gives long rope but no second chances. It has endowed woman with qualities of strength and endurance to fit her for her special reproductive functions. Fail in this, and nature will wipe her out as casually as it did the mighty dinosaurs. And man without his mate would be a useless biological anachronism. If woman uses her special strengths to break out of the systemic bondage imposed by man, nature will, I suspect, approve or be indifferent, as long as she fulfils her basic task of being the nurturing vessel of life. Nature would be as indifferent to the replacing of the male by the female as top-dog of the species as it has been while she was the under-dog.

Woman, after all, is the oldest victim of exploitation and abuse, predating anti-Semitism and slavery. Nature tolerated those, why not woman in control of the world? But what if man fought back by withholding his contribution to the process of natural reproduction? He has fought wars for much less cause. What if he were to use his clever scientific and technological skills to try and by-pass the female and develop some *Dolly*-type cloning process to create legions of warrior-males to retake control from women? Any such aberration would, I suggest, unleash nature's wrath on a scale our species has not dreamt of. Men without women, women without men, is no part of nature's scheme of things; it is not naturally viable, therefore to be discarded as pointless to the natural scheme of things. There is no future in the dominant half holding on to its position at any price, even to the point of a violent gender war. Equally, there is no point in the dominated female half fighting back until it becomes the obverse side of its male half; as brutal, as insensitive, as intolerant, as harsh a coloniser of bodies and minds. To be whole it must find another way. The two halves must join together easily, harmoniously if the results are to be good.

What I hope men will do, especially in places like Africa, the Middle East, Latin America and Asia is to not resist the surging impulse to freedom among the world's women. I hope men will become part of the struggle to emancipate women from the special kind of bondage they have suffered through the centuries. That would be part of the all-important process of human emancipation, reconciliation and atonement without which peace and harmony are not possible.

How do we, who are not personally responsible for what happened in the past, atone for the cruelties and injustices of the past? Why should we? Because the individual has to come to terms with himself/ herself before he/she can come to terms with anyone or anything else. That eliminates the formula solutions which have become the great cop-outs of our time. Race (whatever we think it is), colour, class, gender, wealth, poverty, status, have all been used to define us and explain, excuse and justify what we have done or not done. Behind the racist skinheads of Europe are a history of violence, prejudice and exploitation. Yet, in these days of enlightenment, it is the individual who is blamed and denounced, not the forces which shaped him. Would he have been the same skinhead if the forces which shaped him were different? What would have made those forces different enough to shape a different type of person? Do we go back to the beginning to reshape the forces to reshape the individual? That is not possible. So why are not all young men of Western Europe racist skinheads? They share a common shaping experience. The formula solutions of ideologies cannot answer that one because they do not, or do not want to, admit the singular importance of the individual and of individual choice.

In an ocean of social and political uniformity there are always individuals who are different, who resist the norm, have different ideas, pursue nonconformist paths. They are the ones who say, often in the face of fierce opposition, 'It is wrong to persecute Jews, exploit women, enslave blacks. They are your neighbours.' That wisest of the world's teachers called these 'the salt of the earth'. Learn to pay heed to them — critically, to be sure; but do not cast them out or crucify them. That has been the beginning of wisdom in our long human story. Which is not the same as taking them over, institutionalising them, thus rendering them harmless and ineffective. We need to be alert to the skills we have developed at the taking over and institutionalising and thus nullifying of important visions, dreams and ideas coming from 'the salt of the earth'. Learn from them without fencing them in. That would be emancipating our minds from mental slavery; and that has to be an act of conscious will brought about by the individual in concert with other individuals. The leader or would-be leader, in this context, becomes the potential or actual enemy of that emancipation. Nature needs order; society needs parties and structures and institutions to affirm and sustain that order. Leaders manage that order; in the process, they acquire the taste for power and the will to hold on to it. That is the dilemma inherent in all organised movements. At some point the agent of change becomes the enemy of change. There are no easy ways out of real dilemmas. Being aware of them helps. The heightened consciousness of the individual to the forces at work in his/her society is key to that awareness. No quick fixes; no pet ideological dogmas as substitute for careful thought and feeling and humility in the presence of an extraordinary, complex and infinitely delicate, yet brutal, natural scheme of things.

To have life and to have it more abundantly, and to do no harm become, out of the necessity to survive, imperatives for the new century. They begin with atonement for past wrongs and injustices: those of men to men, men to women; men and women to the environment; to Jews for anti-Semitism; to blacks for slavery and prejudice. All atonement begins with confession and the plea for forgiveness. Restitution is part of atonement.

In our time the post-war German state has paid reparation to the Jews for the horrors of the holocaust in which millions of Jews were systematically destroyed by the Nazis. Money does not cancel such horrible crimes, but it can be an expression of remorse: I am sorry my people did this to your people, take this as a token of our collective guilt and regret at what was done to you in our name. It tells all humanity that a crime has been committed, the guilty ones have admitted it, and have made restitution as an act of contrition. It opens the possibility of reconciliation, without which peace and harmony are not possible. It makes possible the coming together of Jew and German in mutual recognition of each other's common humanity. If you meet thus and say I am sorry, it means that particular piece of inhumanity is recognised and is less likely to be repeated. So it is with racism.

From the long perspective of history, exploitation based on skin colour is the most recent of the tools of exploitation in human affairs. Three hundred years is a fleeting second in nature's scheme of things; it is many generations in the affairs of man, and for those at the receiving end one generation is an eternity. Twenty-seven years as a political prisoner is one-third of the average life span of a strong healthy man. When one-third of the best years of a man's life are taken from him for just cause, it is bad enough. When it is because he refused to accept institutionalised exploitation based on skin colour, that man is entitled to rage against those who inflicted this iniquity on him. Yet he does not. He does not, when he gains the power, inflict the same hurt and humiliation on his former oppressors. He offers instead reconciliation and a new beginning in partnership. Is there something mad about such a man? Would it not be more 'human', more 'reasonable' to repay three hundred years of 'racism' and exploitation measure for measure? If that path were chosen, the cycles of oppression, repression and exploitation would be endless. The weak, grown strong, would do to the strong grown weak, what had been done to them: an endless cycle of human degradation. If that is how it is to be, then it does not matter who does what to whom because there can be no hope of enriching the quality of human life, no hope of reaching the point of doing no harm. The cycle has to be broken. The most important post-Apartheid action in South Africa up to this point was, for me at least, the establishing of the Truth and Reconciliation Commission, which addressed the question of the crimes of Apartheid, the need to confess, the hope for reconciliation.

The fact that those responsible for Apartheid were, with a few exceptions, generally hostile to the enquiry was to be expected. It is a human tendency to try to suppress or gloss over past bad actions, crimes and cruelties. That which was good when it served our interests becomes deplorable when it ceases to do so. Nationalism which was good in the service of European power becomes deplorable in the service of the former colonies. Aggression, the hallmark of European power at its peak, is bad when used by militants of former colonies. Values change; those who were unforgiving demand automatic forgiveness as the token of good intentions. Forget the past, forget slavery, forget discrimination, forget expropriation. Show your good intention by leaving old iniquities, old injustices, old crimes unredressed; leave the expropriated land in the hands of the expropriators, or compensate them in ways they did not compensate you for their seizures. This is how the strong, everywhere, of all 'races' and colours, in all parts of the world, have always dealt with the weak. Always, when fortunes are reversed, they say forget the past, let's get on with the future. So Archbishop Tutu's Commission found those most responsible for Apartheid least interested in appearing before it. They wanted reconciliation, to be sure, but without any looking back, without any serious accounting or apportioning of guilt and responsibility; above all, without atonement and reparation. Forget the past, leave everything as is, and let us move on to a better future.

So the Commission's Report said:

It is the view of the Truth and Reconciliation Commission that the spirit of generosity and reconciliation enshrined in the founding Act was not matched by those at whom it was mainly directed. Despite amnesty provisions extending to criminal and civil charges, the white community often seemed either indifferent or plainly hostile to the work of the Commission, and certain media appeared to have actively sought to sustain this indifference and hostility. With rare individual exceptions the response of the former state, its leaders, institutions and the predominant organs of civil society of that era, was to hedge and obfuscate. Few grasped the olive branch of full disclosure.

Even where political leaders and institutional spokespersons of the former state claimed to take full responsibility for the actions of the past, these sometimes seemed to take the form of ritualised platitudes rather than genuine expressions of remorse. Often, it seemed to the Commission, there was no real appreciation of the enormity of the violations of which these leaders and those under them were accused, or of the massive degree of hurt and pain their actions had caused.

I was reminded of those vivid pictures of the responses of the Nazi leaders at the Nuremberg War Crimes trials of 1945 when the victors sat in judgement over the vanquished of the Second World War.

We spent the best part of one whole night downloading huge chunks of the Commission's report on the day Archbishop Desmond Tutu ceremonially handed it to President Nelson Mandela. A minor miracle of technology made the report available to us, and the world, almost as soon as the President received it. Our world had indeed become one, and the censorship and control of information was coming to an end. We spent the next day going through the near-book-length summary of the Report, its Findings and Recommendations. The world now had the stark facts of the meaning of Apartheid. That, and the spirit of reconciliation which informed the Report, were the key elements of a new beginning. You cannot begin anew without knowing and facing all the facts. Most white South Africans are not yet ready to face those facts and what they say about them; they prefer a quick, embarrassed side glance and say we have accepted the change, the defeat, if you like, so let us get on with the reconciliation without further change. Some of them say you need us more than we need you; do not push us too hard. There is a stubborn refusal to admit guilt, which is no basis for true reconciliation. It is reminiscent of the mulish resistance of the defeated Confederate soldiers of the American Civil War who sang *I won't be reconstructed and I do not give a damn!* But time longer than rope, and they will be. There is a sufficiently sizeable minority of white South Africans who have responded positively for reconciliation to come with time. What is more important is that the blacks have themselves, without prompting from the outside world, chosen this course. The Promotion of National Reconciliation and Unity Act was South African in every respect. It was what the ANC took to the nation's Parliament. The blacks were not driving their former enemies into the sea or out of the country; they were not imposing reverse Apartheid. I am not become like my enemy.

But there has to be confession and atonement for past wrongs. It has to begin with the land, for land is life. They may not be able to go back to the old pre-European forms of land tenure. They are, in Zimbabwe and elsewhere, seeking new ways to deal with an old problem. The land which was 'alienated' during colonialism cannot remain 'alienated' in perpetuity. The problem lies with the terms for restoring the land to the people. To pay for it at today's market value would be to beggar national economies. A strong case can be made that the whites have, over the years, benefited so greatly from an asset questionably acquired, that there is no moral need to compensate them for it. Consider the case of colonialism itself: do the British or French or Dutch or Belgian governments have a right, either in law or in morality, to demand compensation for the 'loss' of their colonies? Those colonies were once their 'possessions'. The 'alienation' of vast pieces of land from native to white settler possession was part and parcel of that colonial process.

Logically, then, when the colonies ceased to be possessions of Europe and reverted to native control, the land, too, which was forcibly alienated, should revert to its original owners. Colonialism was an imposition, like the Nazi occupation of Europe was. Just as you paid no compensation to the Nazis for having lost what they had occupied by force, so there can be no compensation for the colonisers and their beneficiaries.

On what grounds, then, do the white settlers demand 'market' prices for forcibly seized land? There is a dubious legality and morality at work here. I think the white settlers and the white native South Africans with vast land holdings should, as part of the process of reconciliation and atonement, negotiate to retain the land they are using productively and return the rest to those from whom it was 'alienated' in the first place. In the past the slave-owners in the Caribbean were compensated for the loss of their slaves; the slaves were not. The morality, then, said beasts of burden were not compensated for loss. Only human beings. The slaves were human, Morality was stood on its head. You cannot do that in today's or tomorrow's world. The victims, not the perpetrators of injustice, are entitled to make the claims. The restoration of the 'alienated' land is critical to atonement and reconciliation. The leaders of Africa have shown their willingness to deal with it reasonably. So should the white minorities.

And so to slavery. That, too, needs to be put behind us if reconciliation and harmony between black and white is to be a normal relationship between people of equal humanity. The Jews were compensated for the horrors of the holocaust in which an estimated six million human beings were methodically slaughtered. Estimates are that upwards of twenty million human beings perished in the enforced Middle Passage. Does time make the one crime more serious than the other? Certainly not for the millions of the descendants of the slaves who cannot, and will not, forget this most ugly and painful chapter of their history. Generations of angry black men and women, unable to 'bury' this hard and painful part of their history, have called for compensation as part of the atonement for plantation slavery. The beginning of a new millennium is an appropriate time to settle accounts on this one, too. The Rastafarian dream of shiploads of black folk from every corner of the earth being repatriated back to Africa is unlikely to be fulfilled. Where would they be settled? Who would receive them? Would it be a latter-day variation of the colonisers of Liberia? An attempt was made under Norman Manley's government to establish a small settlement in Ethiopia. The Ethiopian government of Haile Selassie provided a small piece of land. Not much came of the enterprise. I do not think this is the way. I think the 'Back to Africa' cry is a deep psychological and emotional attempt to try to wipe away the terrible scars of the past; it is escapist, rejectionist, a desire to return to the imagined African 'womb'. The Africa they dream of is as idealised as the 'Promised Land' of the Jews in the Old Testament. There is no end to this kind of pain and alienation until wherever they are becomes 'home'. Wise old Frederick Douglass understood that better than most.

What is possible is to offer atonement for that hurt. So how do Europe and North America make the atonement? The people of today's Europe and North America can justly say they are not responsible for the sins of their forebears so why should they atone for what they did not do? This argument is logical and reasonable until we ask if they benefited from the deeds of their forebears. Would today's Europe and North America be what they are if there had been no slavery, no colonial empires, no plundering and exploitation of natural resources wherever they found them? Can you be a beneficiary without any responsibility for how the great benefits you enjoy were acquired? I think not. The sons and grandsons of the slave masters do have a responsibility to discharge toward the sons and grandsons of those their forebears enslaved. To free their own children and grandchildren of that historic responsibility, they must atone and seek reconciliation.

Only thus will they be able to say with the poet: *The past has been a mint of blood and sorrow/ That must not be so for tomorrow.*

Where do you begin to wipe the slate clean and start anew? With the admission that slavery, plantation slavery in particular, was as gross a crime against humanity as was ever committed. No great statesman of the Western world has ever expressed regret, or ever offered an apology for slavery. Europe and North America need to say for the record:

'Slavery was wrong; slavery was a crime against humanity; we have benefited from that crime; we are sorry for the part our forebears played in it.'

That would be the beginning of reconciliation. I think if the West were to do that, the darker people of the earth would be disarmed and be able to purge themselves of the great historic hurt of many generations. I hope the people of Europe and North America, especially the young, will come to see and understand the importance of this. To move to a point beyond the inherited memories of the pain and hurt and horrors of the past, there must be recognition, admission, forgiveness and atonement.

Let there be a memorial to slavery as a permanent reminder of the human capacity, when pointed in certain directions, for cruelty and wickedness. There is an impulse to good and an impulse to evil in the nature of things. The need is to recognise both: the negative and the positive, the creative and the destructive; then to choose consciously to do that which is creative, good, kind, tender, caring and to reject, equally consciously, that which is destructive, bad, cruel, harsh, without feeling. In short, there is the need to re-impose on ourselves the ancient precepts and taboos which helped our species to survive to this point. Choose and pursue the impulse to good and you may survive; choose the opposite and you may perish. Any new slavery, as both the Nazis and the *Gulag* have shown in our time, is likely to make the black slavery of the plantation seem benign. So raise a memorial to slavery, not for the sake of the blacks, but that it may never recur because it may recur in more monstrous forms. Do it not for one group but for all humanity, so that it may have a future of decency and hope.

The sceptic may ask: 'what new forms of slavery?' The new political and economic order has already created conditions of power without responsibility. The world's one remaining superpower exercises all the powers of past empires without the corresponding responsibilities. It can coerce any small nation to do what it wants and walk away if things go wrong. It has no responsibility for the consequences of failed policies. The British and French empires assumed responsibility for the administration of their colonies — for good government, education, health, law and order. The new imperialism dictates policy but assumes no responsibility. The new multinationals exploit as did the business arm of the old imperialism, but without the same respect for labour laws and the rights of colonial workers. Trade unions are often prohibited, the workers are forced into low wage 'contract' work from which they can be dismissed without compensation or legal redress, there are no retirement benefits, no pension rights. In some sweatshops of the Far East, female garment workers are locked into factories to fulfil production quotas for a pittance. On the banana plantations of Central America the vast dollar-a-day US-owned companies, using non-union labour, are undercutting and destroying the banana industry of the free and independent small growers of the tiny Eastern Caribbean islands. The great gains won by the workers of the former colonial countries in the earlier years of this century are steadily being eroded by the new economic imperialism of the multi- and trans-nationals which accepts no responsibility for anything. Whatever and whoever is not profitable is discarded. Where growth and productivity cease to be up to their requirements, they shut up shop and move on to other places to seek profits from other people. The chaos and unemployment they leave behind is none of their business; the poverty and instability which follow are blamed on the bad management of native governments. There is a downward spiral into greater poverty while the rich get richer.

These are some of the possibilities of new types of slavery: the Nazi-type forced labour of the politically and economically defeated; that of the coldly brutal Soviet *Gulag*; that of migrant and plantation labour; all exploited by a marauding, buccaneering capitalism behaving like plundering pirates. The meaning of life, investing life with meaning, is an act of will, an act of choice. Choose one direction and it will, almost inevitably, lead to future forms of slavery. Choose another and it will, with almost equal inevitability, lead away from the impulses which make for slavery, exploitation, oppression. Raising a memorial to slavery, as a lasting warning and reminder of where the drive for power and profit can lead, will be choosing the direction which may help turn us into the caring creative humans history shows us capable of being. The meaning of life so many of us seek after, often all our lives, is, I suggest, to be found in the growing awareness that we ourselves can give meaning to life by the choices we make as individuals, communities and societies. This rounds off the circle: it is an act of will to have life and to have it more abundantly; and to do no harm. Shape our lives in accordance with that choice and we can acculturate ourselves out of the impulse to greed, destructiveness, disharmony into caring for each other. This is humanity's choice. Nature gives only so much time, so much rope, before it decides 'this does not work, does not fit into my scheme of things' so, as with other species, let it go. On the other hand, if we make it, if we fit into its delicate balance of forces, we may achieve through long generations of survival, that immortality which is part of the human dream.

Those who repent make amends for wrongs done by offering restitution. Those who gave twenty million pounds in compensation to the slave-owners in the Caribbean for the loss of their slaves have surely made the case for proportionate compensation for the slaves

— in these days when we accept that the slaves were as human as the slave-owners. So let the International Court of Justice convene a special sitting to determine how this matter should be finally resolved. There are those in the Third World who argue that the resolution of this matter should include, as part of it, the cancellation of all Third-World debt. I have mixed feelings about this. Would not we, the descendants of the slaves, be piggy-backing on their bleached bones out of messes of our creation? Would we not be blurring the responsibilities for colonialism with the greater ones for slavery? I think any debt write-off should be related strictly to the issue of compensation for colonial exploitation and the transfer of resources from the poor to the rich countries. Slavery, the owning of one person by another, must be dealt with as an historic crime of transcendent importance, as a manifest evil in terms of morality. It must be resolved on its own. It must be unrelated to some of the questionable actions and wasteful extravagances of some modern-day Third-World leaders. So let us have a judicial ruling from the International Court of Justice on the crime of slavery, and let us have the appropriate punishment for that crime. Let the Court establish a Commission to compile and bring together all the records and facts of the slave trade and of slavery itself as the basis for its findings.

For myself, I would want the Court, if it finds slavery to have been and to be a crime against humanity, to levy one-time fines against all those countries which took part in the slave trade. The reparations paid to the victims of the Nazi holocaust and the compensation made to the slave-owners of the Caribbean after abolition should provide guidelines to the size and nature of the fines to be levied. The money thus levied should be placed in an Anti-Slavery Foundation, under the strictest supervision possible. There should be a small staff under an unpaid board of directors to administer the operations of the Foundation and the use of its resources. It should not be turned into yet another costly international bureaucracy. Salaries and office expenses should be a tiny fraction of its spending. Grants should only be for development purposes: education, infrastructural development, protection of the eco-system, and promoting the safety and protection of women, children and the old. The countries which had suffered most from slavery should be the primary beneficiaries. This should be the final resolution, the final settling, of the long and painful emotional stand-off between the lighter and the darker peoples of the world. Admission of culpability, judgement, penalty, reparation, expression of atonement: the opening to healed new beginnings. I hope this will be done quickly, before the end of the year 2000 and the start of the new century and the new millennium. It would give special meaning to South Africa's reaching out to truth and reconciliation, however reluctant the response of the majority of its present-day white citizens. It could signal the historic turning point of 'race' and colour. It is uniquely touching that it is the black victims of the grossest form of institutionalised racism of this century who are today, in their moment of power, offering truth and reconciliation as the way forward. This is the promise of the possibility of a better future.

It is on this note of muted hope that I end these remembrances and reflections on the events and people who helped to shape and influence my life and outlook over these past eighty years. It is not quite the whole century, but close enough to make no big difference. It took a lifetime to come to a full understanding of the importance of family and community. They are the foundations of stable society, of humans living together in relative peace and harmony. My greatest concern is for the children who grow up today without knowing family and the deep and magical feel of the protectiveness of the extended family, flowing into the whole community, making your world a safe and caring place in which every adult is protector/teacher/guide ensuring your safety and your good behaviour. Nothing else I know ensures that sense of security. It is only now, toward the end of a long life, that I can look back and realise how warmly I was protected by this blanket of community, even in the climate of the harsh institutionalised racism into which I was born.

We found much of that same community protectiveness here when Daphne and I first came to Jamaica. It made for the peace and harmony which made life in Jamaica good, even for the poorest. Being poor in your community is different from being poor in a ghetto yard or shanty shack. The community protects and shares out of caring; love is never far away. Not so in the urban ghetto, not so in the political garrison, not so under the control of the manipulative zone or area Don. Not even so under the itinerant 'crusading' churches of the 'televangelists' from 'Up North'. Their concerns are not with family and community; they can offer no real comfort for the children growing up without the warm protective blanket of family and community. I remember how it was with me and I worry about these children without love. The need to rediscover or reinvent family and community is important. If we cannot do better for our young — envelope them in love and security and prepare them for the future — then we will have failed, or performed poorly, in the primary task of ensuring the easy progression of the generations from one to the other. This, too, is an imperative of nature, one we neglect at the peril of the generations and even at the peril of the long-term survival of the species.

One of the less pleasant aspects of longevity is that we have outlived most of our friends. Most of those who were near and dear to us, with whom we have shared fun and games and joys and sorrows, and special intimacies, are no longer with us. So our high days and holidays are tinged with nostalgia and we think and talk of friends long gone. On Daphne's seventy-second birthday in July, one of the three bottles of Italian red wine Biddy brought from Milan for my eightieth birthday in March, proved too rich in histamines and we both had terrible head and bellyaches the next morning. Was it because we had no friends to share and we drank most of the bottle of wine by ourselves? Does it mean no wine next year? Never mind; the cool soft water from Chocho Bottom, when we get it, these days, tastes as good as some of the finest French wines we drank in the Paris of our youth. These are the days of remembrances, and they are surprisingly, unexpectedly good.

We thought we would have more time now to do the things we had not been able to do in our busy younger years. Daphne has painted all her life — in-between being my friend, companion, sister, lover, home-maker, the mother of our children. But there was never quite enough time; and still there is not enough time for all the painting she wants to do. Looking after ourselves, even though it is only the two of us and the dogs, and we share the chores, still takes up too much of our time. The head-dog, Charley, father of the current pack, refuses to accept strangers in the house — and so do I, especially when I am writing. And the solitary nature of writing is made tolerable by Daphne's understanding and desire for me to write and by the companionship of our afternoons and evenings shared with our happy ageing canine family. It is one of nature's cruel ironies that we have had to bury so many generations of dogs we have come to love because their natural life span is so much shorter than ours; so we have watched them be born, cared for them as little puppies, watched them grow into adulthood, grow old, and die. We have experienced the pain of their dying again and again. But we have also cherished the boundless joy with which they relished life. Their love, extraordinary loyalty, friendship and sheer joy of living form part of the riches of our joint memory bank. Some of them are remembered as part of Daphne's collection of sketches and drawings and the occasional paintings she did of our children and their pets when they were small in Paris and Paley and Debden and here at Coyaba; they hang in my study, in our bedroom, in what were the children's rooms, in the large living room. Many more are stacked away in storage areas. Would she have become a full-time professional artist if I had not come into her life? It is safe to speculate on this now that it cannot be changed. I know she does not want her paintings to be seen and used as commercial 'property'. How to ensure against that?

We are lucky to still have each other as life's time clock runs down. I am older and likely to leave her behind. We have talked about when I will no longer be around and she has to cope by herself. No problem about our possessions, for we own everything jointly and when I die, all goes automatically to her with little or no legal fuss involved. I have asked my publishers to ensure all royalties pass to her. Things cannot fill the personal and emotional void after the end of a lifetime together. This is the one point where we cannot reach out to each other and clasp hands as we have always done in times of trouble or difficulty. Oh, how we will miss what we have shared; the love and deep friendship we have found with and in each other. Thanks to my Daphne my personal life has been rich and beautiful. I can wish no better for any young dream-seekers of the future. May they live in a wiser world of family and community, free of the divisions and hatreds our generation, and earlier generations had to cope with. May they have the good sense to respect, nurture and cherish nature so that nature, in its turn, may judge them worthy of survival as a species. Such are an old man's hopes for the people of this beautiful earth.

I worry over the dangerous human impulse to manipulate and re-order nature. We want to rearrange its building blocks, to fiddle with natural selection, take over its handiwork. Nature's tolerance has boundaries; push beyond those and nature turns clinically brutal. Can we, with our clever new scientific and technological skills, improve on the works of nature and, say, change the composition of this one blood? And if we can, and if we do, will it be within the range and scope of nature's rules for survival? If it is not, if we push too hard, too far, if we upset the balance too critically, all human life as we know it today may be as casually wiped out as you swat a fly. It has happened before with other species. Take care lest it happens with us.

A final thought, a last question for those who may read these chronicles: If all human life as we know it today began in Africa, as the scholars tell us, then who is, and who is not, an African?

So we spend what remains of our time in peace and harmony, doing the small daily chores of our lives, writing and painting. During the writing of these chronicles I have grown stiff in the joints. Now I must try and exercise them a little more. The land needs clearing and it is not easy to find young people to work the land. They prefer to go down to Kingston or look for big money for little work, to pay for the new gadgets and designer clothes and franchise foods the Americans unload on us. For the moment P.J. Patterson is having his work cut out to awaken the new values and attitudes without which moving forward is so hard. But I sense a gradual, almost imperceptible, mood change. I hope it is the remembrance of a time, not all that long ago, when Jamaica — and indeed, all the Third World — had a vision of where we wanted to go and how we needed to get there. If we can get back to that, rekindle that vision, stop tearing each other down, stop destroying the little we have, we may yet begin again the long and slow but steady process we call progress and development.

If people, if the individual and the community are placed at its centre, then it will be good. I pray it will be so for all people, especially the poor, everywhere. The struggle continues but at a higher level, a more human plane, above the race and colour which bedevilled our century. There are new dimensions to tomorrow's challenges. May tomorrow's people deal with them with greater wisdom than most of us showed. But we had our 'men of vision' too, and they helped us through some difficult times of the heart and the mind and the spirit. I have tried to pay homage to some of them in these pages, primarily those of the darker peoples because they have been most neglected in our century. There were 'men and women of vision' from other colours who served humanity as well in their different ways. I hope there will never again be the need for this type of reflection on this type of problem in the centuries ahead. Race and colour, in themselves, are not worth the pain and suffering they have called down on humanity in our time. They are human aberrations never to be repeated: mindless foolishnesses with which man destroyed and side-tracked his brother man.

To the young of all colours and of all lands who must take up the struggle to have life and to have it more abundantly, and to strive to do no harm, I urge respectful recognition of your common humanity. You are all of one blood. Peace and love.

Coyaba
Jamaica, August 1999